EAST INDIAN FORTUNES

EAST INDIAN FORTUNES

The British in Bengal in the Eighteenth Century

BY

P. J. MARSHALL

King's College, London

OXFORD
AT THE CLARENDON PRESS
1976

Oxford University Press, Ely House, London W. 1

GLASGOW NEW YORK TORONTO MELBOURNE WELLINGTON
CAPE TOWN IBADAN NAIROBI DAR ES SALAAM LUSAKA ADDIS ABABA
DELHI BOMBAY CALCUTTA MADRAS KARACHI DACCA
KUALA LUMPUR SINGAPORE HONG KONG TOKYO

ISBN 0 19 821566 5

*Printed in Great Britain
at the University Press, Oxford
by Vivian Ridler
Printer to the University*

Acknowledgements

All historians owe immense debts to librarians and archivists, and I am no exception. To single out for special mention two of the many institutions on whose efficiency and helpfulness the writing of this book has depended is therefore highly invidious. But to include the services which the India Office Library and Records render to their readers in a general acknowledgement would be an act of gross ingratitude on my part. Special thanks are also due to the officials of the High Court at Calcutta and to the staff of the record room of the Original Side, who on two visits to Calcutta permitted me to take up a great deal of their time and to make unreasonable demands on their services.

For permission to consult unpublished material I am grateful to the Chief Justice of the Calcutta High Court, the committee of the Calcutta Bar Library Club, Mr. Boyd Alexander, and Sir Anthony Rumbold.

Generous grants of leave of absence in 1964–5 and 1975 by King's College enabled me to undertake research in India. On the first occasion I was given financial help by the Central Research Fund of London University and by the Drapers Company, for which I owe a special debt to the late H. C. Boddington.

Over the years I have been privileged to learn a great deal, especially on matters concerning Asian trade, not only from the writings but also from the conversation of Dr. K. N. Chaudhuri and Dr. Ashin Das Gupta. Both of them have been kind enough to read large parts of the first draft of this book and to subject them to searching and most valuable criticism. Somen Nandy, Maharajkumar of Cossimbazar, generously permitted me to read his forthcoming study of his ancestor, Krishna Kanta Nandy (Cantu Babu), and has shown me many other kindnesses. I am very grateful to Dr. Indrani Ray and Sri Gautam Bhadra for helpful suggestions made after reading certain chapters in draft.

Contents

Maps and Tables

LIST OF MAPS

LIST OF TABLES

Abbreviations

Note

The currency system of eighteenth-century Bengal was extremely complex; several different denominations of rupee with different values were in use. In general, however, Europeans kept their accounts in what were known as 'current rupees'. Whenever values in rupees are given in this book, unless clear indications to the contrary are shown, they will be in current rupees. The sterling equivalent of the current rupee varied throughout the eighteenth century, as the table on p. 223 shows. For the purposes of this book the current rupee has been converted into sterling at approximately 2s. 3d. until 1770 and at 2s. thereafter. The English method of counting in hundreds of thousands and millions has generally been preferred to the Indian method of counting in lakhs and crores. The term 'a lakh of rupees' is, however, indispensable. Before 1770 a lakh has been given the rough equivalent of £11,000 with £10,000 after 1770.

Original spelling and punctuation has generally been preserved in quotations. Capitalization has been modernized and abbreviations expanded.

The place of publication of all books is London unless otherwise indicated.

Introduction

During the eighteenth century Bengal occupied a central place among British interests in Asia: by the early decades of the century a very large volume of trade was being transacted between Britain and Bengal; in the later eighteenth century British political power grew to the point where Bengal became the first substantial area on the Asian mainland to pass under direct European control; and once the British had secured Bengal's resources they could sustain their other Indian settlements and extend their territorial empire into northern India and South-East Asia. This deepening British involvement had what might be called both a public and a private side to it. The public side was the concern of the East India Company and to some extent of the British government who increasingly intervened in the Company's affairs towards the end of the century. The great bulk of trade between Britain and Bengal passed through the hands of the East India Company. The battles which led to conquest were fought by the armies of the East India Company with some assistance from the forces of the crown, and the first experiments in constructing a British administration for Bengal were made in the name of the Company by its officials with spasmodic supervision by the national government. The pursuit of their own advantage by individual British subjects in Bengal, some of them employed by the East India Company, some not in its service, constituted the private side.

This book is about the efforts of such men to make their fortunes in Bengal. It will try to show how money was made and to estimate the sums involved and the number of successful individuals. Such questions intrigued contemporaries, who often had highly coloured notions about the disruptive effects of what they supposed to be large infusions into Britain of 'Nabob' wealth, and they have attracted the more sober curiosity of historians of eighteenth-century society. But the book is concerned with issues that go beyond British social history.

Partly because of deliberate policies pursued by the East India Company and partly because it was extremely difficult to exert any kind of control from Britain, Englishmen in Asia enjoyed a

great deal of freedom in their pursuit of wealth during the eighteenth century. The ways in which they used this freedom constitute
an extremely important part in the process of British expansion.
Acting on their own account, British subjects were able to
build up a network of so-called private trade within Bengal itself
and by sea throughout Asia which supplemented the Company's
activities and in the nineteenth century replaced them altogether.
In trying to unravel the very complicated events which led to the
conquest of Bengal, it is impossible to ignore the influence which
the personal ambitions of individuals exerted on them: conquest
and the early attempts to rule Bengal were certainly made to
yield enormous private advantages.

With the exception of the Company's trade, the public side of
British expansion, especially the campaigns and the beginnings
of an administration, have been intensively studied. The private
side has, however, received less systematic study, at least until
the very end of the century when a number of distinguished works
have acknowledged its importance and analysed its working in
detail.[1] This book will try to trace the growth of the private
British stake in Bengal from early in the eighteenth century (the
merging of the operations of what had been two East India
Companies in 1704 is an appropriate starting point) until 1784.
In 1784, with the passing of Pitt's India Act and the decision of
Warren Hastings to leave Bengal after a career that had begun
before Plassey, a new order for British India began to come into
being. How this new order worked together with the role of
private interests in it have received authoritative treatment.[2] This
book tries to throw light on the old order.

Since the eighteenth century, most writing about private British
activities in India has been concerned with passing judgement on
them. Controversies began early as genuine public concern about
what appeared to be serious abuses in India was fed by personal
vendettas, as the enemies of men like Clive and Warren Hastings
did their utmost to discredit them in Britain. In the nineteenth
and early twentieth centuries, critics and defenders of British rule

[1] H. Furber, *John Company at Work* (Cambridge, Mass., 1951); A. Tripathi,
Trade and Finance in the Bengal Presidency, 1793-1833 (Calcutta, 1956).
[2] For a recent survey, see V. T. Harlow, *The Founding of the Second British
Empire, 1763-93* (1952-64), vol. ii.

in India continued to join issue about the rights and wrongs of the origins of the *raj*. As far as the history of empire continues to attract a wide audience, it still seems to be seen largely in terms of attributing blame or establishing justification.

This book will not, however, be concerned with drawing up a moral balance sheet or with trying to prove that men were or were not corrupt. In part this is because the definition of corruption is by no means self-evident. The early history of British India has to a large extent been written by Englishmen who were either themselves members of the Indian Civil Service or who were in close sympathy with its ideals as they had evolved by the later nineteenth century. As historians they were naturally interested in tracing the origins of these ideals back into the eighteenth century: early manifestations of them they commended; the pursuit of personal gain they dismissed as 'corruption', a disagreeable facet of the eighteenth century, but largely irrelevant to the history of the Indian empire. But for most of the eighteenth century the British community in Bengal, whether they were employed by the East India Company or not, regarded themselves as a community of merchants, comparable to those in the West Indies, Portugal, or the Levant. They were in India to get rich and, so long as they dealt fairly with the Company and did not infringe its monopoly, contemporaries regarded success in making fortunes as highly praiseworthy. Even Edmund Burke hoped to see men come back from India 'rich and innocent'.[1]

The question of standards apart, there still seem to be very strong reasons for not embarking on yet another attempt to discredit or rehabilitate the Nabobs. Such an approach obscures the great importance of the activities which were the subject of so many polemics. The nature of contemporary British society and the history of the East India Company both combined to ensure that the pressures which were leading to commercial and political expansion in Asia would come in large measure from private initiatives. Territorial empire and commercial hegemony, with all their consequences for Britain and India, were to grow out of the pursuit of private fortunes in Bengal.

[1] *The Correspondence of Edmund Burke*, v, ed. H. Furber (Cambridge, 1965), 257.

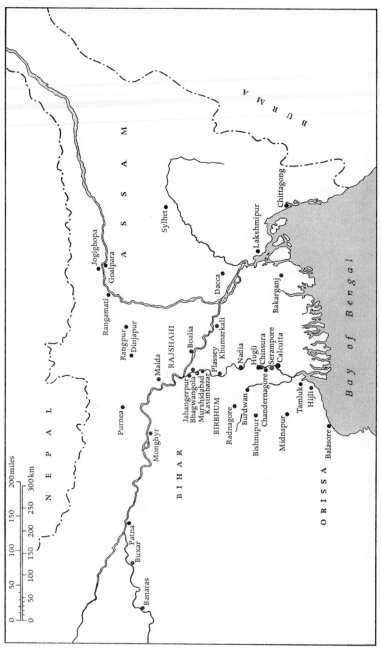

MAP I. Eighteenth-century Bengal

I

The British Community in Bengal

The major part of Bengal is a flat alluvial plain created by two great rivers, the Ganges and the Brahmaputra, which empty themselves into the sea through a maze of channels. Much of the land is extremely fertile. By the eighteenth century parts of it were under intensive cultivation and gave an immediate impression of prosperity. In Mughal documents Bengal was conventionally described as 'the paradise of the earth'. The French traveller François Bernier wrote of 'well peopled villages and boroughs', and thought Bengal even more fruitful than Egypt.[1] A Scot who served there described it as one of 'the richest, most populous and best cultivated kingdoms of the world'.[2]

For centuries a large volume of trade had passed between Bengal and other parts of Asia, either by sea or overland along the river valleys. Groups of Asian merchants, such as the Gujaratis from western India, Marwaris from the north or Armenians, had settled there, and in the sixteenth century they were joined by the first Europeans, the Portuguese. From the mid-seventeenth century Dutch and English ships began to visit Bengal regularly. French and Danish ships followed at the end of the century, and in the eighteenth century the polyglot organizations sponsored by the Holy Roman Emperor and the King of Prussia as the Ostend or the Royal Prussian companies also appeared in Bengal.

In the eighteenth century the authority of Bengal's rulers extended beyond the delta plains or the area inhabited by people who speak the Bengali language. The province of Bihar, stretching along the Ganges to the west, was joined to Bengal intermittently from 1697 and permanently after 1733. To the south-west the province of Orissa was also annexed to Bengal, although most of it

---

[1] 'Mr. F. Bernier's Voyage to Surat', *A Collection of Voyages and Travels* (1745), ii. 240–1.
[2] A. Dow, *The History of Hindostan* (1768–72), iii, p. lxviii.

was to be lost during the course of the century. By 1707 this enlarged Bengal was beginning to emerge as an autonomous political entity. It had been incorporated as a *subah*, or province, of the Mughal empire in the sixteenth century. Like other Mughal *subahs* Bengal was ruled on behalf of the Emperor by twin Governors who divided the functions of government between them. The *Subahdar* was responsible for the *nizamat*, the maintenance of law and order, the command of the armed forces, and the administration of criminal justice. The *Diwan* controlled finance and taxation and administered civil justice. By about 1717 the two offices were combined by Murshid Kuli Khan, an extremely able administrator, who had already been *Diwan* for several years when he obtained the office of *Subahdar*. Murshid Kuli Khan has come to be regarded as the first Nawab of Bengal, that is its first unchallenged ruler. By the time of his death in 1727, Bengal had become a virtually self-contained state, although this was apparently not Murshid Kuli Khan's conscious purpose.[1] Tribute was still paid to the Emperor, but effective imperial intervention in Bengal ceased and the Nawabs recognized no practical obligations outside their provinces. The Nawabs were eventually to lose Bengal, not to the Emperor or to any Indian rival, but to a group of European merchants.

Regular English contact with Bengal began in the 1630s, after the Mughal administration had broken the control over the province's seaborne trade which the Portuguese had been able to exert. Like other merchants, the English sought permission to set up a 'factory', in which they could manage their trade without direct interference, and concessions limiting the customs duties which they were required to pay. The first factories were established in 1651 and 1658, and the first grants fixing customs payments were obtained in 1651 and 1656, commuting all duties for a lump sum of Rs 3,000 (about £350) per annum. From the Mughal point of view this was a reasonable bargain for a small volume of trade in the 1650s; by the 1670s, when the East India Company's exports from Bengal were worth more than £50,000 a year, it was obviously inadequate. Not unnaturally Mughal officials began to demand increased payments. Tortuous and protracted negotiations followed, interrupted by an entirely unsuccessful attempt launched by the British in 1686 to seize

[1] A. Karim, *Murshid Quli Khan and his Times* (Dacca, 1963).

strong points in Bengal and to coerce the Emperor by waging war on Mughal shipping. In spite of the abject failure of the attempted coup, the Company were allowed to establish new settlements in Bengal and even won confirmation of their customs exemption for the annual payment of Rs 3,000. The most important of the new settlements was at Calcutta on the river Hugli. Calcutta quickly became for all practical purposes an English town where English law of a kind prevailed. In 1696 the English began to fortify Calcutta and in 1698 they were able to extend the area under their control by purchasing certain villages in the neighbourhood. A number of subordinate factories were also established in other commercial centres in Bengal.[1]

Although they had made significant gains in Bengal by the early eighteenth century, both on paper and in practice, the English sought additional security. In 1717 they were rewarded with the most spectacular confirmation of privileges ever to be obtained by a European nation. In 1717 a *farman*, or imperial grant, was issued by the Mughal Emperor Faruksiyar to an English embassy which had gone to his court at Delhi from Calcutta. The Emperor confirmed yet again that the English had the right to trade in Bengal without paying customs for an annual payment of Rs 3,000. The prestige of a Mughal *farman* was enormous and the grant of 1717 represented a remarkable British triumph. There were to be bitter disputes in the future as to whether all British goods were covered by the 1717 *farman*, but the principle that the major part of British trade was exempt from customs was never to be challenged. Nevertheless, the British continued to depend much more on the good offices of the Nawabs of Bengal, a few days' journey up-river from Calcutta, than on the benevolence of a remote Emperor. The 1717 grant contained a number of promises which the Nawabs had no intention of carrying out and the British could still be subjected to pressure if the Nawabs chose to apply it. In 1727, 1731, 1732, 1736, 1740, 1744, and 1749 the British had to make extra payments to buy off the Nawabs' interference with their trade. That they were not subjected to even more harassment probably owed more to the Nawabs' appreciation of the

[1] On the early history of English trade in Bengal, see S. Chaudhuri, 'Trade and commercial organisation in Bengal . . . 1650–1720' (London Ph.D. thesis, 1969), and 'The Myth of the East India Company's trading privileges in Bengal', *B.P.P.*, lxxxix (1970), 287–91; A. Chatterjee, *Bengal in the Reign of Aurangzīb* (Calcutta, 1967).

contribution which their trade made to Bengal's revenue than to any immunity conferred by Faruksiyar.[1]

In 1756, however, a new Nawab, Siraj-ud-daula, succeeded who was not prepared to exercise the same restraint. Provoked by an unusual degree of contumacy by the British, he carried a dispute with them to the point of actually attacking and overrunning Calcutta. Unfortunately for him, by 1756 the British had built up armed forces in southern India to fight their wars against the French. A detachment from Madras was sent to Bengal under Colonel Robert Clive. After a skirmish with the Nawab's troops, Clive was able to retake Calcutta. Negotiations followed in which Clive began by trying to re-establish British trade in Bengal through a new agreement with Siraj-ud-daula, but gradually became aware that there were yet higher stakes for which he might play. Siraj-ud-daula's position was a weak one. He had alienated many of his most powerful subjects, who were willing to see him overthrown and to use Clive's army as their instrument. For his part, Clive was prepared to give his support to the conspirators in return for a promise of a huge indemnity for the loss of Calcutta and important new privileges for British trade in the future. Siraj-ud-daula was defeated by the British army at the battle of Plassey in 1757 and a new Nawab was placed on the throne, who agreed to all Clive's demands.

In 1757 Clive and his colleagues had intended to do little more than re-establish British trade on an extremely favourable footing and to ensure the co-operation in the future of a well disposed Nawab. But they had in fact fatally undermined the authority of the Bengal Nawabs. Clive believed that the Company must intervene in the government of the new Nawab when the Company's interest required such intervention. His successors thought the interests of the Company required a change of Nawab in 1760. In 1763 there was renewed fighting between the British and their new Nawab, Mir Kasim. The causes of the war of 1763 are extremely controversial and will be examined in detail later on,[2] but one element in them was undoubtedly Mir Kasim's determination to protect his authority from fresh British incursions. His defeat inevitably led to yet another change of Nawab and to the further

---

[1] On the *farman* of 1717 and its consequences, see S. Bhattacharya, *The East India Company and the Economy of Bengal* (1954); Karim, *Murshid Quli Khan*.
[2] See below, p. 124.

discrediting of any alternative source of authority to the British. The collapse of the Bengal Nawabs was formally recognized by the Mughal Emperor's grant in 1765 of the title and function of *Diwan* of Bengal to the East India Company. A succession of Nawabs might survive for a time as nominal *Subahdars*, but the British now openly ruled Bengal. In the following years more and more important offices were actually to be filled by Englishmen, and the British began slowly to impose their own systems of law and administration on Bengal. Bengal had become the first large area on mainland Asia to be subjugated by a European power, and was to be the base for much further British expansion.[1]

In both the seventeenth and the eighteenth centuries trade between Britain and India was formally a monopoly of the East India Company chartered in 1600. Thus the agents or 'servants' of the East India Company naturally made up a large part of the British community in Bengal in the eighteenth century. Occupying pride of place were the so-called 'covenanted' servants, men to whom the term 'civil' servant was beginning to be applied by the end of the century. They were the men responsible for managing the Company's trade, buying and selling its goods, administering the first settlements and ultimately taking over the government of the whole province. It was from them that the nineteenth-century Indian Civil Service was to evolve.

To become a covenanted servant a man had to be nominated by one of the Directors of the Company. From 1697 candidates had to convince a committee of three Directors 'of their abilityes, and capacityes, as of their morals and good conversations'.[2] Once appointed, a servant was required to sign his covenant. The form of covenants varied during the period, but in general they bound servants to obey the Company's orders, to deal fairly with their employers, to pay their debts to 'black merchants' before they left India, and above all not to trade in ways which infringed the Company's monopoly.[3] A servant had also to give two securities in Britain, who would make good any claims up to £500 which the

---

[1] For a distinguished account of the fall of the Bengal Nawabs, see A. Majed Khan, *The Transition in Bengal 1756–1775* (Cambridge, 1969).

[2] Report of Committee of Directors, 5 Jan. 1697, I.O.R., B/41, p. 284.

[3] For covenants in force in 1756 and 1770, see 1st Report, Select Committee of the House of Commons, 1772, *Reports from Committees of the House of Commons* (1803–6), iii. 176–83. There are covenants from 1740 in I.O.R., O/1/1.

Company might have against him. The sum was increased as a man rose in the service, a Governor's securities being bound for £10,000.[1] In the early years of its operations the Company seems to have chosen experienced merchants to act as its 'factors' in Asia.[2] But by 1668 very young men or boys, called 'apprentices' or 'writers', were also being sent out. The Directors explained that they had enough men of 'age, abilities and quallity' in India and intended in future 'only to send from home young men or youths, to be trayned up in our business, for wee have observed the advantages, that others have by this way, in the knowing and well manadgement of affairs, by encouraging young men, in hopes of preferment, to be sober, industrious and faithfull'.[3] By the eighteenth century most servants going out to India on their first appointment were young men with the rank of Writer. In 1751 the qualifications for a Writer were formally fixed at a minimum age of sixteen with proof being required that the boy had been through 'a regular course of arithmetick and merchants' accounts'.[4] The Company continued, however, from time to time to appoint more senior men to Bengal as Factors, such appointments finally ceasing in the 1770s.

As the generally accepted means of entry became appointment as a Writer, the covenanted service began to take on a strongly hierarchical character. A series of graded ranks were fixed in 1706 into a form that was to last for over 100 years. A man served for five years as a Writer before becoming a Factor; three years later he would become a Junior Merchant; three years later still he would reach the highest rank in the service, that of Senior Merchant.[5] Within these grades there was strict observance of seniority according to year of arrival. In due time the most senior of the Senior Merchants became members of the Bengal Council, a body until 1774 of some ten men who directed the Company's affairs. Until the 1760s, when special appointments began to be made, the most tenacious survivor of all could expect to end up as Governor. The Directors' instructions were invariably that promotion and preferment should be by seniority. They made, however, the conventional exception that outstanding merit might be

[1] See copies of bonds in I.O.R., O/1/1.
[2] K. N. Chaudhuri, *The English East India Company* (1965), pp. 80–2.
[3] Directors to Fort St. George, 20 Nov. 1668, I.O.R., E/3/87, p. 199.
[4] Directors to Bengal, 23 Jan. 1751, I.O.R., E/3/111, p. 79.
[5] Directors to Bengal, 15 Feb. 1706, I.O.R., E/3/95, p. 530.

rewarded, and the much more significant one that they themselves could alter the succession of servants when they thought fit
to do so. Well organized campaigns by the friends of a servant
in Bengal in the Company at home could bring orders that he be
given extra seniority, a lucrative appointment or some other
favour. But the general trend throughout the century seems to
have been for the claims of seniority to become more and more
strongly entrenched. A newly-appointed Writer found in 1771
that the Governor of Bengal 'pays in general great regard to
seniority of service . . . and indeed in the service here supercessions
are not common. In an office if one is put over the rest all those
are provided for and nobody serves under his junior.'[1] Warren
Hastings reflected at the end of his career in Bengal that 'the whole
history of the world affords no example of a service . . . conducted
so strictly according to the rule of seniority'.[2]

The Company servants considered themselves to be the aristo-
crats of the British community. They exercised on the Company's
behalf the authority vested in it by the charters granted by the
British crown or the *farmans* of Indian rulers. Other British
subjects must obey them. They also tried to ensure that the most
lucrative opportunities for personal enrichment were confined to
them. Writerships were by far the most eagerly sought appointments to India. Many civil servants had younger brothers or
other dependants under their patronage serving in less favoured
situations.

Biographical information about Bengal servants in the early
eighteenth century is not very easy to obtain.[3] What is available,
however, suggests that most servants came from a commercial
background and could be called 'merchants'. Entry by nomination
of the Court of Directors inevitably meant that many sons or close
relatives of the Directors were chosen. Connections with the
Company tended, as in the nineteenth century, to be hereditary.
Men who had served in India sought election to the Directors and
used their patronage to send their sons to India, who became
Directors in their turn. Again as in the nineteenth century, East
India Company families frequently intermarried. Thus many

---

[1] G. Bogle to R. Bogle, 22 Feb. 1771, Mitchell Library, Bogle MSS.

[2] Notes in Add. MS. 29204, ff. 19–21; see also Hastings to Lord North,
2 Apr. 1775, Add. MS. 29125, ff. 205–6.

[3] There is much valuable material in the appendices to C. R. Wilson, *Early
Annals of the English in Bengal* (1895–1917), II, i.

members of the pre-Plassey Bengal service were closely related. An obvious example of three interrelated Bengal dynasties is the Russells, the Franklands and the Eyres, who between them provided four Governors and five other members of the Bengal Council before Plassey.

In the eighteenth century the term 'merchant' was an extremely elastic one, covering a huge range of occupations from retail shopkeepers to bankers and financiers. Men connected with the East India Company were among the most socially aspiring of merchants. Directors of the Company who had been useful to the Stuart kings had been rewarded with knighthoods, and Directors often lived in considerable state with large town houses and country residences, usually in the home counties. Many Bengal servants came from this sort of background and intended to live this kind of life when they retired. Thomas Pitt might complain in 1706 that the Company 'generally give more countenance to Blew Coat boys and such fellows than to gentlemen's sons',[1] but even in 1706 the covenanted service was in its own eyes a career for 'gentlemen'. Civil servants carried swords and fought or threatened to fight on points of honour. An application for a Bengal Writership in 1754 felt it necessary to assure the Directors that while he was at Edinburgh University, he had 'behaved himself regularly as became a gentleman'.[2]

From 1749 'Writers' Petitions', that is applications for Writerships, survive.[3] Candidates were required to produce certificates certifying their age, and from these certificates biographical information can easily be deduced. For the last years before Plassey a majority of applicants still seem to have come from commercial families, often with previous Bengal connections. But there is also evidence that men of rather different origins, who were to be important in the future, were already seeking careers in the Bengal service. In 1750, out of eight Writers appointed to Bengal, three were Scottish. Scotland's connection with Bengal had evidently begun, many years before Henry Dundas took over the management of Indian affairs and, according to legend, filled India with Scotsmen. Highly educated and commercially enterprising Scots had presumably been drawn to Bengal in the early

---

[1] T. Pitt to J. How, 11 Sept. 1706, Add. MS. 22849, f. 77.
[2] Petition of G. Gray, I.O.R., J/1/2, 1754, no. 16.
[3] I.O.R., J/1/1 to 1/8 cover the period of this book.

eighteenth century as they had been drawn to so many other parts of the world. Once established there, what has been called their 'innate clannishness'[1] no doubt drew others after them. In 1773 a young Scot reported that his countrymen 'grow so numerous' in Bengal 'that I am afraid that I shall not be able to enumerate them with that exactness I have hitherto done'.[2]

The appearance of three sons of the Anglican clergy among the Writers for 1752 suggests that another major source of recruits for the later civil service was also already in existence before Plassey. It is not necessarily the case that a boy from a rectory was socially very different from a boy from a counting-house. Well established English families would find it perfectly acceptable to put their sons into socially presentable branches of trade as well as into professions and the Church, while in Scotland there was even more mobility between trade, land, and the professions.[3] Nevertheless, the presence of an increasing number of sons of the clergy in Bengal suggests that Indian service was becoming an object of interest to widening sections of the British upper classes even before Plassey.

Interest quickened after Plassey, as stories of great fortunes to be made in Bengal circulated in Britain. Intense competition for Writerships forced up the social level of the Bengal service. By 1787 a pamphleteer could describe the Bengal servants as 'all, or the majority . . . gentlemen or the sons of gentlemen'.[4] A few came from families which would not normally have contemplated trade of any kind as a career for their sons. Frederick Stuart, son of Lord Bute, went to Bengal as a Writer, as did Henry Ramus, a young man with Court connections in whose career George III was interested,[5] and Robert Cholmondeley, cousin of the First Marquis Cholmondeley. Standards of formal education were also rising. In the 1780s Warren Hastings used to preside over annual dinners of old Westminster boys, twenty-seven attending in 1784.[6] Many of the Scots were clearly men of formidable intelligence and

[1] T. C. Smout, *A History of the Scottish People 1560–1830* (1969), p. 364.
[2] T. Graham to J. Graham, 28 Jan. 1773, S.R.O., GD 29/2136.
[3] Smout, p. 283; R. H. Campbell, *Scotland since 1707* (Oxford, 1965), p. 5.
[4] *An Appeal from the hasty to the deliberative judgement of the people of England* (1787), pp. 28–9.
[5] *Later Correspondence of George III*, ed. A. Aspinall (Cambridge, 1962–70), i. 604.
[6] *Memoirs of William Hickey*, ed. A. Spencer (1913–25), iii. 245–6.

accomplishments. Most writers were too young to have been to an English university, but a few had done so, such as Robert Maddison, who came 'well stocked with classical learning' from Cambridge,[1] Edward Pote from Eton and King's, or Nathaniel Halhed from Harrow and Christ Church. The qualities in which the nineteenth-century Indian Civil Service took such pride, gentility, and a high intellectual tone, were already matters of pride in eighteenth-century Bengal.

Even in the early eighteenth century, the Bengal servants tried to maintain a standard of life which they thought appropriate to gentlemen. At the beginning of the century, a visitor found 'gentlemen and ladies' in Bengal living 'both splendidly and pleasantly'.[2] In 1730 the Directors complained about an 'expensive and extravagant way of living, particularly in equipage and show'.[3] The Governor, they believed, 'had a sett of musick at his table and a coach and six with guards and running footmen'.[4] The servants might reply that they merely had 'dancing twice a week to keep up a social spirit',[5] but they were not believed and various sumptuary regulations were sent out to Calcutta. These clearly had no effect. The expense of life for Europeans in Bengal became notorious. By 1735 it was being said that 'no one at present from the hightest to the lowest can live conveniently on his allowance',[6] a complaint which became universal later in the century as the cost of housing, food, and servants continued to rise, especially in Calcutta. Some men felt themselves trapped in a world where 'expences . . . are so excessive, and no person choosing to retrench, lest it impair his credit, . . . a very few years will reduce a man from opulence to beggary should he meet with misfortune'.[7] Others clearly took a pride in the scale of the routs, gambling, and drinking marathons, which William Hickey later remembered with such relish.[8]

In 1707 the servants of what had come to be known as the 'old' East India Company in Bengal together with those of its rival, the

[1] Clive to J. Carnac, 23 May 1765, N.L.W., Clive MSS., 218, p. 28.
[2] A. Hamilton, *A New Account of the East Indies* (Edinburgh, 1737), ii. 12.
[3] Directors to Bengal, 23 Jan. 1730, I.O.R., E/3/104, p. 674.
[4] Directors to Bengal, 3 Dec. 1731, I.O.R., E/3/105, p. 337.
[5] Abs. Bengal to Directors, 10 Feb. 1731, I.O.R., E/4/3, p. 138.
[6] Abs. Bengal to Directors, 28 Dec. 1735, I.O.R., E/4/4, p. 139.
[7] R. Barwell to A. Beaumont, 1 Sept. 1774, *B.P.P.*, xii (1916), 63.
[8] The fullest edition of Hickey is in 4 vols., ed. A. Spencer. There is a single vol. edition, ed. P. Quennell (1960).

'new' Company, formed a united service of twenty-nine. Over the next three years new appointments brought the Bengal service up to about fifty, a level which it was to retain for several decades, until it rose to over seventy in the 1750s. A dramatic increase began in the 1760s: twenty-eight were appointed to Bengal in 1762, twenty-six in 1764, thirty in 1765, and no fewer than forty-six in 1770. The service continued to be flooded with new Writers until 1773, when a halt was called. By then the number of covenanted servants in Bengal had risen to about 250.[1] The service had become so over-inflated that by the 1780s many men were forced either to accept unemployment in India or repatriation on a pension. The flood of new Writers sent to Bengal after 1762 showed that the Directors were aware that new administrative tasks would require more European manpower. But as one of them candidly admitted,[2] it owed much more to the importunities to which the Directors were now being subjected to send young men out to the supposed riches of Bengal, and to the outbreak of faction fighting within the Company, which made the Directors especially anxious to cultivate support at their annual elections by adding to their stock of patronage in India. In 1766 both the Chairman and the Deputy Chairman of the Company objected to a proposal to send more Writers to Bengal, but they were unable to resist 'the general cry'.[3]

The covenanted civil service was by far the most prestigious part of the East India Company's service, but at any time in the eighteenth century civil servants would have made up only a relatively small part of the Company's European personnel in Bengal. The army was by far the largest part. In the early eighteenth century two companies of nominally European soldiers were employed by the Company in Bengal to guard its trade and its factories. At full strength this force consisted of some 200 rank and file and five or six officers. The number was increased to over 500 soldiers and between ten and twenty officers by the middle of the century. The racial and national composition of the Company's troops was extraordinarily diverse. A muster roll of 1750 shows that only a quarter of the men were actually British, while over a half appear to have been Indian Christians or Eurasians, mostly

[1] There are annual returns of the Bengal establishment in I.O.R., L/F/10/1–2.
[2] L. Scrafton to Clive, 1 July 1768, I.O.L., MS. Eur. G. 37, box 53, f. 162.
[3] G. Dudley to Clive, 21 Nov. 1766, ibid., box 43, f. 68.

Catholics with Portuguese names. There were also about 100 Dutch, over fifty French and odd individuals from Italy, Switzerland, Flanders, and Scandinavia.[1]

When put to the test, the old Bengal army collapsed ignominiously in 1756 and, following Plassey, a new and much larger army had to be built up with great rapidity. A very large part of this new army consisted of Indian sepoys under European officers, but the Company was determined to maintain a strong European element. Three European infantry regiments with a target strength of 3,000 rank and file were created and there was to be an artillery train with 300 Europeans, later increased to 900. Although 6,500 recruits were shipped out between 1762 and 1772, the appalling losses from disease from which European soldiers in Bengal suffered meant that they were always well under strength.[2] The figure of 3,000 rank and file of all arms was not attained until 1769,[3] and by 1784 there were only 603 fit European artillerymen and 1,114 fit infantry serving in Bengal.[4] There was, however, no shortage of sepoys. Clive thought a proportion of two sepoys to one European was a safe one, and so he recommended a sepoy force of 6,000.[5] In fact the number of sepoys was already 8,000 in 1763, became 25,000 by 1768[6] and nearly 40,000 by 1784.[7]

Nor was there any shortage of men willing to become officers in the Company's army: the total number rose from 114 in 1763 to 500 in 1769[8] and 1,069 in 1784,[9] an even more remarkable rate of increase than in the civil service. Many of the new officers were of course needed to fill posts created by the growth of the army as a whole. But the supply of officers clearly outran needs. A large number of 'supernumarary' officers, beyond the quota allowed for by the military establishment, were serving in Bengal by 1784.[10]

Pressures of patronage had evidently contributed to the growth of the officer corps in Bengal, as they had done to the flooding of the civil service. In the early 1760s the Court of Directors recruited a number of experienced officers in Britain or from the

---

[1] See muster rolls in I.O.R., L/MIL/10/130.
[2] 9th Report, Secret Committee, 1773, *Reports*, iv. 629–36.
[3] Ibid., iv. 592.   [4] I.O.R., Home Miscellaneous, 361, p. 209.
[5] 9th Report, *Reports*, iv. 577–8.   [6] Ibid., iv. 592.
[7] I.O.R., Home Miscellaneous, 362, p. 141.
[8] 9th Report, *Reports*, iv. 592.
[9] I.O.R., Home Miscellaneous, 361, p. 97.
[10] Ibid. 348, pp. 87 ff.

royal regiments serving in India to provide senior officers in Bengal. Within a few years, however, the military service came to resemble the civil service. Very young men were recruited in Britain by nomination of the Court of Directors to serve as Cadets in the Bengal army, the equivalent of the civilian Writers. On occasions Cadets were also appointed in India. Cadets were promoted according to strict seniority, gradually rising to fill the very limited number of higher ranks allowed in the Bengal army. The Directors seem to have shown some restraint in the appointment of Cadets during the 1760s, although they allowed 73 to be nominated in 1768. But the military service was flooded with young men in the 1770s. In 1777 71 were chosen; 75, 107, and 110 in the three following years; and no fewer than 163 in 1781. At the same time Cadets were being created in large numbers by the Governor and Council in Bengal, about 100 of them in 1778 alone.[1] With so much competition, prospects for promotion began to look very poor.[2]

From early in the eighteenth century the Company maintained an establishment of chaplains, to minister to the European community, not to act as missionaries,[3] and of surgeons, whose numbers grew with the increase in the civil service and the army. The two surgeons and two 'mates' of the early eighteenth century became 40 by 1763 and 140 by 1783.[4]

The professional competence of the army officers was at least sufficient to ensure that the eighteenth-century Bengal army suffered no defeat of any consequence after 1756, and there is no reason to believe that the standard of the majority of chaplains or surgeons fell below what contemporaries regarded as acceptable. Nevertheless, professional ambition alone is not likely to have brought many to Bengal. Those who wished to shine or who had shone in their professions would stay in Britain for obvious reasons. Those who came to Bengal were likely either to be men who despaired of promotion or preferment elsewhere or who wished to get out to India in some capacity or other in the hope of making a fortune. Most of the early Cadets were probably not boys who felt drawn to army life so much as the sons of families who had

---

[1] V. C. P. Hodson's transcripts of military records, National Army Museum, MSS. 6404/69/64, 6404/69/89.

[2] See below, p. 208.

[3] On them see H. B. Hyde, *Parochial Annals of Bengal* (Calcutta, 1901).

[4] D. G. Crawford, *A History of the Indian Medical Service* (1914), i. 199–204.

failed to send them out as Writers but were willing to take second best.

Men were prepared to risk the hazards of eighteenth-century Bengal above all because they hoped to improve their position in life. All employees of the Company received salaries. But until salaries were greatly increased in the last few years of the period covered in this book,[1] they made up a comparatively small part of what the ambitious, especially the civil servants and more senior army officers, hoped to earn; the greater part came from perquisites and unofficial profits attached to offices and above all from trading. For most of the eighteenth century virtually all the civil servants were also private merchants, while many army officers, surgeons, and even chaplains[2] traded. In the early eighteenth century the Governor and the Councillors were the leading European merchants of Calcutta. They appear to have maintained their own 'counting houses' with staffs of European clerks and assistants. The right to trade within limits laid down by the Company 'without any lett, hindrance or interruption' was included in a Writer's covenant. At least until the 1760s private trading by its servants was accepted and generally approved by the Company.

The Company's regulations about private trade were based on the distinction commonly made by Europeans between trade from Europe to Asia and vice versa and the 'country' trade within Asia. By the late seventeenth century it had become the East India Company's policy rigidly to exclude all private participation in trade between Europe and Asia, while allowing its servants in India to have considerable latitude in Asian trading. Protection of the monopoly of trade to and from Europe meant that no English merchant ship was allowed round either the Cape of Good Hope or Cape Horn unless it belonged to the East India Company. With the merging of the two companies and the suppression of 'interloping', the monopoly was kept more or less intact throughout the eighteenth century. Englishmen in Bengal could only trade directly with Europe if they could obtain a share of the limited space allocated on the Company's ships for 'privilege', or private goods,[3] or if they were prepared to entrust their goods to foreign ships.

[1] See below, pp. 180 ff.
[2] See, for instance, inventory of the Revd. H. Butler's estate, 5 Dec. 1761, I.O.R., Mayor's Court Records, I.O.R., Range 154, vol. 63, ff. 100–2; the Revd. J. Burn to G. Graham, 25 Nov. 1775, S.R.O., G.D. 29/2062/1.
[3] See below, p. 220.

They had, however, almost complete freedom in trading with the rest of Asia. This freedom came relatively late in the Company's history. From the Company's point of view, inter-Asian trade was potentially a valuable way in which funds might be earned to pay for return cargoes to Europe, and so at first it tried to reserve the country trade for itself. It was, however, always extremely difficult to prevent the servants from trading on their own behalf, and in 1667 they were given formal permission to do so. 'To encourage persons to undertake and proceed cheerfully in the management of the Company's affairs', Company servants were now to be permitted to trade in Asia in all commodities except calicoes and pepper, the twin staples of the Company's own trade.[1] The privilege of free trade in Asia was defined in a series of 'indulgences' issued in 1670, 1674, and 1675,[2] so that in 1679 the Company could claim that 'in effect the whole trade of those vast countries . . . lies free and open to our servants to improve their own stocks by'[3]. Once the concessions had been made, they were never revoked and survived into the later eighteenth century with only minor amendments and restrictions.

British Company servants enjoyed a freedom of trade in Asia which was denied by the French company until the 1720s, while the Dutch gave no significant concessions to their servants until 1742. As private British trade spread over Asia in the eighteenth century some Englishmen liked to reflect complacently on their superior wisdom. But the grants of free trade had, in fact, arisen from the weakness of the Company, not from its foresight. The Company could engage in the country trade on its own behalf either by maintaining a special fleet of ships in Asian waters or by putting off the return of its regular ships while they went on country voyages. Both alternatives were costly and in the 1660s, when the 'indulgences' to its servants began to be issued, the Company felt it could afford neither. 'Trading in the countrie from port to port hath produced rather loss than proffitt to us', the Directors wrote, and they announced that henceforward they

---

[1] *A Calendar of the Court Minutes of the East India Company 1664–7*, ed. E. B. Sainsbury (1925), p. 396.

[2] Ibid., *1668–70* (1929), p. 381; *1674–6* (1935), p. 24; *The Diaries of Streynsham Master*, ed. R. C. Temple (1911), pp. 195–6, 264.

[3] Directors to Fort St. George, 3 Dec. 1679, I.O.R., E/3/89, p. 116.

would concentrate on 'trade out and home'.[1] In more affluent times ships were allowed to spend extra seasons in Asia on country voyages or were instructed to make circuitous trips trading from port to port, but the Company was always wary of the demurrage charges, which it had to pay the owners of its ships four months after they arrived in Asia;[2] most ships were sent directly to their destinations with orders to return as soon as possible. The major part of the British stake in the country trade was left to private individuals.

A policy begun in weakness was eventually invested with principle. Freedom of trade, it was argued, would enable the servants to earn fortunes which cost the Company nothing, while at the same time it would turn the English settlements into thriving ports from which the Company could collect a large revenue in customs and taxation. The Madras servants were told 'to have as well a regard to the generall good of the Company by encreasing the trade and revenue of Fort St. George as the encrease of your profitts'. Successful private trade would make 'your place great and famous in a short time strong and defensive' and 'a mart for nations . . . That being the means to which God Almighty of old promised to make Jerusalem great'.[3] 'We shall always be glad when trade flourishes in India, as well for the opportunity it affords our servants to get estates honestly, as that our own settlements are bettered thereby', the Directors wrote in 1717.[4]

It was ostensibly to 'better their settlements' that the Directors permitted men who had no connection with their service to settle in Bengal. From a few 'Free Merchants', permitted to go to India on sufferance in the seventeenth century, the 'unofficial' European community of the later British India derived its origins. By 1784 this community was growing rapidly in numbers and in wealth.

By the terms of the Company's monopoly no Englishman not in its employment was allowed to go to Asia without its express permission. In the early seventeenth century the Company was not inclined to give permission, but it still proved impossible to prevent private Englishmen going to India on their own account.

[1] Directors to Surat and Fort St. George, 27 Mar., 31 Aug. 1661, I.O.R., E/3/86, pp. 19, 49–50.
[2] 5th Report, Secret Committee, 1773, *Reports*, iv. 274.
[3] Directors to Fort St. George, 13 Feb. 1685, I.O.R., E/3/90, p. 425.
[4] Directors to Fort St. George, 25 Jan. 1717, I.O.R., E/3/99, p. 113.

In the 1660s the Company decided, as it had done over private trade by its servants, to accept what it could not effectively prevent, and to allow such men 'to live peaceably and quietly without disturbance or discouragement'.[1] They were given the same privileges of free trade in Asia that the Company servants now enjoyed, but they were obliged to live in the Company's settlements under the authority of its Governors and to sign covenants to be of good behaviour. For the future, individuals who wished to go to India on their own behalf might apply to the Directors for a licence. They too would be required to sign a covenant[2] and to give security, fixed in 1705 at £1,000.[3] Throughout the eighteenth century a steady trickle of so-called Free Merchants, fifty-nine were licensed between 1736 and 1756,[4] went to Bengal with the Directors' permission. They seem generally to have been men disqualified, either because they were too old or because they had too little influence in the Company, from obtaining Writerships. The Directors also licensed Free Mariners to go to Bengal, that is men who were needed to act as officers or to fill crucial positions in the crew of ships used in the country trade. By licensing Free Merchants and Free Mariners the Directors hoped to contribute to the 'encrease of our settlements and of the countrey trade'.[5]

The Directors intended that a limited number of private Englishmen should be added to their settlements under close regulation and control. In fact, there was an indiscriminate migration to Bengal during the eighteenth century of Europeans of all kinds, who did not have the Company's licence and about whose numbers and occupations reliable information was very hard to obtain. There was no effective means of stopping enterprising individuals from going to India. By 1751 the Directors were well aware that 'abundance of people are now in India without our licence'.[6] In 1787 the Bengal Council reported that 'a great number' of unlicensed Englishmen were to be found 'all over the country'. They came out on foreign ships, overland via the Persian Gulf, or by enlisting in the crew of the Company's

<hr>

[1] Directors to Fort St. George, 20 Feb. 1662, I.O.R., E/3/86, pp. 98–9.
[2] A Free Merchant's covenant is reproduced in W. Bolts, *Considerations on India Affairs* (1772–5), i. 115–17.
[3] Directors to Fort St. George, 12 Jan. 1705, I.O.R., E/3/95, p. 372
[4] I.O.R., Home Miscellaneous, 78, pp. 49–51.
[5] Directors to Bengal, 19 Oct. 1716, I.O.R., E/3/99, p. 4.
[6] Directors to Bengal, 23 Jan. 1751, I.O.R., E/3/111, p. 80.

own ships and deserting when they got to India.[1] Threats of
punishment against those who went to India and the captains who
took them there, issued from the 1720s,[2] clearly had little effect.
The obvious remedy was for the Company's servants to deport
unlicensed Europeans whom they caught in the British settlements.
The Company considered that they had full legal power to do so,
and a test case lodged in the British courts against a Governor of
Bengal who did deport individuals by force was decided in his
favour.[3] But previous legal advice had been that deportation, unless
carried out very soon after an illegal immigrant arrived, would
raise 'no small clamour against the Company',[4] and Governors
seem to have been very reluctant to use their powers. The advice
given to anyone who wanted to stay in India without official
permission was 'to keep in with Governours, by which you may
be tolerated by them, without the expence of purchasing a licence'.[5]
Warren Hastings admitted that he would 'by no means desire,
nor would I consent to exercise the rigour of the Company's
orders on every unlicensed person who may be found in India and
has demeaned himself peaceably and quietly to the inhabitants of
the country and obediently to the orders of government.'[6]

It is no easier for historians than it was for the Directors to
guess at the number of private Englishmen who may have been
living in Bengal at any time in the eighteenth century. The Company's government did not begin to keep official lists until 1794.
For 1800 the total number of Europeans in Bengal not employed
by the Company was put at under a thousand.[7] A careful reconstruction of the European community in Bengal in 1756 suggests
a total of 751, including the Company's personnel.[8] A list of
Calcutta 'inhabitants', presumably prepared for Clive in 1766,
gave 232 names for what seem to be male heads of families.[9] There

[1] Bengal to Directors, 19 Feb. 1787, I.O.R., E/4/45.
[2] Correspondence Reports, 4 Oct. 1726, I.O.R., D/18, f. 125.
[3] Directors to Bengal, 27 May 1779, I.O.R., E/4/625, p. 367.
[4] Opinion of J. Browning with which C. Yorke agreed, 9 Nov. 1757, I.O.R.,
Home Miscellaneous, 824, pp. 57–8.
[5] R. Adams to G. Gray, 28 Nov. 1735, I.O.R., Home Miscellaneous, 37,
p. 275.   [6] I.O.R., B.P.C., 4 Mar. 1776, Range 2, vol. 12, f. 358.
[7] S. C. Ghosh, *The Social Condition of the British Community in Bengal 1757–
1800* (Leiden, 1970), p. 60.
[8] S. C. Hill, *A List of Europeans and others in the English Factories in Bengal*
(Calcutta, 1902).
[9] Copies in N.L.W., Clive MSS., 184; I.O.L., MS. Eur. G. 37, box 18,
no. 9.

were, however, obvious incentives for many unlicensed Europeans to have kept out of the way of the counters, and it seems reasonable to add a considerable number to each of these totals.

The 1766 list gives interesting details as to nationality and occupation. A very polyglot European community was clearly living under British protection in Calcutta. Of the 232 named, 64 were not of British origin, 19 Germans, 16 Dutch and 13 French being the largest foreign contingents. The list does not include Armenians, whose numbers in Bengal in the late eighteenth century have been put at three or four thousand,[1] nor the sizeable Greek community, nor those conventionally described as 'Portuguese', a term which covered a multitude of sins, including genuine Portuguese, Eurasians,[2] people of Hindu and Muslim origin who had adopted a European manner of life, 'women kept as concubines by the English . . . which are many', and slaves employed by Europeans and 'called Portugueze and considered as Christians merely because they are made to eat all kinds of meat, and to do such things as neither Mussalmen nor Hindoos will do'.[3] The occupations of those in the 1766 list can roughly be divided into 15 merchants, 43 shopkeepers and craftsmen (including some catering for a clientele with luxurious and sophisticated tastes, such as a pastry-cook, a wig-maker, jewellers, goldsmiths, and watchmakers, and a 'draftsman and painter'), 34 personal servants and clerks, 17 practising professions (attorneys and undertakers inevitably well to the fore but a teacher of the French horn also included), and many seamen. Outside Calcutta in 1766 there are likely to have been a few private Europeans acting as clerks or personal servants to the Company servants and a small sprinkling trying to trade on their own in various parts of Bengal.

Another list of the same period gives the names of seventy Free Merchants trading in Bengal.[4] In the 1760s they were still very much the poor relations of the Company's servants, and private Europeans were not to be freed of restrictions on their residence in Bengal or from the threat of deportation until 1833. But the future was bright for them. As more and more prohibitions were laid on the activities of the Company's servants, the bulk of private

[1] N. K. Sinha, *Economic History of Bengal* (Calcutta, 1956–70), i. 72.
[2] For more material on them, see Ghosh, *Social Condition*, pp. 81 ff.
[3] Calcutta Bar Library Club, Supreme Court Reports, iv. 192–3, Hyde's note.
[4] I.O.L., MS. Eur. G. 37, box 18, no. 5.

European business enterprise in Bengal came to be managed by Free Merchants. Within a few years they were to set up the Houses of Agency,[1] which were to control the new plantations and the fleets of ships based on Calcutta, and to develop new European banks and insurance businesses. A little later still they were to help to destroy the monopoly of the East India Company itself and all British trade in India was to pass into their hands.

At any time before 1784 the British were a miniscule element in Bengal's vast population. They lived in tiny enclaves in the great cities and commercial centres of Mughal Bengal, such as Murshidabad, Dacca, Kasimbazar, or Patna, where on an evening in the 1770s 'may be seen thirty or forty carriages on the course or plain w[h]ere the gentlemen ride out for an airing'.[2] As Bengal passed under British control, much of the army was stationed in barracks or camps 'up-country', and a sprinkling of administrators, commercial agents and planters set up their bungalows in the countryside. But only in Calcutta during the eighteenth century was the British presence in Bengal unmistakable. Calcutta was virtually the creation of the East India Company after 1690, but its population grew with extraordinary rapidity. As early as 1730 one observer guessed that it might contain 300,000 people,[3] and another was prepared to hazard 400,000 by 1750;[4] 600,000 has been suggested for the end of the century.[5] These estimates are no doubt grossly over-inflated, but a critical reduction of them to 120,000 for 1750 is still a very striking figure.[6]

The European quarter of Calcutta contained some public buildings. Two Fort Williams were constructed: the old one that failed completely in 1756 and a vast new one that was never put to the test. The first Anglican Church was built in 1709, a Catholic or 'Portuguese' Church in 1727 and the Mission Church of the Society for Promoting Christian Knowledge in 1770. A building for a charity school in 1731 was also used by the Company's courts, as an exchange and a post office and for 'public entertainments

---

[1] See below, pp. 47–8.

[2] E. Law to J. Law, 15 Dec. 1775, P.R.O., 30/12/17/2, p. 59.

[3] *Antwerpsch Archievenblad*, v. 48.

[4] J. Z. Holwell, *India Tracts*, 3rd edn. (1774), p. 209.

[5] Sinha, *Economic History*, ii. 220.

[6] A. K. Ray, 'A Short History of Calcutta', *Census of India 1901*, vii (Calcutta, 1902), pp. 59–62.

and assembly rooms'.[1] But by far the largest part of Calcutta's
European building was put up to house private individuals, much
capital both British and Indian being invested in bricks and
mortar, especially during a massive rebuilding and expansion of
the city after 1757. The Company acted as landlord under the
grants which it had obtained from the Nawabs and leased out land
at a low ground rent. Those who acquired leases, or *pattas*, were
assured of virtual freehold by indefinite renewals.[2] House building
was on an elaborate scale. European houses gave 'the impression
of Grecian temples . . . with great projecting porticoes, or sur-
rounded by colonades or arcades'.[3] A discerning visitor to Calcutta, however, found in 1773:

The quarter inhabited by the English . . . laid off in regular wide streets
with spacious and showy houses, such as in appearance eclipse, (not to
speak of London) almost any thing in Paris and Italy. I say in appearance
for they will not bear an examination, they are all of brick plaistered
over and whitewashed, but all attempt some order of architecture and
you see nothing but portico's, columnades, galleries, etc. etc., some few
in good taste, several tolerable and many more wretchedly bad.[4]

With the security that Plassey brought, more affluent Europeans
moved out of the city to set up what they called their 'garden
houses' in relative calm and seclusion. The 'black town' for the
most part grew up to the north of the European settlement. In
the eighteenth century it was a sprawl of hamlets, villages, and
bazars, inhabited by separate groups and castes or by the dependants of rich men who had been attracted to Calcutta to do
business with the British, rather than an integrated town.[5] A
considerable part of the population lived in straw and grass
shelters, and 'the closeness of such houses, the same not being
intersected by streets or passages' made them liable to devastating
fires, especially in the dry month of March. In the spring of 1780
'almost the whole of the town of Calcutta . . . excepting that part

---

[1] E. M. Drummond, 'The northern side of Tank Place . . . in the 18th century', *B.P.P.*, i (1907), 64–5.
[2] The system is described in R. C. Sterndale, *An Historical Account of the
Calcutta Collectorate* (reprint Calcutta, 1958), pp. 32–9.
[3] W. Hodges, *Travels in India* (1793), p. 15.
[4] L. S. Sutherland, 'A letter from John Stewart', *Indian Archives*, x (1956), 5.
[5] P. Sinha, 'The city as a physical entity—Calcutta 1750–1860', *B.P.P.*,
lxxxix (1970), 264–71, and 'Social forces and urban growth', ibid., xcii (1973),
288–99.

which is inhabited by the Europeans and the more substantial of the native inhabitants' was destroyed with the loss of over fifty lives.[1]

The inhabitants of Calcutta, Indian or European, lived under a rudimentary system of government, derived from the Company's purchase in 1698 of what were known as *zamindari* rights. This system was not significantly modified when the British became the conquerors of Bengal. There was certainly no attempt to introduce any element of representation for the Europeans. Like other Bengal *zamindars*, the Company collected revenue, administered justice and tried to maintain law and order. The revenue came from the ground rents and from a mass of tolls and market dues, which were usually farmed out.[2] Justice was administered by the British official whom the Company called its *Zamindar*, who presided over 'cutcherry' courts, by the Governor and Council, empowered to sit as Justices of the Peace in quarter sessions after 1726, and by a court set up to administer English law by royal charter in the same year. This court was called the Mayor's Court and was to remain in being until 1774. A Mayor and nine Aldermen were appointed to act as judges in civil cases. The court was subjected to sharp criticisms from some contemporaries and has found few defenders among historians. The Aldermen had no obvious legal qualifications, it was sometimes alleged that they did partial justice in cases where they themselves were involved, and they were accused, especially after 1753 when the charter was revised, of being the tools of the Company.[3] It is, however, likely that the Mayor's Court provided a reasonably serviceable legal framework for Bengal's commercial community, merchants' cases being tried by merchants, which is what the Aldermen were. In retrospect at least, some Europeans came to lament the passing of the Mayor's Court when they had had experience of its successor, the Supreme Court set up by act of parliament in 1774.[4] The judges of the new court were appointed by the crown in Britain, and they inevitably enforced a much more

---

[1] B.P.C., 3, 10 Apr. 1780, I.O.R., Home Miscellaneous, 156, pp. 407, 430–1, 438.

[2] G. Blyn, 'Revenue administration of Calcutta in the first half of the eighteenth century', *India Economic and Social History Review*, i (1963–4).

[3] For the case against the court, see T. K. Mukherji, 'Aldermen and Attorneys—Mayor's Court Calcutta', *Indian Historical Quarterly*, xxvi (1950).

[4] *Remarks on the Petition of the British Inhabitants*, [1780], p. 52.

technically exact system of justice, at much greater expense,[1] than that supplied by the Aldermen. The problem of maintaining order in the city was eventually entrusted to police commissioners, appointed for the first time in 1772 and given new powers in 1778.[2]

Even by the not very exacting standards of contemporary British towns, the Company's rule can have offered little to the inhabitants of eighteenth-century Calcutta. Crime was rampant. 'Common robbers and murderers' were said in 1752 to infest the settlement.[3] In 1777 there were complaints of a 'very great increase of the most heinous offences' with the police more anxious 'to screen than to discover offenders'.[4] Attempts to establish commissions which could levy rates to maintain drainage and clean the streets came to very little. In 1780 the streets were said to be 'in a ruinous state', and 'stagnate water' and 'filth, dirt and rubbish' were creating urgent problems.[5] But for Europeans, the events of 1756 apart, the Company at Calcutta did at least provide security for their persons and their property and a reasonably predictable legal framework within which to conduct their business. For the mass of the population, on the other hand, such administration as existed must at the best have been ineffectual, while at certain times it appears to have been corrupt and tyrannical. In the first half of the eighteenth century serious allegations of oppression were made against the European *Zamindar's* Indian underlings.[6] In 1777 the police were said to extort confessions by flogging, and to levy protection money from 'brothels and gaming houses'.[7] Yet the growth of Calcutta, even at the lowest estimates, is very remarkable. The bulk of the Indian population presumably came to Calcutta in the wake of men who had settled there to do business with the East India Company or with individual Englishmen. Such men seem to have found in the Company's government, for all its obvious faults, a respect for the rights of property which made Calcutta a relatively attractive place to live in compared to

---

[1] This point was strongly made in [G. Smith], 'Observations on the English Possessions in India', P.R.O., 30/11/112, ff. 142–3.

[2] I.O.R., B.P.C., 9 June 1777, Range 2, vol. 19, pp. 460–71.

[3] Holwell, *India Tracts*, p. 193.

[4] I.O.R., B.P.C., 2 June 1777, Range 2, vol. 19, pp. 416–17.

[5] B.P.C., 26 June 1780, I.O.R., Home Miscellaneous, 156, pp. 448–9.

[6] Holwell, *India Tracts*, pp. 179 ff.

[7] I.O.R., B.P.C., 2 June 1777, Range 2, vol. 19, pp. 412–13, 417.

cities under the protection of the Nawabs of Bengal. Long before Calcutta became the capital of British Bengal, more and more of the Nawabs' richer subjects were moving there.[1]

By comparison with other European societies overseas, the British community in Bengal was undoubtedly a weak one during the eighteenth century. It was small in numbers, most of its members did not sink any roots in India but regarded their residence as purely temporary, and, in spite of the problem of distance, it was under fairly tight control from home. Most Englishmen in Bengal were either in the service of the Company or of the crown. They had no representative institutions, or authority over the Indian population which they did not derive from the Company; the *jagirs* of Clive and a few others[2] had nothing in common with the *encomiendas* of the New World. Their trading activities were still subject to the Company's monopoly and they were not permitted to own land outside Calcutta. Even their continued residence in India depended formally on the Company's consent. If such a community was to prosper, it could only expect to do so within conditions already prevailing in Bengal; it had neither the manpower nor the resources to change conditions for itself.

[1] For an account of the Indian notables of late eighteenth-century Calcutta, see P. Sinha, 'Social Change', *The History of Bengal 1757–1905*, ed. N. K. Sinha (Calcutta, 1967), pp. 387–94.

[2] See below, pp. 165–6, 177.

11

Eighteenth-century Bengal:
The View from Calcutta

During the sixteenth century and for much of the seventeenth European commercial activity in India had for the most part been concentrated on the ports of the western coast, such as Surat, Cochin, and Goa, and on those on the south-eastern or Coromandel Coast. In the eighteenth century there is a very marked shift of emphasis. Other centres remained important for the Europeans, but they were increasingly overshadowed by Bengal. This shift cannot simply be explained by a political accident which in mid-century brought Bengal under European rule earlier than any other area in India of comparable size. Bengal's commercial importance for Europeans began long before Plassey. By 1697 one-third of all the exports which the Dutch East India Company sent to Europe from the whole of Asia came from Bengal.[1] The role of Bengal goods in British trade was even more striking. In a normal year in the early eighteenth century up to 60 per cent of British imports from Asia originated from Bengal.[2] Private European enterprise, especially by the British community, was also flourishing in Bengal long before Plassey.

Any explanation of why Bengal became so important to Europeans in the eighteenth century must primarily be in economic terms, but political factors also counted for much. Throughout the century Bengal's rulers, Mughal or British, were able to maintain relatively stable conditions by comparison with the upheavals that took place in western or south-eastern India. Under the Nawabs Bengal was virtually immune from outside invasion, at least until the 1740s, or from serious internal revolts. In the middle of the century, after comparatively brief and limited outbreaks of violence, a stable Indian regime was replaced by a stable

---

[1] K. Glamann, 'Bengal and World Trade about 1700', *B.P.P.*, lxxvi (1957), 31.
[2] Based on figures kindly communicated by Dr. K. N. Chaudhuri.

European one. The British met with very little opposition within the province and, after 1764, were able to keep Bengal secure from invasion once again. It says much for the durability of the institutions of Mughal Bengal that they were able to preserve a more or less ordered life in the provinces, while their new masters were gradually devising institutions to replace them.

Murshid Kuli Khan, the architect of a self-contained Bengal, kept control of the province until his death in 1727. He was succeeded by his son-in-law, Shuja-ud-din, whose reign until 1739 was regarded by Europeans as an 'aera of good order and good government'.[1] In 1740 there was one of the upheavals so characteristic of later Mughal India in which Shuja-ud-din's son was challenged and overthrown by a provincial governor called Alivardi Khan; but the struggle seems to have been brief and to have had no serious effects on economic life.[2] Alivardi Khan was regarded by Europeans as an able and effective ruler, but during his reign from 1740 to 1756 Bengal was to undergo serious disruption for the first time for several generations. In 1742 the province was raided by Maratha armies from the Deccan. Large areas of Bengal west of the Ganges suffered serious devastation before the Marathas were driven out. In 1743 further Maratha incursions took place, the raids only finally coming to an end with the loss of most of Orissa to the Marathas in 1751. The wars by which the British gained control of Bengal began with Siraj-ud-daula's attack on Calcutta in 1756 and ended in 1764 with the final expulsion from Bihar of Mir Kasim and his Indian allies. Thereafter the Company's army was strong enough to ensure that Bengal was not invaded from without or disrupted from within on any large scale.

Whether Bengal was or was not disrupted by war or civil war no doubt depended on the prowess of the Nawabs or later of the East India Company. But for much of the eighteenth century stable conditions in the province owed much more to the Bengal *zamindars* than to the central government, be it Mughal or British. To Europeans the status of the *zamindars* was a puzzling one. By the eighteenth century they appeared in some respects to be appointed officials acting as the agents of the Nawabs, but in

---

[1] H. Verelst, *A View of the Rise, Progress and Present State of the British Government in Bengal* (1772), Appendix, p. 230.

[2] Abs. Bengal to Directors, 4 Aug. 1740, I.O.R., E/4/4, p. 337.

others to be independent proprietors of large estates. They were primarily responsible for collecting the government's 'revenue' from the produce of the cultivators, but in the absence of effective machinery for controlling local administration in the hands of the Nawabs,[1] they performed many other functions. The larger *zamindaris*, such as Burdwan, Rajshahi, Dinajpur, Nadia, or Bishnupur, covered huge areas, over which the *zamindars* maintained law and order and administered justice. *Zamindars* kept their own troops and levied tolls on trade.[2] Before 1784 the British had neither the resources nor the knowledge to impose more than a skeleton administration on Bengal, so the role of the *zamindars* remained an extremely important one.

In general the rule of the *zamindars* seems to have been relatively favourable to the economic life of Bengal. Except in frontier districts and in Bihar, Bengal *zamindars* do not seem to have used their power to enlarge their domains by making war on their neighbours. Nor do they appear to have followed the example of landholders in other parts of later Mughal India, who, according to recent studies, either levied taxation on the cultivators at rates which provoked flight and rebellion or themselves incited revolts.[3] Evidence of widespread depopulation or rural revolt has not yet been produced for eighteenth-century Bengal. The *zamindars* also appear to have been able to ensure that goods and persons could travel along the river system and the roads of Bengal in comparative security. In 1753 an Englishman wrote that merchants could send bullion from one part of Bengal to another 'under care frequently of one, two or three peons only'.[4]

Europeans were sharply critical of certain aspects of Mughal government in Bengal, but they were cushioned by special privileges from their worst effects. The British took a thoroughly jaundiced view of the standards of justice maintained in the *zamindars'* and, where they still functioned, the Nawabs' courts,

---

[1] The relative weakness of the Nawabs' *faujdars* and other local officials is stressed by R. Ray, 'Agrarian change in Bengal, 1750 to 1850' (Cambridge Ph.D. thesis, 1973), pp. 20, 38–9; see also P. Calkins, 'The formation of a regionally oriented ruling group in Bengal', *Journal of Asian Studies*, xxix (1969–70), 799–806.

[2] S. Akhtar, 'Role of *Zamindars* in Bengal 1707–72' (London Ph.D. thesis, 1973).

[3] e.g. I. Habib, *Agrarian System of Mughal India* (Bombay, 1953), pp. 317 ff.; N. A. Siddiqi, *Land Revenue System under the Mughals 1700–50* (Delhi, 1970).

[4] I.O.R., B.P.C., 10 June 1753, Range 1, vol. 26, f. 169.

and regarded the Bengal system of tolls and customs as a major impediment to trade. It was said to be 'a known truth' that one-quarter of the sums in dispute before any of the Nawabs' courts was 'appropriated for the service of the government and officers'.[1] In the 1750s the 'black merchants' in a Bengal town were said to find that 'they got more justice done them by the Company's Chiefs, than by their own country judges'.[2] But even before 1757 the British were able to avoid submitting themselves to these courts. They administered their own justice in Calcutta, 'laying hold' of their Indian debtors and carrying them into the settlement whenever possible, a practice 'tacitly allowed and countenanced' by the Nawabs' officials.[3] It is likely that other powerful groups of merchants enjoyed similar immunities. The customs system of Mughal Bengal will be examined in detail in a later chapter.[4] It was an extremely elaborate one, duties and tolls being collected by the Nawabs' government at certain stated places and by local officials and *zamindars* at subordinate customs posts and at markets. Large impositions were levied on trade and merchants were subjected to much oppression. But as with the jurisdiction of the courts, the privileged and the powerful enjoyed exemptions. Under the 1717 *farman* the British had complete immunity for the bulk of their goods; other merchants who wielded influence could also obtain some relaxation of the rigours of the system.

It would no doubt be misleading to attempt to portray eighteenth-century Bengal as an oasis in a war torn India. It is certainly possible to exaggerate both the beneficence of Mughal or early British rule and the degree to which economic life was being disrupted by violence elsewhere. Nevertheless, an authoritative study of Surat, once the greatest commercial centre of India, shows how its prosperity was strangled in the eighteenth century as its hinterland was cut off by war and disorder which ultimately engulfed the town itself.[5] These things did not happen in Bengal. For most of the century the Nawabs and the British were able

[1] Minute of J. Cartier, 1 Mar. 1763, H. Vansittart, *A Narrative of the Transactions in Bengal* (1766), ii. 362.

[2] Memorial of H. Baillie, I.O.L., MS. Eur. G. 37, box 18, no. 10.

[3] 7th Report, Secret Committee of the House of Commons, 1773; *Reports from Committees of the House of Commons* (1803-6), iv. 325.

[4] See below, pp. 108-9.

[5] I am most grateful to Dr. Ashin Das Gupta for his kindness in allowing me to consult his forthcoming study of Surat.

to maintain some kind of unity over an area extending hundreds of miles up the Ganges valley, at least as far as Patna. Beneath their umbrella the *zamindars* enforced a tolerably stable order. Without this stability Bengal could hardly have played its crucial role in the operations of the European companies or in the personal ambitions of so many individual Europeans.

In the early centuries of overseas expansion Europeans trading in Asia were in a very different situation to those in the western hemisphere. Rather than creating their own economic systems, they had to adapt themselves to complex and sophisticated economies which had been flourishing for centuries and into which Europeans were unable to introduce major changes before the nineteenth century. In America Europeans brought their own capital and labour to develop new mines, ranches, and plantations; in Asia they depended to a considerable degree on Asian capital and generally had little control over the supply of the goods they required, which were produced by artisans and cultivators who were not under their jurisdiction and supplied by Asian merchants. Bengal was no exception. Even after they had conquered the province, the British could not hope to remodel its economy; like other merchants before them, they had to adapt themselves to the conditions they found there. But the rewards for successful adaptation were high. Bengal offered fine communications, abundant cheap labour, a productive agriculture, highly developed handcraft industries and a relatively advanced system of currency and credit.

In the eighteenth century textiles, cotton, or silk, were the most valuable items in Bengal's trade with other parts of Asia and with Europe. Cotton piecegoods were woven at many different *aurangs*, or manufacturing districts, scattered throughout Bengal from Balasore in Orissa to Bihar. The largest concentrations of looms were at Malda in the north and in the east at Lakshmipur, Kalinda, and above all at Dacca, where 25,000 weavers were said in 1776 to produce 180,000 pieces of cloth from thread spun by 80,000 women.[1] Raw cotton grown in Bengal was supplemented by imports by sea from western India and later in the century by consignments brought down the Ganges from the Deccan and the Doab. Cotton cloth was produced in a bewildering variety, which

[1] B.P.C., [Sept. 1776], *Reports*, vi. 219.

the British roughly classified as muslins or the coarser calicoes. Categories were given heavily Anglicized versions of Indian names, such as 'Tanjeebs', 'Mulmulls', 'Cossaes', or 'Gurrahs'. Great quantities of silk were manufactured in certain areas, especially around the Nawab's capital at Murshidabad and the neighbouring town of Kasimbazar, at Radnagur in western Bengal and at Rangpur in the north. Some of the silk was mixed with cotton in the manufacture of cloth in Bengal, but much raw silk was exported to Europe and to other Asian markets, especially to Gujarat in western India.[1]

There was an enormous volume of trade in agricultural produce throughout Bengal during the eighteenth century.[2] Cultivators appear for the most part to have paid their revenue in cash[3] and a large proportion of the population must have used money. Valuable crops, such as sugarcane, indigo, betel nut, tobacco, and poppies, were widely grown, and there appears to have been a very large trade in food grains, often over long distances. Certain districts came to specialize in supplying Calcutta, as others no doubt specialized in supplying older cities, such as Dacca, Murshidabad, and Patna. The great market at Bhagwangola near Murshidabad was said to handle 650,000 tons of rice a year in the middle of the century.[4] Some of Bengal's agricultural produce was exported; rice was shipped to southern India, South-East Asia, and Indonesia; sugar to western India and the Middle East; indigo to Europe; and poppies, manufactured as opium, to Malaya, Java, and China. Salt and saltpetre seem to have been the only indigenous mineral products in which there was any sizeable volume of trade. Great quantities of salt were manufactured by boiling sea water in pans along the coast of the Bay of Bengal from Chittagong to Orissa. Saltpetre was extensively collected and refined in Bihar.

Since the sixteenth century Europeans had been struck by the cheapness as well as by the abundance of Bengal goods.[5] Many

---

[1] For a brief guide to Bengal textiles, see J. Irwin and P. R. Schwartz, *Studies in Indo-European Textile History* (Ahmedabad, 1966), pp. 44–50.

[2] For a fuller discussion, see below, p. 107.

[3] Methods of paying revenue are described in I.O.R., B.R.C., 13 June 1775, Range 49, vol. 53, pp. 614–20.

[4] K. M. Mohsin, *A Bengal District in Transition: Murshidabad 1765–93*, (Dacca, 1973), p. 14.

[5] See Portuguese comments quoted in D. F. Lach, *Asia in the Making of Europe* (Chicago, 1965), i. 416.

Bengal commodities retained their relative cheapness until well into the eighteenth century. An attempt to compare price levels of cereals in Delhi, Gujarat, and Bengal shows those in Bengal to have been distinctly lower.[1] The Company found saltpetre from Bengal to be markedly cheaper than saltpetre from other sources.[2] Bengal silk was consistently cheaper than silk from other Asian countries, such as China or Persia.[3] Bengal sugar undersold Javan sugar in the Persian Gulf and the Red Sea in the 1720s and 1730s.[4] Europeans generally attributed the cheapness, which gave Bengal goods such marked advantages in international trade, to abundant labour and the very low cost of food grains.

By the 1740s, however, Bengal's advantages seemed to be disappearing. Between 1738 and 1754 it was thought that the price of rice in Calcutta had risen by three or four times, and that textile prices had risen by 30 per cent.[5] To two Englishmen writing in 1753 it seemed that the price of 'the necessaries of life' had been 'greatly enhanced' over the previous ten or twenty years.[6] By the 1760s it was universally accepted that prices were rising very rapidly. Piecegood prices in Dacca were thought to have gone up by 70 per cent between 1766 and 1774,[7] while increases in sugar prices between 1756 and 1776 were put at 50 per cent.[8] Many explanations were offered. The greed of unscrupulous European monopolists or Indian middlemen was a favourite one. More plausible suggestions were the shortages of labour caused by the Maratha invasions and the 1770 famine (which had a particularly devastating effect on the silk producers) and the greatly increased demand for certain commodities, as a result of ever larger 'investments' by the European companies, especially by the British, and heavy purchases by private Europeans being added to the requirements of Asian merchants.

---

[1] M. A. Ansari, 'A short survey of cereal prices in Northern India during the eighteenth century', *Proceedings of 31st Session of the Indian History Congress* (Patna, 1970), pp. 255–9.

[2] S. Chaudhuri, 'Trade and Commercial Organisation in Bengal 1650–1720' (London Ph.D. thesis, 1969), p. 278.

[3] Glamann, 'Bengal in World Trade', *B.P.P.*, lxxvi. 34.

[4] Price lists in I.O.R., G/29/15, ff. 135, 156; G/17/1, ff. 448, 523.

[5] B. K. Gupta, *Serajuddaulah and the East India Company* (Leiden, 1966), p. 33.

[6] I.O.R., B.P.C., 7 June 1753, Range 1, vol. 26, f. 165.

[7] Ibid., 7 Mar. 1774, Range 2, vol. 5, f. 277.

[8] I.O.R., B.R.C., 15 May 1776, Range 49, vol. 13, p. 212.

Goods may have been cheap in Bengal for much of the eighteenth century, but there were still formidable hazards to successful trading. Even when prices were relatively low, the system of obtaining goods generally practised in Bengal, as in other parts of India, meant that large amounts of working capital were tied up for long periods. What were called 'ready money goods', finished articles ready for immediate purchase, could certainly be obtained, but most merchants operating on a large scale had to place orders and lay out part of the purchase price before production could begin; further payments would have to be made before it was finished. 'Advances' for cotton piecegoods might begin up to nine or ten months before the cloth would be received. The East India Company sometimes made payments for silk almost a year before they expected to receive it.[1] Poppies took seven or eight months from planting to the point where they could be dried for opium, the cultivator requiring an advance before he sowed the seed.[2] Advances had to be paid to the growers of sugarcane when they planted their canes in May or June to be harvested early in the following year.[3] Even the salt-boilers, who only needed sea water, firewood, and earthenware pots to carry on their craft, received payments several months before the salt was delivered.[4]

The need to lay out money in advance not only made heavy demands for working capital, but it also added appreciably to the risks of trade in Bengal. Payments had to be scattered to a multitude of small producers, living on the edge of subsistence and vulnerable to epidemic, flood, harvest failure, or over-taxation by the government. If they perished or fled, the merchant lost his advances. Even in normal years, merchants were by no means certain of receiving the goods for which they had made advanced payments. Weavers, in particular, were often said to take money from one man which they then used to make cloth to sell to another. All merchants were involved in disputes about 'balances', that is about the extent to which cultivators or artisans owed them money for undelivered goods.

---

[1] Chaudhuri, 'Trade and Commercial Organisation', p. 219.
[2] J. Benn to S. Sulivan, n.d., I.O.L., MS. Eur. E. 9, no. 69; I.O.R., B.R.C., 3 May 1775, Range 49, vol. 52, pp. 528–31.
[3] *Papers Respecting the Culture and Manufacture of Sugar in British India* (1822), i. 99.
[4] See the account of salt boiling in A. Keir, *Thoughts on the Affairs of Bengal* (1772), pp. 64–9.

Having disbursed large sums to impoverished producers, merchants had very strong incentives to try to protect their advances by exercising some sort of coercion. It was contrary to the traditions of Mughal government either to permit individual merchants to use force to further their trade or for the government itself to become a trader. Nevertheless, exceptions occurred. Particular merchants were favoured by the government and Mughal officials sometimes traded on their own behalf with the weight of their office behind them. Such exceptions seem to have become increasingly common during the last years of the independent Nawabs of Bengal. In the years before Plassey, it was said to be the custom for 'country merchants' to 'buy the protection of some person of authority', so that they could 'confine the weavers and picars when they cannot recover their balances from them otherwise',[1] while the English Company claimed a 'right over the weavers . . . by long established custom'. A Governor of Bengal explained to the Directors that 'from time immemorial' weavers working for the Company

are not at liberty to leave your service, and engage with others; nor when the cloths are made, are they permitted to sell them to the best bidder: but they are obliged to bring them to your warehouse, where they are valued by your servants, in the customary manner, according to their quality; and if upon account of the dearness of provisions, or other particular circumstances, a small increase in the price is at any time required, it is your servants who determine at any time what it shall be.[2]

As the new rulers of Bengal, the British were even more strongly committed to the theory of trade without coercion than their Mughal predecessors had been. It was universally accepted dogma that the prosperity of Bengal depended on free trade. But under the British the exceptions were on a much greater scale than they had been under the Mughals. The Company eventually enforced codes of regulations which kept artisans in its employment and laid down their rewards,[3] while private Europeans, especially those in the Company's service, tried to imitate it as far as they were able.

[1] Minute of W. Hay, 1 Mar. 1763, Vansittart, *Narrative*, ii. 327.
[2] H. Vansittart to Directors, 7 Oct. 1767, I.O.R., Home Miscellaneous, 192, p. 344.
[3] 9th Report, Select Committee, 1783, *Reports*, vi. 62–70; N. K. Sinha, *The Economic History of Bengal* (1956–70), i. 160 ff.

Even in the latter part of the century, when the British actually ruled Bengal and when some Englishmen had acquired considerable experience of trading conditions there, it was still extremely difficult for Europeans to make individual bargains with a mass of producers or to keep them under close supervision until the goods contracted for were finished. Earlier in the century the difficulties were even more formidable. Europeans was thus forced to rely to a very large degree for the success of their trade on the skills of Indian middlemen. There was a wide variety of such men, whose services could be used. Production of most commodities appears to have been arranged by men whose commonest title was *dalal* or *pikar*. At Dacca, for instance, descriptions of how the manufacture of cloth was organized show little change between 1670 and 1770. Merchants placed orders with *dalals* and advanced money to them. The *dalals* in their turn commissioned *pikars* to set the weavers to work. Finished cloth was brought in by the *pikars* and its price was finally adjusted by the merchants with the *dalals*.[1] In districts like Dacca, where Europeans had set up their factories, they could deal directly with *dalals* or *pikars*. Elsewhere they had to employ another layer of middlemen, either by making contracts with Indian merchants to deliver goods or by employing salaried agents, called *gumashtas*, to make purchases on their behalf. In either case, large sums of money were inevitably at risk. A high proportion of the purchase price of the goods which they were to provide would have to be paid to merchants in advance. The East India Company paid its so-called *dadni* merchants 75 per cent of the price in advance until 1722 and 50 per cent thereafter.[2] *Gumashtas* put up no money of their own, their employers having to finance all their operations. An elaborate system whereby *gumashtas* who took on service with a European or merchants who entered into contracts had to name securities who would be responsible for their debts can have been at best only a partial safeguard against bankrupts and absconders. It was said to be 'well known to all who have had their concerns managed at the discretion of Bengal gomastahs at a distance, what embezzlements and deceits they are guilty of; and that the temptation

[1] There is an account of methods used in the 1670s in A. Karim, *Dacca the Mughal Capital* (Dacca, 1964), p. 77. Trading conditions in Dacca in the 1770s are abundantly documented, e.g. B.R.C., 3 July 1776, *Reports*, vi. 243–51; West Bengal Archives, Board of Trade Proceedings, 10 Feb. 1775, vol. 2, pp. 57 ff.

[2] Chaudhuri, 'Trade and Commercial Organisation', pp. 227–8.

to make away with their employer's money is stronger than any fear of corporal punishment or imprisonment, which they submit to for years sooner than refund'.[1] Yet in spite of the obvious risks, Europeans employed large numbers of *gumashtas* to act for them, even early in the eighteenth century. A Company servant who died in 1727 left 'adventures' outstanding under *gumashtas* at four different textile *aurangs* worth more than Rs 40,000.[2] In 1737 the Company's servants in general were thought to have *gumashtas* 'all over the country';[3] in 1753 purchase through *gumashtas* was said to be the method generally used by private European merchants.[4]

Selling goods in Bengal was also a complex process with a high degree of risk. Outside the towns goods had to be entrusted to *gumashtas* who disposed of them slowly in small lots. Returns might not be realized for several months. It seems to have been customary to allow long periods for settlement on large sales of goods.[5]

A trading system in which payments for purchases had to be made several months in advance and in which payment for sales was often long deferred made heavy demands on a merchant's capital. Only a small part of the trading capital of an individual European in Bengal in the eighteenth century was likely to come from Europe. Under the Company's monopoly it was, of course, illegal for him to receive goods from Europe whose sale might have produced funds with which to finance his trade. There were, however, some means by which money could be transferred from Britain to Bengal, and these were generally used to provide at least limited amounts with which a newcomer could launch his career as a merchant. As Thomas Pitt put it to a father sending his son to Madras in 1706: 'You would have done well to have sent him five hundred pounds with him and not put him under Egyptian bondage. What is it you propose that they can doe without a stock? And you and I have lived long enough to know 'tis money begets money throughout the world.'[6] Funds could be

---

[1] I.O.R., Bengal Secret Consultations, 21 July 1764, Range A, vol. 5, p. 389.
[2] Statement of H. Harnett's affairs, N.L.W., Clive MSS., 359.
[3] Abs. Fort St. George to Directors, 29 Jan. 1736, I.O.R., E/4/4, p. 170.
[4] I.O.R., B.P.C., 25 June 1753, Range 1, vol. 26, f. 193.
[5] The journal of G. Vansittart, R. Palk and J. Jekyll in 1771–4 shows that they were allowing up to six months (Bodleian, dep. b. 90).
[6] Pitt to E. Ettrick, 19 Sept. 1706, Add. MS. 22849, f. 90.

transferred to India either by dispatching bullion, which the Company was prepared to license on its ships, or, much more commonly, by allowing a man in India to draw bills on his British connections. But few men seem to have come out to Bengal with large amounts at their disposal. The Free Merchant who arrived in 1765 with £10,000 'to begin with' was probably exceptional.[1] Of seventeen shipments of bullion to Bengal between 1714 and 1717 the largest consignment by far was 4,000 oz. of silver, worth rather more than £1,000, while most were under 200 oz.[2] In 1767 Lord Elibank sent his natural son William Young out to Bengal with permission to draw on him for up to £1,000 but no more.[3] John Grose who went out in 1763 also had permission to draw on his father for £1,000.[4] If these sums are typical, it seems likely that most families believed that they had done their duty by their offspring when they had poured out their influence and money to get him to Bengal. Once he had got there, he would have to raise his capital for himself. Until relatively late in the century, when large British fortunes began to be made out of the conquest of Bengal, the major part of the finance for European trade was not only raised in India but actually came from Indians.

By the eighteenth century Bengal, like certain other parts of India, had what has been called a 'fairly advanced' system of mercantile credit.[5] At its apex was the great banking house at Murshidabad, the Nawabs' capital, of the so-called Jagat Seths (Bankers to the World), founded in the late seventeenth century by a Marwari family from Rajputana. The Seths ran a huge business, lending very large sums to the Nawabs, the British, the French and the Dutch companies and to individual Europeans. They controlled the Bengal mint and became a powerful force in politics, intervening effectively in 1740 and 1756–7. After 1756 they collaborated closely with the British.[6] By the late 1760s their business began to decline, and, after an attempt to establish

---

[1] G. Pigot to Clive, 8 Feb. 1765, I.O.L., MS. Eur. G. 37, box 33, f. 122, writing about D. Killican.

[2] Sums mentioned in Directors' letters to Bengal, I.O.R., E/3/98, pp. 219–20, 485, 804; E/3/99, pp. 93, 649.

[3] Letter of 1 Aug. 1767, S.R.O., G.D. 32/24/34.

[4] J. Grose to E. Grose, 10 Feb. 1765, I.O.L., MS. Eur. E. 284 (25).

[5] I. Habib, 'Potentialities of capitalistic development in the economy of Mughal India', *Journal of Economic History*, xxix (1969), 74; 'Usury in Medieval India', *Comparative Studies in Society and History*, vi (1963–4).

[6] J. H. Little, *The House of Jagat Seth*, ed. N. K. Sinha (Calcutta, 1967).

a large Indian bank in Calcutta under the Company's patronage had failed,[1] no Bengal bank was left, capable of rivalling the great houses at Banaras, such as that of Monohar Das, Gopal Das with its fifty-two branches. The large Banaras banks did much business in Bengal with the Company and with British merchants.[2]

Lower down the pyramid were the local money-lenders, changers of money or bankers, called shroffs or *mahajans*, found throughout Bengal. They manipulated the immensely complex currency system, which was based on the silver rupee, whose value varied with the age of the coin and the mint where it had been struck. Many of them were also prepared to advance money to merchants or to arrange remittances by bills of exchange (normally called *hundis*) from one part of Bengal to another.

Indian interest rates were high by British standards and those in Bengal were thought to be highest of all. In the late seventeenth century the Company had to pay 12 or 18 per cent for money taken up in Bengal.[3] During the first half of the eighteenth century the Company could sometimes obtain money at 9 per cent, but individuals usually had to pay more; in 1753 10 or 12 per cent were said to be the rates generally charged.[4] Land interest was fixed in the Company's settlements at 12 per cent in 1766,[5] the maximum rate at which money could be lent by British subjects under the Regulating Act of 1773.[6] By the mid 1770s 12 per cent seems to have been the rate generally charged to European borrowers.

High interest rates, it has been suggested, do not necessarily indicate that Mughal India was 'an intrinsically capital starved economy'.[7] But they do seem to reflect the very high level of risk involved in any form of investment. Excessive as the rates which they had to pay might seem to Europeans, Indian borrowers had to pay even more. Rural indebtedness was already widespread in

---

[1] Mohsin, *Murshidabad*, pp. 143–7.

[2] K. P. Mishra, 'The Administration and Economy of the Banaras Region 1738–95' (London Ph.D. thesis, 1971), pp. 260 ff.; Sinha, *Economic History*, iii. 74, 79–81.

[3] S. Chaudhuri, 'The problem of financing the East India Company's investments in Bengal 1650–1720', *Indian Economic and Social History Review*, viii (1971), 124–6.

[4] I.O.R., B.P.C., 6 Dec. 1753, Range 1, vol. 26, f. 362.

[5] I.O.R., Select Committee Proceedings, 31 Dec. 1766, Range A, vol. 7, p. 283.   [6] 13 Geo. III, c. 63, sec. 30.

[7] Habib, 'Capitalist development', *Journal of Economic History*, xxix. 74.

eighteenth-century Bengal. Evidence exists of loans to cultivators at 150 per cent,[1] while the Jagat Seths charged *zamindars* 2 per cent to $3\frac{1}{2}$ per cent per month.[2] News that there was 'an opportunity of plasing out money to good advantage' in Bengal even reached an old gentleman living in retirement in England, who remitted £3,050 (which he was never to see again) to a connection of his who was 'to lend it out among the landholders in different districts'.[3] In 1773 it was said that Indian merchants in Calcutta who could 'give no security' had to pay up to 25 per cent on loans, while even well established ones paid 2 per cent more than Europeans.[4] But loans to Europeans seem to have been popular with Indian investors, even if some interest was lost on them. The prospect of recovering money through the Company's courts in Calcutta may not have been a certain one, but loans which could be enforced under British law were evidently regarded as more secure than those which depended on the Nawabs' justice.

Evidence that Europeans were making extensive and sometimes imprudent use of the facilities for borrowing that existed in Bengal occurs early in the century. In 1714, after they had discovered that the Company was being held responsible for part of the debts owed by one Josias Chitty 'to the Mogul's subjects', the Directors expressed their concern at their servants' borrowing.[5] An obviously ineffective order forbidding members of the Council from contracting loans with Indians in future followed in 1716.[6] In 1727 the Governor reported that several of the Company's servants 'have undone themselves by becoming too bold adventurers, before they had laid any solid good foundations and it is with concern that I must acquaint your Honors that I have had too many complaints of the young gentlemen's not paying their debts. . . . The not paying what is due to the merchants makes them unwilling to trust even those who are industrious and carefull.'[7] His warning was timely. In the 1730s and 1740s a whole series of bankruptcies

---

[1] Habib, 'Capitalist development', *Journal of Economic History*, xxix. 44.
[2] *Proceedings of the Controlling Council of Revenue at Murshidabad* (Calcutta, 1919–24), ix. 191–201.
[3] H. Hastings to W. Hastings, 24 Mar. 1778, Add. MS. 29140, ff. 225–7.
[4] Calcutta High Court Records, Mayor's Court, *Macpherson* v. *Miller*.
[5] Directors to Bengal, 13 Jan. 1714, I.O.R., E/3/98, p. 221.
[6] Directors to Bengal, 15 Feb. 1716, ibid., p. 788.
[7] H. Frankland to Secret Committee, 28 Jan. 1727, I.O.R., Home Miscellaneous, 68, pp. 46–7.

occurred in the British community in Bengal and many defaulted on their debts to Indians.[1] The Directors reacted by imposing further restrictions on borrowing in 1738 and 1741,[2] but they were universally disobeyed. Inventories of estates of men dying in Calcutta were deposited in the Mayor's Court. Surviving inventories from 1758 show that almost every European owed debts of some kind to Indians.[3] They also show that senior Company servants or successful Free Merchants traded on very large capitals, mostly borrowed from Indian sources. For instance, Francis Hare of the Bengal Council, who died in 1771, owed Rs 640,000 (about £70,000) to various creditors, most of whom were Indian. Hare's assets eventually more or less covered his obligations,[4] but the inventory of Samuel Middleton, after his death in 1775, tells a very different story. The first dividend paid out to the twelve creditors who held his bonds, nine of them Indians, was only one anna in the rupee, or one-sixteenth of their claim. Even so, a dividend of one-sixteenth amounted to Rs 95,000, indicating that Middleton had borrowed Rs 1,500,000 in all, or approximately £170,000.[5] By 1783 his creditors had received only half of what was owed to them.[6]

Inventories of Indians who chose to use the Company's courts suggest that those who lent to Europeans liked to spread their risks by lending widely. When 'Ruttoo Sircar's' estate was wound up in 1764 he had loans outstanding to ten Europeans, only two of them for sums exceeding Rs 10,000.[7] Prabhuram Mullick's estate was owed Rs 227,000 by Europeans in 1782, most of the sums again being relatively small.[8] In the 1760s and 1770s there can have been few Europeans of any substance who had not at some time borrowed money from one or more of a relatively small group of Indian businessmen. The bonds of men like Hazari Mal, Gokul Ghosal, Nabakrishna ('Nobkissen' to the English), or Krishna Kanta Nandy ('Cantu Babu') occur over and over again

[1] See below, pp. 232–3.
[2] Letters of 8 Feb. 1738, 3 Feb. 1741, I.O.R., E/3/107, p. 414. E/3/108, pp. 362–3.
[3] I.O.R., Mayor's Court Records, Range 154, vols. 61 ff.
[4] Ibid., Range 155, vol. 1, pp. 238–42.
[5] I.O.R., Supreme Court Records, Range 155, vol. 6, no. 64.
[6] P.R.O., *Barker* v. *Lushington et al.*, C 12/608/22.
[7] I.O.R., Mayor's Court Records, Range 154, vol. 63, ff. 66–7.
[8] Calcutta High Court Records, Supreme Court, Plea Side, *Anderam Mullick et al.* v. *Alexander et al.*

in the inventories, accounts, and correspondence of men from the most junior Writer to the Governor. Four years after his death the estate of Gokul Ghosal still had claims on no fewer than forty-eight Europeans.[1] The size of the sum involved in making even small loans to that number of people suggests that men like Gokul Ghosal may have been acting as agents for a number of Indian investors.

There was thus no possibility of European merchants in eighteenth-century Bengal living in a remote, self-contained world. They were dependent on the Indian commercial community at many points. Without Indian expertise they could not obtain their goods, and without Indian capital they could not carry on their trade. Relations between Indian and British businessmen do, however, seem to have undergone certain changes during the century.

In the late seventeenth or early eighteenth centuries the Europeans were confronted with a rich and powerful group of Bengali and non-Bengali merchants for whom dealings with foreigners were only a relatively small part of the very wide-ranging activities in which they engaged. Such men could resist attempts to dictate terms to them by the East India companies, let alone by individual Europeans.[2] In the middle of the century, the famous Omichund could still undertake to produce a third of the British Company's Bengal goods, costing just under Rs 1,000,000, without needing to receive any payment in advance.[3] But it was inevitable that as the British won more and more political power in Bengal, they should begin to play a more dominant role in their relations with the Indian business community. In the second half of the century Indian merchants still joined in what were ostensibly equal partnerships with Europeans. The extremely wealthy Punjabi, Hazari Mal, for instance, whom one of his British admirers called a 'worthy man' with 'an inclination which he discovers upon every occasion for acts of kindness and generosity',[4] was a full partner in a concern including Warren Hastings.[5] The

---

[1] I.O.R., B.R.C., 26 Nov. 1784, Range 50, vol. 55, pp. 241–5.

[2] They are described in S. Chaudhuri, 'Trade and Commercial Organisation', pp. 105–65; and I. Ray, 'The French Company and the Merchants of Bengal', *Indian Economic and Social History Review*, viii (1971), 46–8.

[3] I.O.R., B.P.C., 8, 10, 25 June, 1747, Range 1, vol. 19, ff. 276, 277–8, 348.

[4] J. Fowke to Hastings, 27 Dec. 1771, Add. MS. 29132, f. 485.

[5] Hastings to T. Hancock and to Hancock and Hazari Mal, 20 Nov. 1769, 8 May 1770, Add. MS. 29125, ff. 17, 35.

characteristic relationship between British and Indian merchants became, however, that of 'master' and 'banian'.

A banian was once described as 'interpreter, head book-keeper, head secretary, head broker, the supplier of cash and cash keeper and in general also secret keeper'.[1] In brief, he was the Englishman's contact with the Indian world, a world with which he lacked the linguistic skill or most of the other kinds of expertise needed to deal at first hand. All Europeans of any consequence employed banians. Nominally their status was servile and they performed some menial tasks, such as managing their master's household and his personal spending. But the banian of a prominent European was a man to be reckoned with. The Governor's banian presided over a court in Calcutta. Men like Gokul Ghosal, banian to Harry Verelst, or Cantu Babu, banian to Warren Hastings, were among the richest and most influential members of the Indian community in Calcutta. By the middle of the eighteenth century men of considerable social standing (Gokul Ghosal was a *kulin* brahmin) and representatives of prominent merchant families were being drawn into European service. Members of the Sett family, one of the oldest groups of Calcutta cloth merchants, who had rarely in the past 'stooped to be banians to the gentlemen', now 'condescended to serve'.[2] Some members of the Basak family, which had a similar background, also appear to have become banians in mid-century.[3]

There were obvious incentives for ambitious Indians to enter European service. When Englishmen gained office in the administration of Bengal their banians were usually able to win a share of their power and of the profits that went with it. For Indian merchants there were also real advantages in becoming a banian. In so doing merchants did not necessarily compromise their independence to any significant extent. They might appear to have become their masters' servants, merely managing their trade for them; but the reality was often less that of master and servant than of trading partners. The banian brought his skill and his capital to the partnership; the European contributed his privileges. So long as the Nawabs' customs system remained in force, the

---

[1] W. Bolts, *Considerations on India Affairs* (1772–5), i. 84.

[2] J. Z. Holwell, *India Tracts* (3rd edn., 1774), p. 427. On the Setts, see B. Ghosh, 'Some old family founders in eighteenth-century Calcutta', *B.P.P.*, lxxix (1960), 42–55.

[3] D. Basu, 'The early Banians of Calcutta', *B.P.P.*, xc (1971), 38–40.

exemptions under the 1717 *farman*, which private Englishmen enjoyed as well as the Company, were coveted by Indian merchants. A banian could expect to have his own goods covered by his master's privileges. As one European put it, he could 'borrow a name and cheat the government of their dutys'.[1] Once the Company had come to power in Bengal, a prudent Indian merchant would have many reasons for wishing to ally himself with one of the new rulers. Yet the terms of the alliance might often leave the European as a purely nominal partner, receiving a commission for the use of his name in transactions with which he was otherwise totally unconnected. A Company servant was said to be able to get '20 or 25 per cent by a trade in which he runs no risque and has no trouble, merely for producing to his banyan permits or dustucks'.[2] In one case of trading ventures in Oudh the banian provided the stock and managed the concern; 'in consideration of the advantages to be derived from the use of the name and influence' of his master, he agreed to make over half the profits to him after deducting 12 per cent interest.[3] In another case, a banian called Ramdulal Mishra told a young Company servant that 'very great advantages were to be made by trade in purchasing various sorts of goods, wares and merchandizes in Calcutta . . . and sending such up the country to various marketts and aurungs'. When the young man pointed out that 'he had not a capital of his own for such a business', he was told that 'it was not material'; he had 'only to execute and deliver his interest bond or bonds to him from time to time'. The master contributed nothing to the partnership beyond putting his signature to various pieces of paper.[4]

If these stories are typical, a fair proportion of what appears to be European trade can only have been European in the most nominal sense. Statements about Indian merchants being driven out of business after Plassey by European competition may also need some reconsideration. Mutual dependence as well as competition seems to have marked the relations of British and Indian merchants in the later eighteenth century. With the British in

[1] J. Z. Holwell, 'Hints on Bengal Affairs', 1757–8, I.O.R., Correspondence Memoranda, D/106.

[2] G. Bogle to R. Bogle, 5 Sept. 1770, Mitchell Library, Bogle MSS.

[3] Calcutta High Court Records, Supreme Court, Equity, *Hyde* v. *Ojagur Mull.*

[4] Calcutta High Court Records, Mayor's Court, *Bateman* v. *Ramdullol Missere.*

political control of Bengal, it was no doubt true, as a witness told a committee of the House of Commons, that 'considerable native merchants' now sought 'the assistance and countenance of some English gentleman'.[1] On the other hand, British trade still depended on Indian skill and Indian capital. The master-banian relation provided a framework within which these needs could be met.

In 1784 European commerce was still heavily dependent on Indian aid, although there are clear indications that the degree of dependence was diminishing. European capital was beginning to accumulate in Bengal. Most men wanted to transfer their fortunes to Britain as quickly as possible, but the means of remitting money did not always match the sums waiting to be remitted,[2] while high interest rates tempted some to leave a part of their fortune behind them after they had returned. Europeans with money to lend could usually place it with the Company, which offered relative security, or they could advance it to private borrowers at higher rates with greater hazards. In 1767 Clive thought that European funds remaining in Bengal either from choice or necessity amounted to £1,500,000.[3] By 1772 the Company's bonded debt, representing its borrowing in Bengal, had risen to over £1,200,000.[4] Much of this was paid off in subsequent years, but the Company began to borrow again on an even larger scale in the 1780s to pay for its wars against the French, the Marathas and Mysore. Even so, it seems reasonable to suppose that substantial sums from Europeans were also offered to private borrowers, making them less dependent than they had been in the past on Indian capital.

European commercial organization was also becoming more elaborate by 1784. For most of the century Europeans had traded on their own, aided by their banians, or in usually short-lived partnerships of two or three individuals. In the 1770s more formal and longer lasting concerns came into being to which the name Houses of Agency was given. In the strict sense agency business involved arranging remittances throughout Bengal or to Europe, buying and selling on commission, and managing the Calcutta affairs of up-country clients. But other functions were acquired.

[1] Evidence of W. Harwood, 9th Report, Select Committee, 1783, *Reports*, vi. 267. [2] See below, pp. 220–6.
[3] Letter to Committee of Correspondence, 28 Aug. 1767, I.O.L., MS. Eur. G. 37, box 46, f. 215.
[4] 5th Report, Secret Committee, 1782, *Reports*, viii. 363.

Houses of agency became rudimentary banking businesses, receiving money on deposit and investing it, and they took over the management of ships and plantations. The rise of the houses of agency and the European banks was largely a phenomenon of the period after 1784. But as early as 1768 four individuals entered into an indenture for establishing a 'house of factory or commission' for at least five years.[1] In the 1770s two substantial concerns, Croftes and Johnson,[2] and Paxton and Cockerell,[3] were operating in Calcutta, while the house of Alexander, Bayne, and Colvin grew out of the business conducted for some years on his own by Claud Alexander, the Company's Paymaster. In 1784 the ending of the wars brought a boom in new 'commission houses', three opening in that year.[4] When the Bengal Bank was enlarged in 1786, it was said to have been 'established in Calcutta for some years past with the approbation and support of many of the most opulent inhabitants of this city'.[5]

The accumulation of European capital and the rise of the new business houses are signs that private British enterprise was beginning to acquire some capacity to shape commercial conditions in Bengal to its own needs. Before 1784, however, British merchants were operating in a world which they could not shape. Even when it was working smoothly, it posed serious problems for them: a high element of risk, heavy demands on trading capital, unstable political conditions, and a cumbersome currency system, thought by the 1760s to be incapable of producing an adequate volume of specie. At certain times the commercial life of Bengal was severely dislocated. In 1746 the Maratha invasions 'occasioned so great a scarcity of money' that even the Company could not borrow.[6] An acute depression began in 1768, whose effects were still being felt in 1773. At its height neither the Company nor private individuals were said to be able 'to borrow money or discharge their debts'.[7] Trade was again at a low ebb in the early

[1] Indenture of Keir, Reed, Cator and Gibson, 18 Aug. 1768, I.O.R., Mayor's Court Records, Range 155, vol. 62.

[2] The firm was dissolved in 1785, see Calcutta High Court Records, Supreme Court, Equity, *Kirkpatrick et al.* v. *Johnson.*

[3] I.O.L., MS. Eur. D. 12 is a volume of their correspondence.

[4] A. Colvin to B. Alexander, 25 Sept. 1784, Alexander MSS.

[5] National Archives of India, Secret Department of Inspection Consultations, 9 Mar. 1786, no. 8.

[6] Bengal to Directors, 30 Nov. 1746, I.O.R., E/4/21, pp. 20, 26, 43.

[7] J. Archdekin to Clive, 22 Nov. 1768, I.O.L., MS. Eur. G. 37, box 55, f. 82.

1780s. 'Our Indian trade is almost annihilated', wrote one merchant, 'The monied men will not lend seeing our public credit so low. . . . Our ships lie by our walls.'[1]

Daunting as the difficulties for Europeans trading in Bengal in the eighteenth century might appear, the rewards of success were very tempting. Profit margins were at least two or three times what a merchant could expect in Britain. 'Normal' commercial profit in late seventeenth-century Britain has been estimated at between 6 and 12 per cent.[2] In 1776 Adam Smith thought 8 or 10 per cent a good profit.[3] In 1767 normal profits in internal trade in Bengal were said to be from 20 to 30 per cent.[4] The 'usual and customary' profit on rice in 'transactions between merchant and merchant' was put at 25 per cent.[5] On certain commodities at certain times profits could be very much higher. In 1764 there was talk of expected profits of 'one hundred per cent or more' from internal trade.[6] In the 1760s 75 per cent was thought to be a fair estimate for profits on dealing in salt, betel nut, and tobacco.[7] Profits from trading at sea could be equally spectacular. Ships trading from British ports to Spain or America were thought to have been earning around 15 per cent in the eighteenth century.[8] The British and Dutch companies reckoned to make between 50 and 80 per cent on Bengal goods carried to Persia.[9]

Trade in Bengal seemed to Europeans to be a lottery in which the prizes were high, but in which there were many blanks. With spectacular profit margins, a man could make his fortune in a few successful seasons. But he ran great risks which left him desperately vulnerable. He had to borrow money at high rates of

---

[1] G. Smith to H. Dundas, 5 Aug. 1785, I.O.R., Home Miscellaneous, 434, p. 140.

[2] R. B. Grassby, 'The rate of profit in the seventeenth century', *English Historical Review*, lxxxiv (1969), 733.

[3] *Wealth of Nations*, ed. W. R. Scott (1921), p. 99.

[4] W. Wynne to H. Strachey, 17 Mar. 1767, I.O.L., MS. Eur. F. 128.

[5] Calcutta High Court Records, Mayor's Court, *Gocul Churn Surmah* v. *Mackenzie*.

[6] *Bengal District Records: Midnapur, 1763-7*, ed. W. K. Firminger (Calcutta, 1914), p. 11.

[7] H. Vansittart's evidence to House of Commons, 1767, Add. MS. 18469, f. 4.

[8] R. Davis, *The Rise of the English shipping industry in the seventeenth and eighteenth centuries* (1962), pp. 378-9.

[9] T. Raychaudhuri, *Jan Company in Coromandel* (The Hague, 1962), pp. 160-1; S. Chaudhuri, 'Trade and Commercial Organisation', p. 367.

interest, which he then entrusted to impecunious cultivators or to Indian middlemen whom Europeans usually regarded with intense distrust. To the normal risks of the sea were added the depredations of pirates and the unpredictable behaviour of Asian governments in ports over which Britain had no control. In these conditions slow, systematic accumulation was difficult. Men either made their fortunes quickly or lost everything.

III

Seaborne Trade:
(I) The Calcutta Fleet

Before the nineteenth century the Europeans believed that the sea was their element in Asia. They might be vulnerable on land, but since the great Portuguese naval victories of the sixteenth century, Europeans were confident in the prowess of their ships and their seamen. It is not therefore surprising that when individual Englishmen began to trade on their own behalf they should at first have concentrated on trading by sea rather than trading by land. Englishmen in Bengal were no exception. For centuries there had been a large volume of trade in and out of the ports on Bengal's principal navigable river, the Hugli, and in the late seventeenth century private English ships began to compete in this trade with the ships of Asian merchants and of other Europeans. So successfully did they compete that during the eighteenth century Calcutta became Bengal's busiest port, and the British became the biggest carriers of Bengal's trade with other parts of Asia.

The size of Bengal's seaborne trade in the seventeenth century can only be guessed at, but the indications are that it was very large. An Englishman thought that 60 to 100 Portuguese ships used to call annually at the port of Hugli before 1632, the year in which it was captured by Mughal forces.[1] In the second half of the seventeenth century, part of the trade once carried on by the Portuguese passed to the Dutch; in a busy year twenty or more Dutch ships called at Bengal in the later seventeenth century.[2] Apart from the ships of Europeans, there was also a sizeable fleet based in Bengal which was operated by the Nawab, his officials and courtiers, and by Hindu, Muslim, and Armenian merchants who lived in the province. In the 1670s Bengal's Asian-owned

[1] S. Chaudhuri, 'The rise and decline of Hugli', *B.P.P.*, lxxxvi (1967), 41.
[2] Pieter Van Dam, *Beschryvinge van de Oostindische Compagnie*, II. ii, ed. F. W. Stapel (The Hague, 1932), 50.

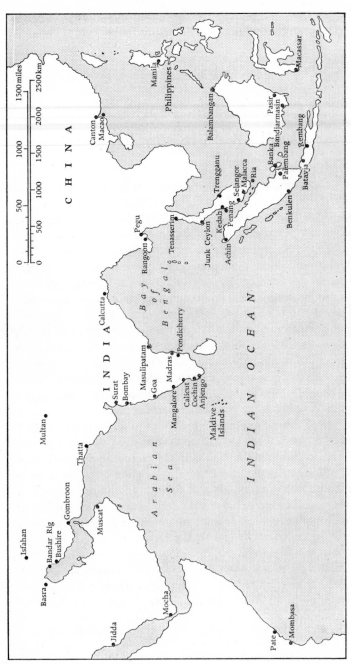

MAP 2. Calcutta's seaborne trade in the eighteenth century

fleet was thought to consist of '20 saile of ships of considerable burthen'.[1] Bengal was also visited by many Asian ships from other ports. In the last three shipping seasons of the seventeenth century the number of arrivals recorded at Hugli from the great port of Surat in western India was twelve, ten, and ten respectively.[2] English sources in the 1690s also noted sporadic appearances at ports in Bengal of Arab ships from the Persian Gulf.

The size of the merchant fleet owned in the eighteenth century by the British community living in Bengal can be estimated with more confidence. The best indication of the number of ships seems to be the figures for 'tonnage' duties collected by the Company in Calcutta. Tonnage was a duty of Re 1 per ton levied annually on 'all the English ships that sail as English, or upon the English priviledge or protection in India'.[3] Records of tonnage paid at the new factory at Calcutta begin in 1694.[4] In any one year the list of ships paying the duty is likely to include some that were not owned by Europeans and some that were not based on Calcutta. The Company's servants did not try to collect tonnage on what they called 'Moors' ships, that is ships owned by Muslims, or on other ships whose owners were under the direct jurisdiction of the Mughal authorities:[5] but Hindu or Armenian shipowners who chose to take up their residence in Calcutta were apparently made to pay. Other Company settlements collected tonnage on their own ships, but if an English ship from another port in India arrived at Calcutta without a certificate showing that it had paid tonnage, it would be made to pay in Bengal. These exceptions apart, and allowing for the fact that a ship could have owners of more than one race and in more than one port, the annual tonnage lists seem to be a reliable indication of the size of the British-owned merchant fleet operating from Calcutta up to 1760, when the duty appears to have lapsed. The figures for the actual tonnage of the fleet are much less reliable. The servants who collected the duty were usually the owners of the largest ships and had an

[1] T. Bowrey, A Geographical Account of countries round the Bay of Bengal, ed. R. C. Temple (1905), p. 179.
[2] Om Prakash, 'European trading companies and the merchants of Bengal', Indian Economic and Social History Review, i (1963–4), 44.
[3] Directors to Bombay, 13 May 1687, I.O.R., E/3/91, p. 298.
[4] They appear at first in the Calcutta Factory Records, I.O.R., G/7/1–8 and later in the Bengal Public Consultations, I.O.R., Range 1.
[5] Abs. Bengal to Directors, 10 Jan. 1705, I.O.R., E/4/1, p. 29.

obvious interest in under-assessing them. There can be no doubt
that the Company was systematically defrauded in the early
eighteenth century. Before 1720 no ship was ever admitted to be
more than 200 tons. More accurate measuring led to some ships
suddenly doubling their displacement, but the tonnage figures
were probably suspect throughout the period.

Early records of ships paying tonnage are defective, but 3 are
listed in 1694–5, 2 in 1695–6, 7 in 1698–9, 5 in 1699–1700, 6 in
1702–3, 4 in 1703–4, 11 in 1705–6, 8 in 1706–7, and 5 in 1707–8.
Figures for the tonnage duties become regularly available from the
shipping season 1714–15, and from the season 1718–19 a new
indicator of the volume of private English seaborne trade is provided by returns for the 'consulage' duties collected at Calcutta.
Consulage was a levy of two per cent laid by the Company on
exports from Calcutta.[1] It was to be paid by all Europeans and
by 'Jentues, Moors or Armenians' who did not pay the Mughal
government's customs.[2] The consulage figures should be treated
with some caution. They were again collected by Company servants who, as the largest exporters, had no incentive to see them
strictly enforced. The Council admitted in 1726 that many people
defrauded the Company and evaded payment.[3]

Much less evidence about Calcutta shipping is available after
1760. The collection of customs duties replaced consulage in
1759,[4] but the bulk of the Calcutta customs records, with the
exception of lists of imports for 1761 to 1765,[5] do not appear to
have survived. By the 1770s there are, however, clear indications
that the port was being used by a greatly increased volume of
shipping. Warren Hastings reported that 88 ships (including the
Company's ships from Europe) with a total tonnage of 22,475

[1] Directors to Bengal, 8 Jan. 1718, I.O.R., E/3/99, pp. 378–9.
[2] I.O.R., B.P.C., 23 May 1726, Range 1, vol. 6, f. 215.
[3] Ibid., f. 215.
[4] I.O.R., B.P.C., 26 Apr. 1759, Range 1, vol. 31, f. 191.
[5] The figures for imports are:

Rs 37,684 for 1761	Rs 29,205 for 1764
Rs 55,612 for 1762	Rs 52,028 for 1765
Rs 52,695 for 1763	

All imports into Calcutta paid 4 per cent, except for those which had paid duties
at other British settlements. Comparison with the figures for the 2 per cent consulage on exports does not suggest any striking increase in Calcutta's trade in
the early 1760s (I.O.R., Miscellaneous Revenue Records (Customs), Range 98,
vols. 3–8).

TABLE I

	Number of ships	Declared tonnage	Consulage in Rupees
1714/15	23	1,435	—
1715/16	19	1,320	—
1716/17	26	2,185	—
1717/18	30	2,265	—
1718/19	32	2,165	21,941
1719/20	32	2,570	20,688
1720/1	28	4,023	17,179
1721/2	32	4,783	28,343
1722/3	40	5,501	21,423
1723/4	31	4,732	22,833
1724/5	41	5,650	23,881
1725/6	28	4,225	24,648
1726/7	35	5,632	41,561
1727/8	32	5,142	44,612
1728/9	38	5,895	40,861
1729/30	27	4,809	48,734
1730/1	38	7,025	36,950
1731/2	41	5,645	17,104
1732/3	39	5,638	27,872
1733/4	—	—	45,740
1734/5	29	7,901	41,453
1735/6	—	—	36,858
1736/7	25	4,860	24,851
1737/8	—	—	27,402
1738/9	18	2,650	17,316
1739/40	23	4,170	18,560
1740/1	—	—	22,592
1741/2	28	4,310	29,661
1742/3	25	4,535	27,993
1743/4	24	4,160	24,321
1744/5	22	3,875	20,826
1745/6	22	4,735	22,661
1746/7	21	3,770	6,691
1747/8	20	3,540	6,035
1748/9	20	3,160	8,851
1749/50	23	3,470	10,449
1750/1	29	2,980	18,411
1751/2	31	3,350	18,729
1752/3	—	—	24,078
1753/4	30	3,225	14,880
1754/5	—	—	—
1755/6	—	—	—
1756/7	—	—	—
1757/8	29	2,190	—
1758/9	—	—	—
1759/60	30	3,598	—

Source: I.O.R., B.P.C., supplemented by I.O.R., Bengal General Journals.

called at Calcutta in 1770. His figures for the following years were:
101 ships of 24,140 tons in 1771, 119 ships of 26,184 tons in 1772,
and 161 ships of 37,187 tons in 1773.[1] 102 of the ships arriving in
Calcutta in 1773 were described as 'country ships under English
colours'.[2] In 1777 Calcutta's exports to other Asian ports were
valued at Rs 2,562,367;[3] assuming that the consulage figures are
a reliable indication of exports, Calcutta's trade in 1777 was
roughly equal in value to its trade in 1729–30, easily the most
successful year between 1718 and 1754. War seriously disrupted
trade in the following years; in 1783 the total of clearances of
private English ships in and out of Calcutta was only 128, but the
number of clearances climbed spectacularly after the war to 575
by 1791.[4]

Taken together, the tonnage duty, consulage, and customs
figures tell much the same story. A private English merchant
fleet based on Calcutta came into existence at the end of the
seventeenth century. From about 1715 the number of ships began
to increase rapidly and the port of Calcutta enjoyed some twenty
years of more or less continuous prosperity. But from 1735 the
indications for the next thirty years are much less encouraging.
The earlier successes were not consistently repeated until the
1770s. But if the history of Calcutta's trade in the eighteenth
century was not a simple one of uninterrupted growth and success,
a large fleet operated from Calcutta carrying a large volume of
goods, in good years and in bad. If, as certainly seems likely, the
total of Bengal's Asian trade grew markedly for most of the
eighteenth century, success for British ships need not necessarily
have meant loss for the ships of others. But until relatively late in
the century a considerable proportion of the cargoes carried by
British ships were provided not by the British themselves but by
Asian merchants. A comparison of the lists of British ships given
in Table I with the arrivals at Hugli, formerly the premier port of
Bengal, of Asian and Portuguese ships given in Table II suggests
that Asian merchants were increasingly inclined to entrust their
goods to the British. In part they may have done this, not because
of any superior merit in British shipping, but because there were

[1] *Memoirs of the Right Hon. Warren Hastings*, ed. G. R. Gleig (1841), i. 393.
[2] H. T. Colebrooke, *Remarks on the Present State of Husbandry and Commerce
of Bengal* (Calcutta, 1795), p. 152.
[3] This valuation was included in the Bengal Commercial Report for 1797,
I.O.R., Range 174, vol. 13.   [4] Colebrooke, *Remarks*, pp. 152–4.

fewer Asian ships available. Many Indian ships which had come to Bengal in the past had been based on Surat, where deteriorating political conditions in the eighteenth century were putting ship owners out of business.[1] Nevertheless, it seems undeniable that there was much direct competition between Asian and British ships and that in this competition the British were tending to prevail.

TABLE II

The arrival of Asian and Portuguese ships at Hugli from Dutch records

1715/16	16	1728/9	16	1736/7	9
1716/17	14	1729/30	11	1737/8	10
1717/18	18	1730/1	12	1738/9	15
1718/19	16	1731/2	15	1739/40	12
1719/20	20	1732/3	—		
1720/1	29	1733/4	11	1747/8	11
1721/2	26	1734/5	—		
1722/3	26	1735/6	—		

Source: Koloniaal Archief, 1755–2603.

By 1715 more ships were visiting Calcutta than called at Hugli. In the good years for Bengal's trade of the early 1720s Hugli evidently prospered, but Calcutta kept her lead. In the lean years of the 1730s and 1740s the disparity became even more marked, Calcutta usually receiving at least twice as many ships as Hugli. Various possibilities have been suggested to explain the success of private British shipowners over Asian rivals. Coercion would seem to be an obvious one. The elimination of competition by force based on the superior fire-power of the European ships on the high seas, was a practice resorted to in the past by the Portuguese and the Dutch. The Portuguese pioneered a system of controlling Asian ships by issuing 'passes'. A vessel without a pass was liable to be seized. By withholding the issue of passes on certain routes it was theoretically possible for the Portuguese to clear them of Asian ships. The British also issued passes, but they never felt themselves strong enough in Bengal before 1757 to force Asians

[1] Dr. A. Das Gupta has argued that the decline of indigenous shipping throughout India owed more to political conditions than to the effectiveness of the Europeans ('Trade and Politics in 18th century India', *Islam and the Trade of Asia*, ed. D. S. Richards (Oxford, 1970). Convincing as this argument is, it may apply less to Bengal where political decline was not so marked and a large volume of seaborne trade was maintained.

to take their passes and thus to use them as a device for regulating
competition. At least in the Bay of Bengal, the British did not
attempt to penalize ships not carrying their pass. Passes seem
rather to have been regarded as a source of revenue. By purchasing
a British pass an Asian merchant could buy a limited degree of
protection. He could hope that the British would help him if he
fell foul of another European power. The British government, for
instance, made representations to Lisbon on behalf of a Bengal
Armenian whose ship was molested by the Portuguese in 1747.[1]
The Company had issued passes fairly widely early in the eighteenth century,[2] but in 1728 the Directors strictly forbade the
giving of a pass to any ship which owed allegiance to the Nawab of
Bengal.[3] Fear of the Nawab was the obvious reason why the British
could not seriously attempt to eliminate their competitors by
force. When the Royal Navy seized a ship under French colours
at the mouth of the Hugli in wartime in 1745, the Company were
obliged to make restitution under threat of having their trade to
Calcutta blockaded by the Nawab.[4]

If the private British shipowner could not eliminate his Asian
rivals by force, could he undercut them by offering a cheaper
service? All the evidence suggests the opposite. Asian ships
offered much lower freights, and even by European standards
British country ships were expensive. In 1699, for instance, the
Calcutta Council let out freight on one of the Company's ships
to Persia at Rs 8 per maund (about 80 lb.) for 'bale goods' (textiles),
while an Armenian ship was offering Rs 5.[5] In 1718 a Company's
ship was charging Rs 9 per maund to an Arab's Rs 6 or Rs 7.[6]
Freighters in 1727 had to pay Rs 10½ per maund on goods sent
from Bengal to Surat on a ship belonging to the British Governor
of Bengal, whereas the rate on Asian ships was said to be Rs 5.[7]
A year later the Bengal Council admitted that the British ships
could never hope to offer cheaper rates than those charged by 'the
Moors', who could always 'afford to take less' than they could.[8]

---

[1] Correspondence Report, 5 May 1749, I.O.R., D/20, pp. 115–16.
[2] Abs. Bengal to Directors, 10 Jan. 1705, I.O.R., E/4/1, p. 29.
[3] Directors to Bengal, 14 Feb. 1728, I.O.R., E/3/104, p. 173.
[4] I.O.R., B.P.C., 6 Nov. 1745, Range 1, vol. 17, ff. 734–5.
[5] Calcutta Diary, 20, 27 Nov. 1699, I.O.R., G/7/3.
[6] Abs. Bengal to Directors, 16 Feb. 1718, I.O.R., E/4/2, p. 144.
[7] Bombay to Directors, 21 Apr. 1727, I.O.R., E/4/460, p. 125.
[8] Abs. Bengal to Directors, 28 Jan. 1728, I.O.R., E/4/2, p. 583.

Freight rates on British ships were higher than those on Asian ones, but it may be that Asian merchants who used them could make considerable savings in what they paid in customs. Under various agreements culminating in the 1717 *farman*,[1] British goods coming into or going out of Bengal did not pay customs to the Nawabs. At most other Asian ports the British had also succeeded in negotiating concessions allowing them to pay customs at rates lower than those paid by Asian traders. Thus, although British-owned goods had to pay consulage to the Company at Calcutta and customs or consulage to the Company at most other Asian ports, they had clear advantages all over Asia. The official policy of the Company was rigorously to exclude Asian merchants from British privileges, even though they placed their goods on board British ships. The Calcutta Council was always anxious to reassure the Nawab of Bengal that they would not connive in any evasion of his customs by Indian merchants passing off their goods as entitled to British immunities. In 1704 and 1705 Asian goods landed at Calcutta were immediately sent up to the customs house at Hugli,[2] while in 1710 a special warehouse, in which goods for the Nawab's customs could be stored under proper inspection to prevent malpractices, was being planned.[3] Similar precautions were taken at Surat, Asian-owned goods placed in error in the Company's 'latty' in 1727 being handed over immediately to the Mughal customs.[4] Two of the greatest users of British shipping from Bengal, the Gujaratis and the Armenians, assured the Company in the 1750s that they were paying the Nawabs' customs before their goods were loaded on to British ships.[5] On the other hand, large-scale evasion must have been fairly common. Many Englishmen were known to be willing for a consideration to assume ownership of Indian goods. As early as 1732 a Governor of Bengal was prepared to admit that customs exemptions were sold by Company servants,[6] while an English agent from Bengal, who lived at Surat, was said to carry on a trade worth two lakhs of rupees

---

[1] See above, p. 7.
[2] I.O.R., B.P.C., 8 July 1704, 5 July 1705, Range 1, vol. 1, ff. 58–9, 219–20.
[3] Abs. Bengal to Directors, 8 Jan. 1710, I.O.R., E/4/1, p. 243.
[4] Surat Diary, 13 June 1727, I.O.R., G/36/12.
[5] I.O.R., B.P.C., 21 Nov. 1751, 17 Dec. 1759, Range 1, vol. 24, f. 389, vol. 31, f. 529.
[6] J. Deane's examination, 23 Nov. 1732, I.O.R., Correspondence Reports, D/19.

(about £22,000) a season, which involved passing off the goods of 'a junto of country merchants' as British and therefore entitled to British privileges.[1] If this practice was very widespread, it may have been a factor of some importance in attracting business to British ships.

Contemporary Englishmen were in little doubt that their success in winning freights was largely due to their skill and their valour. They believed that English ships were handled more dexterously and were much less likely to fall into enemy hands than those of their Asian rivals. If it really was the case that the sailing and fighting qualities of the British ships were higher than those of their competitors, it would not be very difficult to explain why Asian merchants should have chosen them. Speed was a factor of great importance in the country trade. The capacity of most of Bengal's markets was limited and they were easily glutted; so those who arrived first made the best voyages in most cases. With money to finance a venture often borrowed at as much as 30 per cent interest,[2] a delayed voyage could mean heavy loss. The timing of voyages round the Indian Ocean was determined by the monsoon system. In the northern part of the Indian Ocean and in the China Sea the winds generally blow from the north-east from October to May. November to March was the season for leaving Bengal and for voyages across the Arabian Sea from India to the Persian Gulf or the Red Sea. From May to October the winds blow in the opposite direction, taking ships up the Bay of Bengal to Calcutta or up the China Sea to Canton. A well-conducted voyage would take advantage of the change of winds to make the fastest progress possible; a badly conducted one which missed the normal sailing seasons would either be slow and hazardous or would have to be abandoned at some point until the winds changed, the ship being said 'to have missed her passage'. A ship bound from Bengal to the Red Sea, for instance, which did not get off the west coast of India before April, might well have to wait there (the crew faring sumptuously at their owner's expense, and his creditors in Calcutta gratefully clocking up their interest) until October when the monsoon changed, an event said to depend on a 'gilded cocoa nut' being thrown into the sea by a brahmin.[3]

---

[1] Bombay to Directors, 1 Jan. 1728, I.O.R., E/4/460, p. 146.
[2] See below, p. 71.
[3] A. Parsons, *Travels in Asia and Africa* (1808), p. 213.

Seamanship could make all the difference between success and failure.

Fighting qualities were needed to deter or beat off attacks by pirates. 'Piracy' is a subjective term, and those Asian powers who were branded as pirates by Europeans were no doubt merely doing what the Portuguese and Dutch tried to do, that is levying a tribute from merchant ships. Nevertheless, whatever the pretext used to justify them, attacks on shipping were a very serious hazard to trade in certain parts of the Indian Ocean, especially in the early decades of the eighteenth century. The chief offenders were certain Maratha coastal chieftains, above all the extremely formidable dynasty of the Angrias, who preyed on shipping off the west coast of India from the 1690s until the capture of their main stronghold in 1756,[1] the Arabs of Muscat, who harried ships in the Persian Gulf in the early eighteenth century, and the shaikhs Mir Mahanna of Rig and Salman of the Ka'ab who were active in the Gulf in the 1760s and 1770s.[2] The danger of piracy was also high off Malaya and Sumatra. Finally, there were European pirates, mostly apparently led by Englishmen, including for a time the dreaded Captain Kidd, who operated from bases in the Red Sea or off Madagascar from the 1690s to the 1720s.[3] In bad years European shipowners suffered crippling losses from piracy. In 1706 and 1707 'not less than ten sails of ships of all nations' were taken by 'country pyrates', the settlement of Madras alone losing 200,000 pagodas or about £80,000.[4] Against a European pirate, or a powerful squadron belonging to Kanohji Angria, some of whose 'grabs' were said to mount up to thirty large guns,[5] there was presumably little that an unprotected merchant ship could do, but a well-armed and resolute ship could no doubt save its skin when confronted by lesser marauders.

Shipowners who could offer high standards of seamanship and a greater degree of security could perhaps charge high freight rates and still defeat their competitors; but before it is assumed

[1] W. S. Desai, *Bombay and the Marathas* (New Delhi, 1970); C. R. Low, *History of the Indian Navy* (1877), i. 97 ff.
[2] A. A. Amin, *British Interests in the Persian Gulf* (Leiden, 1967), pp. 73 ff.; Low, *Indian Navy*, i. 78, 162 ff.
[3] J. Biddulph, *The Pirates of Malabar* (1907).
[4] T. Pitt to R. Bolton, 30 Aug. 1707, to J. Dolben, 11 Sept. 1707, Add. MS. 22850, ff. 35, 50.
[5] Low, i. 97.

that skill and valour were the secrets of British success, it should be recognized that the British used for the most part the same ships, with the same weight of armament, the same crews and even the same officers as Asian shipowners did. Nearly all the Calcutta ships were built in Asia by Asian craftsmen, and some were actually bought or hired from Asian owners. India had a shipbuilding industry of great antiquity, capable by the seventeenth century of constructing large ships of up to 1,000 tons, built according to European designs, even if critics found 'something clumsy, unfinished and un-artist-like' about their appearance.[1] Europeans obtained many of their ships from yards on the west coast of India, near the supplies of teak and the 'poon' masts of the Malabar forests. But in the early eighteenth century, when the Calcutta fleet was undergoing its most rapid expansion, most of the new ships seem to have been laid down at Pegu in Burma, where teak was also abundant. In the 1720s shipowners from both Calcutta and Madras maintained their own 'Residents' at Pegu with staffs of European carpenters to supervise shipbuilding.[2] Later in the century the Bengal shipowners returned to western India for most of their ships, taking advantage of the new yards being opened at Bombay.[3] Later still they began to build their own in Bengal: a 250-ton ship was completed at Chittagong in 1763,[4] and the first ocean-going ship to be launched on the Hugli river for many years sailed from Calcutta in 1781. There appears to have been nothing in the design and construction of these ships to distinguish them from other Indian-built ships owned by Asian merchants.

Nor does there seem to have been any obvious difference in their capacity to defend themselves. European ships' guns could be obtained fairly readily in India and both Asian- and European-owned ships carried them. Two Arab ships seen at Hugli in 1705 of 330 and 200 tons respectively were thought to carry twenty-two and twenty guns.[5] Large Muslim ships from Surat were

[1] A. Jan Qaisar, 'Shipbuilding in the Mughal Empire during the seventeenth century', *Indian Economic and Social History Review*, v (1968); J. Grose, *A Voyage to the East Indies*, new edn. (1772), i. 108.

[2] Directors to Madras, 23 Jan. 1730, I.O.R., E/3/104, p. 671; D. G. E. Hall, *Early English intercourse with Burma* (1928), pp. 222–3.

[3] R. A. Wadia, *The Bombay Dockyard and the Wadia Master Builders* (Bombay, 1955).

[4] H. Verelst to S. Court, [Feb. 1763], Ames MSS., I.O.L. Microfilm, reel 606.

[5] I.O.R., B.P.C., 18 Sept. 1705, Range 1, vol. 1, f. 243.

similarly armed. Lists of the armaments of British and Asian ships in the Red Sea and the Persian Gulf do not reveal any significant difference, at least in quantity.[1] The fighting quality of the crews is likely to have been identical, since they were both manned by the same Indian seamen. The number of Europeans available in the East was never sufficient to provide more than the officers and a few key members of the crew, such as gunners.

Where Europeans were most confident of their superiority was in the quality of these officers. By contrast with the superior 'courage, conduct and art of navigation' of the British,[2] Asian commanders were thought to be incompetent and dilatory in their sailing and unenterprising in accepting the limitations of the monsoons. 'Their navigators' were called 'very indifferent artists' who 'seldom put to sea but in fair season'.[3] 'Their navigators are so ignorant as often to loose their passage', the Calcutta Council thought.[4] On another occasion they comforted themselves that although conditions were making it difficult for their own ships to get out of the Hugli, 'the Moors' ships will not attempt it'.[5] Granting that recent advances in navigational techniques, such as greater precision in estimating longitude, may have enabled a skilled European master to sail his ship better than a *nakhoda* could do, the advantage of European officers was not confined to European-owned ships. 'The Mogul's subjects' offered 'very handsom salaries and indulgences' to persuade Europeans to serve on their ships.[6] They appear to have had some success. In 1708 the Calcutta Council believed that they could cripple 'the Moors and Gentue shipping' if they were to recall all British subjects employed in it.[7]

In competition with Asian ships, the Calcutta shipowner had no clear-cut advantages based on greater force, sharper commercial acumen, better ships or more skilled men. They were competing on more or less even terms and the benefits which Asian merchants hoped to get from paying higher European freights can have been at best marginal. Their most powerful inducement was perhaps the feeling that in entrusting their goods to a private English ship

[1] Shipping lists in I.O.R., G/29/14, f. 17; G/17/1, ff. 451–2; G/17/2, f. 65.
[2] A. Hamilton, *A New Account of the East Indies* (Edinburgh, 1737), i. 233.
[3] Grose, op. cit., i. 109.
[4] Abs. Bengal to Directors, 3 Dec. 1717, I.O.R., E/4/2, p. 125.
[5] Ibid., 25 Jan. 1721, p. 293.   [6] Hamilton, op. cit., i. 233.
[7] I.O.R., B.P.C., 22 Nov. 1708, Range 1, vol. 1, f. 461.

they were in fact entrusting their goods to the Company, whose privileges private Englishmen enjoyed and from whom they must have seemed inseparable in Asian eyes. Even if Asian goods on British ships were not treated as British, they still had some extra security against the hazards of trade. The behaviour of customs collectors and other officials in nearly all ports was, to say the least, unpredictable; but it required some resolution to detain or to levy exactions on goods in which the East India Company appeared to have an interest. Pirates no doubt attacked all ships indiscriminately; but an attack on an English ship was an act which could have serious consequences.

Asian ships were not Calcutta's only rivals. There was also stiff competition for Bengal's carrying trade from European antagonists, a category which the Calcutta shipowners readily extended to include Englishmen at other settlements in India and even their own employers. In normal circumstances during the eighteenth century the British community at Calcutta did not regard either the Dutch or the Portuguese as serious commercial rivals. During the seventeenth century much of Bengal's trade with Indonesia and Malaya had been handled by the Dutch. Two Dutch fleets a year were expected to come to the Hugli from Batavia.[1] During the eighteenth century, however, Dutch shipping between Java and Bengal declined to a trickle, while their attempts to keep the ships of other Europeans out of the Archipelago became more and more ineffective; by the end of the century far more Bengal goods were going to Batavia in private English ships than were being carried by the Dutch themselves.[2] Direct Dutch trade between Bengal and their factories in the Red Sea and the Persian Gulf, which had been sizeable up to the 1680s,[3] dwindled to insignificance. The Dutch Company would not permit individual Dutchmen to operate ships in Asia on their own behalf until 1742. The prospect of competition from private Dutch ships alarmed the Calcutta Council, who forbade British subjects to co-operate with them in any way in 1745.[4] But the private voyages were not a success. The first Dutch 'freight ship' from Bengal to

[1] C. R. Wilson, *Early Annals of the English in Bengal* (1895–1917), i. 400.
[2] See below, p. 103.
[3] K. Glamann, *Dutch Asiatic Trade 1620–1720* (The Hague, 1958), p. 159; Om Prakash, 'European trading companies', *Indian Economic and Social History Review*, i. 58.
[4] I.O.R., B.P.C., 24 Oct. 1745, Range 1, vol. 17, f. 718.

the Persian Gulf 'lost her passage' in 1746, arrived late, and either she or another one caught fire and was lost.[1] Calcutta only feared Portuguese competition during periods of European war, when the Portuguese as neutrals enjoyed obvious advantages. A Portuguese 'freight ship' from Bengal apparently made a successful voyage to the Persian Gulf in 1747 during the War of the Austrian succession.[2] During the War of the American Revolution a considerable part of the trade between Bengal and China, which usually went on British ships, was carried by the Portuguese.[3]

Spasmodic Dutch or Portuguese competition with Calcutta's shipping caused the British relatively little concern. French competition was quite a different matter. For some years it was formidable and sustained, causing acute anxiety in Calcutta. The French company relaxed prohibitions on private shipping in 1722. By 1727 the British in Bengal were beginning to complain that the French were taking their customers by offering 'half freight'.[4] When Dupleix became Governor of Chandernagore, the French settlement on the Hugli above Calcutta, in 1731, he immediately launched a massive private trading offensive to virtually all the Asian ports visited by English ships. In 1731–2 Dupleix was concerned in six ships, in 1732–3 in eight, and in nine in 1734–5, the momentum being kept up until his departure for Pondicherry in 1740.[5] A Dutch comparison of the major ships of the Calcutta and Chandernagore fleets put them at nineteen to nine in 1734.[6] In 1742 the Calcutta Council urgently discussed how to limit 'the great disservice to the private trade of this place' inflicted by French competition, and decided to prohibit all dealings with the French by Calcutta merchants 'white or black'.[7] War brought more effectual relief. In the periods of European war from 1744 to 1748, 1756 to 1763, and 1778 to 1783 the Royal Navy could generally disrupt all French trade in the Indian Ocean, even if it could not prevent French raiders inflicting great damage

[1] Basra to Directors, 26 May, 16 Oct. 1747, I.O.R., G/29/15, ff. 577, 591.
[2] Basra to Directors, 14 July 1747, I.O.R., G/29/15, f. 585.
[3] Canton to Directors, 29 Dec. 1782, I.O.R., G/12/76, p. 227; Canton Consultations, 24 Aug. 1783, I.O.R., G/12/77, p. 59.
[4] Abs. Bengal to Directors, 28 Jan. 1727, I.O.R., E/4/2, p. 525.
[5] These voyages are analysed in great detail by A. Martineau, *Dupleix et l'Inde française* (Paris, 1920–8), i. 300–47, 515–30; see also I. Ray, 'Dupleix's trade at Chandernagore', *Indian Historical Review*, i (1974).
[6] Koloniaal Archief, 2196, pp. 211–12.
[7] I.O.R., B.P.C., 7 Oct. 1742, Range 1, vol. 15, pp. 327, 390.

on the British. French trade in Bengal ceased altogether after 1757 and 1778 when the British took Chandernagore. In the intervals of peace later in the century French private trade revived, but never on the same scale as in the 1730s and 1740s.

The English community in Calcutta were prepared to guard their seaborne trade against all comers, including their fellow countrymen. In the late seventeenth century the main private English fleet in India had been based on Madras. By 1727, however, the Madras Council sadly recognized that the situation was very different. 'Not so many years since', they wrote, the Bengal servants had been content with receiving a commission on Bengal goods which they provided for the Madras ships to take to Surat and the Persian Gulf and with having a share of one-third in the voyages. Now the ships were owned at Calcutta and the Madras fleet was dwindling away.[1] The Bombay servants had already protested that they too had 'very unjustly from our fellow servants been excluded from any share in the benefit' of Bengal trade.[2] The complaints from Madras and Bombay were in essentials the same. They alleged in the first place that free competition for freight was not allowed at Calcutta. The Bengal servants ensured that goods requiring freight were only offered to Calcutta's own ships. Secondly, it was said that anyone who wanted to export Bengal goods on his own account was not permitted to obtain them for himself at the *aurangs* where they were made, but must receive them from a Bengal servant who would charge so high a commission on them that they would easily be undersold at their destined port by goods provided by the Bengal servants for themselves. The Bengal servants did not deny that they regulated freights or kept other Englishmen away from the *aurangs*, a practice which they defended by referring to orders issued by the Directors in 1692,[3] but they insisted that they did not charge excessive commissions.[4] Whatever the truth may have been, the Calcutta servants achieved the effect they wanted: in January 1735 the Madras Council wrote that they would send no more ships to Bengal to collect cargoes until they were given better treatment.[5]

[1] *Records of Fort St. George: Despatches to England 1727–33* (Madras, 1929), p. 18.   [2] Bombay to Directors, 8 Nov. 1723, I.O.R., E/4/459, p. 213.
[3] Directors to Fort St. George, 22 Jan. 1692, I.O.R., E/3/92, p. 176.
[4] Abs. Bengal to Directors, 10 Feb. 1731, I.O.R., E/4/3, p. 136.
[5] Fort St. George to Directors, 22 Jan. 1735, *Records of Fort St. George: Despatches to England 1733–5* (Madras, 1931), p. 55.

A final opponent to be worsted if possible was the Bengal servants' own employer, the East India Company. Although their cost limited their use in Asia,[1] the Company's own ships from Europe with their British crews, their great size and their heavy fire-power were most formidable competitors in the country trade. For much of the eighteenth century at least one European ship a year was normally available in Bengal to be sent on an Asian trading voyage before being returned to Britain. The disposal of these ships caused an acute conflict between public duty and private interest for the Calcutta Council. On the one hand, they were responsible for letting the ships on the best possible terms for the Company; on the other, it was obvious that freights gained for the Company would be lost to their private ships. On occasions Company servants freighted the European ship themselves, but they were also tempted to use their powers to divert freights away from their employers. In 1714 the Directors complained that a Company's ship had been sent away empty from Calcutta, although her master knew that there was freight waiting for the private ships.[2] Matters came to a head over the *Bouverie*, which according to the Directors, was not allowed to take freight for the Persian Gulf in 1718 until all the private ships had been served. As a result it sailed late with an indifferent cargo and lost its passage. The Directors later heard that one of the Council had said, 'Let our orders be never so strict, none of our ships should be employed in India.'[3] They therefore decided to take action to penalize private ships which might compete with the Company in future. Private Bengal ships of more than 300 tons were to pay an extra tonnage duty of 10s. a ton, and all such ships were to be sold off as soon as possible.[4] The extra duty does not seem to have been collected with any strictness, as was admitted when it was finally abandoned in 1759,[5] ships of over 300 tons were certainly not sold off, and conflicts between private and Company ships still recurred. But the Council became more cautious in their defiance and appear to have regarded the regular sailing of Company ships between Bengal and western India as a form of competition in which they had no option but to acquiesce.

[1] See above, pp. 19–20.
[2] Directors to Bengal, 13 Jan. 1714, I.O.R., E/3/98, pp. 194–5.
[3] Directors to Bengal, 2 Feb. 1725, I.O.R., E/3/102, p. 483.
[4] Directors to Bengal, 29 Jan. 1724, ibid. 221–2.
[5] I.O.R., B.P.C., 6 Aug. 1759, Range 1, vol. 31, f. 314.

The special problems posed by Asian conditions forced Calcutta shipowners to conduct their operations in a manner unlike that of British shipowners in other parts of the world. Calcutta ships were extremely expensive to run. Late in the century it was thought that the 'expences attending ships with their charges' were greater in India than they were in Europe.[1] For all the cheapness of Indian labour, shipbuilding was still very costly. Indian shipwrights fitted their timbers together with great care and precision, but, as a Dutch visitor to Surat commented, 'the tediousness of their method, together with the dearness of timber they employ, which must be brought hither from distant places, make shipbuilding very dear here'.[2] If Asian substitutes were not used, imported ships' stores, sailcloth and iron were another expensive item. In 1758 there were complaints that the cost of ships built in Pegu was rising steeply.[3] An 800-ton ship laid down at Bombay in 1775 cost £16 per ton,[4] while it was said that new 400-ton ships were costing £12 to £16 per ton at Calcutta in the 1790s.[5] By comparison with the £6 or £7 which appears to have been the average cost on the Thames[6] and the £4 per ton in colonial America,[7] these figures are very high. Guns were an added expense.

Teak-built ships were exceptionally durable and did not require frequent repair, but in other respects 'the charges of sailing' Indian ships were said to be very heavy.[8] In 1710 an attempt was made to fix the wages of lascars at Rs 5 per month while they were at sea.[9] Although this was under half the monthly wages paid in peacetime to seamen on British ships throughout the eighteenth century,[10] it is likely that larger numbers of Indian seamen had to be em-employed. European officers were another source of expense. In 1768 a first and a second mate were paid Rs 100 and Rs 70 a month

[1] J. Robinson to W. Hastings, 15 Dec. 1777, Add. MS. 29139, f. 444.

[2] J. S. Stavorinus, *Voyage to the East Indies*, trans. S. H. Wilcocke (1798), iii. 22.

[3] J. C. Long, *Selections from the unpublished records of Government from the year 1748 to 1767* (Calcutta, 1869), i. 169.

[4] I.O.R., B.P.C., 24 July 1778, Range 2, vol. 24, p. 57.

[5] Colebrooke, *Remarks*, p. 214.

[6] R. Davis, *The Rise of the English shipping industry in the seventeenth and eighteenth centuries* (1962), p. 374.

[7] G. M. Walton, 'A measure of productivity change in American colonial shipping', *Economic History Review*, 2nd ser. xxi (1968), 276–7.

[8] J. Grose to N. Grose, 7 Feb. 1770, I.O.L., MS. Eur. E. 248 (54).

[9] Wilson, *Early Annals*, II, i. 1.

[10] Davis, *Shipping Industry*, p. 137.

respectively while at sea;[1] the sterling equivalents would be about £11 and £8, compared with £5 which was the most that a mate on a British ship could normally expect to earn.[2] In addition to wages, it was customary to reward masters and officers of country ships with grants of 'privilege', that is with a proportion of the profits of the voyage or with cargo space in which they could carry goods on their own account. Privilege could be quite a heavy charge on the owners: one-eighth seems to have been commonly allowed to masters by 'Calcutta custom',[3] but evidence of payment of one-sixth also exists.[4] By the 1770s captains of two-masted 'snows' were expecting to earn up to Rs 300 a month and those of larger ships Rs 400 or Rs 500.[5]

Having obtained his ship, fitted it out and engaged his crew, a Calcutta shipowner could then let it out for freight or purchase a cargo for it on his own account. In Britain during the eighteenth century it was becoming increasingly uncommon for the same man to be both a shipowner and a merchant importing and exporting goods; in most trades ownership of the ship and of its cargo were likely to be in separate hands.[6] In India this was not necessarily so. On routes long used by Asian merchants a large volume of freight was available in Bengal, its owners sometimes travelling with their goods, appointing supercargoes to do so, or consigning them to their agents at the port of destination. By the end of the century European-owned freight was also available in considerable quantities to be shipped from Calcutta to large British settlements like Bombay, Madras, Penang, or Canton. But for voyages which lay off the traditional arteries of Bengal's trade it was often necessary for the owner to provide a large part of his ship's cargo himself; even on well established routes he was often tempted to do so by the prospect of large profits on the sale. Thus it was very common for Calcutta shipowners to be deeply concerned in the cargo as well as in the ship itself.

Expensive ships with high operating costs, in whose cargo the owner often had a large stake, made shipowning in Bengal an

---

[1] Calcutta High Court Records, Mayor's Court, *Bryant* v. *Grant*.

[2] Davis, p. 150.

[3] Calcutta High Court Records, Mayor's Court, *Chevalier* v. *Polier*; *Mitchell* v. *Vivanca*.

[4] Ibid., Account of the Owners of ship *Golconda*.

[5] Ibid., Supreme Court, Plea Side, *Starkey* v. *Blackwell*; *Gow* v. *Colvin*; *Witham* v. *Douglas*.   [6] Davis, pp. 90–8.

enterprise that demanded large outlays. To make matters more difficult, the means most commonly used to finance the Calcutta fleet added greatly to the owners' costs. In Britain shipowners met the cost of their ships directly themselves. If extra funds were needed, the owners either increased their own stake or enlisted more owners, ownership of a vessel often being subdivided into small fractions held by a large group of investors. But in eighteenth-century Calcutta there were definite limits to the number of potential owners and to the funds at their disposal. The British community was neither big enough nor rich enough to sustain on its own a merchant fleet of the size that had grown up by the 1720s, while the Indian business community, with some exceptions, appears to have been unwilling to assume the direct owner-ship of shares in European ships. On the other hand, Indians were certainly prepared to invest in shipping on their own terms. The type of investment which they favoured, loans on respondentia, became the chief means by which the Calcutta fleet was financed. As a case submitted to counsel in 1746 put it, 'the trade carried on by the Company's servants in India is for the most part with money borrowed at respondentia, few of them having sufficient capitals of their own without assistance'.[1]

A respondentia loan was a loan secured on the cargo of a ship at a rate adjusted to the risk and the length of the voyage, the risk being on the lender. In Europe they no doubt originated in the sea loans of the ancient Mediterranean,[2] and were recognized in English law from the sixteenth century.[3] Although they had become obsolete in the western hemisphere by the eighteenth century,[4] perhaps originating from a different source, they re-mained very much alive in Asia. Europeans encountered them in Japan[5] and in Java,[6] while a very similar system appears to have been in operation at Surat in the seventeenth century.[7] Money was raised on respondentia not only by shipowners to finance their voyages, but those who were sending cargo on freight also borrowed

[1] Case to counsel, 30 Apr. 1746, I.O.R., Home Miscellaneous, 824, no. 20.
[2] R. S. Lopez and I. W. Raymond, *Medieval Trade in the Mediterranean World* (1955), p. 168.
[3] W. S. Holdsworth, *History of English Law* (1903–52), viii. 261–2.
[4] Davis, pp. 84–5.
[5] C. R. Boxer, *Fidalgos in the Far East* (The Hague, 1948), pp. 116, 119–20.
[6] J. C. van Leur, *Indonesian Trade and Society* (The Hague, 1955), p. 328.
[7] I. Habib, 'Usury in Medieval India', *Comparative Studies in Society and History*, vi (1963–4), 405.

on its security. Respondentia loans became a very popular form of investment in Calcutta both with Europeans and with Indians. A newly arrived Writer was advised in 1756 to begin his trading by lending on respondentia, 'which on average will produce annually 25 per cent at least'.[1] Shipowners themselves, if they had money to spare, became lenders on respondentia. It was common practice for owners to lend to those who wished to freight with them on the security of the goods. The manager of a ship going to Bengal was told that 'the merchants in that place will be glad to freight goods when they can have money on the bottome'.[2]

The obvious disadvantage of the respondentia system from the point of view of shipowners was the very high rates which they were required to pay. Comparison of rates quoted at Madras at the beginning of the century[3] with those in Calcutta in the 1750s and 1760s suggests a slight fall, but a very high price was still being charged for money borrowed on respondentia. Between 18 and 30 per cent was charged on loans for voyages to the Persian Gulf; from 18 to 22 per cent to the Red Sea; 18 or 19 per cent to Surat; 18 per cent for destinations the other side of the Straits of Malacca; with up to 30 per cent for Canton or Manila. Money could be borrowed for voyages to Madras at 12 per cent for six months or 5 per cent for two.[4]

Since the risks of the sea were borne by the lender, respondentia bonds were a form of insurance for shipowners. By the 1770s it was said to be fairly common for owners to give respondentia bonds as a means of diminishing their risk rather than as a means of raising money. If the voyage was successful, no money changed hands apart from the interest on the bond.[5] High interest rates on respondentia made this an expensive way of insuring, but the premiums on ordinary insurance policies were also high. Policies could be laid either in India or in Britain. An insurance office seems

---

[1] S. Dalrymple to H. Dalrymple, 9 Jan. 1756, S.R.O., Hamilton-Dalrymple MSS., bundle 76.

[2] Instructions to J. Scattergood, 25 Jan. 1718, I.O.R., Home Miscellaneous, 822, p. 194; see also the account of Sir G. Mathews's voyages in Directors to Bengal, 5 July 1710, I.O.R., E/3/96, pp. 791–2.

[3] C. Lockyer, *An Account of the Trade in India* (1711), pp. 17–18.

[4] Many bonds survive in the Calcutta High Court Records, Mayor's Court and Supreme Court; see also Bond Book for 1757, I.O.R., Mayor's Court Records, Range 155, vol. 60.

[5] There is much information on this in Calcutta High Court Records, Supreme Court, Plea Side, *Bondfield* v. *Guinand*.

to have been opened in Madras as early as 1687,[1] but no comparable institution appears to have been set up at Calcutta until relatively late in the eighteenth century. By 1773 policies were being drawn up at Calcutta with 'as much force and effect as the securest writing or policy of assurance made in London',[2] and an insurance broker was operating there in 1775.[3] There are references to an insurance society with five superintending members in 1777,[4] and to another in 1778 with four lakhs of rupees at risk and another five lakhs in reserve.[5] A new insurance society was founded in 1780 with twenty-four members (half of them Asian)[6] and yet another, formally called the Bengal Insurance Society, came into existence in 1783 with twenty-five.[7]

In the second half of the eighteenth century peacetime premiums on short voyages round the Bay of Bengal were 4 or 5 per cent,[8] while policies from Calcutta to China appear to have run at 6 per cent.[9] Those who wanted the greater security of insuring in London, as many Calcutta shipowners did, had to pay for it. In 1773 Warren Hastings lent money on respondentia on three ships going in peacetime from Calcutta to Canton; he was told by his London agents that ten guineas per cent was the cheapest they could obtain for him.[10] Even the lowest Calcutta premiums at 4 per cent were markedly higher than the 2 per cent which was common on runs across the Atlantic to North America or $2\frac{1}{4}$ to 3 per cent charged on voyages to Jamaica.[11]

The very high cost of mounting trading voyages from Indian ports meant that their success depended on a high level of profits. High profits could certainly be made, but the element of uncertainty in Asian trade was much greater than in the western

[1] Directors to Bengal, 12 Dec. 1687, I.O.R., E/3/91, p. 470.

[2] I.O.L., MS. Eur. D. 17, no. 20.

[3] Calcutta High Court Records, Supreme Court, Plea Side, *Bondfield* v. *Guinand*.   [4] *B.P.P.*, xiv (1917), 9.

[5] J. Fergusson to C. Alexander, 1 Aug. 1778, Add. MS. 45433, f. 69.

[6] Calcutta High Court Records, Supreme Court, Equity, *Blume* v. *Blythe et al.*

[7] *B.P.P.*, xiv (1917), 22.

[8] e.g. I.O.L., MS. Eur. D. 17, no. 20; Calcutta Bar Library Club, Supreme Court Reports, xxiv. 753.

[9] Ibid. xxviii, 135; Calcutta High Court Records, Supreme Court, Equity, *Bayne and Colvin* v. *Elliot et al.*

[10] J. Woodman to Hastings, 26 Dec. 1774, Add. MS. 29135, f. 411.

[11] G. M. Walton, 'Sources of Productivity changes in American Colonial Shipping 1675–1775', *Economic History Review*, 2nd ser., xx (1967), 71.

hemisphere. Political conditions were unstable in most of the ports visited by Calcutta ships, and even in favourable conditions demand was limited. Complaints of overtrading leading to glut and falling prices constantly recur.[1]

One obvious way to counter uncertainty and to protect the very large sums invested in shipping was to try to reduce competition, not only from Asians, other Europeans or other Englishmen, but within the Calcutta fleet itself. Various schemes were devised for keeping up freight rates and the price at which it was hoped that goods could be sold by limiting the number of ships allowed to proceed from Calcutta to any particular port. At their most ambitious, such schemes aimed at uniting 'the trading partys by making a general stock of the ships belonging to Bengal'.[2] Plans of this kind were proposed by successive Governors and Councils, who invariably allocated the largest share of the freight or of the cargo space to themselves. They eventually found favour with the Directors who attributed 'the badness of trade all over India' to 'competition among yourselves and clogging the markets'.[3] But they were vigorously opposed by junior servants and Free Merchants who were not prepared to see their trade regulated by others. Calcutta's ships were never united into any kind of joint body, although the Governor and the senior servants did succeed in cornering the most lucrative freights for themselves.

It appears to have been relatively easy for the Governor and Council to regulate the distribution of goods brought to Calcutta to be shipped as freight on British ships. Regulation began early. In 1706 a Free Merchant was warned by the Governor against 'being a fellow troubled with the spirit of interlopping, in buying goods and taking freights where he could best get them'.[4] In 1717 the Governor had proposed an official limitation on the number of ships permitted to take on freight.[5] The Directors refused to sanction the scheme, but some kind of unofficial regulation clearly was enforced. In 1719 a Free Merchant reported that the 'country ships that belong to the gentlemen at Bengal . . . gets all the

[1] This problem is discussed at greater length in the following chapter, see below, pp. 90–1.
[2] Abs. J. Stackhouse to Directors, 20 Feb. 1732, I.O.R., E/4/3, p. 204.
[3] Directors to Bengal, 12 Feb. 1731, I.O.R., E/3/105, pp. 208–9.
[4] Hamilton, *New Account*, ii. 15.
[5] Wilson, *Early Annals*, II. i. 284–5, 295–300; E. Page etc. to Directors, 3 Dec. 1717, I.O.R., E/4/20, no. 6.

freight etc they are able'.[1] In 1725 a junior servant found that
'when he did freight out a ship he was threatened to fare the worse
for it and did'.[2] By 1731, however, the Directors were prepared to
give official approval to what they could not prevent by ordering
that 'the direction and management of the freight shall be in the
Governour and Council for the time being'.[3] The term 'freight
ships' came to be used to describe an arrangement that was to
remain in force until the early 1770s. All freight for certain ports
was divided up between the ships of a consortium headed by the
Governor and Council. Any other servant 'inclinable to put his
goods into their stock is allowed so to do',[4] and many small
investors seem to have placed money in the freight ships.

Freight to the most lucrative destinations was brought under
regulation, but in other respects Calcutta's seaborne trade could
not be controlled. Many ships, owned by Company servants, Free
Merchants, and some Indian merchants living in Calcutta, continued to operate outside the ring of the 'freight ships'. Most of
them seem to have been owned by small partnerships of two,
three, or four men, but single ownership, often by a man who
sailed as master of his own ship, was by no means uncommon.
Even outside the 'freight ships' there was hierarchy and discrimination. Company servants were particularly jealous of Free
Merchants and did all they could to hamper them. The Directors'
orders that only Company servants should be allowed to travel
outside Calcutta were strictly enforced,[5] so that Free Merchants
were prevented from dealing directly with the producers. If they
obtained goods through Indian agents, exemption from paying
the Nawabs' customs under the 1717 *farman* seems normally to
have been denied to them. Thus they had no alternative but to
buy through the Company's servants and to pay their commissions,
said to be 'full twenty per cent'.[6] In 1753 the Council even tried to
stop the issue of 'passes', signifying British protection, to Free
Merchants' ships.[7]

[1] J. Scattergood to F. Chamberlain, [Nov. 1719], I.O.R., Home Miscellaneous,
822, p. 377.

[2] Directors to Bengal, 1 Dec. 1725, I.O.R., E/3/103, p. 71.

[3] Directors to Bengal, 12 Feb. 1731, I.O.R., E/3/105, p. 208.

[4] Abs. Bengal to Directors, 26 Dec. 1733, I.O.R., E/4/3, pp. 342–3.

[5] Directors to Bengal, 7 Apr. 1708, I.O.R., E/3/96, p. 269.

[6] Directors to Bengal, 1 Apr. 1760, *Fort William–India House Correspondence*
(New Delhi, 1949–), iii. 29.

[7] I.O.R., B.P.C., 15 Jan. 1753, Range 1, vol. 26, f. 24.

By endurance in adversity Free Merchants were ultimately to gain control of Calcutta's shipping. The 1760s and the early 1770s were years of stringency for Bengal shipowners. The 'freight ships' association finally broke up,[1] and Company servants, for whom more profitable outlets were opening in internal trade in Bengal or in holding offices in the new administration of the province, generally sold their shipping. 'You must positively have no more sea concerns, for they are much more likely to reduce than encrease your fortune . . . an inland one will have the greatest probability of success', was typical of advice being given in Calcutta in the 1760s.[2] Sound as this advice might be, Free Merchants could not usually take it. They were not eligible for office or for the plums of the inland trade. In 1772 Clive told the House of Commons that trading by sea was now 'not worth the attention of the servants. It was carried on chiefly by Free Merchants and Free Mariners and they could scarcely live by it.'[3] When Calcutta's seaborne trade began to expand again in the mid 1770s, Free Merchants were far too well entrenched in it to be displaced by Company servants. Some Free Merchants, like Joseph Price (who once had twenty-four 'ships, snows and sloops, navigating the seas on my own credit')[4] or John Fergusson,[5] built up very large shipping businesses, which are clearly the forerunners of the chains of ships owned by the Houses of Agency from the 1780s.[6]

---

[1] See below, p. 97.
[2] W. Ellis to J. Carnac, 10 Dec. 1762, I.O.L., MS. Eur. F. 128, box 3/5.
[3] *The Parliamentary History of England*, xvii. 338.
[4] [J. Price], *Some Observations and Remarks on a late publication, entitled Travels in Europe, Asia and Africa* (2nd ed., 1783), p. 71.
[5] See below, p. 249.
[6] S. B. Singh, *European Agency Houses in Bengal 1783–1833* (Calcutta, 1966), pp. 18–23.

IV

Seaborne Trade:
(II) From West to East

The figures for tonnage duties, consulage and customs given in the previous chapter do not suggest a simple story of growth and sustained prosperity. They seem rather to indicate that the private British merchant fleet at Calcutta passed through two phases of expansion during the eighteenth century with a period of contraction or stagnation in between. From about 1715 until about 1735 the number of ships based on Calcutta, their total tonnage and the consulage paid on exports generally show an upward trend. From 1735 until the late 1760s the number of ships, their tonnage and the consulage receipts all remain well below the best levels of the previous decades. By the 1770s, however, better times had clearly arrived. Recovery was to be checked by the European war from 1778 to 1783, but after 1783 it was to be resumed at full speed.

These fluctuations between expansion and contraction coincide with major shifts in the geographical distribution of Bengal's trade. In crude outline Bengal traded during the eighteenth century with two areas where profits, high even by Asian standards, could be made by the use of large ships with valuable cargoes such as silk, fine piecegoods, or opium. These markets lay either to the west of Cape Comorin: the ports of western India, especially Surat, and those on the Persian Gulf or the Red Sea; or to the east of the Straits of Malacca: ports in Malaya and Indonesia and above all Manila in the Philippine Islands and Canton in China. Around the Bay of Bengal itself, south-eastern India, Burma, and the west coast of Sumatra, Calcutta ships traded extensively; but the voyages were short and frequent, the cargoes bulky and cheap, such as rice, salt, timber, or coarse piecegoods, and the profits relatively low. Trading round the Bay provided employment for a large part of Calcutta's shipping throughout the whole eighteenth century. But if it was the constant element in Calcutta's trade, it evidently could not of itself sustain a large merchant fleet at a high level of prosperity. Up to 1735 the Bay trade was supplemented by a large volume of trade to the west of Cape Comorin. After 1735 trade to the westward experienced serious difficulties which are clearly reflected in the tonnage duty and consulage returns. When recovery came in the 1770s, it was based on expanding trade to profitable markets to the east.

Immediately to the west of Cape Comorin is a string of ports on the Malabar Coast of south-western India. Bengal ships normally called at the Dutch settlement at Cochin, the English factories at Tellicherry and Anjengo, the independent city of Calicut, or the Mysore port of Mangalore. The Malabar Coast was a major pepper producing area, as well as a source of other spices, such as cardamom and coarse cinnamon, and sandalwood.[1] Calcutta ships took on Malabar pepper either as part of their return cargo (Bengal was thought to import 700 tons of Malabar pepper in the 1760s)[2] or to sell in China, the Red Sea or the Persian Gulf. From the Malabar ports some ships left the coast and struck across the Arabian Sea, but most proceeded further north, to Goa, capital of Portuguese India, to Bombay, for much of the eighteenth century a relatively unsuccessful settlement, but one whose trade was to grow very rapidly indeed from the 1780s, when its private fleet began to rival Calcutta's,[3] and to Surat.

At the beginning of the eighteenth century Surat was the most important port in India.[4] Some Europeans thought that it had a population of half a million. It was the main outlet for the very rich province of Gujarat and had an extremely cosmopolitan and wealthy merchant community. A large volume of trade passed between Bengal and Surat, partly by sea, partly overland via the Ganges valley. Bengal exported sugar, certain kinds of piecegoods and above all raw silk, needed for the great silk manufactories at Ahmedabad and Surat itself. Every year a number of Gujarati silk merchants travelled to Bengal, their silk and the goods of many

[1] For the Malabar ports, see A. Das Gupta, *Malabar in Asian Trade* (Cambridge, 1967).

[2] R. Gregory's evidence to the House of Commons, 1767, Add. MS. 18469, f. 38.

[3] P. Nightingale, *Trade and Empire in Western India 1784–1806* (Cambridge, 1970), pp. 16–24.

[4] A. Das Gupta, 'The Merchants of Surat', *Élites in South Asia*, ed. E. Leach and S. N. Mukherjee (Cambridge, 1970).

other Asian merchants providing valuable freight for Calcutta's ships. In return Bengal imported much raw cotton from Gujarat. In an average year in the 1760s it was said that 15,000 bales of Gujarat cotton worth £1,500,000 would reach Bengal.[1] Surat's extensive connections with other markets in northern and western India and its highly sophisticated commercial organization also encouraged Europeans to ship cargoes there on their own account. Jain and Hindu brokers of 'invincible phlegm and coolness' were said to buy a ship's cargo 'in half an hour's time with very few words, and the amount paid down upon the nail, either in ready money or by barter'.[2] In trying to win a share of the trade between Bengal and Surat the British at Calcutta faced formidable competition from Asian shipowners. In the early eighteenth century the Dutch listed over fifty sizeable ships sent to sea by the merchants of Surat,[3] many of them employed in the Bengal trade. In 1698 the English believed that about sixteen Asian ships from Surat came into the Hugli.[4] The Dutch recorded fifteen in 1701–2 with declining numbers thereafter until there was a recovery to ten in each of the seasons 1708–9 and 1709–10.[5] Decline followed again; apart from relatively good years in 1718 and 1722 of eight and nine respectively, the average number of Surat ships returning from Bengal each season between 1715 and 1735 was about five. By the late 1730s the number of Asian-owned ships trading between Bengal and Surat had been reduced to a trickle.[6]

While the number of Asian ships on the Surat run was declining, the number of private British ships was gradually increasing. In the first twenty years after the founding of Calcutta, most of the private ships which took Bengal goods to Surat appear to have been owned at Madras or by the Company's servants stationed at Surat or by unattached Free Merchants. But by 1711 three or four Calcutta-owned ships 'of good force' were said to be going yearly to Surat.[7] In 1717 the Governor estimated that Calcutta ships were carrying 1,000 tons of freight and cargo a year to

---

[1] Gregory's evidence, Add. MS. 18469, f. 38.
[2] J. Grose, *Voyage to the East Indies* (new edn., 1772), i. 105–6.
[3] Das Gupta, 'Surat Merchants', *Élites*, p. 208.
[4] Calcutta Diary, 25 July 1698, I.O.R., G/7/3.
[5] Om Prakash, 'European trading companies and the merchants of Bengal', *Indian Economic and Social History Review*, i (1963–4), 44–5.
[6] Figures from Dutch records kindly communicated by Dr. Das Gupta.
[7] Abs. Bombay to Directors, 19 Jan. 1711, I.O.R., E/4/449, p. 150.

Surat and named five ships which were to sail there in the current season.[1] By 1725 Calcutta British ships were outnumbering Asian-owned ships by eleven[2] to five. In 1728 it was said that trading to Surat 'generally engrosses all those whose schemes are not deep enough to take in a large compass, and even for those who are no great schemers Suratt is a very convenient port'. Some ten ships from Calcutta were said to be bound there that season.[3] By the late 1730s British dominance over the carrying trade between Bengal and Surat was very marked. In 1738 the figures were nine British[4] to four Asian ships with seven[5] to none in 1739. The Gujarat silk merchants, who offered the most valuable freights for Surat, complained in 1731 to the Nawab of Bengal that they would be 'very great sufferers' from any interference with British shipping.[6] In 1745 and 1746 thirteen and ten Calcutta ships respectively were listed as travelling between Bengal and Surat.[7] By the 1760s it was being alleged that the Calcutta 'freight ships' (the joint stock run by the Governor and Council) had so complete a monopoly over the main return cargo from Surat, Gujarat cotton, that their owners could fix its selling price in Bengal.[8]

Sind, to the north and west of Gujarat, was another rich coastal province with important inland communications up the Indus valley, especially to the great commercial city of Multan.[9] Sind imported metals, sugar, rice, and silk by sea from Bengal. The goods were normally landed at anchorages on the Indus Delta to be sold at Thatta some 200 miles up the river, where from 1758 until 1775 the East India Company had a small factory. For some years before the Company had been established there, one or two private English ships from Calcutta had been calling at Sind. The trade seems to have been most active in the 1740s, but to have dwindled away in the 1760s.

For centuries the Persian Gulf ports had received goods from all over Asia destined not only for Persia itself but by river and

---

[1] Abs. R. Hedges to Directors, 20 Dec. 1717, I.O.R., E/4/2, p. 147.

[2] Recorded in Surat Diary, I.O.R., G/36/11.

[3] R. Upton to R. Cowan, 16 Nov. 1728, Northern Ireland Public Record Office, D/564/B1/5E, no. 13.

[4] Recorded in I.O.R., B.P.C., Range 1, vol. 13.

[5] Koloniaal Archief, 2347, f. 294.

[6] I.O.R., B.P.C., 17 Oct. 1731, Range 1, vol. 8, f. 477.

[7] Ibid., Range 1, vols. 17, 18.

[8] W. Bolts, *Considerations on India Affairs* (1772–5), i. 196.

[9] S. P. Chablani, *Economic Conditions in Sind 1592–1843* (Bombay, 1951).

caravan for the Ottoman Empire. Bengal's part in this trade was an ancient and important one. Up to fifty different kinds of piece-goods,[1] silk, rice and sugar were all shipped to the Gulf in large quantities. Return cargoes were less easily obtained: copper was a staple for much of the eighteenth century, lesser items being rose water, Shiraz wine, dates, almonds, horses, and asafoetida. But payment for a very large part of Bengal's exports to the Persian Gulf, up to nine-tenths by the end of the century,[2] was made in bullion. There was much valuable freight to be carried between the Persian Gulf and India. An English ship making a successful voyage between Surat and the Gulf in the early eighteenth century hoped to be as 'deep loaden as she can swim, full of passengers, and . . . vast quantitys of pearl and treasure on board; some-times to the value of two or three hundred thousand pounds'.[3] An extremely important community in trade between India and Persia was the Armenians. Settled since the early seventeenth century at Julfa, a suburb of the Persian capital at Isfahan, they had connections spreading throughout the Middle East and India. In Bengal many wealthy Armenians came to live in Calcutta as well as in their own privileged settlement at Saidabad.[4] In the correspondence of the Company's agents in the Persian Gulf 'Armenian freight' is repeatedly described as a major element in trade with Bengal.

For most of the eighteenth century Bengal ships used two main ports on the Gulf, Basra in Turkish Iraq, and Gombroon (as the English called Bandar Abbas) in Persia itself. Basra is seventy miles up the Shatt al-Arab at the head of the Gulf. It was in the Ottoman *vilayet* of Baghdad and throughout most of the eighteenth century was considered by the British to be a well administered city. Occasional English ships had visited Basra in the seventeenth century, but with the establishment of an agency on the Company's behalf in 1723 formal agreements began to be made with the Ottoman authorities about trading conditions and customs. In 1731 a rate of 3 per cent was fixed for the goods of British private merchants as well as for the Company.[5] But private merchants were required to pay a consulage and other dues to the Company

[1] Report on trade with Persia and Arabia, 1791, I.O.R., G/29/21, p. 247.
[2] Ibid., p. 335.
[3] C. Lockyer, *An Account of the Trade in India* (1711), p. 251.
[4] M. J. Seth, *Armenians in India* (Calcutta, 1937), pp. 333, 472–3.
[5] Basra to Directors, 14 June 1731, I.O.R., G/29/15, f. 89.

which amounted to a 6 per cent addition to the Ottoman customs.[1]
At the height of the trade between Calcutta and Basra agents of
the Bengal shipowners lived at Basra throughout the year. The
chief purchasers of Bengal goods were Turkish or Armenian
merchants, described as 'very prying into a man's behaviour:
a complaisant courteous behaviour with a dissembling countenance, is a mighty taking with them, as they are a very polite people,
so they expect the aforesaid behaviour in us'.[2] Bengal goods from
Basra were either taken directly across the desert by caravan to
Aleppo, or shipped up the rivers to Baghdad from whence
caravans also went on to Aleppo. Two caravans a year usually took
the direct route with four going up to Baghdad.[3]

Gombroon developed as a port after the capture in 1622 by the
Persians and the English of the Portuguese island base of Hormuz.
As a reward for their services the English were permitted to trade
custom-free, and the East India Company opened a factory there.
Private traders therefore paid no customs but they were required
to pay a 2 per cent consulage to the Company and to make extra
payments to the Company's Chief at the factory and to his broker.[4]
The Chief had also been able to enforce a rule that all private sales
must be made through him, a rule which no doubt enabled him
to collect large commissions, but which was much resented by the
Bengal shipowners.[5] During the eighteenth century Gombroon
suffered severely from the political disorders which periodically
broke out in Persia. Eventually it was abandoned by the Company
who moved their main factory further up the Gulf to Bushire in
1763. Private ships also tried to find other outlets in Persia. They
too visited Bushire, and from 1752 some of the Bengal ships tried
their luck at Bandar Rig, north of Bushire.[6] But by 1772 the
Company's agents regarded the 'whole Persian Coast as an hostile
one'.[7] Late in the century English ships started going in some
numbers to Muscat on the southern shore of the Gulf, the port
of the Imam of Oman. In the early eighteenth century the Muscat

[1] A. Parsons, *Travels in Asia and Africa* (1808), p. 157.
[2] *An Account of the Navigation between India and the Gulf of Persia*, ed.
A. Dalrymple (1786), p. lv.
[3] *The Desert Route to India*, ed. D. Carruthers (1929), p. 62.
[4] Lockyer, *Account of Trade*, pp. 225–6.
[5] Gombroon to Directors, 31 Mar. 1739, I.O.R., G/29/15, ff. 346–7.
[6] Basra to Directors, 28 May 1752, I.O.R., G/29/15, f. 788.
[7] Basra to Directors, 8 Jan. 1772, I.O.R., G/29/16.

Arabs, with their fleet of 'fifty large ships', were feared as marauders;[1] later they began to be feared as rivals who were thought to be cornering much of the trade of the western Indian Ocean.[2] They were said to maintain 'the strictest and civelest' government 'of any in either Persia or Arabia'. Boys in the streets of Muscat became so accustomed to the sight of British sailors that they would call out 'God dammy' to them, which 'through ignorance of the word they thought to be a compliment'.[3]

As in their trade with Surat, private Calcutta ships faced keen competition on the routes between the Persian Gulf and Bengal from the ships of Asian merchants. It has been suggested that the number of Asian ships operating in the Persian Gulf was seriously reduced at the end of the seventeenth century by the depredations of pirates, thus making the Europeans' task easier.[4] In the 1694–5 season, however, the Calcutta factory recorded three Muslim and two Armenian ships leaving the Hugli for the Gulf.[5] Most of the English ships trading between Bengal and Persia in the 1690s and in the first decade of the new century seem either to have been based on Madras or to have been the 'separate stock' ships allowed to come out from England. But from 1702 to 1704 the Governor of Bengal sent his ship the *Monsoon* on three successive voyages to the Persian Gulf and by about 1710 the practice of sending at least a single Calcutta ship and sometimes two or three had become firmly established. In 1717 the Governor estimated that two ships a year carried about 500 tons of Bengal goods to Persia.[6] A large Bengal ship, such as the famous *Shah Alam* which made so many voyages from Calcutta in the early eighteenth century, could take 600 bales of piecegoods and 4,540 bags of sugar to the Persian Gulf.[7]

In 1722 the whole course of the Gulf trade was violently upset by the Afghan invasion of Persia. Trade at Gombroon became virtually impossible for some years, forcing many of the merchants who bought Bengal goods to move to Basra.[8] Calcutta ships quickly

---

[1] Abs. Bengal to Directors, 11 Dec. 1714, I.O.R., E/4/1, p. 538.

[2] J. Long, *Selections from the unpublished records of Government from the year 1748 to 1767* (Calcutta, 1869), i. 170.

[3] J. McLuer in *Account of the Navigation*, ed. Dalrymple, p. 11.

[4] R. W. Ferrier, 'British–Persian relations in the seventeenth century' (Cambridge Ph.D. thesis, 1970), p. 441.   [5] Calcutta Diary, I.O.R., G/7/2.

[6] Abs. R. Hedges to Directors, 20 Dec. 1717, I.O.R., E/4/2, p. 147.

[7] I.O.R., G/29/14, f. 17.

[8] Bombay to Directors, 15 May 1723, I.O.R., E/4/459, p. 195; Basra to Directors, 29 Nov. 1723, I.O.R., G/29/15, f. 145.

followed them, two arriving in 1723 to begin a long connection between the two ports. The opening of Basra seems greatly to have stimulated Calcutta's trade with the Gulf. The Company's agents at Basra recorded a steady stream of private ships arriving from Calcutta: two more in 1723/4, three in 1724/5, three in 1725/6, four in 1726/7, three in 1728/9; a decline to one or two took place in the early 1730s with a recovery to four in 1737/8 and five in 1738/9.[1] A large Calcutta ship, like the 300-ton *Deane Frigate*, which went to Basra virtually every season in the 1720s and 1730s, could bring up to 1,000 bales of piecegoods and 1,000 bags of sugar.[2] European ships began to call at Gombroon again by 1727, but most of the visits of Bengal ships appear either to have been on the way up to Basra or on the way back. From the point of view of the Bengal shipowners, Basra was clearly a much more satisfactory port. Indeed, the Company's servants at Gombroon believed that 'trade will not turn back into its own channel . . . so long as the Bengallers resort thither', even though 'the merchants who buy the goods of them there are the same who formerly purchased here and at Spahaun' [Isfahan].[3] A comment which, if it was true, shows how important Bengal trade was to the Gulf ports. Gombroon only attracted a large volume of Bengal trade when there was serious disruption at Basra, as in the season 1730–1 when six Bengal ships called at Gombroon.[4]

The Red Sea was the other great highway by which Asian goods could reach the Middle East. Ships from India generally called either at Mocha, the port of the Imam of the Yemen, or at Jidda, the pilgrim port for Mecca, in Turkish-controlled Arabia. Mocha was a considerable port through which large quantities of coffee from the Yemen were exported to Europe and Asia, but eighteenth-century Jidda was described as 'no more than a mart between Egypt and India'.[5] Goods from India were carried away from Jidda either by camel caravan, particularly on the caravans returning to Egypt from the *Hajj* to Mecca, or on a fleet of some forty small ships which plied between Suez and Jidda.[6] Suez

---

[1] Recorded in I.O.R., G/29/14–15.
[2] Basra to Directors, 20 May 1731, I.O.R., G/29/15, f. 83.
[3] Gombroon to Directors, 28 Jan. 1737, ibid., f. 297.   [4] List in ibid., ff. 34–5.
[5] C. Niebuhr, *Travels through Arabia and the Countries in the East*, trans. R. Heron (Edinburgh, 1792), i. 235.
[6] *The Red Sea and Adjacent Countries at the close of the seventeenth century* ed. W. Foster (1949), pp. 63–4.

itself was officially closed to Indian ships by the Ottoman authorities, although a number of Calcutta ships did succeed in opening
up a brief trade there in the 1770s.[1] The greater part of Mocha's
demand for Indian goods in the eighteenth century was supplied
from western India, particularly from Surat,[2] but some Bengal
piecegoods, sugar, and rice sold there. Bengal seems, however,
to have had a large share of the Jidda market. Piecegoods of
medium and coarse quality, especially 'cheap white muslins . . .
used by the Turks for summer dresses', sold well there, as did
sugar, rice, ginger and silk.[3] Bengal ships normally brought back
little from the Red Sea apart from bullion. At Mocha British goods
paid 3 per cent customs compared to 9 per cent generally paid
by Asian merchants;[4] at Jidda the British paid 8 per cent to the
Sharif of Mecca, while Asians paid 10 per cent on an artificial
valuation which was said to bring them up to 12 or 17 per cent.[5]
Egyptians, Armenians, and banias from western India were the
chief purchasers of Bengal goods. Europeans regarded trading
conditions as hazardous in both ports. There were frequent
complaints about the behaviour of the port authorities and about
the difficulties in obtaining prompt payment for goods sold.

Evidence about the number of Calcutta ships going to the Red
Sea is somewhat fragmentary, but the pattern seems to be similar
to that of the trade with Surat or the Persian Gulf. Single Calcutta
ships belonging to the Governor are recorded as having left for
Mocha in 1702/3 and 1705/6.[6] No evidence survives for the
following years, but from 1720, when reports sent by a British
Resident at Mocha become available, it is clear that a regular trade
had been established, and it seems likely that the greater part of
Bengal's exports to the Red Sea were being carried in private
English ships. In 1720 three Bengal ships were reported to be at
Mocha, together with some twenty Muslim ships from different
parts of India and the ships of the Bombay servants that traded

---

[1] See below, p. 96.

[2] See lists of sales in 1721 and 1722, I.O.R., G/17/1, ff. 104–5, 173.

[3] See answers to queries on the Jidda trade provided for Hastings by
J. Price, J. Robinson, and C. Thornhill in 1776, Add. MSS. 29138, ff. 86–8;
29199, ff. 25, 66.

[4] Mocha to Directors, 20 July 1721, I.O.R., G/17/1, f. 59.

[5] I.O.R., Mayor's Court Records, 16 Feb. 1754, Range 155, vol. 28; Niebuhr,
Travels in Arabia, i. 235.

[6] Calcutta Diary, 15 Jan. 1703, I.O.R., G/7/4; I.O.R., B.P.C., 3 Jan. 1706,
Range 1, vol. 1, f. 273.

between Surat and Mocha.[1] Thereafter two or three and sometimes even four Bengal ships are recorded in the Red Sea every
year throughout the 1720s and 1730s. In 1724, apparently after
an interval of some years, trade was re-established with Jidda.[2]
For many years after that at least one large ship a year was specifically consigned to Jidda. When a Jidda ship was lost, the whole
Calcutta mercantile community, both 'white and black' were said
to be involved.[3]

There are occasional records of private Bengal ships trading
with East Africa. In the middle decades of the eighteenth century
at least three ships called at Pate, a more or less independent
sultanate on the Kenya coast. Cowries were said to be the main
item of the return cargoes.[4] Other ships, sometimes one a year in
the 1740s, went much further south to the Portuguese settlements
in Mozambique, presumably in search of slaves.

The success of the Calcutta shipowners on the routes between
Bengal and the ports of the western Indian Ocean, and the degree
to which the continuing prosperity of the Calcutta fleet depended
on the continuing prosperity of western trade, are strikingly illustrated by a Dutch analysis of the English country trade from
Calcutta in 1734.[5] A list of ships returning to Calcutta in 1735
kept by the English themselves tells an almost identical story.[6]
The Dutch believed that nine ships left Calcutta for Surat in
1734 (eleven returned from Surat in 1735); two sailed for Basra
and Gombroon and one to Basra alone; two to Mocha and one to
Jidda (the 1735 figures are the same both for the Persian Gulf
and the Red Sea); with one to Sind. By contrast with the sixteen
ships trading west of Cape Comorin, the Dutch thought that only
three ships and a sloop were employed on the Madras trade with
four ships (three in 1735) going to the eastern side of the Bay of
Bengal. The Dutch also hazarded a guess at the value of the ships
trading to particular destinations. Conjectural as these obviously
were, the contrast between west and east is even more marked.
The Dutch believed that the English-owned goods on a Surat
ship were likely to be worth some Rs 70,000 over and above the

[1] Mocha to Directors, 20 July 1720, I.O.R., G/17/1, f. 20.
[2] Mocha to Directors, 12 July 1724, ibid., ff. 319, 327–8.
[3] Abs. Bengal to Directors, 24 Jan. 1735, I.O.R., E/4/4, p. 74.
[4] I.O.R., Mayor's Court Records, Range 155, vol. 69, p. 305.
[5] Koloniaal Archief, 2196, p. 211.
[6] I.O.R., B.P.C., 1735, Range 1, vol. 11.

value of its Asian freight; the cargo on the Persian Gulf ships might be worth Rs 200,000 to Rs 150,000 and on the Red Sea ships Rs 300,000 (with Asian freight again to be added). Cargoes to the eastern side of the Bay of Bengal were put at Rs 60,000 and those to Madras as only Rs 25,000.

Insignificant as trade round the Bay of Bengal might appear in the lists of 1734 or 1735, it was in fact the staple for much of Calcutta's shipping throughout the eighteenth century. Profits might be low, but the demand for shipping was constant and dependable. A large volume of trade passed between Calcutta and Madras. Madras imported considerable quantities of Bengal rice, 3,500 tons were thought to have been transported by sea in 1737,[1] and other food stuffs. There was too a constant shuttling of stores and highly miscellaneous cargoes between the Company's largest settlements. Many Bengal ships also called at other Coromandel Coast ports, such as Masulipatam, well to the north of Madras. Ceylon trade was closely regulated by the Dutch who tried to exclude the ships of other European countries. This prohibition was not particularly effective, but in the early part of the century only occasional Calcutta ships appear to have called at Ceylon.[2] There was, however, a considerable trade in cowry and chank shells between Bengal and the Maldive Islands, to the west and south of Ceylon. There was also a brisk trade between Bengal and Burma, Calcutta ships calling at the ports of Syriam, near Rangoon, and Pegu. Burma was a major source of supply for timber for ship repairs and for building in Calcutta. Calcutta ships also traded with Tenasserim on the western coast of Siam and with islands off the Siamese coast, especially with Junk Ceylon. Tin and sandal and sapan wood could be obtained at Tenasserim,[3] and there were thought to be large deposits of tin at Junk Ceylon.[4]

By trading further southward into the Straits of Malacca Calcutta ships could obtain tin and pepper in both Malayan and Sumatran ports. They could also hope to make contact with ships that would both bring them goods from further afield and carry their Bengal goods to distant markets. Both Chinese junks and the

[1] Abs. Bengal to Directors, 31 Dec. 1737, I.O.R., E/4/4, p. 246.
[2] S. Arasaratnam, 'Dutch commercial policy in Ceylon and its effects on Indo-Ceylon trade', *Indian Economic and Social History Review*, iv (1967).
[3] 'Account of Trade in the Streights of Mallacca', I.O.R., Home Miscellaneous, 823, p. 354.
[4] F. Light's accounts, Add. MS. 29210, ff. 217–21, 226.

perahus of the Bugis from Celebes frequented the Straits of Malacca and would distribute Bengal piecegoods and opium throughout Indonesia and the ports of mainland South East Asia. But trade in the Straits of Malacca was likely to encounter Dutch opposition. The Dutch claimed that most of the tin and pepper of Malaya and Sumatra was pledged to them by treaties signed with the local rulers and that they had an exclusive right to deal in opium in the Straits of Malacca.[1] The East India Company did not accept such claims,[2] which the Dutch had no real power to enforce. Even in Malacca itself, which was under direct Dutch rule, British country captains believed that they could trade as they wished with the aid of a little discreet bribery,[3] and Dutch control over the Malay sultans' trade was clearly very tenuous. Nevertheless, in the first half of the eighteenth century Bengal ships seem in the main to have concentrated on ports which were safely outside the Dutch sphere. Deeper penetration of the Straits to secure much bigger pepper and tin supplies was not to begin on a large scale until the 1760s.[4]

In the early eighteenth century the Malayan port most frequented by Bengal country ships seems to have been Kedah, well to the north of Malacca, whose ruler could keep the Dutch at arm's length.[5] Tin and pepper could be bought at Kedah and opium and piecegoods sold there. Achin at the northern tip of Sumatra was completely outside Dutch control. The English had long enjoyed cordial relations with its rulers; they were still trading in the eighteenth century under the privileges granted to them on the East India Company's first voyage in 1602. Achin was a pepper-producing area and a considerable entrepôt for trade further afield. In the season 1704/5 four departures were recorded from Calcutta for Malacca, Achin or 'to the eastward'; four in 1705/6; and three in 1706/7.[6] In 1718, after some sort of interruption, the ruler of Achin invited the British back to his port, 'above twenty sail' accepting his invitation.[7] When recordings of departures

---

[1] I.O.R., B.P.C., 5 Sept. 1746, Range 1, vol. 18, f. 355.
[2] Directors to Fort St. David, 17 June 1748, *Records of Fort St. George: Despatches from England 1748–9* (Madras, 1933), p. 11.
[3] Lockyer, *Account of Trade*, p. 68.
[4] See below, p. 101.
[5] R. Bonney, *Kedah 1771–1821* (Kuala Lumpur, 1971), pp. 19–20.
[6] I.O.R., B.P.C., Range 1, vol. 1.
[7] J. Williamson to J. Scattergood, 12 Feb. 1718, I.O.R., Home Miscellaneous, 822, p. 212.

begin again in the Bengal Public Consultations, the number of ships going to Malaya or Sumatra is listed at:

1735/6	2	1739/40	5
1736/7	3		
1737/8	7	1741/2	3
1738/9	3	1742/3	3

The East India Company's settlement at Benkulen on the west coast of Sumatra played little part in this trade. It was too remote from the main shipping routes to attract Chinese or Bugi ships or to enable the Company to use it successfully as an outlet for Bengal opium, as they planned to do as early as 1707.[1]

In any trading voyage round the Bay of Bengal Calcutta ships faced stiff competition from Asian-owned ships, which could offer cheap freights for cargoes whose profit margins were generally much lower than those on silk or high quality piecegoods sent to Surat, the Red Sea or the Persian Gulf. To make a profit on his operations a captain had to keep his ship fully employed, either in frequent voyages (the 'whole success, emolument and advantage' in trading in timber between Rangoon and Calcutta was said to lie in getting two voyages in before the monsoon changed)[2] or in carefully worked-out circuits of ports. For instance, the *Katharine* was instructed in 1714 to go from Calcutta to Junk Ceylon for tin and dried fish, to truck the fish at Malacca for sugar and rattans, which would be sold at Anjengo and Calicut on the Malabar Coast of India, where pepper would be taken on to be sold at Madras.[3]

During the first half of the eighteenth century the eyes of most Bengal shipowners were fixed well to the west of Cape Comorin, but to the east of the Straits of Malacca there were potential markets available for Indian country ships as rich as any in Persia or Arabia. These were at Canton and Manila. In both ports conditions were laid down for trade of the most stringent kind, even by Asian standards. For most of the eighteenth century Canton was the only Chinese port at which Europeans were permitted to trade. There they had to pay duties on their ship according to a

---

[1] Directors to Bengal, 7 Feb. 1707, I.O.R., E/3/96, p. 196.

[2] Calcutta High Court Records, Mayor's Court, *Waple et al.* v. *Mitchell.*

[3] J. Scattergood to Hurst, [Apr. 1714], I.O.R., Home Miscellaneous, 821, p. 300.

scale based on measurement, as well as duties on exports and imports and substantial 'cumshaws' or presents.[1] A European merchant's freedom to buy and sell in Canton was also severely restricted by the rise of a virtual monopoly of the so-called 'Hong' merchants through whom all purchases and sales had officially to be made. Manila was formally closed to Protestant Europeans altogether. It was a Spanish colony, whose inhabitants were forbidden to have any direct trade with the Asian mainland but were permitted to trade across the Pacific with Spanish America on the famous Acapulco galleons. The galleons brought American silver and returned with Chinese silk and Indian piecegoods. In theory, the Indian piecegoods were carried to Manila in ships owned by Portuguese, Armenian, or Asian merchants; in practice, many of the Indian ships were British under their Portuguese or Armenian colours.

At the beginning of the eighteenth century English trade with Canton and Manila was largely in the hands of the Madras ship-owners, who were able to hold their own very much more success-fully in these trades than in the trade to the western Indian Ocean. Bengal ships were said to be at Canton in 1725[2] and 1736,[3] while the largest ship of the Calcutta fleet, the *Shah Alam*, was being fitted out for a voyage to China via Surat in 1730.[4] But such ventures were unusual. Apart from opium, few Bengal commodi-ties could be sold directly in China, while the tutenag, porcelain, and other Chinese items which the Bengal ships needed for their western trade could either be obtained from the junks in the Straits of Malacca or at Madras. While Madras ships seem to have made more or less annual voyages to Canton, Calcutta did not develop her own Chinese trade on a large scale until after Plassey, when the accumulation of private British fortunes and the willing-ness of the Company to grant bills of exchange on London for money delivered at Canton provided the incentive.[5] Bengal piece-goods found a ready sale at Manila and, although Madras with

---

[1] The system of duties is described in E. H. Pritchard, *Anglo-Chinese Rela-tions during the seventeenth and eighteenth centuries* (Urbana, 1929), pp. 78, 86, 221.

[2] Abs. Fort St. George to Directors, 26 Jan. 1727, I.O.R., E/4/2, p. 509.

[3] H. B. Morse, *Chronicles of the East India Company trading to China* (Oxford, 1926–9), i. 247.

[4] W. Mitchell to R. Cowan, 17 Nov. 1730, Northern Ireland Public Record Office, D/564/B1/5E, no. 69.   [5] See below, p. 98.

an average of three ships a year kept a clear lead,[1] Calcutta ships
were much more involved in the Philippine trade in the first half
of the eighteenth century than in the trade to China. In 1717 the
Governor of Bengal listed Manila among places which the Madras
shipowners had 'most to themselves',[2] and there were some
examples of co-operation between the settlements in fitting out
ships jointly.[3] By 1727, however, Madras was beginning to complain of Bengal's competition at Manila.[4] The records of arrivals
kept by the Spanish authorities,[5] together with the surviving
shipping lists in the Bengal Consultations, suggest that ten Bengal
ships went to Manila in the 1720s, six or seven in the 1730s, and
seven in the 1740s up to 1748, when sailings seem to have stopped
for twelve years. A successful Manila ship returning with its
Mexican silver was an extremely valuable object; a ship that came
back to Calcutta in 1742 was said to be worth $300,000 (about
£75,000).[6]

The existence of a large volume of trade round the Bay of
Bengal and the bringing off of some successful voyages to Manila
did not significantly alter the extent to which the Calcutta fleet
depended for its prosperity on markets in the western Indian
Ocean. When the number of ships based on Calcutta and the
Company's consulage receipts from exports declined or at best
remained static from the mid-1730s, the causes were to be found
to the west of Cape Comorin.

Asian seaborne trade was a vulnerable business at any time.
With expensive ships, high operating costs and heavy interest
charges, success depended on large profits. To the normal hazards
of the sea were added the dangers from piracy and from French
attack during the periods of Anglo-French war. The practice of
concentrating trade to certain ports, such as Jidda or Manila, on
one or two very rich ships accentuated the risk. If such a ship was
to be lost or to suffer a lesser misfortune, like missing its passage

[1] S. D. Quiason, *English Country Trade with the Philippines* (Quezon City,
1966), pp. 67–70.

[2] Abs. R. Hedges to Directors, 20 Dec. 1717, I.O.R., E/4/2, p. 147.

[3] Fort St. George to Directors, 28 Aug. 1732, *Records of Fort St. George:
Despatches to England 1727–33* (Madras, 1929), p. 104.

[4] Abs. Fort St. George to Directors, 26 Jan. 1727, I.O.R., E/4/2, p. 509.

[5] P. Chaunu, *Les Philippines et le Pacifique des Ibériques* (Paris, 1960–6),
i. 180–9.

[6] Abs. Fort St. George to Directors, 11 Sept. 1742, I.O.R., E/4/4, p. 399.

across the Arabian Sea and arriving at Jidda after the Egyptian merchants on their *Hajj* had left, the consequences would be serious for many people in Calcutta. Even without mishap, many voyages failed to show a profit. The capacity of most of the markets with which Calcutta traded was strictly limited. Reports of a successful trading season at a certain port would lead to that port being oversupplied in the following season. Surplus goods unsold in the year they arrived would have to be left for the following year, and loss would be inevitable. Even in the early decades of the eighteenth century, when Calcutta's trade was generally expanding and when more and more ships were going to Surat, Basra, and Jidda, there were frequent complaints of bad years. So long as prosperous years followed, losses could generally be made good, but by the mid-1730s certain factors were making the frequent recurrence of good years less likely and were leaving their mark on the tonnage and consulage figures.

Political instability was a deadly disrupter of trade. The merchants who bought Bengal goods were at the mercy of exactions by the rulers of the ports where they traded, while the ports and their lines of communication by camel, bullock, or river boat were highly vulnerable to war or disorder. By the middle of the eighteenth century all Bengal's markets in western Asia were threatened by political instability. In the 1720s the Maratha drive to the north brought to Gujarat what its historian has called 'a period of civil strife and foreign invasion, involving progressive deterioration in the administrative system and continuous warfare', culminating in the final overthrow of Mughal rule in 1758.[1] Violence was even to spread to Surat itself. Eighteenth-century Iran suffered from Afghan invasion, wars against Turks and Russians, the usurpation of Nadir Shah, and the rivalry of Zand and Kajar. Basra, which provided Bengal with an alternative port on the Persian Gulf in the 1720s, was later to be in the front line of the Turkish-Persian wars and was threatened by Arab insurrections against the Turks. There was civil war in the Yemen, and the British believed that the rapacity of the port authorities at Jidda and Mocha made trade to the Red Sea more and more hazardous. A report of 1771 spoke of 'the most barefaced impositions' at Mocha and of 'oppressions . . . not less unjust and cruel' at Jidda.[2]

---

[1] M. S. Commissariat, *A History of Gujarat* (Bombay, 1938–57), ii. 383.
[2] T. Mathewson to Bombay, 8 Apr. 1771, I.O.R., G/17/3, no. 533.

To the damage being done by adverse political conditions in the western Indian Ocean was added from the 1740s the effect of rising prices in Bengal itself.[1] By the 1760s Bengal traders were convinced that their goods were pricing themselves out of their markets. In 1773 the Council considered that Bengal commodities 'have risen in their price to a degree that greatly exceeds the medium of trade in foreign markets'.[2] Bengal sugar, which had been cheaper than sugar from other sources in western India, the Persian Gulf, or the Red Sea in the early eighteenth century, was thought to have increased in price by 50 per cent,[3] and was now being undersold by sugar from Java[4] and from China.[5] By the 1770s Bengal raw silk, whose price was said to have risen by 40 per cent between 1765 and 1780,[6] was also suffering from the competition of Chinese silk in western India.[7] Even Bengal's cotton piecegoods, thought in 1776 to have risen by 30 per cent over recent years,[8] were losing their markets in western India and the Persian Gulf.[9]

Mounting political disturbances and rising prices began to erode Bengal's trade to the western Indian Ocean from the mid-1730s, but the speed of the decline varied from area to area. A large part of the Calcutta fleet continued to go to Surat during the 1740s; thirteen ships returned from there in 1745 and ten in 1746,[10] but conditions were steadily deteriorating as the Marathas moved north. To make matters worse, Surat's Mughal rulers levied increasing exactions from its merchants, provoking them to unavailing revolt in 1732, while the port's nominal protectors, the Siddis, raised their demands as well.[11] The British at Bombay

---

[1] See above, p. 35.

[2] I.O.R., B.R.C., 23 Mar. 1773, Range 49, vol. 38, p. 1034.

[3] See above, p. 35.

[4] K. Glamann, *Dutch Asiatic Trade 1620–1720* (The Hague, 1958), pp. 165–6.

[5] *Papers Respecting the Culture and Manufacture of Sugar in British India* (1822), i. 51.

[6] Directors to Bengal, 12 May 1780, I.O.R., E/3/626.

[7] Observations on 'the Company's concerns on the other side of India', Add. MS. 29210, f. 80.

[8] J. Robinson to W. Hastings, 20 Apr. 1776, Add. MS. 29137, f. 169.

[9] [J. Price], *Five Letters of a Free Merchant in Bengal to Warren Hastings* (1783), p. 29.

[10] I.O.R., B.P.C., Range 1, vols. 17, 18.

[11] A. Das Gupta, 'The Crisis at Surat', *B.P.P.*, lxxxvi (1967) and 'Trade and Politics in 18th-century India', *Islam and the Trade of Asia*, ed. D. S. Richards (Oxford, 1970).

finally sent a naval expedition to take control of the port in 1759, but by then it was too late. During the 1750s Calcutta's trade with Surat began a sharp decline. Only two ships were recorded there in 1754 and 1755,[1] and for the whole decade the value of British-owned silk and piece goods paying the Company's duties was only one-tenth of what it had been in the peak years of the 1730s.[2] There may have been something of a recovery in the 1760s,[3] but in 1772 a shipowner complained that he could not 'carry any thing from Bengal to the other side that will answer',[4] and an even more dismal account came from Surat in 1779:

The stagnation to trade in general which we have for some time laboured under on this side has almost entirely put an end to the intercourse betwixt this place and Bengall, except solely by the channel of the shroffs, for the Armenians and other merchants here have their houses full of goods unsaleable and no encouragement whatever to send their property to Bengall for investing.[5]

Even in the 1720s, when a thriving trade with Calcutta was being built up, Basra could prove a fickle market. In 1729, for instance, it was reported that the 'vast quantity of goods imported last year and this had quite sunk the market'.[6] By 1739, after several years of political disturbance, it had acquired the reputation of being 'a grave for so many people's estates'.[7] In 1731 routes into Basra were disrupted by the Arabs. In 1732 and 1733 trade virtually ceased and the Bengal ships were obliged to lie at Basra 'laden near twelve months together without landing their goods', as the invading Persians attacked Baghdad.[8] In 1735 both the Arabs and the Persians attacked Basra itself. Basra's difficulties and the return of relative peace to Iran with the expulsion of the Afghans in 1730 brought some Bengal ships back to Gombroon; but the outlook remained generally discouraging in both ports. The seasons 1741 and 1742 were said to have been good ones in the Persian Gulf, but they were followed by four bleak years in succession due to renewed war between the Turks and the Persians.

---

[1] Surat Diaries, I.O.R., G/36/39, G/36/40.
[2] H. Furber, *John Company at Work* (Cambridge, Mass., 1951), p. 163.
[3] Customs figures for Bengal goods at Surat, I.O.L., MS. Eur. D. 281, f. 14.
[4] G. Stratton to Hastings, 24 Sept. 1772, Add. MS. 29133, f. 244.
[5] R. H. Boddam to Hastings, 8 Mar. 1779, Add. MS. 29143, f. 134.
[6] Basra to Directors, 14 Aug. 1729, I.O.R., G/29/15, f. 3.
[7] J. Fullerton to W. Weston, 10 Dec. 1739, I.O.L., MS. Eur. D. 602, f. 73.
[8] T. Waters to Directors, 22 Feb. 1736, I.O.R., G/29/15, f. 276.

Prospects seemed to be so bad in 1747 that the Bengal Council decided not to send a freight ship at all to Basra.¹ Another revival in the early 1750s was followed by years of 'small trade and low consulage'.² Gombroon was captured in 1759 by the French and formally abandoned by the Company in 1763. Yet another revival of Calcutta's trade with Basra began in 1760, but navigation in the Gulf was becoming increasingly hazardous. In 1765 two Calcutta ships were captured by an Arab chieftain, the Shaikh of the Ka'ab, who was an enemy of the Turks at Basra and evidently regarded the British as their allies.³ The Company's Bombay Marine failed conspicuously in attempts to quell the Shaikh or to ensure the safety of other ships. In 1768 the *Speedwell* from Calcutta, alleged by its owners to be carrying 'native freight' worth £60,000,⁴ was taken by Mir Mahanna of Bandar Rig in Persia, and in 1772 royal Persian ships took the *Britannia*. Nevertheless, a considerable trade between Calcutta and Basra continued until 1773, the year in which Basra was devastated by the plague. For the previous ten years it was estimated that an annual average of 3,000 to 3,500 bales of Indian piecegoods had been shipped to the port.⁵ After the plague came the Persians, who finally captured Basra in 1776. Calcutta's connections with Basra were not renewed until 1780.

Calcutta's trade with the Red Sea seems to have followed a similar course to its trade with the Persian Gulf. There were bad seasons, even in years when the trade was generally buoyant, and the difficulties eventually became more and more acute, until the Red Sea was generally reckoned to be an unprofitable market. At the best of times trade there was uncertain. As the Company's Resident at Mocha explained in 1721, 'this markett is very precarious, a very small surplus of any thing before in demand immediately falls the price occasioned by there not being above four or five substantial merchants in the place that can be trusted to buy a considerable bargain'.⁶ The British frequently complained that the competition was narrowed even further by a single merchant's being able to buy the favour of the Governors of the

---

¹ Basra to Directors, 14 July 1747, I.O.R., G/29/15, f. 585.
² Abs. Basra to Directors, 14 Oct. 1756, I.O.R., E/4/451, p. 202.
³ 'Narrative of the Rise and Progress of the Troubles in the Gulph of Persia', I.O.R., G/29/16.
⁴ Memorial of F. Douglas, 30 Aug. 1769, I.O.R., G/29/21.
⁵ Report on British Trade with Persia and Arabia, 1791, ibid., p. 261.
⁶ I.O.R., G/17/1, f. 105.

ports, which enabled him to have a monopoly of dealings with Europeans and to fix the prices at which they might sell. At Jidda in 1727 one of the remarkably few cases of an attack by the local population on English private traders took place. The so-called massacre involved the murder of four officers and supercargoes, a gunner, and three Portuguese from two of the Bengal ships by an enraged crowd who believed that the Europeans had been responsible for the deaths of Muslim seamen. The ships' treasure was plundered and, although protests by the British ambassador at Constantinople brought restitution, considerable sums were never recovered.[1] For all its hazards, a regular trade between Calcutta and the Red Sea of at least one ship a year to Mocha and one to Jidda seems to have been maintained with some consistency until the 1760s.

In the 1770s European trade between Calcutta and the Red Sea was largely abandoned. The perennial problems of oppression by the port authorities and of obtaining prompt payment for goods sold got worse. Merchants were asking for credit for one or two years,[2] and huge debts were piling up at Jidda, 'which are deemed irrecoverable, for notwithstanding the Bashaw of Judda and the Xerif of Mecca become guarantees for the payment, every solicitation for redress and satisfaction have been treated by that government with the utmost neglect'. The 'uncertainty of payment' was said to make the trade 'totally ineligible'.[3] A last attempt was, however, made to revive the Red Sea trade by by-passing Mocha and Jidda and sailing straight to Egypt, always the ultimate market for most Red Sea goods. In the past, voyages by Christian ships beyond Jidda had been strictly forbidden by the Ottomans, but when Calcutta ships reached Suez they were for a time well received by the Egyptian authorities. Proposals for a voyage to Suez were canvassed in Calcutta in 1772 and two ships were fitted out in 1774, neither of which reached its destination.[4] In the following year the Calcutta ship *Minerva* did succeed in reaching

---

[1] For accounts of the massacre, see the papers of John Fullerton, I.O.L. Microfilm, reel 674; A. Stanyar to Newcastle, 6 Oct. 1727, P.R.O., SP 97/25, ff. 295–7; I.O.R., B.P.C., 31 Oct., 13 Nov. 1727, Range 1, vol. 6, ff. 517–18, 526.

[2] H. Verelst to Constantinople, 10 Jan. 1768, Ames MSS., I.O.L. Microfilm, reel 606.

[3] G. Moore to R. Gregory, 29 Jan. 1778, Add. MS. 29140, f. 52.

[4] Add. MS. 29210, ff. 426–8; F. Charles-Roux, *L'Angleterre, l'isthme de Suez et l'Egypte au dix-huitième siècle* (Paris, 1922), chaps. ii iii.

Suez, where her captain was able to sell his cargo and to sign
a trade agreement with the Bey on behalf of the Bengal Council.[1]
In 1776 an 800-ton ship, the *Alexander*, owned by five Calcutta
merchants, carried a very rich cargo to Jidda. Her captain eventually came back with the treasure paid to him for his goods, but
only after he had threatened to 'reduce Juddah to ashes' with the
Alexander's guns.[2] The *Alexander*'s owners were not prepared to
risk her at Jidda again, and sent her to Suez in 1777 and 1778. The
1777 voyage was certainly a successful one. Her captain was able
to obtain bills of exchange on London for part of his sales and thus
to open a new channel for the remittance of fortunes from Bengal
to England.[3] Other ships followed in the *Alexander*'s wake,
inevitably attracting the attention of the Ottoman government,
who protested to the British ambassador at Constantinople, and
of the Levant Company, who complained that their sales were
damaged by the direct shipment of Bengal goods to Egypt. The
East India Company in London yielded to pressure. Instructions
were sent to Bengal forbidding further voyages to Suez. In 1779
two private Calcutta ships evaded the prohibition by hoisting
Danish colours, but by doing so they put themselves outside
British protection when the Egyptians plundered the cargo of one
of the ships and murdered seven of its Europeans.[4] With this
disaster the Suez trade, and with it hopes of a revived Red Sea
trade, came to an end.[5]

Thirty years of generally low profits did not destroy all trade
between Bengal and the western Indian Ocean. European-owned
ships might find it increasingly unprofitable to go beyond Bombay,
but Asian ships which operated on lower costs and were prepared
to accept lower returns continued to ply between Calcutta and
Surat, Basra (after 1780), Muscat, Mocha, and Jidda in some
numbers.[6] Low profits did, however, deter Europeans and above

---

[1] See the captain's account of his voyage in Add. MS. 29198, ff. 329–38, with
a copy of the treaty, ibid., ff. 191–6; also the proceedings in Calcutta High
Court Records, Supreme Court, Equity, *Holford et al.* v. *Shaw*.

[2] D. Scott to B. Marlow, 28 Apr. 1776, I.O.R., G/17/5, pp. 7–27.

[3] J. Robinson to Hastings, 15 Dec. 1777, Add. MS. 29139, ff. 438–45.

[4] [G. Baldwin], *Narrative of Facts relative to the Plunder of the English
merchants by the Arabs*, [1780].

[5] Trade with Suez is examined in greater detail in my 'The Bengal Commercial
Society', *Bulletin of the Institute of Historical Research*, xlii (1969).

[6] Furber, *John Company*, pp. 166–8.

all the Company servants. Few of them had the phlegm of Harry Verelst, who was 'eternally losing by water what he gains by land' and who when told that 'a vessel of his worth Rs 14,000 had foundered at sea . . . called for a glass of wine and said he would get up the loss'.[1] After a life of at least forty years the 'freight ships' association was finally abandoned in 1771, shares in the ships having been 'offered on very low terms and rejected'.[2] Company servants had more profitable openings available to them in the inland trade or in their new offices, but Free Merchants had no alternative in many cases to trying to make a living from the sea. When better times came in the 1770s, Free Merchants were firmly in control of Bengal's shipping.

That better times came in a pattern of trade radically different from that revealed in the Dutch and the English surveys of Calcutta's shipping in 1734 and 1735 is strongly suggested by an analysis of the value of Calcutta's exports for 1777.

Exports to Basra and Muscat were worth				Rs	107,100
„	Sumatra	„	„	„	29,284
„	'Malabar' (presumably all ports in western India, including Bombay and Surat) were worth			„	828,149
„	Coromandel were worth			„	980,254
„	Penang and Eastwards were worth			„	289,900
„	Pegu	„	„	„	23,180
„	China	„	„	„	283,500
„	Suez	„	„	„	21,000
	Total			Rs	2,562,367[3]

Trade to China and to Indonesia and Malaya had to a large extent replaced trade to the Persian Gulf and the Red Sea.

The rise of Calcutta's trade with China was a response to two developments: to the increasing need of the East India Company for funds at Canton with which to purchase cargoes of tea for London, and of the makers of fortunes in Bengal to find new ways of transferring money to Britain. On the arrival of news of the

[1] A. Campbell to H. Strachey, 18 Aug. 1765, I.O.L., MS. Eur. G. 37, box 35, f. 109.

[2] Bengal to Directors, 2 Apr. 1771, *Fort William–India House Correspondence* (New Delhi, 1949–), vi. 292.

[3] I.O.R., Bengal Commercial Reports, 4 Aug. 1797, Range 174, vol. 13.

granting to the Company of the *diwani*, the Directors ordered the
Bengal Council to ship Rs 4,000,000 annually to Canton, out of
what was assumed to be the surplus of Bengal's revenue, to
finance the purchase of tea.[1] After 1768, however, the Bengal
Council was in no position to provide sums of this order, and by
1773 it had decided that money remitted to Canton must largely
be provided by private individuals.[2] A number of schemes were
devised to attract private money from Bengal to Canton. In 1776,
for instance, the Council gave bills on London for £105,129 in
exchange for bullion subscribed by individuals in Calcutta for
shipment to Canton.[3] In 1781 the Company sent two ships from
Calcutta to Canton loaded with opium which had been bought
with money advanced by individuals in return for bills on London
worth £200,000.[4] But it soon became apparent that if bills on
London at a reasonable rate of exchange were freely available at
Canton, large sums from Calcutta would find their own way there.
The men responsible for bringing the money from Calcutta to
Canton were the Calcutta shipowners. A man in Bengal, who
wished to send part of his fortune to London via Canton, lent
money on respondentia to a shipowner, who used it to buy a
cargo for China. When the cargo was sold, its proceeds were
offered to the Company's agents at Canton in exchange for bills
on London. In 1773, for instance, Warren Hastings lent three
lakhs of rupees at 12 per cent on respondentia to the shipowner
Joseph Price, to be secured on the cargoes of three of his ships
sailing to Canton. Had the ships all arrived safely, Hastings would
have realised £36,000 in London.[5] In all bills for some 9,000,000
taels, about £3,000,000, were issued at Canton between 1770 and
1783 for money received from India;[6] in 1780 alone $1,200,000
(about £300,000) was received at Canton from Madras and Bengal.[7]
Those who could not obtain bills through the English Company
could usually give their money to the agents of the Dutch, the
Danes, the Swedes, or the Portuguese at Canton or Macao. They

[1] Bengal to Canton, 24 Feb. 1767, I.O.R., R/10/6.
[2] Bengal to Canton, 21 June 1773, I.O.R., R/10/7.
[3] Bengal to Canton, 13 Feb. 1777, I.O.R., G/12/61, pp. 3–4.
[4] Morse, *Chronicles to China*, ii, chap. xxxvii.
[5] P. J. Marshall, 'The Personal Fortune of Warren Hastings', *Economic History Review*, 2nd ser., xvii (1964–5), 290
[6] E. H. Pritchard, *The Crucial Years of Anglo-Chinese Relations 1750–1800* (Washington, 1936), p. 400.
[7] Canton Consultation, 31 Oct. 1781, I.O.R., G/12/72, p. 163.

would receive bills on Amsterdam, Copenhagen, Gothenburg or Lisbon, usually at a more favourable rate of exchange than that offered by the British.

From 1759 a ship called the *Muxadavad* began a series of voyages under the patronage of successive Governors of Bengal from Calcutta to western India and then to China. In 1764 the *Muxadavad* struck a rock off Hainan and sank with the loss of forty-four lives, including ten of her twelve Europeans.[1] In 1768 and 1769 a single Bengal ship visited Canton. Regular records of the arrival of Indian ships in China begin in 1772. They show that Calcutta established a valuable trade with Canton, but that the majority of British country ships now going there were no longer those of her old rival, Madras, but of a new rival, Bombay, which was taking advantage of sharply rising cotton prices in China by exporting large quantities of Gujarat cotton.[2]

	Indian country ships at Canton[3]	Probable Bengal ships
1772	2	2
1773	4	2
1774	15	4
1775	8	3
1776	16	5
1777	9	4
1778	10	3
1779	9	3
1780	11	3
1781	7	2
1782	2	2

Opium was the only Bengal commodity which sold extensively in China. Since the sale of opium was officially forbidden by the Chinese, the quantities imported are not listed in the records of cargoes of country ships which survive from 1775. Yet there can be little doubt that Bengal opium went regularly to China. It could be disposed of more or less without restriction at Macao, and in Canton in 1779 a country captain was said to have sold it

---

[1] Canton Diary, 16 Dec. 1764, I.O.R., R/10/5, p. 86.
[2] L. Dermigny, *La Chine et l'occident. Le commerce à Canton au xviiième siècle* (Paris, 1964), ii. 803–5.
[3] Taken from I.O.R., R/10/9, G/12/58–9, 61, 64–5, 71, 74, 75.

openly after paying suitable bribes.[1] Consumption was, however, relatively limited. In 1782 1,200 chests, or about 80 tons, were thought 'to have supplied the present demand'.[2] Apart from opium, the cargo lists show that the three commodities which made up the bulk of imports into Canton on Indian ships were raw cotton, tin, and pepper. A Bengal captain would have to obtain these either by going first to western India for Malabar pepper or Gujarat cotton or by trading in the Straits of Malacca on his way to China for Indonesian and Malayan tin and pepper. Tutenag and alum were the largest items in a highly miscellaneous list of commodities taken back to Calcutta on the Bengal ships. During the 1770s Europeans had rather more freedom in making sales and purchases at Canton than would have been the case a few years previously, when the Hong monopoly was functioning effectively. But in 1780 and 1781 price-fixing was said to be enforced again; country captains were 'hurt in their property; their prospects of success disappointed and the dispatch of their business delayed'.[3] By 1780 war was in any case making the Canton trade very hazardous, especially when the Dutch joined the coalition against Britain. A French privateer took two Indian ships on the way to China as well as 'several other small vessels'.[4] A rich Bengal ship was lost in 1781 and trade under English (but not under Portuguese) colours virtually came to an end, to be resumed at a much higher level after the ending of the war.

In the 1777 list of exports the value of Calcutta's trade with Indonesia and Malaya appears as roughly equal to the value of its trade with China. This was not a new trade, but it had increased considerably from the 1760s. The tactics of the English country traders also became much bolder. They no longer kept out of the way of the Dutch, but took their ships deeper and deeper into the Straits of Malacca, beyond the Straits to Borneo and to eastern Malaya, and to Java.[5]

Increasing trade with Indonesia and Malaya was in part the

[1] T. Fitzhugh to R. Gregory, 7 July 1782, *Reports from Committees of the House of Commons* (1803–6), vi. 297.

[2] Canton Consultations, 29 Oct. 1782, I.O.R., G/12/76, p. 128.

[3] Canton to Directors, 16 Dec. 1780, I.O.R., G/12/70, p. 267.

[4] Ibid., pp. 269–70.

[5] For the wider context of British penetration of the area see the illuminating essays in D. K. Bassett, *British Trade and Policy in Indonesia and Malaysia in the late eighteenth century* (Hull, 1971).

consequence of increased Chinese trade. Calcutta ships going to Canton needed to take on pepper and tin on their way there, and in the East India Company's Canton Diaries they are recorded as having called at ports like Selangor, Riau, Palembang and Trengganu. But it was also a direct consequence of British military success in Bengal. Many more Bengal goods, above all, opium, became available for export 'to the eastward' as a result of the conquest. Before Plassey the Dutch, who were usually able to obtain the pick of the Bihar poppy crop,[1] had been the chief exporters of opium. After Plassey control of Bihar's opium quickly passed to Englishmen serving the East India Company at Patna, who were able to establish an unofficial monopoly on their own behalf.[2] In the 1750s the licensed Dutch Opium Society operating from Batavia received about 1,200 chests of Bengal opium a year. In 1762/3 they only got 210 chests, and only 418 in 1763/4,[3] while private British traders were said to have sold 500 chests in 1764 in the Straits of Malacca.[4] The unofficial monopoly over Bihar opium was replaced by an official Company one in 1773. The Dutch were given a fixed share of 450 chests a year,[5] compared to the annual average of 3,139 chests which the English Company sold at Calcutta for private British shipowners to export.[6] An estimate for the 1790s put Calcutta's shipments of opium to Java at 1,000 chests a year with 800 to Sumatra, 700 to Malaya, and 500 to Borneo.[7]

By the 1760s not only did the British have more incentives to trade in the Straits of Malacca and more to sell there, but political developments were opening more ports to them. The Bugis had succeeded in extending their influence over much of the Malay coast and were systematically defying Dutch trade restrictions. In 1765 the Raja of Selangor wrote to Clive at Calcutta welcoming British ships. The Dutch retaliated by seizing the opium off two

[1] G. Sanyal, 'Ramchand Pandit's Report on opium cultivation in 18th-century Bihar', *B.P.P.*, lxxxvii (1968), 183.
[2] See below, pp. 118–19.
[3] *De opkomst van het Nederlandsch gezag over Java*, ed. M. L. van Deventer, viii (The Hague, 1883), 112–15. Dutch opium exports from 1764 to 1774 are listed in I.O.R., Bengal Secret Consultations, 7 Feb. 1776, Range A, vol. 34.
[4] Bassett, *Trade and Policy*, p. 14.
[5] I.O.R., Bengal Secret Consultations, 7 Feb. 1776, Range A, vol. 34.
[6] I.O.R., Home Miscellaneous, 209, p. 148.
[7] H. T. Colebrooke, *Remarks on the Present State of Husbandry and Commerce in Bengal* (Calcutta, 1795), p. 185.

Calcutta ships which had traded at Selangor, but under threats from the Bengal Council made restitution.¹ The most important new outlet for trade was, however, the port of Riau on Bintang Island off the tip of Malaya. By the 1780s it was said to have carried on more trade over the previous twenty years than 'all the others in the different parts of the Streights of Malacca put together'.² Up to 1,500 or 2,000 chests of opium could be sold there,³ and much pepper and tin, from the rich deposits on Banka Island further south, could be obtained. The Bugis and the Sultan of Johore had opened Riau to the English from about 1768, and trade there was said to be well established by 1773.⁴ In eastern Malaya Trengganu, where tin was plentiful, was the port which most interested Bengal traders.⁵ In all in 1778 six Calcutta ships and four 'snows' (ships with fewer than three masts) were trading on 'the Malay Coast'.⁶ The American War and a Dutch counter-offensive in the Malacca Straits, which closed Riau in 1784, temporarily checked Bengal's commercial expansion into Malaya, but in 1786 it took a more concrete form with the annexation of Penang, the first British settlement in Malaya.

Calcutta's renewed interest in Indonesian trade took her ships beyond the Straits of Malacca to Borneo and even further east. In the early eighteenth century the Company had maintained a settlement for some years at Bandjarmasin in southern Borneo, but it does not appear to have attracted private ships from Bengal. By 1766, however, they were beginning to visit what was to be called 'that general mart in the East', Pasir in south-eastern Borneo.⁷ The volume of Calcutta's trade with Pasir by 1772 was said to be such that it had brought down the 'prices of opium and piecegoods, even below prime cost'.⁸ In 1773 a Calcutta private

---

¹ I.O.R., B.P.C., 16 Dec. 1765, 12 Mar. 1767, Range 1, vol. 38, ff. 531 ff., vol. 41, f. 100.
² D. Cumming to H. Dundas, 18 Feb. 1787, P.R.O. 30/11/199, f. 5.
³ H. Cox to Cornwallis, 12 June 1787, ibid., 30/11/17, f. 61.
⁴ J. Bastin, 'Historical Sketch of Penang', *Journal of the Malayan Branch of the Royal Asiatic Society*, xxxii (1959), 5; K. J. Fielding, 'James Scott's report on the settlement of Penang', ibid. xxviii (1955), 41; see also B. Harrison, 'Trade in the Straits of Malacca, 1785', ibid. xxvi (1953).
⁵ Cox to Cornwallis, 12 June 1787, P.R.O., 30/11/17, f. 64.
⁶ I.O.R., B.P.C., 5 Oct. 1778, Range 2, vol. 28, ff. 273–4.
⁷ Bassett, *Trade and Policy*, p. 20.
⁸ I.O.R., B.P.C., 2 Oct. 1772, Range 2, vol. 1, f. 270.

ship took opium to the Company's brief and ill-fated settlement at Balambangan Island to the north of Borneo.[1] Ambitious men at Calcutta even considered plans for possible trade with the Celebes, where the Dutch tried to enforce a rigid exclusion;[2] a Bengal ship which was forced to put into Rembang in northern Java in 1768 seems actually to have been aiming for Macassar.[3]

Even Batavia, the capital of the Dutch Indies, was being drawn into Calcutta's orbit. The Dutch permitted foreign ships to trade with Batavia, but certain commodities, including opium and most Bengal piecegoods were reserved to the Dutch Company.[4] By the 1760s, however, so few Dutch ships traded between Bengal and Java that Batavia became dependent on private English shipping for the great bulk of its Bengal imports, whether the commodities were officially restricted or not. In 1775 the Dutch admitted that, whereas they had in the past sent twelve or thirteen ships a year to Bengal, two ships now called there to take cargo to Europe and one to make the return voyage to Batavia.[5] By contrast, the English factory at Benkulen noted two or three private Bengal ships a year on their way to or from Batavia in the late 1760s, eight in 1773, six in 1774, and six in 1776.[6] It became notorious that restrictions on the import of opium and piecegoods could be defied, with the connivance of the Batavia authorities.[7] In 1762 a Bengal country captain blockaded by the French in Batavia was able to sell his piecegoods and opium in the port.[8] In 1773 the Dutch Opium Society with official approval gave a contract to the Calcutta shipowner Joseph Price to deliver 200 chests of opium at Batavia on his ship the *Sarah*.[9] From 1783 to 1785 the Opium Society got all its opium from private British sources.[10]

---

[1] I.O.R., B.P.C., 15 Nov. 1773, Range 2, vol. 4, f. 303.

[2] Bassett, *Trade and Policy*, pp. 39–40.

[3] Batavia to Benkulen, 30 Dec. 1768, I.O.R., G/35/77, pp. 155–7.

[4] *Nederlandsch-Indisch Plakaatboek 1602–1811*, ed. J. A. van der Chijs (Amsterdam, 1885–1900), vii. 257–60.

[5] K. K. Datta, *The Dutch in Bengal and Bihar* (2nd edn., Delhi, 1968), p. 140.

[6] I.O.R., G/35/74–83.

[7] J. S. Stavorinus, *Voyage to the East Indies*, trans. S. H. Wilcocke (1798), i. 367–8.

[8] J. Edwards to A. Senior, 1 Mar. 1762, I.O.R., Mayor's Court Records, Range 155, vol. 61.

[9] Bodleian, dep. b. 94, pp. 50–2.

[10] *De opkomst van het gezag*, ix (1884), 316–17.

Calcutta's trade with Manila in the years when its eastern trade as a whole was developing so rapidly seems to have languished. Spanish records list the arrival of ships from Bengal in 1760, 1764, and 1767.[1] Thereafter direct trade seems to have lapsed until 1787, when the subterfuge of Portuguese or Asian colours could at last be abandoned. Contracts were officially made between Calcutta merchants and the new Spanish Royal Philippine Company for Bengal goods to be delivered openly at Manila in English ships.[2]

Intrepid Calcutta captains were shortly after 1784 to sail even further east. With the colonizing of New South Wales, a regular trade developed between Bengal and Australia, while one or two Calcutta ships were to make colossal voyages across the northern Pacific to the coast of British Columbia in search of the sea otters whose pelts could be sold in China.

The shift in the emphasis in Bengal's trade through Calcutta from west to east during the eighteenth century was clearly demonstrated by Professor Furber some twenty-five years ago.[3] The account given in this chapter abundantly confirms his findings, while possibly offering some modification in detail. Professor Furber suggested that the rise of the eastward trade was 'the almost simultaneous concomitant' of the decline of trade to the west.[4] It would seem, however, that as far as Europeans were concerned there may have been an interval of some thirty barren years. The western trade was thought to be in serious decline by the 1740s; the eastward trade was not providing substantial compensations until the 1770s.

The shift from west to east is perhaps an indication of the importance which the British were beginning to acquire in Asian trade at the end of the eighteenth century. In the early part of the century the activities of the Calcutta shipowners were determined by Asian needs. They operated along routes which had been established by the ships of the Asian merchants, carrying Asian freight or goods which would be sold in Bengal's traditional markets. But after the conquest of Bengal, the wealth which the British acquired and the control which they won over some of

[1] Chaunu, *Les Philippines*, i. 188–93.

[2] W.-E. Cheong, 'Some Aspects of British Trade and Finance in Canton' (London Ph.D. thesis, 1962), pp. 47–57.

[3] Furber, *John Company*, pp. 160–8.   [4] Ibid., p. 164.

Bengal's commodities, such as opium, enabled them to begin to carve out routes of their own. Trade between Calcutta and Canton and the greatly increased trade between Calcutta and Malaya and Indonesia were essentially British creations in response to British needs. Much of the old pattern of Asian trade remained in 1784, but there were clear portents of the future.

V

The Internal Trade of Bengal:
(I) The Boom after Plassey

In the title of this and the following chapters the term 'internal trade' has been preferred to the frequently used alternative 'inland trade'. This is because 'inland trade' was a term that acquired a special connotation. It came more and more to be applied to trade in articles produced and consumed within Bengal itself, and and even to be confined to certain commodities, such as salt, over which there was bitter controversy. These chapters are, however, concerned with Bengal's internal trade in the widest sense: with the movement of all goods within the province's boundaries, regardless of where they originated or of their ultimate destination.

Bengal had a highly developed system of internal trade, linking to some degree virtually every part of the province in an extremely intricate pattern. A huge volume of goods was moved by water, bullock cart, or pack animal, handled by merchants and traders who varied from great wholesalers to the holders of a single stall, and disposed of in markets covering several acres, such as those at Bhagwangola, near Murshidabad, or Rajbari, near Dacca, at one extreme, or village *hats* and *ganjs* at the other. Parts of this system offered profits at a level to tempt the participation of Englishmen.

Precise information about the composition and volume of Bengal's internal trade is very difficult to obtain. Most of what is available relates to the end of the century, after the East India Company had begun to administer the customs system in 1773. Figures for collections made at Murshidabad, the Nawabs' capital situated at a strategic point on the river system between the ports of the Hugli and the cities of the Ganges valley, have recently been analysed. They reveal that for the 1770s at least, 'if trade was in total important, it was nevertheless conducted in very small parcels; . . . most consignments are worth less than a thousand rupees'. The items were extremely varied, with food grains by far the largest, but salt, betel nut, cotton piecegoods and silk also figured largely.[1] Also in 1773 two Company servants tried to give an estimate of the value of the trade of the districts in eastern Bengal to which they had been posted. Given that these figures must be largely guesswork and that the pattern of trade for each district is likely to be very different, they are still of some interest. Lakshmipur, which roughly corresponds to modern Noakhali, was thought to export 115,000 maunds of paddy or unhusked rice out of a total output of 500,000 maunds. Allowing thirty maunds to a ton, this means that about 3,850 tons a year out of a crop of 16,500 tons were sent out of the district. Lakshmipur was also thought to export some 650 tons of betel nut, 5,000 tons of salt and small quantities of 'jaggery' (coarse sugar), vetch, raw cotton, and chillies.[2] The main exports of Chittagong, further to the east, were considered to be 2,000 tons of salt, 500 tons of sawn timber, as well as chillies and raw cotton, but only a small part (some 550 tons) of its total paddy crop of 40,000 tons.[3]

From these and other indications, certain generalizations can be hazarded about the pattern of Bengal's trade. Cotton piecegoods of the finer qualities and silk travelled from the *aurangs* where they were made to Calcutta or the other ports on the Hugli for export by sea, up the Ganges to the markets of northern India or to centres of conspicuous consumption within the provinces, such as Patna or Murshidabad. Opium and saltpetre came down the river system from Bihar to the ports. European manufactured goods, spices, and pepper from Indonesia or Malabar, and raw cotton from western India moved outward from the ports. Some districts in Bengal regularly produced grain surpluses which fed other parts. The grain surplus areas seem generally to have been in the north and the east: Calcutta drew much of its rice from Bakarganj, Dacca, and the south east, while districts in the north such as Dinajpur, Rangpur, and Purnea also exported much rice and wheat. Tobacco, betel nut, sugar, and vegetable oils were also carried over considerable distances. But apart from food grains, salt seems to have been the largest and most highly organized of the trades in articles of common consumption. It

[1] K. M. Mohsin, *A Bengal District in Transition: Murshidabad 1765–93* (Dacca, 1973), chap. 2
[2] I.O.R., Board of Customs, appendix, 14 July 1773, Range 98, vol. 15.
[3] Ibid., 21 Apr. 1773, Range 98, vol. 15.

was produced in coastal districts and distributed under an elaborate system of controls maintained both by the Nawabs and the British.

Regulations and controls for public and private profit were very widely enforced on trade of all kinds under both regimes. The Nawabs' government levied duties on goods passing certain customs posts at $2\frac{1}{2}$ per cent on their current price for Muslims; Hindus paid 5 per cent on 'a fixed appraisement' and Armenians $3\frac{1}{2}$ per cent. When the Nawabs' officials had collected their duties at the appropriate rates, they still had not finished with their clients. For instance, a Hindu merchant bringing fifty-five bales of broad cloth to Patna in 1773 paid 5 per cent on them but was then required to pay fees, charges and extra duties amounting to a further $2\frac{1}{2}$ per cent.[1] In addition to the Nawabs' customs, dues were collected on goods in transit by officials and by *zamindars*, both on the government's and on their own behalf, at what were called *chauki* posts: on the 150 or so miles of river between Calcutta and Murshidabad there were seventeen *chauki* posts collecting dues in 1768;[2] in the rich district of Burdwan there were 114 main posts in 1773 with 410 subsidiary ones.[3] Charges of many kinds were levied at markets, the grant of a right to open one and collect dues from it was a very valuable perquisite for a local dignitary. The list of market dues collected at Dacca suggests the complexity of the system: duties were paid on the sale of arms, cattle, gram, cotton, betel nut, articles made of copper and brass, vegetables, leather, paper, red paint, and 'every thing that bears the denomination second hand'.[4] Burdensome as the payment of the duties was, Europeans often implied that peculation and harassment by those who manned the various tolls and collection posts could be worse. The obvious mitigating factor was that the system was riddled with exemptions and reductions, of which the privileges granted to the European trading companies were only the best known.

Trade in certain commodities or the trade of certain districts was regulated either by the government or by individuals in Mughal Bengal. Tobacco and betel nut 'farms' existed in the

---

[1] I.O.R., Board of Customs, 21 Apr. 1773, appendix 3 June 1773, Range 98, vols. 14, 15.

[2] Mohsin, *Murshidabad*, p. 104.

[3] I.O.R., Board of Customs, appendix, 12 May 1773, Range 98, vol. 15.

[4] A. Karim, *Dacca, the Mughal capital* (Dacca, 1964), pp. 214–23.

areas where these crops were produced.[1] The Nawabs collected a duty on the manufacture of salt, and granted a monopoly of its sale throughout Bengal, held in the years before and after Plassey by the great Armenian trader, Khwaja Wajid, who was thought to pay nearly £200,000 a year for it.[2] Bihar's saltpetre was also a monopoly, in the possession of a Muslim, Mir Afzal, from 1749 until 1755, when it too passed to Khwaja Wajid.[3] The *faujdar*, or local governor, of Chittagong was said to monopolize many articles of trade in his district, while similar monopolies were operated at Sylhet, on the eastern border of Bengal, over trade between Bengal and Assam,[4] and over certain commodities at Purnea in northern Bengal.[5]

Early in the eighteenth century private fortunes in Bengal were generally made or lost at sea. But internal trade, to obtain goods for export and to dispose of imports, was an inevitable adjunct to trading by sea and quickly became an object in itself for many Englishmen. In 1727 the Governor assured the Directors that every Company servant was free to improve his fortune in any way that he chose, 'either inland or by sea'.[6] Before Plassey internal trade was conducted either through Company servants stationed at the Company's factories outside Calcutta or by employing Indian *gumashtas* to travel up-country. The scale of such operations, even in the early eighteenth century, is suggested by the papers of one Harry Harnett who died in 1727. He had a series of 'adventures' in tin, tutenag, pepper, and cotton sent for sale to Dacca; tutenag and sandal wood consigned for sale at Patna; Indian *gumashtas* were selling goods for him at four different *aurangs* and buying for him at three more, while a European was also buying goods on his behalf at Dacca.[7] The Company reestablished a factory at Patna in 1718. By 1723 the Directors had heard that private trade

---

[1] For their working at Chittagong, see A. M. Serajuddin, *Revenue Administration of the East India Company in Chittagong, 1761–85* (Chittagong, 1971), pp. 165–8.

[2] Clive to Directors, 14 Nov. 1767, *Reports from Committees of the House of Commons* (1803–6), iii. 529.

[3] I.O.R., Bengal Secret Consultations, 29 Jan. 1774, Range A, vol. 25.

[4] J. Reed's minute, 20 Dec. 1770, *Proceedings of the Controlling Council of Revenue at Murshidabad* (Calcutta, 1919–24), ii. 106.

[5] Mir Kasim to H. Vansittart, 31 Jan. 1762, Add. MS. 29099, f. 1.

[6] H. Frankland to Secret Committee, 28 Jan. 1727, I.O.R., Home Miscellaneous, 68, p. 46.

[7] N.L.W., Clive MSS. 358, 359, 362.

in piecegoods, opium, and saltpetre by the servants stationed at Patna was bigger than the Company's own trade there.[1] In 1725 the Calcutta Council put the value of private sales and purchases at Patna at Rs 600,000 (about £68,000).[2] A single partnership between Hugh Barker of the Company's service and the great Indian merchant Omichund was selling goods worth more than Rs 60,000 at Patna in 1729.[3] There are also indications of extensive private dealings at Dacca well before Plassey. Estimates of private English cloth purchases are available for the years 1736/7, 1737/8, 1743/4, 1744/5, and 1747 at Dacca; in three out of the five years they were thought to have exceeded Rs 200,000.[4] Individuals became deeply involved in trade: a Company servant called Thomas Cooke, who was arrested for defrauding the Company in 1737, had Rs 76,663 'at the aurungs' at Dacca;[5] another servant borrowed Rs 80,000 at Dacca from 1750 to 1752 from 'sundry shroffs' to enter into 'a very extensive scene of business'.[6]

Englishmen naturally wished to secure their private trade from the expense and hazards of the Bengal customs system and so invariably claimed the right to have their personal property covered by the concessions obtained from the Nawabs by the Company for itself. Above all they insisted that private English goods should be granted the Company's *dastak*, or seal, signifying that they were exempt from search or payment under the 1717 *farman*. Extension of the Company's privileges to cover the private activities of individual Englishmen was accepted by the Directors, although their instructions that these privileges should be available to all Englishmen[7] were in practice set aside in Bengal. The Company servants claimed an exclusive right to *dastaks* for themselves and refused to give them to Free Merchants.[8]

The extent of private Englishmen's privileges in pre-Plassey Bengal was, however, determined not by what the Directors in London would accept but by what the Nawabs in Bengal would concede. The 1717 *farman* was somewhat ambiguous. The crucial

---

[1] Directors to Bengal, 14 Feb. 1723, I.O.R., E/3/101, p. 472.

[2] Abs. Bengal to Directors, 9 Jan. 1725, I.O.R., E/4/2, pp. 438–9.

[3] *Omichund* v. *Bell*, P.R.O., C 11/1055/16.

[4] Karim, *Dacca*, p. 87; 'An Account of the District of Dacca dated 1800', *Journal of the Asiatic Society of Pakistan*, vii (1962), 308–9.

[5] I.O.R., B.P.C., 28 Dec. 1736, Range 1, vol. 12, f. 40.

[6] Calcutta High Court Records, Mayor's Court, *Cooke* v. *Pearkes*.

[7] Directors to Bengal, 3 Oct. 1684, I.O.R., E/3/90, p. 381.

[8] Abs. Bengal to Directors, 18 Jan. 1723, I.O.R., E/4/2, p. 360.

phrase in the English translation was that 'All goods and necessaries' which the Company's 'factors . . . bring or carry away either
by land or by water' should be exempt from customs.[1] Whatever
may have been intended by 'all goods' in 1717, the Nawabs and
their officials quickly made it clear that they were going to impose
limitations. In disputes over a consignment of English-owned salt
sent up to Patna in 1727 they began to make a distinction between
articles for import or export by sea, which, they argued, were
covered by the *farman*, and 'inland' articles, moved from one part
of Bengal for sale in another, which were not.[2] Since the Company
did virtually no inland trading in this sense, the chief sufferers
from this distinction were private individuals. In 1731 the issue
was raised again, when the Nawab denounced the English for
trading 'in all the country merchandize besides what are proper
for the Europe markets, as well salt as every other commodity'.[3]
The complaints were followed up by a blockade of the Company's
trade at several points, which was only lifted when the Company's
Chief at Kasimbazar promised that the English would not in
future 'trade in any goods but what are proper for Europe and
intermeddle with such part of trade as belong to the natives of
Indostan'.[4] This distinction between 'inland' and 'import and
export' commodities does not bear close examination. Articles
such as sugar, food grains, or certain kinds of piecegoods, which
were never challenged by the Nawabs, were used in both types of
trade. To Englishmen it seemed clear that what the Nawabs were
really trying to do was to protect the exclusive grants and special
duties which provided a considerable part of their revenue: salt
paid an extra duty, and dealing in betel nut, salt, and tobacco
were 'farms' sold by the government. These were the articles which
the Nawabs' officials were particularly anxious to deny to the
English.[5] Attempts to apply the *dastak* to any of them, especially
to salt which was often carried up to Patna in English boats,
provoked confiscation and protests.

[1] Facsimile in S. Bhattacharya, *The East India Company and the Economy of
Bengal* (1954).
[2] I.O.R., B.P.C., 18 Sept., 9 Oct. 1727, Home Miscellaneous, 92, pp. 55–7.
[3] I.O.R., B.P.C., 17 Oct. 1731, Range 1, vol. 8, f. 476.
[4] Bhattacharya, *East India Company*, p. 56.
[5] S. Batson's evidence, 3rd Report, Select Committee, 1772, *Reports*, iii.
301; P. Amyatt's minute, 1 Mar. 1763, H. Vansittart, *A Narrative of the Transactions in Bengal* (1766), ii. 377–8.

To keep the peace with the Nawabs, it became official policy, reinforced by orders from home, that Englishmen should not deal in 'inland' commodities. In fact they did, although the usual practice seems to have been to do so under a Muslim name, paying duties at Muslim rates.[1] Evidence of servants stationed at Dacca trading on their own behalf in betel nut exists for 1737[2] and for the years immediately before 1756,[3] while salt was still being smuggled up to Patna in 1741.[4]

Before Plassey Englishmen were certainly involved in the internal trade of Bengal, but the scale of their operations seems to have been relatively limited. Without some major political upheaval it is unlikely that these limits could have been significantly enlarged. Successful trade on a very large scale in eighteenth-century Bengal required the effective exercise of political power. Power to claim exemption from customs and local dues or grants of monopolies; power to maintain control over weavers and cultivators to whom large sums had to be advanced;[5] power to enforce debts without having to resort to uncertain and apparently corrupt courts. The Company had acquired a degree of power before Plassey: it did not submit to the Nawabs' customs or their courts, and it applied coercion to those who worked for it without reference to the government. Private Englishmen claimed and exercised these privileges too. But they could only be exercised in Calcutta or in the immediate area of the Company's factories (at Dacca, Kasimbazar, Patna, Balasore, and Lakshmipur in the 1750s), and where they could be exercised they still depended on the tolerance of the Nawabs. The events of 1756 showed the ultimate weakness of the British position in Bengal. A massive expansion of British inland trading would require the extension of British influence to many new areas in Bengal and the placing of this influence on a much surer foundation; it would in short require a political revolution.

Plassey brought about such a revolution, although this was not at first apparent. Formally Mir Jafar, the new Nawab placed on the throne by British arms, exercised all the powers of his

---

[1] *A Defence of Mr Vansittart's Conduct in concluding the Treaty of Commerce with Mhir Cossim Aly Chawn . . . by a Servant of the Company* (1764), p. 5.

[2] I.O.R., B.P.C., 1 Mar. 1737, Range 1, vol. 12, f. 122.

[3] Calcutta High Court Records, Mayor's Court, Account of N. Clerembault's estate.   [4] I.O.R., B.P.C., 21 Jan. 1745, Range 1, vol. 17, ff. 466–7.

[5] See above, p. 36.

predecessors. He had ceded a small area south of Calcutta called the Twenty-four Parganas outright to the British, but in theory at least he had not abdicated any part of his authority over the rest of Bengal. His successor, Mir Kasim, owed his throne even more explicitly to the intervention of the British in 1760 and made much larger cessions of territory, but he too retained full power over the rest of Bengal. In 1757 Mir Jafar issued a new grant confirming British trading privileges in Bengal. Once again they were given a guarantee that goods bearing the Company's *dastak* would pass without paying customs;[1] but nothing was said to resolve the ambiguities about the type of goods which could be covered. It would seem that in negotiating the new settlement with Mir Jafar Clive had not sought any new concessions in this respect. 'The utmost care should be observed in granting dustucks', he told the Council; for 'as the Nabob readily allows us every proper advantage, and will preserve us in the same, it is equally our duty to avoid all deviations or encroachments contrary to the real intent and meaning of the priviledges enjoyed by the English'.[2] The Nawabs soon made it clear that they stuck to their predecessors' interpretation that certain kinds of goods were excluded from the British customs exemptions.

On the surface it might appear that little had been changed by 1757, but the conditions which would enable a large expansion of inland trading to take place were in fact being created: British influence was reaching out into new areas of Bengal and Englishmen were increasingly able to disregard the Nawabs' officials and to enforce for themselves the terms on which they traded. One of the immediate consequences of Plassey was that more and more Europeans came to be stationed outside Calcutta or the traditional up-country factories of the Company. The new Nawabs were obliged to accept a Company's Resident living at their court, a post which gave its holder extremely lucrative opportunities for private trade. Within a short space of time the Company's army virtually became the Nawabs' army, which meant that the majority of troops were no longer confined at Calcutta but were stationed at new cantonments near Murshidabad and Patna or even outside

[1] C. U. Aitchison, *A Collection of Treaties, Engagements and Sanads* (Calcutta, 1930), ii. 203.
[2] Clive etc. to Council, 31 July 1757, I.O.L., Orme MSS., 'India', x, pp. 2450–1.

Bengal altogether in Oudh. Army officers were thus given entirely new opportunities for trade. When Mir Kasim ceded the extremely rich districts of Midnapur, Burdwan, and Chittagong to the Company in 1760, civil servants moved into them to establish the new administration and also set up their private trade there. The grant of the *diwani* put the remaining parts of Bengal and Bihar under the Company's rule in 1765. Especially after 1769, the *diwani* lands came under an increasing degree of European administration; European administration meant European trade.

In the lands ceded in 1757 and 1760 the Nawabs' ability to control European traders collapsed overnight. Among other consequences of the cessions, some of the largest salt producing areas in Bengal began to be exploited by Europeans. Outside the ceded districts the Nawabs tried up to 1765, often with great stubbornness, to maintain some degree of authority over European traders. But Plassey had seriously weakened their prestige with Europeans, and with each change of Nawab it became more obvious where the real source of power in Bengal lay. In any dispute between a European trader and one of the Nawab's officials, the official's chances of prevailing became less and less. European trade could only be regulated by Europeans themselves. This fact was, however, only accepted slowly by the Company and its servants, and when it was accepted, systems of regulation proved very difficult to devise.

If internal trading could be supported with some degree of effective political power, many of its risks could be significantly reduced and its potentially high profits[1] could be realized with much more certainty. With Calcutta's seaborne trade generally at a low ebb, it is not therefore surprising that many Europeans should have decided to try their luck inland under the new conditions that were coming into existence after Plassey. The size of internal ventures grew spectacularly. European trade had always been financed by extensive borrowing, mostly from Indians,[2] but after 1757 individuals were raising ever larger sums for the internal trade. The number of Indian *gumashtas* buying and selling on their masters' behalf multiplied and European agents began to be sent out of Calcutta to supervise trading concerns, a practice said in 1764 to be 'of very late date' originating 'within these two years'.[3]

---

[1] See above, p. 49.   [2] See above, pp. 42–4.
[3] Bengal Secret Consultations, 21 July 1764, *Reports*, iii. 495–9.

In pre-Plassey Calcutta the Governor of the settlement was normally the largest private trader. Robert Clive, who was more than adequately provided for by the bounty of the new Nawab, showed little interest in trading during his Governorship from 1757 to 1760. Indeed, he urged moderation in trading on other servants.[1] Clive's successor Henry Vansittart was, however, involved on a huge scale in internal trade during his administration from 1760 to 1764. One of Vansittart's many enemies even accused him of 'trying to encircle the general trade of Bengal under his own immediate direction'.[2] His share in the salt trade was said to be 'equal to that of all the other servants of the Company put together'.[3] In 1762 he was employing at least four European agents to manage various ventures.[4] A concern comparable to Vansittart's and in bitter competition with him was that run by three senior servants, John Johnstone, William Hay, and William Bolts. One of the partners, William Hay, was killed by Mir Kasim's troops who took the English factory at Patna in 1763, when his third of the 'principal or capital engaged in that partnership' was Rs 190,805,[5] which suggests that the concern was trading with a capital of some £67,000. The partnership had huge transactions in salt and at least three Europeans working for it in northern Bengal and Bihar. William Ellis, another senior servant who was killed by Mir Kasim, owed Rs 164,852 on bond at his death in 1763, but by January 1766 his executors had been able to pay Rs 583,430 into his estate and estimated that another Rs 265,440 were still outstanding.[6] Warren Hastings, whose trade was usually managed by his partner, the surgeon Tysoe Saul Hancock, was involved in salt, opium, tobacco, timber, and boat-building, employing five Europeans in 1763.[7] He still had Rs 300,000 sunk in various concerns when he left India in 1765.[8]

Lesser Company servants, whose credit was less good, traded

[1] Letter to W. Sumner, 4 June 1758, N.L.W., Clive MSS. 208, p. 50.

[2] H. Verelst to R. Becher, 7 Feb. 1763, Ames MSS., I.O.L. microfilm, reel 606.

[3] *Facts relating to the Treaty of Commerce concluded by Governor Vansittart* (1764), p. 28.

[4] I.O.R., B.P.C., 10 May, 11 Oct. 1762, Range 1, vol. 34, ff. 246, 462.

[5] I.O.R., Mayor's Court Records, Range 154, vols. 64, f. 3; 66, pp. 147-52.

[6] Ibid., Range 154, vols. 64, f. 21; 65, pp. 96-103, 106-9.

[7] I.O.R., B.P.C., 14 Apr., 23 May, 6 June 1763, Range 1, vols. 35, f. 391; 36, ff. 39, 52-3.

[8] Letters to Hancock, 20 May, 25 July 1770, Add. MS. 29125, ff. 37, 48.

according to their means, employing a single European, if they could afford one, or relying on Indian *gumashtas*. In May 1762 thirty-three Europeans were listed as being employed on private business outside Calcutta.[1] The number of Indian *gumashtas* in the service of European traders is impossible to calculate, but it must have been very considerable. An experienced trader later wrote that he had employed fifteen 'head gomastahs'.[2] Several Englishmen must have had staffs of this size, while a junior Company servant may have employed two or three *gumashtas*. In 1762 Mir Kasim complained that four or five hundred new 'factories', by which he meant places from which a European or a *gumashta* operated, had been set up in Bengal.[3] This was no doubt an exaggeration, but it may not have been an altogether grotesque one. The most reliable indication of the extent of British internal trade within six years of Plassey is perhaps the claims for losses incurred in the war against Mir Kasim in 1763. British control had temporarily collapsed over much of Bengal outside Calcutta, allowing much plundering of trade. Claims for restitution were submitted to a committee, which was supposed to scrutinize them very closely, and Rs 5,300,000 were eventually passed.[4] Doubts about the severity of the scrutiny would probably be very well justified, but on the surface British participation in Bengal's inland trade by 1763 was worth well over £500,000.

Even if it could be kept within the conventions that had grown up round European trade before Plassey, British internal trading on such a scale posed a very serious threat to the Nawabs' government. In the first place, their customs receipts were likely to be drastically cut. A huge volume of trade would now travel customs-free covered by the Company's *dastak*. Not only was the *dastak* used by all Europeans and by their Indian employees, but it was also being used by many Indians who had no real connection with the British. This was an old problem. As early as 1726 it was admitted that Armenians and 'black merchants' moved 'vast quantitys of goods . . . by virtue of our dustucks'.[5] In 1732 a former Governor acknowledged that Company servants sold

[1] I.O.R., B.P.C., 10, 13, 24, 31 May 1762, Range 1, vol. 34, ff. 246, 250, 266–7, 277.
[2] W. Bolts, *Considerations on India Affairs* (1772–5), ii. 192.
[3] Vansittart, *Narrative*, ii. 100–1.
[4] I.O.R., Bengal Secret Consultations, 24 Sept. 1764, Range A, vol. 5, p. 508.
[5] I.O.R., B.P.C., 10 Apr. 1726, Home Miscellaneous, 68, p. 49.

dastaks to Indian merchants.[1] Abuse of *dastaks* was one of the reasons that Siraj-ud-daula gave for his attack on Calcutta in 1756.[2] After Plassey the Nawabs' officials complained repeatedly about unauthorized use of *dastaks*. On a journey up the Ganges to Bihar in 1762 Warren Hastings hardly found a single boat which was not flying an English flag and claiming customs exemption.[3]

Under existing conventions, an increase in British inland trade would also involve an undermining of the authority of the Nawabs' government in many parts of Bengal. The 1717 *farman* had promised that those owing obligations to the Company should be dealt with by its servants rather than by the Nawabs' courts and officials.[4] The Company came to regard the weavers and brokers whom it employed as its dependants, rather than being the 'dependants of the circar' [the government].[5] Private Europeans claimed such privileges as well. 'The Company have ever protected their gomastahs and those of their servants', it was said.[6] So long as these claims were exercised within the comparatively limited areas of the traditional factories, serious conflict could perhaps be avoided. But it is hard to see how any Nawab could have accepted claims for immunity from the authority of his government for scores of new trading-posts sprouting up all over Bengal.

The manner in which some Europeans conducted their trade went far beyond previous convention. Within two years of Plassey the Council found it necessary to forbid 'sepoys being employed in the private business of the gentlemen at the subordinates'.[7] Armed men were still used to support trade. A party of sepoys sent from Dacca to Sylhet 'on account of some private dispute' were alleged to have 'fired upon and killed one of the principal people of the place, and afterwards made the zemindar prisoner and forcibly carried him away'.[8] Once they had established their authority, by force if need be, European agents or *gumashtas* could

---

[1] J. Deane's evidence, I.O.R., Correspondence Reports, D/19.

[2] S. C. Hill, *Bengal in 1756–1757* (1905), i. 4.

[3] Vansittart, *Narrative*, ii. 80. See also account of conditions in Malda in I.O.R., B.P.C., 28 June 1762, Range 1, vol. 34, f. 309.

[4] Bhattacharya, *East India Company*, p. 28.

[5] B.P.C., 1 Feb. 1763, Vansittart, *Narrative*, ii. 256.

[6] B.P.C., 1 Mar. 1763, ibid. ii. 343.

[7] I.O.R., B.P.C., 5 July 1759, Range 1, vol. 31, f. 265.

[8] Ibid., 14 Oct. 1762, Range 1, vol. 34, ff. 466-7.

use it to drive out rivals and to regulate prices. 'Very certain it is', Vansittart wrote, 'that many English agents and gomastahs . . . have practised a method of carrying on business called in this country Barja and Kichavat, that is, forcing the merchants and shopkeepers to take their goods at 30, 40, or 50 per cent above the market price.'[1] A European sent to report on conditions at Bakarganj in 1762 found that *gumashtas* were having those who refused to trade with them on their terms flogged and were taking goods at prices 'a considerable deal less than another merchant'.[2]

There are many reasons why stories of abuses in European private trade should be treated with caution. Several people had an obvious interest in exaggerating them. Mir Kasim was trying to make the strongest possible case against the Company, while Vansittart and Johnstone and his friends were engaged in a campaign of mutual vilification, trying to portray one another's trading activities in the worst possible light. Nevertheless, it is hard to believe that abuses, amounting on occasions to atrocities, were not widely committed. In 1764 a Council, most of whose members were not noted for tender-mindedness, agreed that European agents could no longer be trusted to operate outside Calcutta without behaving oppressively and must therefore be recalled.[3]

The way in which private Englishmen could bring important trades under their control, even without formal authority, in the years immediately after Plassey is strikingly illustrated by the case of Bihar opium. Before Plassey a number of Indian merchants dealt in opium,[4] although Omichund had tried to establish a monopoly in 1756.[5] Plassey gave the English Company's servants stationed at Patna the chance to bring opium production under their control, to the detriment of the Dutch in particular, whose shipments of Bengal opium to Batavia were seriously cut.[6] In 1761 the Nawab's deputy at Patna agreed to a request by William McGwire, the Chief of the Patna factory, that an order should be issued forbidding purchases of opium until McGwire had completed what he called his 'investment', which seems to have been virtually the whole crop. Although he was offered a share in the

[1] B.P.C., 1 Feb. 1763, Vansittart, *Narrative*, ii. 245–6.

[2] B.P.C., 14 Oct. 1762, ibid. ii. 113.

[3] Bengal Secret Consultations, 3 May, 21 July 1764, *Reports*, iii. 494–9.

[4] G. Sanyal, 'Ramchand Pandit's Report on opium cultivation in 18th-century Bihar', *B.P.P.*, lxxxvii (1968), 182–6.

[5] Hill, *Bengal 1756–7*, ii. 63.   [6] See above, p. 101.

deal, Vansittart disapproved of it, and ordered McGwire to with-draw the order.[1] Vansittart might like to believe that he had made 'all the world free . . . to buy opium',[2] but the truth was otherwise. In 1762 and 1763 the new Chief at Patna, William Ellis, was buy-ing up most of the opium, keeping the Dutch short and warning off other English traders.[3] Private monopolies of opium by the servants at Patna continued to be operated with varying degrees of intensity until the Company established its own monopoly in 1773.

European trading was not only being conducted with a use of force that would have been impossible before Plassey, it was also openly invading areas which the Nawabs had previously tried to protect. Salt was by far the most important. Bengal's total salt output was estimated at 2,800,000[4] or 2,500,000 maunds[5] (about 95,000 or 85,000 tons). Since salt water and firewood were the essential constituents of salt-making in the Bengal manner, most of the salt was made in well-wooded areas close to the sea. The Nawabs had levied a revenue from salt by collecting a duty on it and by selling a monopoly of its distribution. But in 1757 important salt-producing areas immediately around Calcutta were ceded to the Company and after 1760, with the cession of Chitta-gong, Burdwan, and Midnapur, about two-thirds of all Bengal's salt came under direct British control.[6] The rest followed in 1765 with the grant of the *diwani*.

As the Company's frontier was extended to include more and more salt lands, its servants were quick to involve themselves in the production of salt. In 1761, for instance, when John Johnstone was appointed to Midnapur he hoped to persuade the salt boilers to work for him, only to find that they were engaged to another servant, who had got in first and had been able to 'engross the whole salt trade in those parts'.[7] The firm of Johnstone, Hay and Bolts did, however, succeed in getting salt from Midnapur in 1762 and in Burdwan, where Johnstone was later stationed, in

---

[1] I.O.R., B.P.C., 3 Oct. 1763, Range 1, vol. 36, ff. 274–81.
[2] Letter to Hastings, 27 June 1762, Add. MS. 29132, ff. 224–5.
[3] Vansittart to Council, 13 Jan. 1763, *Reports*, iii. 343; Hastings to Capt. Johnstone, 12 June 1763, Add. MS. 29097, f. 102; W. Ellis to P. Amyatt, 7 July [1762], I.O.L., MS. Eur. G. 37, box 29.
[4] W. Sumner's evidence, 4th Report, Select Committee, 1773, *Reports*, iii. 463.
[5] I.O.R., B.R.C., 19 Jan. 1773, Range 49, vol. 38, p. 589.
[6] Sumner's evidence, *Reports*, iii. 466.
[7] I.O.R., Mayor's Court Records, Range 155, vol. 61.

1763.[1] The servants appointed to Chittagong immediately took over its salt production, including the large quantities of salt made on Sandwip Island.[2] The biggest speculator in salt on the Company's new lands seems to have been a Free Merchant called Archibald Keir, who in 1762 and 1763 employed 13,000 men to manufacture 12,000 tons of salt on his behalf.[3] In the early 1760s Europeans were even making salt in areas outside the Company's direct jurisdiction. By 1762 the salt pans at Dacca[4] and at Lakshmipur were under European control, much to Mir Kasim's annoyance.[5] Up to 1765 the two largest salt-producing districts in the whole province, at Hijli and Tamluk, south-west of Calcutta, remained at least nominally out of European hands under the management of the *faujdar* of Hugli. But much Hijli and Tamluk salt was obtained by private traders.[6]

Having taken control of so much of Bengal's salt production, private traders inevitably began to make their own arrangements for selling it not only at Calcutta but throughout the province. Large convoys of boats took salt to the Company's factories or to other places where private traders intended to dispose of it. This was a direct defiance of the Nawab's monopoly to which even Mir Jafar was not inclined to submit. Immediately after Plassey, the *faujdar* of Hugli reminded Clive that the British did not trade in salt.[7] Clive's view appears to have been that individuals might take part in the salt trade but that they should not try to carry the salt duty-free under the Company's *dastak*; they should pay the Nawab's duties at Muslim rates and get his pass through the customs.[8] On these terms large shipments of European-owned salt were moved in 1758 to places like Patna.[9] Under Vansittart

---

[1] I.O.R., Mayor's Court Records, Range 154, vol. 64, f. 12; B.P.C., 2 Sept. 1765, *Reports*, iv. 206–7.

[2] J. Carnac to Clive, 19 Nov. 1761, I.O.L., MS. Eur. G. 37, box 29.

[3] A. Keir, *Thoughts on the Affairs of Bengal* (1772), pp. 61, 70; letters to Select Committee, 17 Oct. 1765, 12 Jan. 1766, *Reports*, iii. 502–4.

[4] K. Petrus's protest, 14 July 1762, I.O.R., Mayor's Court Records, Range 155, vol. 61.   [5] B.P.C., 1 Mar. 1763, Vansittart, *Narrative*, ii. 165, 167–8.

[6] See the shipment of 200,000 maunds of Hugli salt to Patna in 1763, I.O.R., Mayor's Court Records, Range 154, vol. 64, f. 20.

[7] Amir Beg Khan to Clive, rec'd 10 Sept. 1757, N.L.W., Clive MSS. 369, p. 109.

[8] This emerges from letters from Hastings to W. Sumner, [Feb. 1759], and to J. Holwell, 19 Feb. 1760, Add. MS. 29096, ff. 112, 224; see also L. Scrafton to Clive, 14 Nov. 1764, I.O.L., MS. Eur. G. 37, box 32.

[9] e.g. Clive to Amir Beg Khan, 8 Oct. 1758, N.L.W., Clive MSS. 248, pp. 17–18.

after 1760 many more Europeans took part in the salt trade ('the English inhabitants in general' were said to be trading in salt by 1763),[1] and the volume of transactions grew even larger; Archibald Keir had 700,000 maunds (about 25,000 tons) of salt awaiting sale at Patna by 1765.[2] The revenue from customs on trade on this scale was of course a matter of great importance to the Nawab. Vansittart wrote that 'the gentlemen of Calcutta' still invariably applied for 'the Houghly dustuck' and paid the Nawabs' duties.[3] Later he went even further, saying that he himself had paid the 'government duties . . . on every maund I ever dealt in . . . nor did I ever grant a dustuck for this trade'.[4] Neither statement seems to be strictly true. In 1761 it was rumoured that Vansittart had obtained 'an exemption for the country duties' for a large consignment of salt to Patna in which he had a half share.[5] There are two recorded instances of his ordering the Nawab's officials to release boats with a Company's *dastak* which were carrying salt on which they presumably had not paid duties.[6] In June 1762 he admitted that he had 'lately' begun to issue *dastaks* for salt.[7] Even if they paid the Nawabs' duties, European salt-traders at Calcutta still had significant advantages over their Indian rivals. The duties paid by Europeans were the nominal Muslim $2\frac{1}{2}$ per cent, in reality about $4\frac{1}{2}$ per cent because of over valuation, whereas Muslims actually paid 9 per cent, but most 'country merchants', liable to local tolls, were thought in reality to pay at least 20 per cent if not more.[8] Europeans outside Calcutta also conducted a trade in salt. The servants stationed at Dacca were said in 1758 and 1759 to be refusing to pay any duties,[9] but by 1763 they were generally paying $3\frac{1}{2}$ per cent.[10]

Tobacco and betel nut were other farmed commodities from which the Nawabs had tried to exclude the British. As with salt,

---

[1] I.O.R., B.P.C., 22 Feb. 1763, Range 1, vol. 35, f. 188.

[2] Letter to Clive, 10 Nov. 1765, I.O.L., MS. Eur. G. 37, box 36, f. 132.

[3] B.P.C., 1 Feb. 1763, *Reports*, iii. 345.

[4] Letter to Directors, 7 Oct. 1767, I.O.R., Home Miscellaneous, 192, pp. 336–7.

[5] J. Carnac to Clive, 19 Nov. 1761, I.O.L., MS. Eur. G. 37, box 29.

[6] *Calendar of Persian Correspondence* (Calcutta, 1919–49), i. 174–5, 185.

[7] Letter to Hastings, 23 June 1762, Add. MS. 29132, f. 219.

[8] H. Vansittart, *A Letter to the Proprietors of East India Stock* (1767), pp. 83–4.

[9] Hastings to P. Pearkes, 1 Apr. 1758, to W. Sumner [Feb. 1759], Add. MS. 29096, ff. 9, 111.

[10] B.P.C., 1 Mar. 1763, Vansittart, *Narrative*, ii. 398.

such prohibitions could no longer be maintained after Plassey. Company servants at Dacca and other places in eastern Bengal where betel nut was grown not only traded extensively in it, but refused to pay any duties.[1] Europeans also insisted on their right to trade in tobacco, although they were prepared to pay a small duty on that.[2]

Under the Nawabs the trade of particular areas was also subject to monopolies and farms. Most of these areas were frontier ones, remote from Calcutta, into which Europeans had rarely penetrated. But after Plassey Europeans wandered much further afield, breaking into monopolies and even trying to take them over themselves. The most obvious example occurred in the Brahmaputra valley where Bengal's trade passed into the kingdom of Assam. At Rangamati and the neighbouring towns of Goalpara and Jogighopa private traders were locked in bitter conflict with the Nawab's *faujdar* and with one another. The prizes at stake were the import from Assam of a kind of cloth called *mughaduties* and the export of Bengal salt and European metals and woollen cloth.[3] The *faujdar* of Rangamati had 'engrossed' parts of the Assam trade,[4] but in 1755 the French Company sent one of its servants called Jean-Baptiste Chevalier to trade at Goalpara. After Plassey Chevalier became the agent of the English Company's servants at Dacca and later of John Johnstone and his partners. Chevalier remained on the Assam border until 1762, carrying on his trade with what seems to have been extreme ruthlessness. In 1759 he was said to be behaving in 'a very violent and arbitrary manner', establishing 'monopolies of several commodities, particularly salt and tobacco'.[5] When he was finally recalled to Calcutta, a new agent was sent to the Assam border by the Johnstone partnership. Since 1759 another European had also been active in the area. This was a man called Paul Pearkes, who settled at Jogighopa where he matched Chevalier, paying no duties, driving off competititors, and defying the *faujdar*.[6] Yet another European, acting for Vansittart and

---

[1] B.P.C., 2 Mar. 1763, Vansittart, *Narrative*, ii. 415.

[2] B.P.C., 1 Mar. 1763, ibid. ii. 398.

[3] There is a very informative account of the Assam trade in S. K. Bhuyan, *Anglo-Assamese Relations 1771–1826* (Gauhati, 1949), pp. 50–3.

[4] I.O.R., B.P.C., 1 Feb. 1763, Range 1, vol. 35, f. 106.

[5] Hastings to W. Sumner, 26 July 1759, Add. MS. 29096, f. 156.

[6] 'Complaints to be transmitted to the gentlemen at Dacca', Add. MS. 29096, ff. 260–1.

'some other gentlemen' was sent up to the Assam border in 1762. It is hardly surprising that the Council should have been bombarded with protests and counter-protests from the *faujdar* and the European trading interests involved.

Similar conflicts broke out in other frontier districts, such as Sylhet in the east or Purnea in the north. These were both areas previously outside the range of European traders where the *faujdars* enjoyed special powers, including commercial monopolies. The chief attraction of Sylhet was its *chunam*, or lime made from shells, which was used extensively in building. *Chunam* was a monopoly of the *faujdar*, but the boom in building materials, created by the huge programme of public and private works in the reconstruction of Calcutta after 1756, brought agents of the Company and private traders to Sylhet to buy *chunam*. The *faujdar* also found that his salt monopoly was invaded by the *gumashtas* of the English at Dacca.[1] Saltpetre and opium of inferior quality to the produce of Bihar could be obtained in Purnea, and large timbers for building could be cut in its forests. In 1762 Mir Kasim began to complain of *gumashtas* being sent by Europeans to trade in Purnea in items reserved for the government.[2] Shortly afterwards, European agents were dispatched to Purnea on behalf of the Johnstone partnership and on behalf of Vansittart. Disputes inevitably broke out as the *faujdar* tried to protect his interests by preventing the Europeans or the *gumashtas* from advancing money for goods.[3] Disputes spread to the neighbouring district of Rangpur, where one James Moore, who acted for Vansittart, became so well entrenched that he set up his own opium monopoly and used violence to drive out rival *gumashtas*.[4]

The spectacular growth of European private trade after Plassey was highly damaging to the Nawabs of Bengal. As more and more trade travelled under British auspices, they lost a sizeable part of their customs revenue. British trade in salt, betel nut, and tobacco presumably made it virtually impossible for the Nawab to sell monopolies. The revenue of the outlying *faujdaris* was much diminished by the invasion of monopolies there. Claims to

[1] Vansittart, *Narrative*, ii. 106–7.
[2] Letter to Vansittart, 31 Jan. 1762, Add. MS. 29099, f. 1.
[3] I.O.R., B.P.C., 17 Jan. 1763, Range 1, vol. 35, ff. 48–53.
[4] Calcutta High Court Records, Mayor's Court, *Bollackey Doss* v. *Moore*; I.O.R., B.P.C., 6 June 1763, Range 1, vol. 36, f. 52; H. Vansittart to Hastings, 11 June 1762, Add. MS. 29132, f. 210.

immunity from the normal rule of the government were being asserted over ever wider areas. Finally, Europeans were openly defying the Nawabs' authority and committing violent acts in places like Rangamati or Rangpur. Mir Jafar protested on several occasions either to Clive or the British Resident at his court about the excesses of the private traders. But Mir Kasim, who was both a more resolute and more ambitious character, and had been subjected to a much larger and more vigorously sustained volume of private trade, was prepared to take action.

From the action which he took events moved quickly to full-scale war with the British, and war ended in his defeat and deposition. Among contemporaries there were at least two schools of thought about the role of the trade disputes in the outbreak of war in 1763. To some Englishmen it seemed that Mir Kasim had been plotting war against the Company for some time and that he simply used the alleged abuses of trade as a pretext for it.[1] Others, like Vansittart himself, were inclined to believe that he had been provoked beyond endurance by repeated insults and acts of aggression by the European private traders.[2] It seems most improbable that the Nawab was seriously contemplating making war on the Company. On the other hand, his grievances against the traders were only one of several grievances which he had against the British. He was evidently determined to halt the increasing assertion of British power over Bengal and was also pessimistic about British intentions towards him, whatever he did; he cannot have been ignorant of the fact that many senior servants who regarded themselves as loyal to Clive hoped to see him deposed. Had he not taken his stand on the extension of British trade, it is still likely that he would have brought on a conflict by seeking to resist British pressure on him from some other direction.[3]

Vansittart, in whose name the replacement of Mir Jafar by Mir Kasim had been engineered in 1760, took an optimistic view of the Nawab's intentions. Deeply involved in trading himself, he believed that rules for private trade could be worked out that would reconcile both the interests of the traders and those of the

[1] e.g. H. Verelst to R. Becher, 30 Sept. 1763, Ames MSS., I.O.L. microfilm, reel 606.

[2] *Narrative*, ii. 78–9.

[3] For contrasting views of Mir Kasim, see N. L. Chatterjee, *Mir Qasim* (Allahabad, 1935) and B. K. Chowdhury, 'Political History 1757 to 1772', *History of Bengal 1757–1905*, ed. N. K. Sinha (Calcutta, 1967), pp. 32–8.

Nawab. He tried to persuade Mir Kasim that 'trade cannot be hurtful to the country, but beneficial'.[1] Harmony could be preserved, he thought, if Europeans paid duties on the traditional 'inland' articles and if their *gumashtas* and British agents could be kept under proper discipline. Whether any lasting settlement could have been achieved on this basis, given the nature of trade in Bengal with its close connection with political power, and given Mir Kasim's fears and mistrust of the British, is perhaps doubtful. But in any case Vansittart lacked the authority over his Council and over the servants in general which he needed to put his plans into effect. In October 1762, after several months of complaints, Mir Kasim decided to bring matters to a head by having the boats of European traders stopped at many points throughout Bengal. Vansittart tried to resolve the crisis by paying a visit to the Nawab at his new capital at Monghyr in Bihar. There an agreement was reached by which Europeans who traded in 'inland' items in future would pay customs to the Nawab at 9 per cent and would be obliged to make their Indian *gumashtas* answerable to the jurisdiction of his officials and his courts. When the terms of the so-called Treaty of Monghyr were made known, most Europeans greeted them with outrage. The servants at Dacca complained that 'all our privileges, all our fortunes and future prospects' were at risk.[2] The Treaty was referred for ratification to the whole Council, where after a long debate a majority overruled Vansittart and declared that the agreement must be annulled. In place of the Monghyr terms the majority decided to offer Mir Kasim a duty of $2\frac{1}{2}$ per cent on salt alone (all other commodities were to travel free under the *dastak*), and to reaffirm that in future all English *gumashtas* were outside the jurisdiction of the Nawab and could only be disciplined by the Chiefs of the English factories.

In the widely read *Narrative of the Transactions in Bengal* which Vansittart published in Britain in 1766 he put a most persuasive case on his own behalf. His enemies have met with little sympathy. For men like John Johnstone or William Ellis, who had shown themselves to be completely ruthless in the pursuit of their fortunes, sympathy is difficult. Having borrowed huge sums and laid them out all over Bengal, they stood to lose much by an interruption of trade. The Dacca servants complained that the Monghyr treaty

---

[1] Letter to Hastings, 15 Apr. 1762, Add. MS. 29132, f. 147.
[2] B.P.C., 17 Jan. 1763, Vansittart, *Narrative*, ii. 221.

'must entirely ruin most of us at this place',[1] and Johnstone reckoned that 'the best part' of his fortune was at stake.[2] But Vansittart and his dealings with Mir Kasim were also criticized by men like the future Governor Harry Verelst, who were capable of taking a more far-sighted view.[3] So the case put by those who opposed the treaty perhaps merits some consideration. In the first place, however unfairly, Vansittart aroused deep mistrust. He was the trading rival of many and it was widely rumoured that he had struck deals for his own advantage with Mir Kasim, rumours which had real foundation.[4] His trade was spared while others' was blockaded. Many were also disturbed by his apparent grovelling to the Nawab, and believed that only by standing firm on private trade could the British maintain the ascendancy which they had won at Plassey. Of the terms of the treaty, the actual rate fixed for 'inland' commodities of 9 per cent probably caused least misgiving. Johnstone called it 'exorbitant',[5] but with very high profit margins on salt, such a charge could easily be absorbed. Nine per cent would still give Englishmen a marked advantage over Indian salt traders. One critic of the treaty estimated that with all the various charges and duties which were levied on them Indian salt merchants paid 30 or 40 per cent;[6] Vansittart put it at 20 per cent.[7] What the private traders really valued was their complete independence from the Nawab in not having to submit to his customs and ask for his pass, and above all the freedom of their *gumashtas*. As one of them put it: 'Let em grant the encrease of duties, it won't hurt—but to oblige us to withdraw our protection from our gomastahs and sacrifice at once the privilege of our dusticks must ruin us all.'[8]

Once the Monghyr agreement had been rejected, events gathered momentum. Mir Kasim first of all insisted that no further European trade in inland articles could be permitted. Then, as a final gesture of defiance, he exempted all traders, Indian and European, from all duties, thus at a single stroke annulling all the privileges which the British had cherished for so long. A new delegation was

---

[1] B.P.C., 17 Jan. 1763, Vansittart, *Narrative*, ii. 218.
[2] Letter to J. Carnac, 7 Jan. 1763, I.O.L., MS. Eur. F. 128, box 3/15.
[3] See Verelst's letters to R. Becher, Ames MSS. I.O.L., Microfilm, reel 606.
[4] See below, p. 169.   [5] B.P.C., 1 Mar. 1763, Vansittart, *Narrative*, ii. 335.
[6] L. Scrafton, *Observations on Mr. Vansittart's Narrative* (1766), p. 40.
[7] See above, p. 121.
[8] R. Leycester to J. Carnac, 10 Jan. 1763, I.O.L., MS. Eur. F. 128, box 3/1.

sent to negotiate with the Nawab, but fighting broke out at Patna in June 1763. In the war that followed private trade at first suffered severely. Isolated Englishmen, their *gumashtas*, and the advances they had made to weavers and cultivators, were all vulnerable. Some of the most ambitious traders, including Hay and Ellis, were killed, and trading concerns throughout much of Bengal were plundered.

But disaster soon turned to triumph. British influence was quickly restored over the whole of Bengal, even while Mir Kasim was still resisting in Bihar, and a new Nawab was installed who was obliged to pay liberal compensation to the private traders and to grant them new privileges. The new Nawab was Mir Jafar, reinstated after an interval of three years. Vansittart apparently at first asked him to pay Rs 1,000,000 to the 'sufferers' in the late war, but then raised his demands to Rs 4,000,000; another Rs 800,000 was subsequently added.[1] Even Rs 4,800,000 (about £520,000) was less than some Europeans thought themselves entitled to; a committee, which had 'taken all possible care to reduce the claims to the lowest rate, estimated that they might amount to Rs 5,300,000.[2] Three-quarters of the Rs 4,800,000 had been paid off by May 1766, when the Directors ordered an inquiry.[3] The rest was paid off by 1775.[4]

After his restoration Mir Jafar was in no position to cavil about terms. The Council insisted on the same conditions for European trade as had been offered to Mir Kasim as an alternative to the treaty of Monghyr: all goods were to be covered by the Company's *dastak* and to have immunity from the Nawab's customs, except for salt, which was to pay him $2\frac{1}{2}$ per cent.[5] With the inevitable weakening of the Nawab's government, European agents and *gumashtas* seem to have enjoyed even more freedom than under Mir Kasim. In September 1764 Mir Jafar delivered a remonstrance against abuses said to have been committed at Rangamati, Bakarganj and Dacca.[6] Publicity was given to events in Rangpur and

[1] I.O.R., Select Committee Proceedings, 19, 26, 30 Aug. 1766, Range A, vol. 7, pp. 83–91, 94–5, 126–8; Bengal Secret Consultations, 10 Sept. 1764, Range A, vol. 5, p. 473.

[2] I.O.R., Bengal Secret Consultations, 24 Sept. 1764, Range A, vol. 5, p. 509.

[3] I.O.R., B.P.C., 19 May 1766, Range 1, vol. 39, f. 201.

[4] Bengal to Directors, 24 Feb. 1775, I.O.R., E/4/33, p. 321.

[5] I.O.R., B.P.C., 6, 11 July 1763, Range 1, vol. 36, ff. 141, 166.

[6] I.O.R., Bengal Secret Consultations, 10, 17 Sept. 1764, Range A, vol. 5, pp. 471, 487–8.

Dinajpur in northern Bengal by the rivalry of European trading concerns who accused one another's agents of malpractices. Stories of *gumashtas* employing sepoys, of flogging and of forced contracts, were relayed to the Council.[1]

The downfall of Mir Kasim not only strengthened the position of private traders in Bengal, but it also gave them a chance to move out of Bengal altogether into new and profitable pastures. Mir Kasim had been able to win the support of the Wazir of Oudh in his war with the British. When he was defeated in Bihar, he withdrew into the Wazir's territory, where he was pursued by the Company's army. Parts of the Wazir's dominions were occupied for some months, and after peace was made in 1765 a permanent link between the Wazir and the Company began to evolve which was to take numerous Englishmen into Oudh. Many of those who entered Oudh had an eye to trade. The great city of Banaras was one of the areas briefly occupied. The Company servants fortunate enough to be posted there imported broad cloth and silk from Bengal, took over the Raja of Banaras's opium and saltpetre monopolies, and began an extensive diamond trade.[2] The British administration was withdrawn from Banaras in 1765, but several private traders continued to operate there. Others moved further into Oudh, where the Wazir apparently felt obliged to issue *parwanas* (similar to the Bengal *dastaks*), which exempted 'the possessor from all duties or impositions', because he was 'afraid of offending the English'.[3] Within a year or two, 500 English *gumashtas* were thought to be trading in Oudh.[4]

By 1765 the prospects for private trade seemed to be excellent. Compensation had been won for the losses of 1763, the traders had regained and even strengthened their position in Bengal, and they had begun to expand into Oudh. Vansittart, who had some scruples about the methods used in trading, even though he had failed to give practical effect to them, had left India and been replaced by an even more pliant Governor, John Spencer, brought to Bengal from Bombay. Only in London was the outlook less promising; but London must have seemed very remote.

[1] I.O.R., Bengal Secret Consultations, 30 Apr., 25, 26, 30 July, 27 Aug. 1764, Range A, vol. 5, pp. 156–61, 408–21, 444–58.
[2] Bolts, *Considerations*, ii. 41–3; Bolts to Verelst, 2 Apr. 1768, *Reports*, iii. 275; R. Marriott to Hastings, 15 Aug. 1765, Add. MS. 29132, ff. 272–3.
[3] T. Rumbold's evidence, 2nd Report, Select Committee, 1772, *Reports*, iii. 268.   [4] R. Smith's evidence, ibid. iii. 289.

VI

The Internal Trade of Bengal:
(II) Regulation and Contraction

The news that the Company's servants, far from having consoli-
dated their immense new gains in Bengal, had quarrelled with
Mir Kasim and involved themselves in yet another war caused
consternation in London. As Vansittart and his enemies refought
their battles on paper in Britain and later combatants joined in,
private trade got much lurid publicity, and it came to be widely
assumed that the greed of the traders was the root cause of Bengal's
instability. Over the next few years there was much clamour for
restrictions to be imposed. The Directors' immediate response
to news of the war was to order that all inland trading cease and
that all European agents and private *gumashtas* be recalled.[1] But
the personnel of the Directors changed so frequently in the bitter
Company politics of the 1760s and the alliances between groups at
home and servants in Bengal were so notorious, that their instructions laid down no consistent policy and carried little weight in
India. Opinion in Britain about abuses of trade in Bengal was not
effectively asserted until these abuses were probed by committees
of the House of Commons and the Directors' orders were reinforced by acts of parliament.

In the meanwhile such regulation of private trading as was
attempted was devised by men actually in India. However strong
the pull of personal interest might be, some action had clearly to
be taken. The Nawabs were no longer capable of maintaining any
control over the activities of European traders; control of some
kind must therefore be applied by the British to themselves.
Before he left India, Vansittart was able to persuade his Council
to accept a modest programme of reform. In May 1764 the
Council heard complaints about malpractices being committed by

---

[1] Directors to Bengal, 8 Feb. 1764, *Fort William–India House Correspondence*
(New Delhi, 1949–), iv. 7.

European agents at Rangpur and eventually decided, after a long
and acrimonious debate, that all Europeans not in the Company's
service must be recalled to Calcutta by 31 December 1764. Trade
would in future be carried on solely through Indian *gumashtas*,
whose misdeeds could be punished more effectively.[1] All Europeans had certainly not left the Bengal countryside by January
1765. The order was to be repeated several times in the future, still
without much success. Eventually a convention seems to have
grown up that unofficial Europeans were tacitly permitted to live
where they liked so long as they did not draw attention to themselves
by misconduct. Vansittart's Council also devised the first scheme
for trying to control Europeans' trade by limiting the commodities
open to them. In October 1764, in response to complaints from
Mir Jafar, the Council ruled that Europeans might not trade in
rice, except to supply Calcutta, might not make salt outside the
Company's own territory, and might not sell it or betel nut,
except at Patna, Murshidabad and Dacca.[2] This plan was never
put into effect and was to be replaced by a much more ambitious
one introduced by Robert Clive.

In 1765 Clive returned to Bengal for his second Governorship
with wide powers from the Company to reform abuses. He was
specifically instructed to devise a 'proper and equitable plan' for
the inland trade.[3] By comparison with other servants, Clive was
capable of taking a relatively detached view of the problems raised
by private trade. He had no real inclination to trade himself and
with his vast fortune no need to. He believed that reform was
urgently needed and had a very unfavourable opinion of current
practices. European agents were, he thought, committing 'actions
which make the name of the English stink in the nostrils of a Jentue
or a Mussalman'.[4] He heard 'numberless complaints . . . of the
black agents and dependants of the black agents making use of the
authority of the Europeans', reflecting that 'It is really very shock-
ing to think of the distress of the poor inhabitants.'[5]

The centrepiece of Clive's reforms of the inland trade was his

[1] Bengal Secret Consultations, 3 May, 21 July 1764, *Reports from Committees
of the House of Commons* (1803–6), iii. 494–9.
[2] I.O.R., Bengal Secret Consultations, 17 Oct. 1764, Range A, vol. 5,
pp. 549, 553–4.
[3] Directors to Bengal, 1 June 1764, *Fort William–India House Corr.* iv. 54.
[4] Letter to J. Fowke, 25 Sept. 1765, N.L.W., Clive MSS., 222, p. 35.
[5] Letter to Sykes, 17 July 1765, I.O.L., MS. Eur. G. 37, box 3.

famous Society of Trade, which he set up in 1765 and which was effectively to last until 1768. The Society was an attempt to regulate the trade throughout Bengal in the most controversial 'inland' articles, salt, betel nut, and tobacco. The Society was to receive the whole of Bengal's output of all three commodities and to market it wholesale to Indian merchants, paying a duty to the government. The scheme's authors believed that it would reconcile all the interests involved in the internal trade of Bengal and end the bitterness and contention of previous years. The members of the Society would be the most senior Company servants, who would be assured of a substantial profit from its operations; the government of Bengal (after 1765 the Company itself) would be guaranteed an adequate revenue from trade by the duties which the Society would pay it; a single monopoly would avoid the disputes between rival agents and *gumashtas* which had led to disorder and oppression in the past; Indian merchants would have a fair field, since retail sale of the Society's goods would be left to them; and finally the fixed prices would be moderate and the mass of the population would be assured of adequate supplies without extortion.[1]

The detailed plan for the Society was drawn up by William Sumner, the second in Council, who sent a draft of it to Clive on 16 July 1765,[2] and the scheme was formally launched on 10 August 1765. The Society was to consist of all the civil servants down to the rank of Factor (that is all those with more than five years standing) and all the army officers with the rank of Major and above, shares being graded according to seniority. Virtually all the Society's dealings were in salt, which they were to obtain by contract from Company servants in districts where the salt pans were situated near the Company's factories, like Dacca or Midnapur, from other Europeans in the Calcutta area, and from the *faujdar* of Hugli for the Tamluk and Hijli districts. The Company would be paid a duty of 35 per cent on a fixed valuation of Rs 90 for 100 maunds of salt. The salt was then to be transported to thirteen centres throughout Bengal, where the Society's European

---

[1] Select Committee Proceedings, 10 Aug. 1765, *Reports*, iii. 509–10. For subsequent defences of the plan, see Clive's speech in the House of Commons, 30 Mar. 1772, *Parliamentary History of England*, xvii. 338–43; H. Verelst, *View of the Rise, Progress and Present State of the English Government in Bengal* (1772), pp. 105–19.

[2] Sumner to Clive, 16 July 1765, I.O.L., MS. Eur. G. 37, box 35, ff. 46–7.

agents, who received a commission of 5 per cent, were responsible for selling it to Indian merchants.[1] The prices at which they were to sell were fixed by Sumner after inquiries into past prices, the Society selling at what was supposed to be 15 per cent below the average price for the district for the last twenty years.[2]

Not without good reason, Clive was apprehensive about how his scheme would be received in Britain by the Company. To protect the money which the Society had committed for its first year of operations, the Governor and Council privately entered into an indenture with themselves to guarantee the Society at least one year's trading 'not withstanding any order or direction be issued to the contrary'.[3] Before the first year was completed, orders were received from the Directors, absolutely prohibiting all trade in salt, betel nut, or tobacco under any circumstances.[4] But Clive had also heard privately from at least one Director that with 'some few amendments' the aims of the Society could be regarded as 'both just and laudable'.[5] He therefore decided to give himself the benefit of the doubt, continuing the Society for a year, while being ready to assure the Directors that 'if they persevere in prohibiting that trade', they would of course be obeyed.[6] 'Some few amendments' were duly made to sugar the pill. The Company's duty was increased from 35 to 50 per cent. To give Indian merchants a bigger share in the trade, the Society decided to limit its sales to Calcutta; to keep down prices to consumers, the retail price of salt was fixed throughout Bengal.[7] Fresh orders from home were received in Bengal on 8 December 1766 specifically condemning the Society of Trade,[8] which was formally wound up on 3 September 1767, after its second year of operations. Abundant evidence, however, later came to light, showing that the Society had continued to deal in salt and to enjoy at least a partial monopoly for yet another year, that is until September 1768.[9]

[1] Select Committee Proceedings, 10 Aug., 18 Sept. 1765. *Reports*, iii. 509–11.
[2] Sumner's evidence, 4th Report, Select Committee, 1772, *Reports*, iii. 466.
[3] Ibid. iii. 532–4.
[4] Directors to Bengal, 19 Feb. 1766, *Fort William–India House Corr.* iv. 146–7.
[5] Sykes to Clive, 5 Aug. 1766, I.O.L., MS. Eur. G. 37, box 41.
[6] Clive to R. Smith, 31 Aug. 1766, N.L.W., Clive MSS., 228, p. 93.
[7] Select Committee Proceedings, 3 Sept. 1766, *Reports*, iii. 523–4.
[8] Directors to Bengal, 17 May 1766, *Fort William–India House Corr.* iv. 189.
[9] The evidence is assembled in the 4th Report, Secret Committee, 1773, *Reports*, iv. 194–5.

The Society of Trade was intended to provide the Company's servants with a profit, the Company with a revenue and the population with salt and betel nut at reasonable prices. (In the event the Society did no trading in tobacco.) The Society certainly succeeded in its first purpose, but it defaulted on its payments of duty to the Company and the available evidence strongly suggests that it kept the price of salt at an artificially high level.

When the Society was instituted, Clive anticipated that at the lowest estimate it would show a profit of 50 per cent on its dealings with 100 per cent as the 'most sanguine' estimate.[1] One of the Society's critics produced figures for its first two years of operation, whose authenticity was never denied, showing that the higher estimate was the more accurate one. On the first year's capital of £262,420 the profit was £238,619; on the second £199,875 was distributed on £260,000. These profits went to sixty and sixty-one persons in the two years. Individual shares varied in the first year from Clive's £21,179, all of which he gave away, to a Councillor's £8,472 and a Factor's £1,412.[2] Handsome as these rewards were for a trade which involved no risk or exertion for most of its participants, Clive and others defended them as a reasonable compensation for the profits which senior servants would otherwise have made in their own private trade. William Sumner, who received nearly £23,000 profit for two years of the Society, argued that he and other Councillors would have done even better trading on their own behalf.[3]

From the point of view of the Company or the consumers of salt the advantages of the Society of Trade were much less obvious. It was calculated that a duty of 35 per cent on the first year of the Society's trade with 50 per cent on the second amounted to £635,000 in all owed by the Society to the Company. By 1771 the Society had in fact only paid £256,342.[4]

The price at which salt was sold to the consumer in Bengal traditionally had very little relation to its cost. The Society's salt was no exception. The Society seems to have paid its contractors between Rs 70 and Rs 90 for one hundred maunds of salt.[5] It

---

[1] J. Malcolm, *Life of Robert Lord Clive* (1836), iii. 102.
[2] W. Bolts, *Considerations*, i. 180–4.
[3] Evidence in 4th Report of Select Committee, 1773, *Reports*, iii. 466.
[4] Ibid. iv. 108–10.
[5] Rs 75 was paid to contractors at Burdwan; Rs 87 at Dacca and Chittagong (B.P.C., 2 Sept. 1765, *Reports*, iv. 206–7).

then had to pay a duty of Rs 31. 8 annas on 100 maunds to the Company in the first year, rising to Rs 45 in the second. The Society also had to meet the costs of transporting the salt to market: in its second year all the salt was taken over comparatively short distances from the coastal salt pans to Calcutta, but in the first year it might have to be carried to destinations as remote as Patna. Transporting salt was costly and it was usual to allow for losses of 10 per cent on long journeys.[1] The Society paid Rs 58 per 100 maunds to a European who was shipping a consignment to Nabobganj in northern Bengal.[2] Allowing for generous margins, it would seem that, at the most, salt ready for sale in Calcutta could have cost the Society Rs 150 per 100 maunds and perhaps Rs 200 at Patna. The price at which the Society began its auctions of salt to Indian merchants at Calcutta was said to be Rs 215 per 100 maunds,[3] although in the second year of its operations the Society limited itself to Rs 200. At Patna prices at the Society's sales were said to vary between Rs 350 and Rs 400.[4] At Midnapur the Society asked for Rs 200 for salt in an area which produced abundant salt.[5] At Dacca, another salt-producing area, the Society's prices varied between Rs 200 and Rs 320.[6] When he set up the Society Clive prophesied that 'salt in general will be sold at a much lower price than formerly'.[7] Most of the evidence is to the contrary. Even Clive's disciple Verelst admitted that prices had sometimes been as low as Rs 100 per 100 maunds at Calcutta from 1760 to 1765.[8] At Dacca, far from selling his salt at 15 per cent below the average price of the past twenty years, as he was officially supposed to do, the Society's agent discovered that prices for the previous ten years had varied between Rs 150 and Rs 175 per 100 maunds,[9] but started his sales at Rs 245. William Bolts, a hostile witness, quoted three sets of prices at which he

---

[1] A. Keir, *Thoughts on the Affairs of Bengal* (1772), p. 77.

[2] Calcutta High Court Records, Mayor's Court, *Grant* v. *Bellah and Kerperam Metre*.

[3] Notes on salt prices, I.O.L., MS. Eur. G. 37, box 81.

[4] Verelst, *Rise and Progress*, pp. 116–17.

[5] *Bengal District Records: Midnapur 1763–7*, ed. W. K. Firminger (Calcutta, 1914), p. 47.

[6] Dr. Semple's evidence, 4th Report, Select Committee, 1773, *Reports*, iii. 470.

[7] Letter to R. Palk, 23 Nov. 1765, N.L.W., Clive MSS., 223, p. 52.

[8] Verelst, *Rise and Progress*, p. 116.

[9] Notes on salt prices, I.O.L., MS. Eur. G. 37, box 81.

personally had sold salt at Patna between 1762 and 1765: the lowest was Rs 268; the highest, Rs 331,[1] was still lower than the Society's price. Indian salt merchants' reaction to the Society's price of Rs 200 at Midnapur was to tell its agent that 'they dare not venture to buy at such an enhanced price'.[2] When the Society was abolished, salt prices fell throughout Bengal. Two Indian salt merchants later described how they had made large purchases 'at a time (it being just after the dissolution of the Society of Salt Trade) when the price of this article was high and would have afforded a large profit to your petitioners. The opportunity of so beneficial a sale did not continue long. The effects of a free and open trade were more extensively felt and were naturally accompanied with a great reduction in the price of that article.'[3] In 1768, when the Company again tried to fix the price at which salt would be sold to Indian merchants, they put it at Rs 140 per 100 maunds (including a duty of Rs 30) for Calcutta and Dacca.[4] Perhaps the most damning epitaph on the Society was written by Clive himself. By 1771 he was prepared to admit in private that 'the price to the natives was too great and so was the advantage to the servants'.[5]

Clive's hopes that private profit and public welfare could be harmoniously combined in the Society of Trade were frustrated by the determination of those who actually managed the Society to ensure that it made the highest possible profits. No doubt Clive was not personally responsible for the detailed running of the Society, but his unwillingness or his inability to impose strict standards on those subordinates whom he trusted, as opposed to the mass of the service whom he chastised with gusto, seriously weakened the effect of his reforms in other areas, apart from trading practices.[6]

Clive's strategy for the reform of private trade was to try to combine the elimination of abuses with an adequate income for the senior servants by regulating trade through the Society, while at the same time curbing opportunities for unregulated trade, where he supposed that abuses were rife. At one point he even

[1] Evidence in 4th Report, Select Committee, 1773, *Reports*, iii. 468.
[2] *Midnapur District Records 1763–7*, p. 47.
[3] I.O.R., B.R.C., 27 July 1773, Range 49, vol. 40, pp. 2646–7.
[4] Select Committee Proceedings, 7 Oct. 1768, *Reports*, iv. 197.
[5] Letter to Hastings, 1 Aug. 1771, Add. MS. 29132, f. 435.
[6] See below, p. 206.

proclaimed that 'the prohibition of a free inland trade . . . must now take place and be confined to imports and exports'. If individuals felt their livelihood endangered, the existence of the Society would 'obviate all complaints'.[1] An over-all prohibition of 'inland trade' was entirely impractical, and Clive's order had no effect. Some more specific limitations were, however, imposed on the trade of individuals outside the Society, which did produce results. Vansittart's orders that all Europeans not in the Company's service must be recalled to Calcutta were repeated.[2] A number of junior servants were also brought back to Calcutta from up-country factories or residencies, where they had enjoyed lucrative opportunities for trading.[3] The cutting of timber in the Purnea forests and the supply of *chunam* to Calcutta from Sylhet, in both of which Europeans had been profitably involved, were again made monopolies of the Nawabs, although those who were now excluded believed that the real beneficiary was Francis Sykes, Clive's nominee as Resident at the Nawab's court.[4] Clive's successor Verelst took action against English commercial penetration into Oudh, which had begun in 1764 after the Wazir had entered the war on the side of Mir Kasim.[5] Both the Raja of Banaras and the Wazir of Oudh complained about malpractices by private traders and their *gumashtas*. Saltpetre farms were being taken by the English, who refused to pay duties or to recognize the authority of the Wazir's officials. In 1768 the Council decided that passes or *dastaks* should no longer be given to *gumashtas* going to Oudh and later ordered that all *gumashtas* be expelled from Oudh. Once the order had been issued, the Wazir seized a number of *gumashtas* and deported them forcibly, much to the annoyance of private traders, who claimed heavy losses; William Bolts, the only member of the Johnstone partnership still in India, put his at Rs 150,000.[6]

In trying to confine trade to a limited group, whose activities could be controlled, Clive and Verelst were acting very much in

---

[1] Select Committee Proceedings, 3 Sept. 1766, *Reports*, iii. 524.

[2] I.O.R., Select Committee Proceedings, 11 May, 5, 25 Oct. 1765, Range A, vol. 6, pp. 395, 653, 688–9.

[3] Ibid., 10 Sept. 1766, Range A, vol. 7, p. 149.

[4] Ibid., 19 Feb. 1766, Range A, vol. 7, p. 14; R. Barwell to R. Leycester, 15 Sept. 1766, *B.P.P.*, ix (1914), 94.

[5] See above, p. 128.

[6] Verelst, *Rise and Progress*, appendix, pp. 183–91; Bolts. *Considerations*, ii. 85–98.

the traditions of the Bengal service. Rewards were graded according to seniority, as they had been in the various schemes to regulate the seaborne trade, such as 'the freight ships'.[1] Restrictions on the inland trade were as much resented by junior servants or Free Merchants as restrictions on shipping had been. Ambitious men were not prepared to see themselves excluded from the salt trade or given only a small part of its rewards, while other opportunities for trade were closed down. To such men it seemed that Clive and Verelst were not trying to provide an equitable solution which would reconcile the very diverse interests involved in internal trade, but that they were simply creating a monopoly for their own benefit and for that of other senior servants. These accusations might be unfair, but Clive and Verelst had liberally supplied their enemies with ammunition. The high prices and high profits on the Society of Trade's salt were one obvious example. The great fortune made by Sykes as Resident at the Nawab's court, a post which gave him every opportunity to exploit the Nawab's trading monopolies was another; yet another was a story that the Council had used the authority of the Nawab to sell a large consignment of their Gujarat cotton through the *zamindars* at a rigged price.[2] There were suspicions that *gumashtas* were thrown out of Oudh and Banaras, not to protect the interests of the Wazir of Oudh but to protect the trade of the army officers stationed there, particularly of Colonel Richard Smith, the maker of another great fortune.[3]

Those with grievances could take their revenge at home. Clive and Verelst were to suffer a great deal from Bolts, who felt that he had suffered much from them. Not only had his trade been brought to an abrupt end in Oudh, but he himself had been forcibly deported from Bengal on Verelst's orders, leaving huge sums uncollected behind him.[4] On Bolts's instigation Verelst was prosecuted in London by two of the Armenian *gumashtas* who had been ordered out of Oudh in 1768. Bolts also linked his cause with those of other enemies of Clive, such as his old trading partner, John Johnstone, whom Clive had forced to leave India in 1765.[5] In 1772

---

[1] See above, p. 74.

[2] Bolts, *Considerations*, i. 196; R. Barwell to T. Rumbold, 15 Nov. 1772, I.O.L., MS. Eur. D. 535, pt. ii, f. 115.

[3] Bolts, *Considerations*, ii. 100.

[4] They are listed by his agents in I.O.R., B.P.C., 16 Jan. 1770, Range 1, vol. 46, ff. 100–3.

[5] See below, p. 175.

Clive and Verelst came under fierce attack from Bolts in the first volume of his *Considerations on India Affairs*, which attracted a great deal of public attention. The Society of Trade was judged unsympathetically by both the Select and the Secret Committee of the House of Commons, which were investigating the affairs of the Company, and it was eventually made one of the charges against Clive which were debated in the Commons.[1]

Clive's attempts to solve the problem, created by Plassey, of how to regulate European private trade in the absence of an effective Nawab were in the end discredited and rejected. But over the next few years solutions were to be devised which were not radically different from his, but which were acceptable to British opinion and were to fix lasting limits within which European participation in Bengal's internal trade could develop. Clive had used two weapons against abuses of trade: prohibitions (on the use of European agents, on trade in Oudh and Banaras, on participation in the *chunam* or timber trades), and carefully regulated monopolies (the Society of Trade). His successors in India, notably Warren Hastings, and the Directors at home, as well as the national government in its Regulating Act of 1773, were to use the same weapons, but in general they were able to avoid the accusations of partiality which had discredited Clive's use of them.

Prohibitions were applied to trading by certain kinds of European and to trade in certain commodities. The majority of the Company's servants were, in the course of time, to be excluded from most forms of trade, commerce being left to those Europeans not in the Company's service, who in the new British Bengal were to trade within a framework of legal restraint enforced on them by non-trading Company's servants. Thus political power and trade were to be kept separate, at least in theory. In addition, no European trade was to be permitted in certain articles. The famous trinity of salt, betel nut, and tobacco was put out of bounds, as was the rice trade. Monopolies were set up over saltpetre, salt, and opium, but this time for the benefit of the Company not of individuals. But outside the prohibited commodities or the Company monopolies a considerable area was still left open for private enterprise. The oldest trades of all, in textiles and in goods imported from Europe were still free, as were items such as

---

[1] The attack on Clive and Verelst is described in L. S. Sutherland, *The East India Company in eighteenth-century politics* (Oxford, 1952), pp. 219–22, 255–8.

indigo or sugar in which Europeans became heavily involved by
the end of the eighteenth century. They were of course also free to
develop new products such as jute or tea in the following century.
Within these limits, devised for the most part in the 1770s, a very
large private European sector to Bengal's economy was to grow
up in the nineteenth century.

The exclusion of Company servants from trading began with
the Governor, traditionally the greatest private merchant in
Calcutta. On 19 September 1766 Clive took an oath to renounce
all trade and thus to put himself on a different footing from
previous Governors, who 'too eager in the pursuit of private
interest have interested themselves in affairs which could not be
reconciled to the strict principles of integrity'.[1] The following
year the Directors issued instructions that all future Governors
were to take a similar oath.[2] Members of the Bengal Council were
permitted to continue trading for the time being, but when a new
Supreme Council was set up by the Regulating Act of 1773, its
members were prohibited from 'any dealing or transactions, by
way of traffick or commerce of any kind whatsoever'.[3]

The increasing administrative responsibilities acquired by the
Company, especially after the grant of the *diwani* in 1765, meant
that, if the principle of preventing those who exercised political
power from using it to further their trade was to be applied
effectively, prohibitions would have to be enforced well below the
rank of Councillor. Clive wanted as many servants as possible
to be kept from temptation by confining the majority of the
service to the large factories. In September 1766 he responded
to 'daily complaints . . . of the violence and insults offered to the
servants of the government and agents of the private merchants
by the Company's servants residing at the different aurungs' by
calling in many of those stationed in outlying districts.[4] After the
grant of the *diwani*, however, more Company servants were again
dispersed over the countryside. In 1769 and 1770 Verelst made
a series of appointments of so-called Supervisors, who assumed
what amounted to direct authority over the administration of

---

[1] I.O.R., Select Committee Proceedings, 19 Sept. 1766, Range A, vol. 7,
p. 160.
[2] Directors to Bengal, 20 Nov. 1767, *Fort William–India House Corr.*, v. 60.
[3] 13 Geo. III, c. 63, sec. 23.
[4] I.O.R., Select Committee Proceedings, 10 Sept. 1766, Range A, vol. 7,
p. 149.

certain districts. Verelst was understandably apprehensive about 'the commercial views' of his new Supervisors.[1] They were certainly in a strong position to control the trade of their new districts, as Mughal *faujdars* had done before them, and it was commonly supposed that they took their chances with both hands. In 1771 a group of Councillors living in Calcutta tried to organize a joint trade to be carried on by Indian *gumashtas* sent up-country, but they found that their efforts were repeatedly blocked by 'the superior advantages of the gentlemen living in the districts'.[2] On his return to Bengal as Governor in 1772, Hastings was told that 'the trade in every district is engrossed by the Supravisor, but more especially rice and the other necessaries of life ... A member of the Board lately declared to me that he could not send an agent into the country for the purchase of a single article in it without applying to the Supravisor for his permission; and if it was granted it was looked upon as an encroachment.'[3] Allegations of this sort are not easy to substantiate, but the papers of one Supervisor, John Grose of Rangpur, show that he was an ambitious trader. He intended his trade 'to proceed to a trot and afterwards to a gallop', but an early death left his estate burdened with debts for money raised from his banian and other Indian creditors.[4]

Like Clive, Hastings felt that the dispersal of Company servants throughout Bengal would, because of their trading activities, do more harm than good. He was able to obtain the recall of some Supervisors in 1773, but in general he could not reverse the trend towards employing more Europeans in the administration of Bengal. If Europeans were deemed indispensable, ways of restraining their trading would have to be devised. Significantly, the members of the so-called Provincial Councils, who replaced the Supervisors in 1773, were bound not to trade by making advance payments for 'any such articles as contribute to the subsistence of the natives, and cannot be dealt in without oppression to them'.[5] When the Regulating Act of 1773 was received in Bengal, it was

[1] A. Majed Khan, *The Transition in Bengal 1756–1775* (Cambridge, 1969), p. 215.
[2] I.O.R., B.P.C., 27 Dec. 1771, Range 1, vol. 49, f. 434.
[3] Letter to Sir G. Colebrooke, 26 Mar. 1772, Add. MS. 29127, ff. 12–13.
[4] J. Grose to N. Grose, 23 Dec. 1770, J. Holme to N. Grose 25 Nov. 1771, I.O.L., MS. Eur. E. 284; his inventory is in I.O.R., Mayor's Court Records, Range 155, vol. 2, pp. 151–2.
[5] I.O.R., B.R.C., 23 Nov. 1773, Range 49, vol. 42, p. 3663.

found that it had gone much further. All servants 'employed or concerned in the collection of the revenues, or the administration of justice' were now to be prohibited from all trade.[1] Other servants could still trade: those employed in the Company's offices in Calcutta (and therefore presumably without any local influence) kept their right until 1789,[2] while the Company's commercial servants were never restricted.

While some servants were having permission to trade taken away from them, all were losing the advantage of the *dastak* the immunity from paying customs duties which Englishmen had cherished for so long. In April 1771 the Directors had ordered that a sweeping attack should be made on the complexities of the Bengal customs system in order to replace it with a system of 'free and equal trade throughout these provinces'. All exceptions and immunities, including the *dastak*, must be abolished.[3] These orders were carried out by Hastings in 1773. The administration of the Nawabs' customs was now placed under European supervision. A flat rate in future was to be collected from all traders, European and Indian, including the Company's servants, at $2\frac{1}{2}$ per cent at a limited number of government customs houses. All *zamindari* or other tolls and duties collected on goods in transit at *chauki* posts were ordered to be abolished.[4]

Not only were some Europeans excluded altogether from trading, but all Europeans were excluded from trade in certain commodities, either because they were specifically reserved for Indians or because they had become monopolies of the Company. Private European dealing in Bihar saltpetre had been officially forbidden since 1758, when it became a monopoly for the Company by grant of Mir Jafar. By 1773 salt, betel nut, tobacco, food grains, and opium were also prohibited.

Under the regulations drawn up for the Society of Trade contracts for salt-making had been given to private Europeans for most of the salt pans, but all the salt which they made had to be supplied to the Society. These regulations were condemned root and branch by the Court of Directors. The Company's Secretary told Clive that 'the natives' had 'a natural right to an open trade'

[1] 13 Geo. III, c. 63, sec. 27.
[2] I.O.R., B.P.C., 4 Mar. 1789, Range 3, vol. 43, pp. 601–3.
[3] Directors to Bengal, 10 Apr. 1771, *Fort William–India House Corr.*, vi. 82.
[4] I.O.R., B.R.C., 16 Feb., 23 Mar. 1773, Range 49, vol. 38, pp. 806–7, 1028–48.

in salt,[1] and in November 1767 orders were sent to Bengal forbidding participation by Europeans either in making or in selling salt.[2] After the Society of Trade had completed the third year of of its operations, the Directors' instructions were complied with. From October 1768 Europeans were to have no concern in the salt trade. The salt pans were to be worked by Indians, who would sell their salt to Indian merchants.[3] But decreeing the exclusion of Europeans and actually enforcing it were quite different matters. At factories and residencies where Company servants were well established, like Dacca, Midnapur or Burdwan, they clearly had no intention of being parted from what they regarded as their salt pans. Continuing European participation could easily be disguised under Indian names. For instance, detailed accounts kept by the Resident at Midnapur show that he and his assistant kept control of the salt production of the district under this form of disguise.[4] The Directors had second thoughts in 1770 and issued fresh instructions that making salt and dealing in it should be free to all, Europeans as well as Indians. These instructions were duly enacted in December 1770,[5] but their chief effect seems merely to have been to enable covert European participation to continue openly. The scale of European participation in the early 1770s is suggested by the experience of members of the Council who tried to order salt in 1771, but found that no salt boilers would accept their money without the permission of the Company servants stationed in the district.[6] Reviewing the situation since the winding up of the Society of Trade, Hastings concluded that 'the abolition of the great monopoly I fear has had no other effect than to establish several lesser ones in its stead . . . the Chief of every southern district and factory then, and the Supravisor now, enjoy the sole benefit of the salt trade.'[7]

Since free competition for the salt pans had proved to be unattainable, Hastings decided to create another 'great monopoly'; this time to be a monopoly for the benefit of the Company rather

---

[1] G. W. Forrest, *The Life of Lord Clive* (1918), ii. 359.
[2] Directors to Bengal, 20 Nov. 1767, *Fort William–India House Corr.* v. 57–8.
[3] Select Committee Proceedings, 7 Oct. 1768, *Reports*, iv. 197–9.
[4] Accounts of G. Vansittart and J. Peiarce, Bodleian, dep. b. 89.
[5] I.O.R., B.P.C., 12 Dec. 1770, Range 1, vol. 47, f. 284.
[6] Ibid., 27 Dec. 1771, Range 1, vol. 49, f. 434.
[7] Letter to Sir G. Colebrooke, 20 Apr. 1772, Add. MS. 29127, f. 35.

than for the benefit of its servants. From October 1772 all the salt pans were to be taken over by the Company, who would sell the right to make salt for five years to the highest bidder. The farmer of the salt pans would deliver his salt to the Company who would auction it to the salt dealers.[1] Hastings believed that the Directors would not accept any proposal which allowed the Company servants to compete for the five-year farms of the salt pans,[2] and so they were expressly excluded. They were, however, free to deal in salt sold at the Company's auctions for another year or so, until the Regulating Act of 1773 finally laid down that no European be 'concerned directly or indirectly' in the salt trade.[3]

The new regulations could be evaded as easily as the old ones had been. Company servants continued to control their local salt pans, as they had done for some years past. When the pans were put up for auction, the successful bids came from Company servants under Indian names. The Dacca salt works were still held after 1772 by the Chiefs, who divided the profits among the servants of the factory.[4] The same thing happened at Lakshmipur,[5] while at Burdwan the Europeans allowed the *zamindar* to hold the contract but collected a commission from him.[6] Such contracts could be extremely profitable. The salt boilers could be made to deliver extra salt for which they did not receive payment, and additional quantities over and above the amount he had contracted for with the Company could be clandestinely sold at his own price by the contractor. By such devices 'a tollerable profit of at least 200 per cent' could be realized.[7] In one instance profits of Rs 30,000 were reported on an outlay of Rs 14,000.[8] By the later 1770s, however, European participation in the salt trade seems to have been declining. In part this may have been due to a vigorous investigation conducted by the Council in 1775, which exposed several fictitious contracts. But the fall in salt prices throughout Bengal, generally attributed to large imports by sea of cheap salt from

---

[1] B.R.C., 7 Oct. 1772, *Reports*, vi. 187.
[2] Letter to J. Graham, 20 Oct. 1772, Add. MS. 29125, f. 162.
[3] 13 Geo. III, c. 63, sec. 27.
[4] I.O.R., B.R.C., 21 Apr. 1775, Range 49, vol. 52, pp. 356–7.
[5] Ibid., 25 July 1775, Range 49, vol. 54, pp. 1337–49.
[6] Ibid., 5, 26 May 1775, Range 49, vols. 52, pp. 618–31; 53, pp. 115–32.
[7] J. Haliburton to D. Anderson, 18 Feb. 1774, Add. MS. 45431, f. 19.
[8] R. Barwell to J. Graham, 24 Mar. 1776, *B.P.P.*, xiv (1917), 234.

Orissa or Madras,[1] was probably a much more effective deterrent. By 1780 the Company could get no satisfactory offers to farm the salt pans near Calcutta,[2] which strongly suggests that Europeans now considered salt-making to be unprofitable and that the prohibitions of 1772 and 1773 were at last effective.

Betel nut and tobacco, commodities traditionally linked with salt since they had also been farmed by the Nawabs, were also forbidden to European traders by the Regulating Act, and rice was added to the list as a result of recent controversy. Trade in food grains was the greatest single element of Bengal's internal trade by a very wide margin. In general the profits on deals in grain were probably too small to attract much European participation, except in the supply of Calcutta or the Company's troops or for export to Madras. In 1773 the Collector of Dacca reported that the profit on the grain trade was 'inconsiderable unless in time of scarcity'.[3] But in 1773 Bengal was recovering from times of dire scarcity, from which arose the controversy about European grain dealings and the prohibition.

In 1769 and 1770 the rains failed over much of Bengal; as a result harvests were pitifully small and there was appalling loss of life. Such rice as was available rocketed in price. In normal years after the famine one rupee would buy 52 seers or about 110 lbs of rice at Murshidabad, one of the places worst affected by the famine;[4] at the height of the famine a rupee at Murshidabad would buy as little as five lbs of rice.[5] It was widely alleged that the situation had been made very much worse by speculators buying up such surpluses of rice as could be gathered in eastern and northern Bengal and forcing up prices at which they sold it in the famine areas. Allegations were specifically directed against two targets: Muhammad Reza Khan, the minister who was conducting the government in the name of the Nawab, and 'gomastahs belonging to the English gentlemen', who were said to be 'monopolising the rice'.[6] An account published in Britain spoke of 'the

[1] I.O.R., B.R.C., 17, 24 Oct. 1775, Range 49, vol. 56, pp. 160–70, 274–98; N. K. Sinha, *Midnapore Salt Papers* (Calcutta, 1954), pp. 5–7.

[2] Hastings to J. Scott, 28 Apr. 1781, Add. MS. 29128, ff. 337–8.

[3] I.O.R., Board of Customs, 21 Apr. 1773, Range 98, vol. 14.

[4] I.O.R., B.R.C., 9 Aug. 1774, Home Miscellaneous, 216, p. 70.

[5] National Archives of India, Secret and Separate Proceedings, 10 Mar. 1773, vol. 2C, p. 57.

[6] R. Becher to Council, Jan. 1770, ibid., 3 Mar. 1774, vol. 3A, p. 221.

English having engrossed all the rice, particularly in the Bahar and Purnea provinces'.[1] Much was to be made of such allegations; it came commonly to be assumed in Europe that private trading had 'caused' the famine. Two inquiries into famine trading were held in Bengal, neither of which produced concrete evidence against Europeans. The charges against Muhammad Reza Khan were examined by the Council who succeeded in exculpating him without implicating any Europeans.[2] The Council also tried to collect evidence on European involvement by asking for a list of *dastaks* issued for grain during the famine period. Perhaps not surprisingly, the replies that they received did not indicate large shipments.[3]

The lack of official evidence does not of course mean that Europeans had not been involved. Trading in grain was very widely diffused indeed, involving thousands of small transactions; so a system of European control comparable to that achieved in the salt trade was quite impracticable.[4] But a fairly high degree of organization existed for moving grain from surplus areas, such as Rangpur or Dacca, to large centres of population by way of markets, like that at Bakarganj, port for shipping the rice of the south east, or Azimganj in Hugli district, which was able to 'intercept the carriage of all grain towards Calcutta'.[5] It was theoretically possible for a European armed with political influence to corner supplies and manipulate prices at such places. But that they did so remains unproven. Such indications of European trading as have been found do not generally seem to have been on a scale to suggest that they were dominating the rice supply.[6] It is perhaps more likely that Europeans joined in rice trading to take advantage of high prices during the famine than that they were the creators of the high prices.

After the famine, a relatively limited trade in grain, especially for shipment to southern India, continued quite openly, in spite of the prohibition of the Regulating Act. Legal sanctions were not

[1] *Gentleman's Magazine*, xli (1771), 402.
[2] National Archives of India, Secret and Separate Proceedings, vols. 2C, 3A.
[3] I.O.R., B.P.C., 6, 26 Feb., 2 Mar. 1772, Range 1, vol. 51, ff. 148, 160, 198, 207–12, 220–1.
[4] There is much material on the working of the grain trade in West Bengal Archives, Committee of Grain Proceedings for 1783–5.
[5] I.O.R., B.R.C., 23 Mar. 1773, Range 49, vol. 38, p. 1088.
[6] Collected in N. K. Sinha, *Economic History of Bengal* (Calcutta, 1956–70), ii. 58–9.

needed to prevent large-scale participation in Bengal's internal grain supply; in normal times profits were too low to make it worth while.

Opium was the last major commodity to be taken out of private European hands. In 1773 Hastings decided, as he had done in the previous year over salt, to turn a private monopoly into a public one. At least since 1761 the servants stationed at Patna had been extending their control over the opium crop grown in Bihar.[1] By 1767 they had succeeded in establishing 'one general agent as manager and purchaser of all the opium produced'.[2] Trading in opium was described as the 'principal emolument' of the Patna factory. The annual crop was divided into shares, according to the seniority of the servants, for sale to the British East India Company, the Dutch, the other foreign companies, or to private shipowners.[3] The profits were enormous. At the very highest estimate opium could be produced at Patna for about Rs 200 per chest;[4] in the early 1770s, when British shipowners were competing avidly for opium in Calcutta, sales were made at Rs 550 per chest in 1772,[5] at Rs 650 in 1773,[6] and even at Rs 800 in 1774.[7]

In 1772 the Patna servants came into conflict with the Company, who insisted on buying more opium from them for export to Madras and Balambangan than they were prepared to sell at a price which they regarded as unreasonably low.[8] In the following year Hastings evidently decided that the Company should no longer be held to ransom in this way. All opium produced in Bihar and later in Bengal as well was declared to be the property of the Company, who would arrange for it to be sold in Calcutta. The opium was provided by official contractors, the contract becoming a valuable piece of patronage in the gift of the Governor General, since the price offered to the contractor was deliberately

---

[1] See above, p. 118.

[2] S. Sanyal, 'Ramchand Pandit's report on opium cultivation in 18th-century Bihar', *B.P.P.*, lxxxvii (1968), 184.

[3] Calcutta High Court Records, Mayor's Court, *Dallas, Stewart and McNeil* v. *Stephenson*.

[4] P. J. Marshall, *The Impeachment of Warren Hastings* (Oxford, 1965), p. 171.

[5] G. Vansittart to J. Price, 25 Oct. 1772, Bodleian, dep. b. 93, p. 38.

[6] Vansittart to J. Holland, 15 Apr. 1773, ibid., p. 132.

[7] Vansittart to R. Palk, 12 Mar. 1774, ibid., dep. b. 94, p. 70.

[8] Vansittart's letters to R. Barwell and to Hastings, 21 Sept. 1772, ibid., dep. b. 102, pp. 64–5.

inflated to give him some of the profits enjoyed for so long by the Patna servants.[1]

By 1773, with the passing of the Regulating Act and the creation of the opium monopoly the limits within which European private traders were permitted to operate in future were more or less complete. Whether they were effective or not was, of course, another matter. The enforcement of regulations in India was an intractable problem for most of the eighteenth century; Governors and Councils showed little relish for cutting off the advantages of their fellow servants, at best cutting them off selectively. So it should not be assumed that Company servants concerned with revenue administration immediately stopped trading after 1773 or that no private European ever again dealt in salt, betel nut, tobacco, rice, or opium.

Those who were trying to reform private trading were, however, fortunate in that the prohibitions were enacted and the monopolies created in a period of generally depressed trading conditions. A European trader had to ask himself not only whether a proposed deal was legal but whether it would be profitable. It is likely that the second consideration was as important in confining trade within narrower limits as the first.

Early in 1768 there were reports of 'a general complaint throughout the settlement of the extreme scarcity of silver'.[2] By the autumn the credit system on which European trade depended was breaking down. 'The scarcity of cash is already so sensibly felt in this country, that the almost universal bankruptcy of the shroffs has taken place', and 'business and trade' were said to be 'at a stand'.[3] In 1769 a group of European traders told the Council that 'the distress is so great, that, every merchant in Calcutta is in danger of becoming bankrupt . . . it being impossible to raise any large sum at any premium on bond'.[4] The famine years of 1769 and 1770 made a bad situation worse. 'An almost total stop . . . as well in publick as in private credit' was said to be continuing in December 1770.[5] In 1772 it was still the case that 'not a man will trust his brother without a trusty English security'.[6]

[1] Marshall, op. cit., pp. 167–71.
[2] Verelst to Clive, 5 Feb. 1768, I.O.L., MS. Eur. G. 37, box 51.
[3] Sykes to Clive, 12 Sept. 1768, ibid., box 54, f. 28.
[4] B.P.C., 20 Mar. 1769, Verelst, *Rise and Progress*, appendix, p. 242.
[5] D. Anderson to his father, 28 Dec. 1770, Add. MS. 45438, f. 24.
[6] T. Hancock to his wife, 23 Sept. 1772, Add. MS. 29236, f. 14.

In such conditions European traders would have been cautious whatever regulations they were obliged to operate under. A senior servant commented in 1771 that Europeans were again permitted to deal openly in salt and betel nut, but 'such is the state of trade that no man can now with safety venture abroad his property'.[1] In the early 1760s newly arrived Writers launched into trade as soon as they could scrape together some credit from their patrons or from their banians; in 1770 a new Writer was warned that trade was 'dangerous even to the most experienced people—from the dullness of the markets, the want of money and credit in the settlement, and the distress the country has suffered from famine'.[2] At Murshidabad another young Company servant found in 1772 that 'trade is at so low an ebb that I really can scarcely employ any sum to advantage here'.[3] At Dacca trade was said in 1773 to be 'very precarious'.[4] Unfavourable conditions took their toll of trading ventures. Detailed accounts survive of a partnership between a civil servant and a Colonel in the Company's army. In four years between 1773 and 1777 the partners lost Rs 60,000 in trading in silk, muslins, sugar and salt under the management of the Colonel's banian.[5] It was in this period that Samuel Middleton's ambitions, supported by a borrowed capital of Rs 1,600,000, came to grief.[6] In November 1775 an experienced Calcutta merchant wrote bleakly that 'no advantages are to be derived . . . from the inland trade'.[7]

This was over pessimistic. But it is undoubtedly true that a combination of closer regulation and trade depression had brought to an end conditions in which Europeans could borrow huge sums and be assured of earning large profits on them by the judicious use of their newly won political power. Such conditions only survived in the remoter parts of Bengal and presumably in Bihar, where there were no effective checks on the activities of isolated Europeans. In the old battle grounds of the 1760s monopolies were still being maintained by force many years later. Robert Lindsay, Collector of Sylhet, has left an engaging account of his

---

[1] T. Kelsall to Clive, 13 Apr. 1771, I.O.L., MS. Eur. G. 37, box 61.
[2] G. Bogle to R. Bogle, 28 Dec. 1770, Mitchell Library, Bogle MSS.
[3] D. Anderson to his father, 12 Sept. 1772, Add. MS. 45438, f. 81.
[4] I.O.R., Board of Customs, 21 Apr. 1773, Range 98, vol. 14.
[5] Calcutta High Court Records, Supreme Court, Equity, *Dow* v. *Dow*.
[6] See above, p. 43.
[7] D. Killican to G. Graham, 30 Nov. 1775, S.R.O., GD 29/2061/4.

trading successes there.[1] The trade of Rangamati was still being described as 'de facto exclusive' in 1780.[2] The old order also survived outside the Company's official boundaries in Oudh and Banaras. In 1771 Europeans were once again allowed to send their *gumashtas* into Oudh and Banaras, but they were not allowed to claim exemptions from the Wazir's customs and from local duties.[3] They thus stood no chance against Europeans who could insist on exemptions and privileges, that is the army officers and the Company's Residents appointed to Lucknow and Banaras in 1773 and 1775 respectively. The Resident at Banaras won opium and saltpetre monopolies for himself;[4] the Resident at Lucknow had a saltpetre monopoly,[5] while one of his entourage who traded with the Resident's 'influence and interest' was able to avoid paying duties, to have his goods escorted by sepoys and to collect his debts by force; by these means his trade showed a profit of 50 per cent.[6]

In most parts of Bengal profits of this order were a thing of the past by the 1770s. But there were still large areas of trade which were both legal and profitable for European merchants. They still dealt extensively in the old staples of Bengal's trade, cotton piecegoods and silk, although there were frequent complaints that the Company's greatly increased exports to Britain were making it very hard for private individuals to get the goods they wanted. After the acquisition of the *diwani*, the Council were under instructions to invest as much of their surplus territorial revenue as possible in goods for London and their purchases doubled in value in five years.[7] Although it was often argued that the Company's cloth, and the textiles bought by private traders for Asian markets were of different kinds, conflicts arose. The Company insisted that it must have first priority: from 1766 no private individual was allowed to buy raw silk until the Company's indent for the year had been met;[8] in 1775 this principle was

[1] *Lives of the Lindsays*, ed. Lord Lindsay (1849), iii. 176 ff.

[2] G. Bogle to Hastings, 16 July 1780, Add. MS. 29145, f. 315.

[3] I.O.R., B.P.C., 26 June 1771, Range 1, vol. 49, pp. 180–2.

[4] J. Benn's evidence, *Minutes of the Evidence taken at the Trial of Warren Hastings* (1788–94), i. 329–30.

[5] W. Paxton's and N. Middleton's evidence, Committee of Managers, Add. MS. 24266, pp. 340–1, 346.

[6] Calcutta High Court Records, Supreme Court, Equity, *Hyde* v. *Ojagur Mull.*   [7] Figures in 3rd Report, Secret Committee, 1773, *Reports*, iv. 61.

[8] I.O.R., Select Committee Proceedings, 27 Dec. 1766, Range A, vol. 7, p. 280.

extended to all goods purchased by the Company.[1] Conflicts also occurred about weavers. The Company insisted that those who accepted its 'advances' or who were in debt to it from previous years were bound to its service; private traders replied that greatly increased purchases by the Company meant that fewer and fewer weavers were ever free to make contracts with them. The actual extent to which private trade suffered is, however, difficult to assess. In 1768 the Governor thought that the 'private trade of your servants at every aurung' had been reduced to 'a degree almost of annihilation'.[2] Probably more realistic assessments of the output of cotton cloth at Dacca in 1776 put its total value at between Rs 2,500,000 and Rs 3,000,000 of which the Company only took Rs 500,000, leaving Rs 600,000 for the purchases of the Company servants and very substantial amounts for Free Merchants.[3]

Increased 'investments' in textiles by the Company may have encroached at times on the private trade of Europeans, but there were ample compensations for them; in the 1770s the Company bought more and more of its silk and piecegoods from European merchants. In the past Company servants had frequently sold their own goods to their employers, but they had been forced to do so clandestinely. The Directors had ruled against purchases from Europeans, since they believed with good reason that servants were not likely to drive hard bargains on the Company's behalf with themselves or their friends.[4] In the 1770s, however, these prohibitions were relaxed and Europeans were permitted to supply the Company.

The first investment contracts openly made with Europeans were for raw silk. Of all the Company's textile exports, silk appeared to be the one with the largest capacity for expansion. While Bengal piecegoods were beginning to encounter competition from an increasingly mechanized English cotton industry, English silk manufacturers were still petitioning for more raw silk shipments. To meet this demand the Company launched an ambitious scheme in 1769 to improve the quality of Bengal silk. Silk was in future to be wound not in the traditional Bengal manner, but in the Italian way. Silk filatures with the necessary equipment

[1] West Bengal Archives, Board of Trade Proceedings, 18 Oct. 1775, vol. 5, pp. 81–2.
[2] Verelst to Directors, 28 Mar. 1768, I.O.L., MS. Eur. G. 37, box 52, f. 123.
[3] B.R.C., 19 July, [Sept.] 1776, *Reports*, vi. 214, 233.
[4] See below, p. 161.

were to be set up, and French and Italian artisans were shipped to India to instruct Bengali silk winders in the new techniques.[1] The new filatures were elaborate undertakings, with large numbers of 'basons', each heated by its own furnace, in which the silk was separated from the cocoon, ovens, and warehouses. The first filatures were built by the Company at its own expense, but individuals soon began to set up their own and to offer the silk to the Company. In 1774 and 1775 the first four contracts were given to Europeans, all Company servants, to produce the new filature silk at Jahangerpur, Malda, Khumarkali, and Radnagur.[2] More Europeans were encouraged to invest in silk works; James Keighley, who was the Company's Commercial Resident at Boalia, put up five separate filatures of his own;[3] a partnership of four Europeans spent £4,000 on buildings for new works at Kasimbazar.[4] By 1782 all but four of the fourteen silk contractors employed by the Company were Europeans, most of them being the Chiefs or Residents at the Company's factories.[5] Those who managed to obtain contracts to provide the Company's silk were liberally rewarded for the expenses they incurred in setting up new works; the full extent of the Company's unwitting generosity was revealed in a series of prosecutions for collusion in making excessive profits begun against the contractors and those who awarded the contracts.[6]

Official sanction for the purchase of cotton piecegoods for the Company from Europeans (as opposed to clandestine purchases which had gone on for many generations) was not given until 1782. In that year a system of purchasing piecegoods by contract, similar to the method used for a time for raw silk, was introduced. Europeans were now permitted to compete 'openly in their own names' for piecegood contracts, and it was agreed that Company servants should in general be given the preference when the contracts were awarded.[7] In the first list there were fourteen

---

[1] *Reports and Documents connected with . . . the culture and manufacture of cotton-wool, raw silk, and indigo in India* (1836), pt. ii, ix–xix.

[2] West Bengal Archives, Board of Trade Proceedings, 24 Mar., 25 July, 12 Sept. 1775, 24 Feb. 1787, vols. 2, p. 236; 4, pp. 134–5, 437–9; 53, pp. 132–5.

[3] *East India Company* v. *Keighley*, P.R.O., C 12/2431/25.

[4] *East India Company* v. *Aldersey et al.*, P.R.O., C 12/175/27.

[5] West Bengal Archives, Board of Trade Proceedings, 8 Aug. 1782, vol. 32, p. 583.   [6] See below, pp. 200–1.

[7] West Bengal Archives, Board of Trade Proceedings, 11, 19 June 1782, vol. 31, pp. 637–50, 698.

European contracts and only four Indians.[1] A valuable piecegood contract could make a man's fortune, as Charles Grant, the Commercial Resident at Malda and later one of the most distinguished Chairmen of the East India Company at home, was to discover.[2] In the manufacture of piecegoods there was less incentive than in silk winding for Europeans to try to introduce any technological innovations. A Free Merchant called John Prinsep, founder of a famous Bengal dynasty, did, however, make an interesting attempt to adapt British methods of printing calicoes to make printed cloth called chintz. In 1773 Prinsep was given a grant of land by the Company with a loan to set up a chintz manufactory. He sold his chintz to the Company from 1773 until 1783, when, after protests from British calico printers against unfair competition, his contract was withdrawn and the factory closed down.[3]

Not only did private British merchants supply a large part of their own Company's exports of textiles, but they were also involved in extensive dealings with the foreign companies. These transactions, although clearly illegal, began early in the eighteenth century, an indication of the ascendancy that British traders had gained over other Europeans long before Plassey. For seven years in the 1740s the Dutch placed a valuable contract for Dacca piecegoods with an English Company servant.[4] Once the British became the effective rulers of Bengal, foreign companies had even stronger incentives to obtain their goods through Englishmen. The Dutch became ever more dependent on the British;[5] in the last trading season before news of the outbreak of the Anglo-Dutch war of 1780 reached India they placed orders worth ten lakhs of rupees (£100,000) with a single British merchant.[6] When the Danes began to increase their exports from Bengal in the 1770s, they too obtained a large proportion of them from British sources.[7]

Throughout the eighteenth century there had been much European trading in sugar because of its importance in Bengal's

[1] West Bengal Archives, Board of Trade Proceedings, 10 Aug. 1782, vol. 32, pp. 620–32.

[2] A. T. Embree, *Charles Grant and British Rule in India* (1962), pp. 76–8.

[3] P. J. Marshall, 'Private British investment in eighteenth-century Bengal', *B.P.P.*, lxxxvi (1967), 59–60.

[4] Capt. Fenwicke's letters [1751], I.O.L., Orme MSS., 'India', vi. 1545.

[5] H. Furber, *John Company at Work* (Cambridge, Mass., 1951), pp. 81–2.

[6] O. Feldbaek, *Indian Trade under the Danish Flag, 1772–1808* (Copenhagen, 1969), p. 56.   [7] Ibid., pp. 26 ff.

exports to western India, the Persian Gulf and the Red Sea. But it was not until after Plassey that Europeans appear to have taken an active part actually in growing sugar-cane or in manufacturing sugar. In 1774 a Free Merchant called James Christie was given a grant of land at Dinajpur in northern Bengal which he tried to clear for sugar-planting. Two much more ambitious projects followed in 1776. At Umedpur, near Calcutta, a group of four Company servants had seventy acres planted with sugar-cane and were distilling rum, as well as making silk at a large filature. At Sukhsagar, north of Calcutta, another group of Europeans, who called themselves 'the Bengal Commercial Society' were awarded a grant of up to 3,000 acres. By 1777 they had about two hundred acres under cane and had set up a sugar mill of the kind used in the West Indies. Sugar and rum made at Sukhsagar, where there was also a large silk filature, were eventually sold in Calcutta. In the long run, however, all three projects failed: Christie was dispossessed of his land and 'died in distress'; Rs 2,000,000 were said to have been spent at the Umedpur plantation with little to show for it; while Sukhsagar was eventually sold at what its proprietors called 'an incredible loss'. Behind all these failures there seems to have been a common delusion: that methods which succeeded in the West Indies would succeed in Bengal. In the West Indies planters had no alternative to growing sugar on their own plantations and crushing the cane in their own mills. In Bengal Indian cultivators could grow the cane and crush and boil it with hand-rollers and clay pots much more cheaply than Europeans could. This lesson was in time learnt by British sugar makers in Bengal. They made advances for coarse sugar to be delivered to them, from which they produced loaf sugar or rum or arrack. In 1791 the first shipment of Bengal sugar was sent to the London market.[1]

European involvement in indigo followed a similar course. It too was a crop indigenous to Bengal and especially to Bihar; but Europeans were not concerned in its manufacture until the British won political control of Bengal. The first European indigo factories seem to have been set up in 1778 or 1779, presumably stimulated by the cutting off of Britain's North American indigo by the revolt in the Thirteen Colonies. Some pioneers, such as John

---

[1] On early European sugar making, see my 'The Bengal Commercial Society of 1775', *Bulletin of the Institute of Historical Research*, xlii (1969), 181–7.

Prinsep[1] and at least one European at Chittagong,[2] tried to acquire land and grow their own indigo plants, but most found it more profitable to buy the plants grown by Indian cultivators, which they then processed at their factories. In 1783 the first indigo factory was opened in Bihar,[3] where much of the European indigo industry was later to be concentrated, and by 1785 there were said to be fourteen factories throughout the Company's provinces.[4] After many failures and tribulations, Bengal and Bihar became the largest suppliers of indigo to the British textile industry.[5] It is a clear indication of the vitality of private enterprise in Bengal and of the decline of the Company as a commercial body that the production of this potentially most important item of its trade was left entirely to individuals.

Other attempts by Europeans to develop Bengal's resources in the 1770s do credit to their optimism and to their versatility, if not necessarily to their sense of commercial realism. What were described as 'large pepper plantations' under the management of a man who had been trained in Sumatra were established at Chittagong.[6] In 1774 a group of Company servants financed the raising of coal from the large seams in western Bengal. They were given an exclusive grant to mine coal in the Birbhum area and a contract to deliver it to Calcutta. At least one consignment of coal was actually provided, but of too poor a quality to be usable, and the enterprise was abandoned.[7] Iron, lead, and copper were all worked for short periods with an equal lack of success. The iron deposits were also found in Birbhum, where attempts were made to cast cannon and shot. Archibald Keir, the great salt-trader of a previous generation, tried to mine lead in Bihar, but his grant was revoked. The copper was also mined in Bihar, the entrepreneur in this case being the ubiquitous John Prinsep, who

[1] I.O.R., B.R.C., 9 July, 2 Nov. 1779, Range 50, vols. 18, 20.
[2] A. M. Serajuddin, *The Revenue Administration of the East India Company in Chittagong 1761–85* (Chittagong, 1971), pp. 201–2.
[3] Calcutta Bar Library Club, Supreme Court Reports, xxxiii, report on *Grant and Pope* v. *Grand*.
[4] [J. Prinsep], *Strictures and Occasional Observations upon the British commerce with the East Indies* (1792), p. 163
[5] Early indigo ventures are described in my 'Private British investment', *B.P.P.*, lxxxvi. 59–61.
[6] E. Impey to Hastings, 26 July 1778, Add. MS. 29141, f. 179.
[7] P. B. Sinha, 'Early History of the Coal Mining Industry in India 1774–1833', *B.P.P.*, lxxxix (1970), 29–32.

proposed to mint a copper coinage for the Company. Some coins were actually produced, but Prinsep's project was showing a loss even before it was closed down on orders from London. The Directors were hostile to any development of Bengal's mineral resources which might detract from British exports of metals.[1]

European trading in Bengal seems to have passed through two more or lesss distinct phases in the later eighteenth century. Following Plassey there were twelve or fifteen years of generally high profits as Europeans invaded and eventually brought under their control certain trades, some of which had been subject to restriction and regulation under the Nawabs. Where this was the case, Europeans were able to maintain and even to intensify restrictions, so that very large profits could be extracted from commodities like salt, betel nut, and opium. Profits of 25 per cent in this period were quoted with pride as a sign of moderation.[2] The Society of Trade realized profits approaching 100 per cent on its salt, while the Bihar opium traders or the clandestine salt farmers after 1772 did even better.[3] By the 1770s, however, the credit system on which European trade depended was functioning uncertainly, the demand for goods at the level of prices which Europeans tried to enforce seems to have been contracting, and the political power which was so necessary to maintain high profits was being taken away from private traders. In the new phase it was no longer possible to seize existing monopolies and to exploit them ruthlessly for easy profits. Europeans had to create opportunities for themselves, often requiring the introduction of new skills or the commitment of fixed capital in new plant, such as silk filatures or indigo vats, for considerable periods. The transitory partnership of two or three Europeans with a trading capital raised for a short period on bond from Indians was beginning to be replaced by the more elaborate and more enduring House of Agency.

The post-Plassey phase has acquired an understandable notoriety. The methods employed in making trading fortunes in this period can hardly be defended. A successful Company servant did not attempt to do so, when he replied to one of his critics: 'We are men of power, you say, and take advantage of it. Why,

---

[1] Marshall, 'Private European investment', *B.P.P.*, lxxxvi, 62–3.
[2] Bolts, *Considerations*, ii. 191. [3] See above, pp. 143, 146.

man, what is the use of station if we are not to benefit from it?'[1]
There is abundant evidence that when violence or intimidation
were thought to be commercially advantageous, some Europeans
were prepared to resort to them. Europeans were able to apply
such methods to a considerable section of Bengal's trade; the
£500,000 claimed for losses in 1763 shows how large this section
was.[2] But European trading, even at this level, may only have
constituted a relatively small part of Bengal's total internal trade.
At the height of his disputes with the British Mir Kasim asserted
that 'every village and district in that province was ruined' by
their trade.[3] Some Englishmen were inclined to agree with him.
In 1769 Verelst wrote that the agents of European traders had
spread 'the baneful effects of monopoly and extortion on every
side of them', so that the provinces 'decline from their ancient
opulence, as from a state of unrivalled splendour, now to groan
under the pressure of indigence'.[4] Such statements have a hallowed
place in British-Indian historical writing. But indications of the
extent and variety of Bengal's internal trade, such as those given
at the beginning of the previous chapter, induce scepticism about
them. Whether any small group of men, however powerful and
ruthless, could have brought so vast and complex a system under
their control seems doubtful.

For the most part British private traders concentrated on certain
trades already under some degree of control. A number of official
government farms and monopolies existed in late Mughal Bengal.
The private enterprise of individuals had probably created others.
The tendency for Mughal noblemen to take an increasing interest
in trade has been noted throughout India, and Bengal appears to
have been no exception.[5] Even Mir Kasim himself, if the English
are to be believed, was a salt trader. He is reported to have bought
salt from an Englishman at Patna at Rs 500 for 100 maunds (a
price high even by the standards of the Society of Trade) with the
intention of 'stuffing it down the merchants' throats' at an even
higher price.[6] There was likely, however, to be a difference

---

[1] G. Vansittart to W. Holland, 27 Oct. 1771, Bodleian, dep. b. 92, p. 124.

[2] See above, p. 116.

[3] *Calendar of Persian Correspondence* (Calcutta, 1919–49), i. 194.

[4] I.O.R., Select Committee Proceedings, 11 Aug. 1769, Range A, vol. 9,
p. 411.

[5] A. Karim, *Murshid Quli Khan and his times* (Dacca, 1963), pp. 3, 217.

[6] H. Lushington to Carnac, 8 Apr. 1762, I.O.L., MS. Eur. F. 128, box 3/6.

between a British and a Mughal monopoly. A prominent Company servant could presumably raise larger sums and enforce restrictions more effectively than an Armenian who had bought a monopoly from the Nawab or a *faujdar* who was uncertain of his tenure. An Englishman, whose service went back well before Plassey, believed that 'English influence', exerted by 'the Company's servants and their banians and dependants', was now more damaging to the 'freedom of trade' than the 'many oppressions from the officers of the court and others' which had taken place under the Nawabs.[1] Within trades which the English succeeded in controlling, the malign effects of their control, so often pointed out then and since, no doubt occurred. Prices were forced up for the consumer, while the rewards of the producer were held down. In the case of salt, the Society of Trade undoubtedly succeeded in raising the price throughout Bengal, while a subsequent inquiry into conditions in the salt pans in the Twenty-four Parganas near Calcutta showed that payments made to the *mulangis* who boiled the salt remained static throughout the 1760s.[2] The same could presumably be said of betel nut, opium, *chunam* excavation, and the cutting of certain timbers. But these occupations did not constitute the whole economy of eighteenth-century Bengal.

From the 1770s European participation in Bengal's internal trade began to take more constructive forms. Some attempts were made to diversify Bengal's products and to develop existing ones. Europeans tried to raise the quality of Bengal's raw silk, indigo, or sugar by introducing new machinery and new expertise. There were a few bold experiments, such as Warren Hastings's botanical garden at Alipore, from which he hoped to spread cinnamon and other spices.[3] But little had been achieved by 1784. There were still too few Europeans with too limited resources. In 1784 Europeans were still for the most part drawing their profits from a traditional structure of trade, even if their activities were less predatory than they had been after Plassey.

[1] Minute of R. Becher, *Proceedings of the Controlling Council of Revenue at Murshidabad* (Calcutta, 1919–24), i. 220.

[2] I.O.R., B.R.C., 13, 20 Dec. 1774, Range 49, vol. 48, pp. 117–18, 186–200.

[3] P. J. Marshall, 'Warren Hastings as Scholar and Patron' in *Statesmen, Scholars and Merchants*, ed. A. Whiteman, J. S. Bromley and P. Dickson (Oxford, 1973), p. 251.

VII

Profits of Office: (I) Presents

So long as the British lacked effective political power in Bengal, the majority of Englishmen who aspired to make more than a bare subsistence paid to them by the Company in salaries or wages, had to do so by trading profits. Most individuals evidently had few inhibitions about supplementing their salaries by helping themselves to the Company's resources or by levying money from those Indians with whom they had dealings. But before 1757 opportunities for doing either were relatively limited. Compared with what it was to win later, the Company's funds were small and only a small section of the Indian population came into its orbit. After Plassey the situation changed rapidly. The Company was quickly enriched by Indian revenue, part of which went to individuals, either in a regular manner through increased official salaries, or in a less regular way through fraud, embezzlement or perquisites. Englishmen who began to wield political power throughout Bengal could now also collect money on their own behalf directly from Indians without having to wait for it to come to them through the Company.

The trade of the British community had greatly benefited from the conquest of Bengal, as previous chapters have tried to show, but from the point of view of private individuals its most important consequence was immensely to enhance the value of office in the Company's service for its own sake. In the short run, the conquest of Bengal set off a scramble among the Company's servants for spectacular presents and opportunities to loot the Bengal revenue system on a large scale. Fortunes were accumulated even more rapidly by these means than from the boom in the inland trade of the early 1760s. But in the long run conquest eventually produced an ordered hierarchy of civil and military offices, which offered security and moderate affluence to many. These developments will be examined in this and in the following chapter.

In the years before Plassey, opportunities for turning office in the Company's service to major personal gain were somewhat limited, but such chances as existed were enthusiastically taken. There is much evidence which suggests that servants had few scruples about defrauding their employers. The administration of the town of Calcutta was made to yield private perquisites in a way that hardly suggested that high standards would be applied to the administration of wider areas in Bengal after Plassey.

Throughout the eighteenth century the formal structure of the civil service remained unchanged. A man served for five years as a Writer, followed by three years each as a Factor and as a Junior Merchant, before attaining the highest rank of Senior Merchant. Basic salaries, which only changed in the 1760s, were attached to each rank. Writers were paid £5 a year, Factors £15, Junior Merchants £30, and Senior Merchants £40, with a special salary of £300 for the Governor at the beginning of the century. Salaries were supplemented by various allowances, for 'diet', servants, housing, cattle, 'washing', and water brought from outside Calcutta. These additions still did not provide a means of subsistence for the mass of the service in the period before Plassey. The total emoluments of a Writer were less than Rs 300, or about £34 a year, while Senior Merchants on the Council could only expect Rs 2,000, or £225, rising perhaps to £600 if they became Chiefs of the out-factories, such as Dacca. The allowances of the Governor were on such a scale, including the pay of eighty-two servants, that he alone received some sort of living wage, about Rs 21,000, or some £2,300.[1]

It was impossible to maintain a genteel standard of life in a settlement already notorious for its expensiveness, let alone to save anything for a return to Britain, on emoluments of this size. In 1754 a new Writer found 'every thing here . . . double the price it is at home'. With 'good oeconomy' he thought that he might be able to make his annual salary pay for six months' living expenses.[2] For 'a man in trade', keeping a house in Calcutta in this period was thought to cost £1,000 a year.[3] Most men tried to supplement their income from trading profits, but the temptation to make a

---

[1] See lists in I.O.R., L/F/10/1.
[2] S. Dalrymple to Sir H. Dalrymple, 3 Jan. 1754, S.R.O., Hamilton-Dalrymple MSS., bundle 56.
[3] Letters of Capt. Fenwick [1751], I.O.L., Orme MSS., 'India', vi. 1552.

position in the Company's service yield more than was officially permitted was clearly a strong one. In the first half of the eighteenth century the majority of the Company's servants were employed in its commercial business, selling its imports from Britain and buying what was called its 'investment' for the London market. The purchase of the silk, piecegoods, or saltpetre for the investment offered a number of opportunities for private profits. Servants making purchases inevitably handled large sums of the Company's money. Outright embezzlement, followed by flight occurred on occasions,[1] but a more common practice was for servants to use the money in their hands to finance their own trade and thus to save themselves the very high interest charges of eighteenth-century Bengal. So long as the individual concerned could fend off inquiries into his accounts and so long as his own trade prospered, he could perhaps hope to go undetected. But disaster often struck. In 1736, for instance, Thomas Cooke at Dacca was found to have disposed of nearly Rs 100,000 of the Company's money, a sum which his surviving assets could not hope to cover.[2] Samuel Browne and Hugh Barker were detected in using the Company's money for their own purposes at Patna in 1719,[3] while a later Chief, called Humphreys Cole, ran the factory there in a highly irregular manner for several years until he was finally exposed in 1744. Cole's accounts were never satisfactorily unravelled, but it is at least clear that he had succeeded in totally confusing his own private business with the official trade of the Company, doing what he liked with the Company's money in the process.[4]

Even if he kept his hands off the Company's money, there were two obvious points in the process of making the Company's investment at which a servant could try to take private profits. The first was when he chose the Indian merchants who were to provide the goods and fixed the conditions and prices at which they were to be delivered, or, if he was stationed at a factory outside Calcutta, when he contracted with brokers who would set the weavers, silk-winders, or saltpetre-boilers to work. The second

---

[1] See below, p. 201.

[2] I.O.R., B.P.C., 4 Oct., 5, 17, 28 Dec. 1736, 14 Feb. 1737, Range 1, vols. 11, f. 320; 12, ff. 10–11, 26–7, 39–40, 108.

[3] Ibid., 8, 21 Dec. 1719, Range 1, vol. 4, ff. 152–7, 163.

[4] 'Papers and Accounts relating to the affairs of Patna', I.O.R., B.P.C., Range 1, vol. 17.

point of maximum advantage or danger (depending on one's point of view) was the 'prizing', when the merchant or the broker produced the goods for their quality to be tested by a sample before the final instalment of the price was handed over.[1] The most obvious temptation for a servant in choosing a merchant to provide goods was to choose himself and to fix the price to his own advantage. This was forbidden, but there were frequent allegations that Company servants sold their own goods to the Company at their own prices, under the cover of Indian names, often using those of their banians. In 1727, when the Chief at Dacca was found guilty of passing off his own goods on the Company, the servants at the factory had a scheme for dividing up the provision of the investment among themselves.[2] Specific allegations were made in 1732 that the Governor and Council 'had appropriated what sale of their own goods to the Company as they pleased'.[3] Company servants who did not make investment contracts with themselves could still expect to receive some gratification from the merchants or brokers whom they did choose. The habit of taking some sort of commission, or 'dastur', seems to have been universal. As early as 1681 the Directors complained about the Chiefs in Bengal collecting a commission from merchants.[4] 'Contoo' Sarma the Company's broker at Kasimbazar, alleged after he had gone bankrupt in 1730 that he had been obliged to make large payments to the Chief for his investment contracts.[5] Another Chief was said to be offering generous contracts on the Company's behalf to merchants who would then 'make good hard bargains they made with him in his private trade'.[6] At particular factories rates were established at which the Company's servants made deductions from the money which they advanced to *dalal* brokers or to the weavers themselves: at Jagdia 2½ per cent was being taken in the 1750s;[7] at Dacca the rate was 5 per cent by the

---

[1] The Committee of Correspondence received an interesting account of how prices were fixed and of the prizing from S. Margas, 19 Dec. 1752, I.O.R., D/103.

[2] I.O.R., B.P.C., 16 May, 14, 21 Aug. 1727, Range 1, vol. 6, ff. 434, 485, 489.

[3] S. Greenhill to Directors, 9 Feb. 1732, I.O.R., Home Miscellaneous, 74, pp. 160–2.

[4] Directors to Bengal, 18 Nov. 1681, I.O.R., E/3/89, p. 422.

[5] I.O.R., B.P.C., 20 July, 3 Aug. 1730, Range 1, vol. 8, ff. 266, 274.

[6] Capt. Fenwick's letters [1751], I.O.L., Orme MSS., 'India', vi. 1530.

[7] Bengal to Directors, 7 Dec. 1754, *Fort William–India House Correspondence* (New Delhi, 1949–), i. 833.

1770s;[1] at Lakshmipur in the 1760s and 1770s it varied between 5 and 7½ per cent.[2] At the prizing, when the price which he received depended on the assessment of the Company servant, who might even 'ferrett' his goods (that is reject them as substandard), a prudent merchant, broker, or weaver would be ready with inducements. It was said in 1775 to have been the custom for many years for weavers at Dacca to pay a commission of one anna in the rupee at the prizing.[3]

It would be difficult to try to maintain that the Company's service suddenly became corrupted by the lure of vast wealth after Plassey or by the example of the Indian officials whom its members had replaced. There is abundant evidence of low standards long before 1757. The sums involved may have increased greatly with the acquisition of political power, but attitudes to exploiting the advantages of office were already formed. Indeed, in the one place where the Company's servants did exercise administrative responsibilities in the early eighteenth century they were already trying to derive private sources of income from them. From 1720 Company servants were appointed to act as *Zamindars* of Calcutta. Their chief function was to collect rents and dues. There were obvious opportunities for taking a commission on what was collected. In 1752 the Directors were given detailed accounts of abuses said to have been committed over many years in the administration of Calcutta. Most of the accusations were directed at Ram Govind Mitra, the famous Indian under-*Zamindar*, but it was also alleged that the European *Zamindars* collected a 10 per cent commission from those to whom they farmed markets or the collection of dues.[4] Other perquisites also existed. In 1765 it came to light that it was 'usual' for the prostitutes of Calcutta to make payments.[5]

Gains from investment contracts, or from Calcutta farms were made to seem very trivial by the great sums accruing to those highly placed in the Company's civil and military service after

<hr>

[1] B.R.C., 3 July 1776, *Reports from Committees of the House of Commons* (1803–6), vi. 243–4.
[2] West Bengal Archives, Board of Trade Proceedings, 13 Oct. 1775, vol. 5, p. 58.
[3] Ibid., 10 Oct. 1775, vol. 5, pp. 43–5.
[4] J. Z. Holwell, *India Tracts*, 3rd edn. (1774), p. 133; Directors to Bengal, 16 Jan. 1753, I.O.R., E/3/111, p. 313.
[5] I.O.R., B.P.C., 14 Oct. 1765, Range 1, vol. 38, f. 403.

Plassey. The most spectacular and the most notorious of such sums came as 'presents' from Indians. For some fifteen years after 1757 the British in Bengal were in the position that their military power could determine who was to be Nawab and who was to fill the major offices in the Nawabs' government. Contestants were generally willing to pay very large sums for British support; in cases where they were not willing, some Englishmen soon learnt how to bring pressure on them to make them do so. By 1772 Bengal had become virtually a British province and its discredited and more or less powerless Nawabs had neither the incentive to go on bribing their protectors nor the means to do so on a large scale. But during the fifteen years while the Nawabs governed under the shadow of the Company, Clive made the biggest fortune to come out of Bengal in the eighteenth century, largely from their generosity, and a flight of lesser men returned to England, enriched by presents far beyond all previous expectations of Indian service. In 1772 a committee of the House of Commons listed over £2,000,000 taken in presents between 1757 and 1765.[1]

The years of affluence beginning in 1757 were preceded by a year of total disaster for the British community in Bengal. Siraj-ud-daula took Calcutta in 1756 and sacked it, his soldiers carrying away most movable valuables. Clive found it impossible to describe 'the distress of the inhabitants of this once opulent and great town'.[2] Deliverance came through an expedition from Madras under Clive's command, which retook Calcutta and forced Siraj-ud-daula to agree to a peace, restoring the Company's settlements and its trading privileges. Had matters ended there, the mass of Europeans would have gained little. Although Clive had 'left no means untried with the Nabob . . . to induce him to consider the unhappy people of Calcutta and he has often promised to do it', no formal stipulation for the restitution of private losses was included in the peace with Siraj-ud-daula.[3] The Nawab only promised to pay 'such a sum of money as his justice shall think reasonable',[4] which in the event seems to have been about Rs 400,000 or Rs 600,000;[5] at the most about £67,500, whereas

[1] *Reports*, iii. 311–12.
[2] Letter to his father, [Feb. 1757], S. C. Hill, *Bengal in 1756–7* (1905), ii. 209.
[3] Clive to J. Payne, 23 Feb. 1757, ibid., ii. 244.
[4] Ibid., ii. 216.
[5] L. Scrafton to Clive, 28 Apr. 1757, I.O.L., Orme MSS., 'India', ix. 2332.

Clive at first thought that about £2,000,000 might in fact have been lost.[1] The agreement with Siraj-ud-daula was not, however, to last; a new agreement which gave very much more to the British community was soon made with a new Nawab. The British were drawn ever deeper into Bengal politics, first of all to eliminate the French settlement at Chandernagore and then to eliminate Siraj-ud-daula himself.

Negotiations began with Siraj-ud-daula's numerous enemies for the Company's army to be used in deposing the Nawab and in putting Mir Jafar on the throne in his place. Europeans had grossly inflated ideas about the disposable wealth of the Nawabs of Bengal (one estimate in 1757 put it at forty crores of rupees, or at least £40,000,000),[2] and so it was made clear to Mir Jafar that he would have to pay a very high price, both to the Company and to individuals, for British support. When the propositions to be put to him were being worked out between Clive and William Watts, who was in personal contact with Mir Jafar, a 'gratuity' for the army and 'restitution' for the losses in 1756 of the Company and of private individuals were included.[3] A few days later the Select Committee of the Company's Council, who were managing its affairs in Calcutta, decided that some provision for them must also be insisted upon, since it was they 'who really set the whole machine in motion'.[4] Taking an 'oath of secrecy upon the Bible', they instructed Watts to demand twelve lakhs of rupees on their behalf.[5] A lakh, or Rs 100,000 (about £11,000), became the standard unit for large presents, as in Macaulay's highly apocryphal story that Clive proposed 'alas and alack-a-day' as a suitable toast for good fellowship in Bengal. On the eve of Plassey, when Mir Jafar finally concluded his agreement for the use of the Company's army, he was formally bound to pay huge indemnities to the Company and to the private sufferers of 1756; fifty lakhs were to go to the Europeans with twenty to the Calcutta Hindu community and seven to the Armenians. He was also privately committed to distributing large presents to the Select Committee and to the army. Once he was placed on the throne, all limits to his generosity

[1] Letter to his father, [Feb. 1757], Hill, *Bengal*, ii. 210.
[2] Watts to Clive, 3 June 1757, ibid. ii. 397.
[3] Clive to Watts, 2, 5 May 1757 and 'proposals', ibid. ii. 373–7. Letter of 5 May in full in N.L.W., Clive MSS., 204, p. 23.
[4] R. Becher's evidence, 1st Report, Select Committee, 1772, *Reports*, iii. 145.
[5] Clive to Watts, 19 May 1757, Hill, *Bengal*, ii. 388.

were broken down. He gave twenty-five lakhs each to the army
and the navy, whose ships had played an important part in the
recovery of Calcutta and the taking of Chandernagore and many
of whose sailors had fought with the army. The Select Committee's
share was finally fixed at seventeen lakhs,[1] and the new Nawab
was persuaded to add a lakh each to the six members of the Council
who did not sit on the Select Committee.[2] Personal presents to
particular individuals followed in lavish profusion. Clive with no
less than sixteen lakhs, over and above his share in the Select
Committee and the army donations, was by far the largest beneficiary, Mir Jafar 'expressing himself that I had been one of the
principal means of not only getting him the subahship but of
saving his life'.[3] Watts received eight lakhs, John Walsh, who had
come to Bengal with Clive from Madras as his secretary was given
five, Major Killpatrick of the Bengal army was given three or four
lakhs, two lakhs went to Luke Scrafton of the Council who had
been an active negotiator in the conspiracy, and there were
smaller gifts.[4] The House of Commons Select Committee was
finally able to compile a list of presents worth £1,238,575, which
were distributed in 1757.[5] Half the sums promised were paid over
immediately in specie or jewels with a promise that the rest would
be paid off in instalments over the next three years.

Some eighteen months after Plassey, Clive seems to have decided
to add a permanent income from India to what he could expect
from investing his presents in Britain. Mir Jafar had already
obtained for him the rank of *Mansabdar* of the Mughal empire
with the title Zubdat ul Mulk (select of the state).[6] In January 1759
he applied to the Jagat Seths, the great Hindu bankers, for a *jagir*,
a grant of revenue, 'equal to my rank'.[7] With some ingenuity the
Nawab worked out a scheme by which Clive would get his income
at the expense of the Company. He invested Clive with a *jagir*
worth approximately £27,000 a year, of which the revenue was
secured on lands in the Twenty-four Parganas, territory which the

[1] The distribution of this sum is set out in H. Doidge to G. Pocock, 30 Oct.
1757, I.O.R., Home Miscellaneous, 192, p. 197.
[2] Clive to Frankland, 8 July 1757, N.L.W., Clive MSS., 206, p. 22.
[3] Clive to G. Pigot, 25 Dec. 1757, ibid., 200, pp. 114–15.
[4] Clive's evidence, 1st Report, Select Committee, 1772, *Reports*, iii. 150.
[5] *Reports*, iii. 311.
[6] A. Majed Khan, *The Transition in Bengal 1756–75* (Cambridge, 1969),
p. 11.
[7] Clive to the Seths, 31 Jan. 1759, *Reports*, iii. 224.

Nawab had already ceded to the Company.[1] The defence of the *jagir* both at home and in India was to cause Clive expense and vexation. At home his enemies harassed him by calling on the Company to cancel the grant, which for a short period they did. In India he was able to obtain confirmation of it from the Mughal emperor,[2] and ultimately the Company permitted him to draw £27,000 a year from the revenues of Bengal for the rest of his life.

Almost at once Clive began to formulate the defence of present taking which was to be used again and again by others as well as himself. Presents were permissible, he thought, if they were a voluntary offering made for genuine services done in the course of duty, and if they did no damage to the Company's interest. They should not be accepted if they were only offered under threat or were held out as the price by which an individual could be persuaded to neglect his obligations to the Company. To receive an unsolicited mark of gratitude for a service done from public motives was honourable; to bargain for rewards and let them influence one's actions was dishonourable. Clive was in no doubt that Mir Jafar had acted 'of his own free will'[3] and that 'motives of gratitude prevailed upon him to do it'.[4] Clive always insisted that he had not bargained in advance for any reward for himself.[5] He had staged the Plassey 'revolution' to win great advantages for the Company and for Britain. Events had proved him right. Presents came to him as an unlooked-for but well-deserved windfall.

This defence is in part convincing. There seems no reason to doubt that Clive entered into the conspiracy with Mir Jafar for the reasons he gave at the time: he was genuinely convinced that 'there can be neither peace nor trade without a change of government'.[6] He was of course fully involved in the negotiations for presents and restitution, but he seems to have regarded them as a subsidiary consideration whose details he was prepared to leave to the generosity of Mir Jafar.[7] Other members of the Select Committee were less single-minded. Indeed Clive later wrote that

[1] Evidence of Clive and Sykes, 3rd Report, Select Committee, 1773, *Reports*, iii. 154–5.

[2] I.O.R., B.P.C., 9 Sept. 1765, Range 1, vol. 38, f. 342.

[3] Clive to J. Payne, 25 Dec. 1757, N.L.W., Clive MSS., 200, pp. 109–10.

[4] Clive to Pigot, 25 Dec. 1757, ibid., pp. 114–15.

[5] I.O.R., B.P.C., 24 June, 28 Oct. 1765, Range 1, vol. 38, ff. 231, 439–40; his evidence in the 1st Report, Select Committee, 1772, *Reports*, iii. 147.

[6] Letter to Pigot, 30 Apr. 1757, Hill, *Bengal*, ii. 369.

[7] Letter to Watts, 2 May 1757, ibid. ii. 373.

'without some such provision' for them, 'I should have found a difficult task to have executed the late glorious expedition.'[1] William Watts later took the credit for insisting that Mir Jafar should be tied down to precise figures, lest 'a false delicacy might produce disputes'.[2]

But if Clive cannot be convicted of staging the Plassey campaign simply to win a fortune for himself, he still overstated the case when he insisted that he had received no prior assurances about presents and that the new Nawab had acted entirely from disinterested gratitude. Clive may not have taken the lead in stipulating precise sums from Mir Jafar for the army and the Select Committee; but once the stipulations had been made, he could be in no doubt that his own share of the distribution would be very considerable, even if he could not foresee the extent of the riches which Mir Jafar would eventually bestow upon him. There seems no reason to doubt that Mir Jafar felt genuine gratitude towards Clive, for whom he later came to have a real personal liking,[3] but it seems hardly credible that in making huge personal presents to him, he was not also trying to buy future British countenance and protection.

The events of 1757 not only taught Nawabs and would-be Nawabs to cultivate British support, but since Clive believed that the Company must concern itself about other appointments in Bengal in order to protect its interests, they encouraged contenders for lesser offices to seek British allies. In 1760 and 1761, for instance, there was a contest for the office of *Naib*, or deputy, in Bihar. Ram Narain, and Rajballabh, the two leading contenders, were both said to have dispensed money to the Company servants to win their support.[4] Other ambitious men in the Nawabs' government were to try to build up a following in Calcutta by similar means on other occasions.

In 1760, barely three years after Plassey, a new contest broke out for the throne of the Bengal Nawabs. Since Clive's departure earlier in the year, leading Company servants had increasingly come to regard Mir Jafar as an unsatisfactory Nawab. In their

---

[1] Clive to J. Payne, 25 Dec. 1757, N.L.W., Clive MSS., 200, p. 110.
[2] [W. Watts], *Memoirs of the Revolution in Bengal* (1760), pp. 83, 87.
[3] Khan, *Transition*, p. 12.
[4] J. Carnac's evidence, 3rd Report, Select Committee, 1773, *Reports*, iii. 300, 332; see also his letter to Clive, 2 Nov. 1760, I.O.L., MS. Eur. F. 128, box 4/1.

opinion he was incapable of governing Bengal effectively, unlikely
to discharge his heavy financial obligations to the Company, and
less than whole-heartedly loyal to the British in seeking other allies
who might balance their influence in Bengal. Clive's temporary
successor as Governor, John Zephaniah Holwell, devised a plan
by which Mir Jafar would be compelled to cede effective power in
his government to his son-in-law, Mir Kasim, although he would
remain as titular Nawab. This plan was actually carried out in
October 1760 by the new Governor, Henry Vansittart. Faced with
an ultimatum, Mir Jafar preferred to resign the throne altogether
and Mir Kasim was duly installed as his successor in name as well
as in fact.

It immediately became apparent that Mir Kasim had been
obliged to pay for his accession with substantial grants of territory
to the Company, the districts of Burdwan, Chittagong, and
Midnapur. It was also strongly suspected that he had made payments to individuals, which was indeed the case. The fullest
accounts of what happened are those related twelve years later
to the Select Committee of the House of Commons by Colonel
John Caillaud, who had been in command of the Bengal army, and
by William Sumner, who had been a member of Council. They
had both seen Mir Kasim offer Vansittart a written obligation to
pay twenty lakhs of rupees (about £225,000) in presents to the
English. Both agreed that Vansittart had refused to accept any
money while the Nawab still had unsettled accounts with the
Company and while the pay of his own army was still in arrears,
but that he had implied that offers made at a later date would not
be refused.[1] News of the offers leaked out, and to embarrass
Vansittart, his opponents on the Council passed a resolution in
March 1762 that Mir Kasim should now be asked to hand over
the twenty lakhs for the Company's use, a proposition which the
Nawab scornfully rejected.[2] In the ensuing discussion, Vansittart
publicly denied that he or his colleagues had received anything
from the Nawab.[3] If this statement was true in March 1762, it
soon ceased to be. At some point in his reign Mir Kasim certainly
disbursed at least part of what he had promised in 1760. The first
definite proof of this was provided by an extraordinarily injudicious

[1] 1st Report, Select Committee, 1772, iii. 161, 163-4.
[2] Undated letter to the Council, Add. MS. 29099, f. 67.
[3] I.O.R., B.P.C., 22 Mar. 1762, Range 1, vol. 34, f. 180.

letter from Holwell, now in England, which he wrote in 1763 and which came to be registered for public edification on the records of the Mayor's Court. In it Holwell complained that Mir Kasim had promised him two lakhs but that so far he had only received Rs 50,000.[1] When Clive returned to India in 1765 he made it his business to find out more about Mir Kasim's presents. He collected a series of depositions from Indians involved in the transactions. Some of these implicated William Sumner, who was still in India. Clive showed him the evidence against him and forced him to resign the service rather than face disclosure,[2] although he later admitted that he had taken £28,000 from Mir Kasim in 1761 and 1762.[3] Clive also collected material which was damaging to Vansittart himself. It appears that Clive would not have made this public if he had not been provoked into doing so by Vansittart at home in 1768. He then handed over a part of what he had found to the Directors.[4] This consisted of two depositions showing that seven lakhs of rupees had been given by Mir Kasim to Vansittart at the time of the signing of the so-called treaty of Monghyr,[5] the attempt to patch up an agreement about private trading.[6] In a letter to the Company Vansittart made no real attempt to contest the truth of the charges.[7] Presumably aware that they might at any time be confounded by some new disclosure from Clive's cornucopia, a number of Vansittart's colleagues confessed to the Select Committee of the House of Commons in 1772. Caillaud admitted that Vansittart had obtained two lakhs for him at the time of the Monghyr treaty (it is not clear whether this was part of Vansittart's seven or an additional payment); William McGwire of the Council admitted to Rs 180,000; and William Sumner added the names of another Councillor, Culling Smith, and another army officer, Major Yorke, both recipients of Rs 134,000.[8] The rest of Clive's depositions, which appear to have included a highly damaging one by Khwaja Petruse, Mir Kasim's Calcutta agent, were suppressed and have evidently been

[1] Holwell to J. Wollaston, 13 Apr. 1763, I.O.R., Mayor's Court Records, Range 155, vol. 62.
[2] Clive to Palk, 3 Aug., 8 Sept. 1766, N.L.W., Clive MSS., 228, p. 74; 229, p. 10; Clive to Walsh, 8 Sept. 1766, I.O.L., MS. Eur. D. 546/5, ff. 149–50.
[3] Evidence, 1st Report, Select Committee, 1772, *Reports*, iii. 163.
[4] Clive to Verelst, 9 Mar. 1768, N.L.W., Clive MSS., 61, pp. 34–5.
[5] Reprinted 3rd Report, Select Committee, 1773, *Reports*, iii. 402.
[6] See above, p. 125.   [7] Letter of 15 Sept. 1768, *Reports*, iii. 403.
[8] Ibid. iii. 161, 164, 310.

destroyed.[1] Of those who escaped publicity, the luckiest was perhaps Warren Hastings. As Vansittart's closest ally and his Resident
at Mir Kasim's court, money must have been offered to him, and
he was certainly on Clive's list. According to someone who had
seen it, Nandakumar and Petruse had put him down for four lakhs,[2]
which seems improbably high. With what was probably incomplete
information the Commons Select Committee could still produce
a list of presents worth £200,000 taken after the 1760 'revolution'.[3]

Vansittart offered the same sort of defence for the presents from
Mir Kasim as Clive had offered for Mir Jafar's presents. They
were voluntary and neither the promotion of Mir Kasim nor the
Monghyr treaty had been influenced by them.[4] Definite evidence
does not appear to have survived, but as far as Vansittart was
concerned, it may well be that presents had not been discussed
with Mir Kasim before the coup against Mir Jafar. Contemporaries
were not, however, willing to make the same assumption about
Holwell, who had begun negotiations with Mir Kasim before
Vansittart arrived in Bengal, and to whom the detailed arrangements were entrusted. Holwell had apparently been boasting
openly of how he intended to put his temporary Governorship to
good account. He had failed to get anything from Mir Jafar, and
to his enemies it seemed that 'since that channel was stopped
from whence it was expected some advantage would flow, it was
necessary that another should be opened' by changing Nawabs.[5]
It seemed to them hardly credible that he should not have struck
a bargain with Mir Kasim.

If Vansittart had not bargained for money, in eventually accepting it from Mir Kasim, he is vulnerable in the same way that
Clive had been. Mir Kasim was not simply showing gratitude; he
was buying future support, knowing that his position was far from
secure and that many important Company servants were bitterly
opposed to the change. Mir Jafar had in a sense bought the whole
Council in 1757; Mir Kasim only bought half of it. The fact that

---

[1] The fullest description of them is in J. Walsh to Clive, 26 Feb. 1768,
I.O.L., MS. Eur. G. 37, box 51, f. 269. One of those never made public, by
Nobkissen, which adds nothing material, is in ibid., box 12, no. 19.

[2] Walsh to Clive, 17 May 1766, ibid., box 40, f. 159; Sykes to Hastings, n.d.,
Add. MS. 29194, ff. 119–21.

[3] *Reports*, iii. 311.   [4] Letter to Directors, 15 Sept. 1768, ibid. iii. 403.

[5] Defence of his conduct by J. Caillaud, I.O.L., Orme MSS., 'India'. xii.
3253–8.

those who supported Mir Kasim's promotion received his bounty, while those who opposed it were ignored, contributed very materially to the bitter factionalism that paralysed Vansittart's government. Every time the Governor tried to improve relations with the Nawab, he was accused of rendering services for which he had already received payment.

In 1763 Mir Kasim took up arms against the Company, was defeated and deposed, Mir Jafar being brought back from retirement to succeed him. Once he was re-established, Mir Jafar was given a list of claims which he must satisfy. He was required to pay a large sum in compensation for losses sustained by private traders throughout Bengal.[1] He was also asked to give money to the troops, who had defeated and driven out Mir Kasim and were now campaigning in Oudh and Bihar, and to the men of a royal naval squadron, whose ships anchored in the Hugli could hardly be said to have made a very decisive contribution to a war being fought several hundred miles up-country. Mir Jafar responded with little enthusiasm to Vansittart's suggestions about donations. He offered to give the army five lakhs, but after making 'many objections and difficulties' finally agreed to dispense twenty-five lakhs, the sum which he had distributed to the army after Plassey. An offer of five lakhs to the navy was rejected as inadequate by the Commodore in command of the squadron, who took over the negotiations himself. Commodore Tinker eventually broke down the Nawab's resistance by 'puffing off his own consequence', in a way that European observers found both odious and ludicrous,[2] and persuading Mir Jafar that he could do him great services with the King of England. The sum of 12½ lakhs was handed over to be distributed throughout the squadron, with two lakhs as a personal present for Tinker.[3] With much more justification, officers in the army also applied for personal rewards for their part in the overthrow of Mir Kasim. Major Hector Munro, who commanded the army at the decisive battle of Buxar, established a claim for two lakhs in compensation for the grant of a *jagir* in Bengal.[4] Major John

---

[1] See above, p. 116.
[2] G. Vansittart to H. Vansittart, 27 Nov. 1766, Bodleian, dep. b. 100, p. 12.
[3] The extraction of the donations for the army and the navy is described in H. Vansittart to Directors, 7 Oct. 1767, I.O.R., Home Miscellaneous, 196, pp. 356–71; and in the evidence of Nobkissen and Nandakumar, Select Committee Proceedings, 27, 29 Aug. 1766, ibid., pp. 167 ff.
[4] His evidence, 1st Report, Select Committee, 1772, *Reports*, iii. 170.

Carnac, Munro's predecessor, collected Rs 50,000 with a promise
of Rs 50,000 more,[1] while Colonel John Caillaud got Rs 150,000
for his part in an earlier campaign.[2]

Mir Jafar's death in 1765 set off yet another scramble for
presents.[3] A new Nawab was made to pay for his accession, while
with the succession going to a minor, candidates for the post of
minister in control of the Nawab's government were willing to pay
high prices for European support. Vansittart's successor, John
Spencer, brought over from Bombay on the orders of the Directors,
was Governor when Mir Jafar died. He and his Council were in
little doubt that the rightful claimant was a boy of sixteen or
seventeen, called Najm-ud-daula. There were, however, three
leading contenders for the office of chief minister: Nandakumar,
who had already dominated the government of Mir Jafar after his
restoration, Rai Durlabh, one of those most prominent in the
conspiracy that led to Plassey, and Muhammad Reza Khan,
a skilled revenue official, who had served at Dacca. All were prepared to bid for the support of prominent Englishmen. At various
times Nandakumar offered Spencer eleven lakhs, if he would
leave him in control;[4] he also offered five lakhs to Ascanius Senior,
another member of the Council;[5] and he actually persuaded
Samuel Middleton, the Company's agent at Murshidabad to take
bills on him worth one lakh.[6] Rai Durlabh made a present to
John Burdett, another Councillor,[7] and was thought to have
distributed money more widely.[8] Muhammad Reza Khan handed
over Rs 40,000 to Spencer.[9] The solution devised by the Council
offered something for everyone, but most for Muhammad Reza
Khan. He was to be the chief minister assisted by Nandakumar
and Rai Durlabh. To confirm the Nawab's accession and the new
arrangement of ministers, what was termed a 'delegation' of the
Council was sent up from Calcutta under the leadership of the

[1] Carnac to R. Gregory, 9 Apr. 1765, I.O.L., MS. Eur. F. 128, box 4/11.
[2] Caillaud to H. Vansittart, 15 Aug. 1760, I.O.L., Orme MSS., 'India', xii.
3168–70.
[3] For an excellent account, see Khan, *Transition*, chap. v.
[4] Spencer to L. Sulivan, 25 Sept. 1765, I.O.L., MS. Eur. E. 302/1, p. 73;
B.P.C., 11 June 1765, *Reports*, iii. 430.
[5] His evidence, 3rd Report, Select Committee, 1773, *Reports*, iii. 309.
[6] F. Sykes to Clive, 25 July 1765, N.L.W., Clive MSS., 53, p. 85.
[7] I.O.R., B.P.C., 16 Sept. 1765, Range 1, vol. 38, f. 362.
[8] J. Carnac to R. Leycester, 26 Feb. 1765, I.O.L., MS. Eur. F. 128, box 4/11.
[9] B.P.C., 6 June 1765, *Reports*, iii. 412.

redoubtable John Johnstone. The delegation made one important change in what had been decided. They were presented with information suggesting that Nandakumar was, from the British point of view, an unreliable ally, and decided that he must be removed from the new Nawab's government and should be forced to leave Murshidabad and go to Calcutta. When he arrived there, he continued to press his money on anyone whom he thought likely to help him; Burdett at least took Rs 50,000.[1] After removing Nandakumar, the delegation duly confirmed Najm-ud-daula as Nawab with Muhammad Reza Khan as his chief minister.

Public business having been accomplished, private business followed. When the delegation was chosen, one observer commented: 'the individuals thereof . . . it may be supposed will receive . . . a considerable present.'[2] What they received was revealed to Clive when he returned to Bengal to begin his second Governorship in May 1765. The Nawab immediately complained to Clive that he had been forced to make large presents, and to protect himself, but no doubt also with an eye to winning the favour of the new Governor, Muhammad Reza Khan produced lists of money distributed to the delegation and to the Governor and the rest of the Council who had stayed in Calcutta. The ever enterprising Nandakumar also offered a list of presents amounting to no less than twenty-one lakhs.[3] Clive decided to conduct a public investigation into the Khan's lists. In the first one, presents paid by the Nawab, Johnstone was shown to have received two lakhs with a lakh each going to the other three members of the delegation and Rs 50,000 to Johnstone's younger brother, Gideon, who had accompanied it to Murshidabad. Of those who stayed behind, Governor Spencer was promised two lakhs, of which he actually received one, and the three remaining Councillors were each promised one lakh, receiving half that amount. The second list consisted of presents made by the Khan personally. He committed himself to giving Rs 150,000 to Johnstone and a lakh each to the rest of the delegation, but in fact only handed over a lakh to Johnstone and Rs 50,000 to two of the others. Finally, the banking house of Jagat Seth was induced to promise Rs 125,000 to the delegation and actually parted with Rs 50,000. In all, over

[1] *Nuncomar* v. *Burdett*, P.R.O., C 12/1334/33.
[2] J. Carnac to R. Leycester, 26 Feb. 1765, I.O.L., MS. Eur. F. 128, box 4/11.
[3] Copy in Clive's hand, I.O.L., MS. Eur. D. 546/5, f. 117.

Rs 1,000,000 or about £112,000 appear to have been levied by Englishmen out of the change of Nawabs in 1765. Johnstone with about £36,000 was the greatest single beneficiary.[1]

The recipients never denied that they had taken the money, but they totally rejected Muhammad Reza Khan's version of how it had come to be offered. The Khan maintained that the initiative had come from the delegation, who had instructed him to raise the matter with the Nawab. Evidence was also produced to show that the Seths were threatened with unpleasant consequences for their business if they did not pay up.[2] In reply, the accused all said much the same. They had been offered presents from Najm-ud-daula as soon as Mir Jafar died. They had refused them then, but once the new Nawab had been formally placed on the throne, there could be no objection to taking presents. Even then, 'we more than once told him we wanted no such offer if it was not entirely with his own inclination, which he repeatedly assured us it was'. Members of the delegation also denied that they had brought any pressure to bear on Muhammad Reza Khan or the Seths to make them presents. The Seths had acted entirely of their own free will, one of them saying that 'his father had made presents on like occasions with a view to raise the credit of his house'.[3]

The most that can be said for Johnstone and his friends is that they had probably not sold their services in advance. Had they been willing to promote the highest bidder, they would presumably have chosen Nandakumar as minister. From the Company's point of view, Najm-ud-daula and Muhammad Reza Khan were probably the best available choice. But the argument that the presents were voluntary is even thinner than usual. The delegation were not receiving the benevolence of an independent ruler moved by gratitude and able to dispose of his own wealth as he wished. The young Nawab and his minister can have had no illusions as to what was expected of them, even if they were not subjected to a list of precise demands backed by threats. They had no option

[1] Select Committee Proceedings, 6 June 1765, *Reports*, iii. 410–14.
[2] Select Committee Proceedings, 6, 8 June, 4 July 1765, ibid. iii. 410–14, 414–15, 424–5.
[3] R. Leycester's defence, B.P.C., 11 June 1765; see also Johnstone, B.P.C., 17 June; Senior, Middleton, Select Committee Proceedings, 21 June 1765, *Reports*, iii. 420–1, 430–1, 433–7; *A Letter to the Proprietors of East India Stock from John Johnstone, Esq.* (1766), pp. 19–35.

but to comply. The only real defence that the delegation could offer was that they were following well-worn precedents. Every time there had been a change of Nawab in Bengal it had been turned to private advantage. The men who were in the Council in 1765 did not intend to let the chance slip. But unfortunately for them, they were legally vulnerable in a way that their predecessors had not been. Constantly repeated stories of present-taking in Bengal had finally provoked the Directors into issuing instructions that their servants must take covenants binding them not to accept presents. The covenants had arrived in Calcutta in January 1765, but with Mir Jafar dying on 5 February and the prospect of profitable dealings with a new Nawab ahead, the Council chose not to execute them. One of them explained that they were not disposed to obey orders from home, which had proved 'so very fluctuating'.[1]

When Clive returned to India he was at first inclined 'to injure the characters of individuals as little as possible'. He believed that Spencer had taken very large presents, but since he was leaving Bengal anyway, he was prepared to 'draw a veil over these proceedings'. The presents from Najm-ud-daula were, however, another matter. 'The cause of them was so notoriously public, that we could not without forfeiting our own reputation do otherwise than we did.'[2] In his mind there was no comparison to be made between what Mir Jafar had done for him after Plassey, without being 'stipulated, required or expected by me or with my knowledge . . . as the reward for real services rendered to the Nabob at a very dangerous crisis',[3] and contributions 'levied' from a weak Nawab and a dependent minister for giving the Nawab what was his right anyway.[4] As the inquiry into the presents proceeded, Johnstone and a number of others implicated thought it best to withdraw from Bengal. The Directors ordered the dismissal of those who were still in their service and began a prosecution of Johnstone, which was soon dropped in response to the pressure of his friends in the Company at home.

In 1765 the British had chosen the Nawab and his ministers entirely as they wished. Later in the year the formal grant of the

[1] R. Leycester, B.P.C., 11 June 1765, *Reports*, iii. 431.
[2] Letter to R. Palk, 14 July 1765, N.L.W., Clive MSS., 219, p. 29.
[3] I.O.R., B.P.C., 24 June 1765, Range 1, vol. 38, f. 231.
[4] Select Committee to Directors, 30 Sept. 1765, *Reports*, iii. 438.

diwani to the Company by the Mughal Emperor carried yet further the degradation of the Bengal Nawabs. Their power was virtually extinguished when Najm-ud-daula's death in 1766 was followed by the accession of two more very young Nawabs in a short space of time. The Nawabs became pensioners on an annuity, while real power was exercised by the Company's Resident at Murshidabad and by the *Naib Subah*, their chosen Indian minister. In 1772 the Nawab's stipend was reduced even further, the machinery of government was moved away from Murshidabad and put under direct British control at Calcutta, and Muhammad Reza Khan, who had kept the post of *Naib Subah* since 1765, was finally dismissed.

Even though the Nawabs now had relatively little left to dispose of, presents were still extracted from them. To maintain his position for so long, Muhammad Reza Khan was presumably required to pay generously to Residents at Murshidabad and to Governors at Calcutta. Precise details cannot, however, be ascertained. Recipients were able to cover their tracks and those instructed to investigate the Nawabs' accounts stopped short at what Hastings called bringing 'more to light than ought to be exposed'.[1] An inquiry into Muhammad Reza Khan's administration, which began in 1772, was said to have been less than complete because 'almost every member of the Board found himself more or less involved in the fate of the delinquent'.[2] One persistent rumour was that Francis Sykes, who made a princely fortune as Resident at Murshidabad, had received 'a lack or upwards in jewels' from the Khan.[3] The rearrangement of the Nawab's affairs in 1772 was the pretext for the last distribution of presents, even if it was a small one compared with what had gone before. Samuel Middleton, the Resident, admitted that he had taken a lakh for 'keeping every body quiet in the city' on the occasion.[4] What the new Governor, Warren Hastings, took is in doubt. He was eventually accused of having accepted three-and-a-half lakhs from those who had benefited from the dismissal of Muhammad Reza Khan and the remodelling of the Nawab's household. The charges were laid

[1] Letter to S. Middleton, 10 Feb. 1774, Add. MS. 29125, f. 267.
[2] L. Macleane to L. Sulivan, 18 Jan. 1774, Bodleian, MS. Eng. Hist. c. 271, f. 3.
[3] Sykes clearly seems to be 'the beast' referred to in R. Maddison to J. Mudie, 20 Jan. 1769, Add. MS. 29132, f. 415.
[4] Middleton to D. Anderson, 25 May 1775, Add. MS. 45431, f. 178.

by Nandakumar at the height of the famous conflicts between Hastings and the new Councillors recently arrived from Britain. They were clearly intended to smear Hastings and to win official countenance for Nandakumar, and so they should be treated with caution. Solid evidence was only in fact produced to substantiate a part of them: the receipt of one-and-a-half lakhs when Hastings went to Murshidabad. Hastings admitted the receipt of this money, implying that such payments were a recognized perquisite for the Governor.[1] The reduced stipend after 1772 can have left the Nawab very little margin for being generous to Europeans, even if he felt any inclination towards generosity. But he was still occasionally called upon for presents, such as one sent in 1783 to John Carnac, now at Bombay and very much down on his luck,[2] and the Resident at his court still made a good living by deducting a commission on the Nawab's stipend from the Company.[3]

As the Company's military power began to be felt outside Bengal, other Indian rulers were drawn into its orbit. They too came to appreciate the advantages of buying the services of prominent Company servants. In 1761 Shah Alam, the exiled Mughal Emperor, surrendered to a British army in Bihar. For several years thereafter he was to maintain close relations with some of the Company's military commanders, trying to persuade them to put their forces at his disposal and offering them imperial titles, *jagirs* in Bengal and presents in return. Eyre Coote became a *mansabdar* of the empire with a promise of a *jagir*,[4] while Carnac, after being offered presents and *jagirs*, finally accepted two lakhs in 1765, which Clive had invited the Emperor to give him.[5] Colonel Richard Smith also took two lakhs, which the Council gave him permission to keep,[6] and a further lakh was acquired by Sir Robert Fletcher, yet another army officer.[7]

---

[1] This episode is examined in my *Impeachment of Warren Hastings* (Oxford, 1965), pp. 132–40.

[2] Hastings to Sir J. D'Oyley, 28 July 1783, D'Oyley to Carnac, 19 Aug. 1783, Add. MS. 29160, ff. 159, 239.

[3] *Memoirs of William Hickey*, ed. A. Spencer (1913–25), iii. 236.

[4] Carnac to Coote, 10 June 1761, I.O.L., MS. Eur. F. 128, box 4/5; see also I.O.R., Home Miscellaneous, 196, p. 17.

[5] Carnac's statement, I.O.L., MS. Eur. F. 128, box 3/15; Clive's letter to the Emperor, I.O.L., Orme MSS., OV, 37, f. 111.

[6] Smith to Orme, 31 Aug. 1767, 16 Nov. 1768, I.O.L., Orme MSS., OV, 37, f. 69; 38, f. 100.

[7] Clive to Sumner, 25 July 1765, to Fletcher, 6 Aug. 1765, N.L.W., Clive MSS., 219, pp. 61, 77.

In 1764 British troops crossed the Karamnasa river for the first time. Thereafter the Wazirs of Oudh and the Rajas of Banaras were to be drawn into very close relations with the Company. Both inevitably became the quarry of present seekers. Balwant Singh, the Raja of Banaras, obviously thought it prudent to give presents to those who were commanding the Company's troops operating in his territory in 1764. Both Carnac and Major Munro received Rs 80,000.[1] Larger sums were apparently promised to Munro, which were still being collected from Balwant Singh's son some years later.[2] From 1773 the Wazir of Oudh had a Resident from the Company permanently stationed with him. Residents at Lucknow were as well placed for receiving presents as those at Murshidabad. Even one of the most high-minded of the Lucknow Residents, Major William Palmer, felt that it was 'both prudent and honourable' for him to receive 'marks of the Vizier's favour'.[3] It was at Lucknow that the last bid was made by an individual to win a fortune for himself by presents from an Indian ruler. This was the attempt made by Warren Hastings to secure ten lakhs (almost exactly £100,000 at the lower rates of exchange then prevailing) from Asaf-ud-daula in 1781. The offer (whether prompted or not cannot be ascertained) was made after an agreement had been signed regulating the Wazir's connection with the Company. More scrupulous than his predecessors and aware that the climate of opinion towards presents was extremely hostile by 1781, Hastings asked for permission from the Court of Directors before he finally kept the money. 'I am now in the fiftieth year of my life', he wrote: 'I have passed thirty-one years in the service of the Company, and the greatest part of that time in employments of the highest trust. My conscience allows me boldly to claim the merit of zeal and integrity; nor has fortune been unpropitious to their exertions. To these qualities I bound my pretensions.' Permission was never given and Hastings derived no benefit from the money.[4]

By 1781 the rich seam of presents from the Nawabs of Bengal, which the Company's servants had quarried so assiduously since

[1] Their evidence, 1st, 3rd Report, Select Committee, 1772–3, *Reports*, iii. 171, 310.

[2] T. Graham to R. Johnson and to E. Coote, 28 May 1779, 7 Jan. 1780, S.R.O., GD 29/2137.

[3] Letter to D. Anderson, 23 Oct. 1782, Add. MS. 45427, f. 129.

[4] Marshall, *Impeachment of Hastings*, pp. 147–8.

1757, was worked out. The rulers of other states now coming into contact with the Company still had the incentive to offer presents and the resources available, but accepting them was now much too risky. Presents were universally condemned in Britain. Covenants against taking them were enforced and their receipt was illegal under the Regulating Act.[1] It had never proved possible for large presents to remain undetected.

The Select Committee of the House of Commons identified presents worth £2,169,665, which had been distributed in Bengal between 1757 and 1765.[2] The total should perhaps be raised to something like £2,500,000 by adding presents taken since 1765 and earlier ones which escaped detection; more was certainly given by Mir Kasim and by the contenders for power after Mir Jafar's death than ever came to light. Some of this wealth went to the rank and file of the Company's armies and the ships of the royal navy, but most of it was acquired in large sums (a lakh or about £11,000 was the unit of measurement in most cases) by senior civil servants or army officers. Presents, which, unlike trading profits, could usually be realized quickly and easily, made a substantial contribution to the fortune of any man who could survive the turmoils of the 1760s and reach the higher ranks of the service.

[1] 13 Geo. III, c. 63, secs. 23, 24.   [2] *Reports*, iii. 311–12.

VIII

Profits of Office:
(II) Salaries and Perquisites

Huge as the sums involved in presents were, they enriched a comparatively small group of men over a relatively short space of time.
Other developments which began after Plassey were to affect many
more people and to set a pattern which was to last until 1947. Put
crudely, the sporadic plundering of the resources of the government of Bengal by a few in the form of presents was eventually
superseded by the regular syphoning off of a considerable part of
these resources to many in the form of salaries. The range of
offices in the Company's service underwent a rapid expansion and
increased greatly in value. Up to 1784 and well beyond a substantial part of what office holders received was not officially recognized, but the Company's allowances became increasingly generous.
For more and more men the uncertainties of trade were replaced
by the predictable certainties of salaries, of regular promotion, and
later of pensions, which were to make Indian service so attractive
to generations of Englishmen of at least moderate ambition.

Immediately before Plassey, the East India Company employed
between seventy-five and eighty civil servants in Bengal, whose
official pay and allowances amounted to about Rs 100,000 a year
in all, an average of under £150 a man.[1] In 1774 238 civil servants
were serving in Bengal, those below the Council earning an average
of £455 each; by 1783 the number of men below Council had grown
to 286 and their average emoluments had jumped to £2,261 a year.[2]
The military service had grown in an even more spectacular way:
the handful of officers before Plassey had swelled to 500 in 1769
and 1,069 in 1784.[3] But the pay of the army officers was much less
generous than that of the civil service. In 1784 only the twenty or
so Colonels and Lieutenant Colonels and the sixty Majors earned

---

[1] See the establishment lists in I.O.R., L/F/10/1.
[2] I.O.R., Home Miscellaneous, 79, p. 105. [3] See above, pp. 16–17.

over £1,000; Captains of sepoy battalions got about £500; but the mass of subalterns were paid under £250.[1] Figures for official earnings do not of course include perquisites and private profits, which liberally supplemented the pay of many of the civil servants and of a few of the more senior or more fortunate army officers.

The great increase both in the number of civil servants and in the rewards which they received might at first sight appear to be a creditable response to the urgent problems created by the annexation of Bengal. It was generally agreed that new administrative responsibilities required the deployment of many more Europeans and that extortion and the levying of private profits could only be curbed if officials were adequately paid by their employers. Men of high quality must be attracted to India to perform extremely exacting duties by the prospect of making at least a competence for their retirement by honourable means. Virtually everyone who thought seriously about the problem of governing a newly acquired province accepted these propositions. But the relatively large and well paid civil service which existed in Bengal by the 1780s had not been created by any coherent attempt to put them into effect. The increase in numbers owed as much to the need to satisfy demands for extra patronage for Company politics at home[2] as it did to serious consideration of the number of men required to administer Bengal. Questions of patronage were also at least as important as any attempt to place men above temptation in bringing about increased emoluments. As a result of the indiscriminate shipping out of men to India, and the manipulation of salaries to satisfy pressure from home, the service was overstaffed and the level of rewards bore comparatively little relation to responsibilities. Hastings's comments on the service towards the end of his Governorship clearly reveal its defects. 'In effect the civil offices of this government might be reduced to a very scanty number', he wrote in 1781, 'were their exigency alone to determine the list of your covenanted servants.'[3] In 1780 he complained of 'a system charged with expensive establishments and precluded by the multitude of dependants and the curse of patronage from reformation'.[4]

[1] 9th Report, Secret Committee, 1773, *Reports from Committees of the House of Commons* (1803–6), iv. 514; I.O.R., Home Miscellaneous, 362, p. 127.
[2] See above, p. 15.
[3] Bengal to Directors, 5 May 1781, I.O.R., E/4/39, p. 443.
[4] Letter to L. Sulivan, 10 Nov. 1780, Add. MS. 29128, f. 296; see also his

The increase in the number of servants was brought about by the unprecedented numbers of Writers allowed to go to Bengal in the years between 1763 and 1773, especially in 1766, 1769, 1770, 1772, and 1773.[1] By 1785 civil servants of between fifteen and twenty years' seniority were so numerous in Bengal that they could neither 'be employed or provided for'.[2]

The increase in the servants' emoluments was a more complex process. The Directors played very little part in it. They consistently tried to enforce economy and retrenchment. They were expressing concern about increasing salaries as early as 1766.[3] In 1774 they ordered that 'the strictest economy' must be applied and that no increases should be granted until their prior approval had been obtained.[4] In 1785 they conducted a long inquiry into increased establishments and ordered many economies.[5]

Whatever the Directors might have intended, very large increases in official rewards were granted in Bengal, most of them in a comparatively short space of time during the last few years of Warren Hastings's administration. As late as 1776 average earnings in the civil service were still only £685; in 1783 they were £2,261.[6] Part of this increase clearly reflects Hastings's idealism. Whereas other men had merely accepted the principle that adequate salaries were an integral part of eliminating abuses, he was actually prepared to take action to bind Company servants 'to the faithful discharge of their duty by the ties of honor and acknowledgement',[7] even at the price of allowing 'ostensible emoluments . . . which will appear enormous'.[8] His preference was for payment by commission. He regarded 'fixed salaries' as 'no incitement to diligence'.[9] Those who collected territorial revenue or customs or

assessment of the service in 'Memoirs relative to the state of India', *Selections from the State Papers of the Governors-General of India, Warren Hastings*, ed. G. W. Forrest (Oxford, 1910), ii. 22–4.

[1] See below, p. 218.
[2] Bengal to Directors, 25 Oct. 1785, *Fort William–India House Correspondence* (New Delhi, 1949–), ix. 590–1.
[3] Directors to Bengal, 19 Feb. 1766, ibid. iv. 155–6.
[4] Directors to Bengal, 29 Mar. 1774, I.O.R., E/4/622, p. 57.
[5] Directors to Bengal, 11 Apr., 8 July, 21 Sept. 1785, *Fort William–India House Corr.*, ix. 205–10, 231, 255.
[6] I.O.R., Home Miscellaneous, 79, p. 105.
[7] Letter to J. Scott, 28 Apr. 1781, Add. MS. 29128, f. 343.
[8] Bengal to Directors, 5 May 1781, I.O.R., E/4/39, p. 441.
[9] Hastings to Lord North, 2 Apr. 1775, Add. MS. 29127, f. 207.

who managed the Company's salt monopoly were rewarded in proportion to their success. Such rewards could be very generous indeed.

But as Hastings himself was perfectly willing to admit, the service which he left also contained a number of highly paid offices, whose duties and responsibilities were not very exacting, and some outright sinecures. He attributed these anomalies to what he called 'the curse of patronage'. Governors of Bengal received a constant stream of letters of recommendation in favour of individual members of the civil service. They ignored these at their peril. In a Company sharply divided into factions, a Governor depended for his survival in office on being able to ensure support in the Court of Directors and among the shareholders at large in their General Courts. The situation was further complicated by the interaction of national and Company politics. The affairs of Bengal were attracting increasing attention from the government and from parliament. It was therefore extremely important for a Governor to maintain friendly contacts with leading politicians. In previous generations once a man had been appointed to the Company's service in Bengal, it could perhaps be assumed that he would be able to launch his own trade and look after himself. By the 1770s, with trading opportunities limited both on land and at sea, it was difficult for a Governor to provide for an individual whom he wished to favour except by creating an office for him or by raising the income of an existing office.

Some recommendations were made publicly by the Directors in their letters to Bengal. The special office of Commissary General of Musters was created by order of the Directors to accommodate the famous bankrupt Lauchlin Macleane, who owed large sums to the veteran Company politician, Laurence Sulivan.[1] A special paymastership in Oudh was created by the Directors to serve a relative of Sir George Wombwell, Chairman of the Company.[2] Most recommendations were private, however, and indicated no specific means by which the protégé was to be helped. During Hastings's administration all contenders for power in Bengal, however much they might disagree about other matters, recognized

---

[1] Directors to Bengal, 7 Apr. 1773, *Reports*, iv. 594; see also L. S. Sutherland, *The East India Company in eighteenth-century politics* (Oxford, 1952), p. 285.

[2] Directors to Bengal, 28 Nov. 1777, I.O.R., Home Miscellaneous, 347, p. 107.

that such recommendations must as far as possible be met. Hastings himself disliked creating offices 'of no kind of use for the sake of serving an individual', but would do so in cases of 'very strong necessity'.[1] By the end of his administration, in addition to looking after a number of men who had connections with leading figures in the Company at home, he had made provision for the protégés of two Lord Chancellors, the Lord Chief Justice, the Archbishop of York and Charles Fox.[2] Philip Francis, who opposed Hastings throughout his six years in India, believed that 'it deserved my attention to gain as many attachments as promised to be useful', and used such patronage as came his way 'to serve my friends'.[3] John Macpherson, who became a Councillor in 1781 and made loud public protestations of his intention to reform the service, began, according to Hastings, by settling nine of his dependants advantageously.[4]

The mixture of motives which had produced increased emoluments is graphically illustrated by the Bengal civil establishment in the 1780s. Among its highest paid members were some who had already acquired great skill in the administration of revenue and were ruling densely populated districts, and others like Stephen Sulivan, who had come to Bengal in middle age to make a fortune with which to rescue his father and had been given the offices of Judge Advocate General, Agent Victualler to the royal naval squadron and opium contractor by Warren Hastings, out of respect for Laurence Sulivan, Hastings's patron in the Company.[5]

The principle that high official salaries should replace dubious unofficial perquisites had been applied in the first instance to the Governors of Bengal. Before Plassey a Governor of Bengal had been paid about £2,300 a year.[6] After Plassey he received a fixed salary of some £3,000, augmented by various allowances and commissions. By far the most valuable of these was a commission on the Company's territorial revenue, beginning in 1761 with 2½ per cent of the revenue of the Twenty-four Parganas, the district ceded by Mir Jafar in 1757.[7] In 1767 an elaborate scheme was

[1] Letter to Sir E. Impey, 22 Feb. 1780, Add. MS. 16261, f. 277.
[2] See my *Impeachment of Warren Hastings* (Oxford, 1965), p. 27.
[3] Letter to W. Ellis, 18 Nov. 1777, I.O.L., MS. Eur. F. 5, p. 221.
[4] Hastings to J. Scott, 15 Oct. 1783, Add. MS. 29129, f. 187.
[5] L. Sulivan to S. Sulivan, 28 Feb., 20 Nov. 1784, Bodleian, MS. Eng. Hist. b. 190, ff. 30, 32–7.   [6] See above, p. 159.
[7] Directors to Bengal, 13 Mar. 1761, *Fort William–India House Corr.* iii. 84.

devised whereby $2\frac{1}{2}$ per cent was deducted from the *diwani* revenues of the whole of Bengal and divided up among the senior civil and military officers, the Governor having 31 per cent. This was intended as a compensation for giving up trade.[1] Vansittart calculated that his revenue commission in the early 1760s amounted to about £15,000 a year,[2] while Hastings was paid £18,516 for his share in 1772–3.[3] With his salary and other commissions the Governor's emoluments must already have been close to the £25,000 a year at which they were fixed by the Regulating Act of 1773.[4] Only the Lord Lieutenant of Ireland of British public officials was paid a comparable sum.

Members of the Council were at first much less well rewarded. Unless they held certain specific offices, they only received the tiny salary of a Senior Merchant with an allowance for housing or the tenancy of a Company house. But in 1767 they were given shares in the revenue commission, varying from $1\frac{1}{2}$ to $4\frac{1}{2}$ per cent according to seniority, which yielded between £300 and £1,000 a year.[5] In 1773 greatly increased salaries for Councillors were introduced, of about £4,000 a year.[6] The much smaller number of members of the Supreme Council were paid £10,000 after 1774 under the Regulating Act.[7]

Below Council the civil service by the 1770s was divided into three sections. A large number of servants were still employed in the Company's commercial work, buying its exports and selling its imports. After 1774 the commercial servants were a more or less autonomous group directly under the authority of an institution called the Board of Trade set up to manage the Company's commerce. The story of how the Company's administrative responsibilities spread beyond Calcutta to the Twenty-four Parganas ceded in 1757, to Burdwan, Chittagong, and Midnapur ceded in 1760 and to the whole of Bengal and Bihar in 1765, and of how European Company servants began to take a direct part in

[1] Directors to Bengal, 20 Nov. 1767, ibid. v. 59.
[2] *A Letter to the Proprietors of East India Stock from Mr. Henry Vansittart* (1767), p. 138.
[3] P. J. Marshall, 'The private fortune of Warren Hastings', *Economic History Review*, 2nd ser., xvii (1964–5), p. 293.
[4] 13 Geo. III, c. 63, sec. 21.
[5] Figures for the commissions from 1767 to 1770 are given in 4th Report, Secret Committee, 1773, *Reports*, iv. 164–73.
[6] Bengal to Directors, 31 Dec. 1773, I.O.R., E/4/32, p. 225.
[7] 13 Geo. III, c. 63, sec. 21.

administration has often been told. Such servants were members
of the Revenue Department, so called partly no doubt because in
administering Bengal the Company was acting as *Diwan* or finance
minister of the Mughal emperor, but in fact an accurate description of the work done: in early British India administration was
synonymous with the collection and assessment of revenue from
the land, although responsibility for civil justice was also among the
Diwan's duties. Members of the Revenue Department served in the
secretariat and treasury in Calcutta after 1772 or were scattered
throughout Bengal with local responsibilities as Supervisors,
Collectors, or members of Revenue Councils, according to the
system then in vogue. The third branch of the service came to be
called the General Department. This consisted of a very miscellaneous range of offices, mostly in Calcutta, such as secretaries,
accountants, paymasters, translators, or storekeepers.

Adequate salaries had obviously to be paid to servants in the
Revenue Department; they were extremely well placed to provide
for themselves out of the revenue if they were not provided for.
The fixing of adequate salaries was, however, a slow process. The
salaries of the Supervisors, the first Company servants sent out into
districts after the grant of the *diwani*, were said to be based on the
principle of 'economy without meanness' in allowing SRs 1,800 a
year, or under £250, a sum which some of its recipients not surprisingly greeted with derision.[1] The members of what were called
the Provincial Revenue Councils of 1774 were laid under restrictions on their trading.[2] but were treated rather more generously
over salaries. The Chiefs were given over £4,000 a year and the
junior members about £500.[3] But the amounts were still regarded
as inadequate and drew further protests.[4] Major increases were not
granted until Hastings was able to remodel the revenue administration in 1781, when he applied his favourite principle of reward by
commission to the five members of a committee which supervised
the whole revenue system. With earnings of about £10,000 a year the
members of the Committee of Revenue and those who managed
the salt monopoly under a scheme also devised in 1781 became the

---

[1] *Proceedings of the Controlling Council of Revenue at Murshidabad* (Calcutta,
1919–24), v. 4, 86–8, 130.

[2] See above, p. 140.

[3] I.O.R., B.R.C., 18 Feb. 1774, Range 49, vol. 44, p. 477.

[4] Ibid., 31 Mar., 7 Apr. 1775, Range 49, vols. 51, pp. 1114–16; 52,
pp. 144–5.

highest paid men in the service.[1] Collectors, who administered individual districts were paid Rs 1,200 a month, or about £1,500 a year, a sum which they, and later Lord Cornwallis, regarded as still inadequate.[2]

Salaries in the commercial branch rose least of all. Private trade was never prohibited to the commercial servants. Many of them were indeed supplying the Company with their own goods, as the prohibition on servants being involved in the provision of the 'investment' was relaxed after 1774.[3] The members of the Board of Trade, senior servants who managed the Company's commercial affairs at Calcutta, were given salaries of £1,500 a year, but the Residents, who were in charge of particular *aurangs*, were only paid Rs 150 a month (£180 per annum), rising in 1778 to Rs 500 a month (£600 a year). Salaries at this level were 'little more than nominal', but it was 'supposed that the Resident had other resources'.[4] Assistants in the commercial departments in Calcutta were paid less than Rs 100 a month, a pittance which was said to make it difficult for them to borrow money even to pay their household expenses.[5]

The General Department provided the most obvious openings for the creation of extra offices with limited duties which could be used to meet the Governor's need for well paid posts to which he could appoint strongly recommended men who lacked experience or capacity. The deputy postmasters at various stations or the compiler of standing orders were obvious examples. But the General Department contained some offices, such as the secretaries, accountants, and translators from oriental languages, which were universally recognized to be extremely laborious and to need a high degree of skill and application; it also included the Residents, who represented the government of Bengal at the court of the Wazir of Oudh or with some of the Maratha generals, where they were often entrusted with very delicate diplomatic negotiations. For many of the offices in the General Department salaries were supplemented by officially recognized fees and commissions, as in

[1] Lists of earnings, I.O.R., Home Miscellaneous, 348.
[2] See their petition, I.O.R., B.R.C., 10 May 1785, Range 50, vol. 58, pp. 361–2, and *Correspondence of Charles, First Marquis Cornwallis* (1859), i. 286.
[3] See above, p. 150.
[4] West Bengal Archives, Board of Trade Proceedings, 30 Dec. 1774, 20 Mar. 1787, vols. 1, p. 183; 54, pp. 245–50.
[5] Ibid., 17 Mar. 1775, vol. 2, p. 312.

public offices in Britain. Secretaries collected fees on issuing revenue *sanads*, warrants, and appointments; accountants collected theirs on passing accounts; and paymasters took a commission on the money they handled. Senior officers in the General Department were relatively well paid. Residents at Indian courts had large allowances for expenses. Paymasters' official emoluments were calculated at between £4,600 and £5,600 and those of secretaries at between £2,500 and £3,500.[1]

Finally, there was a small group of civil and military servants the major part of whose salaries did not come from the Company but were provided by the Wazir of Oudh. The practice of persuading the Wazir to grant salaries and pensions to persons whom the Governor or other important Company servants wished to favour apparently began some time after 1776.[2] In 1781 Hastings yielded to protests from the Wazir and ordered that all Company servants not officially employed in the Lucknow Residency or in the army in Oudh should be recalled. Private importunities seem, however, to have got the better of him. He commented that the Wazir in 1783 was 'loaded with as many pensioners as he was when I agreed and engaged to recall them'.[3] In 1785 a list of those receiving salaries and allowances from the Wazir appears for the first time on the Company's records. It included nine soldiers, eleven civil servants, and two surgeons, all being paid at a generous rate.[4]

By the standards of British public life elsewhere average earnings throughout the Bengal civil service of £2,261 were very high indeed. Chief Clerks in the British Treasury in London who earned £850 have been described as 'unquestionably well-to-do'.[5] An investigation of the Secretary of State's office suggested £1,500 as suitable for an Under Secretary with £800 for a Chief Clerk.[6] High salaries in Bengal were usually defended on two grounds: men must be adequately compensated for the risks they ran and for the separation from their families and friends which they had to endure, and they must be cushioned against the exorbitant expenses of life in Calcutta. New heights were reached after Plassey in the lavish hospitality and display on which the British community

---

[1] I.O.R., Home Miscellaneous, 348.
[2] J. Bristow to P. Francis, 25 Oct. 1785, I.O.L., MS. Eur. G. 4, f. 243.
[3] Hastings to J. Scott, 7 Feb. 1783, Add. MS. 29129, f. 60.
[4] I.O.R., L/PARL/1/20, no. 39.
[5] H. Roseveare, *The Treasury* (1969), p. 105.
[6] M. A. Thomson, *The Secretaries of State 1681–1782* (Oxford, 1932), p. 142.

had prided itself for so long. Clive spent a lakh of rupees (about £11,000) on his 'table' expenses during the twenty months of his second administration.[1] Neither Verelst nor Hastings, men of more modest tastes than Clive, could live on their official earnings of over £20,000.[2] Those who tried to live more frugally constantly complained about the cost of housing, the number of servants that had to be employed and the charges levied on articles imported from Europe. By the 1780s suitable accommodation for a Company servant was said to cost between £300 and £800 a year, while an establishment of servants, 'upon the lowest level of oeconomy' required another £120, in spite of repeated efforts to peg wages.[3] A man who had served in a public office at home thought Indian salaries ought in fairness to be twice as high as British ones;[4] five times as high was even suggested.[5]

When Lord Cornwallis became Governor General in 1786 and began to apply to the Bengal civil service standards of reform that were being slowly applied to public life in Britain, he did not usually object to the level of salaries. What he objected to was the payment of high salaries to men who were manifestly incompetent and were filling offices of little use as well as to able men who filled offices with very great responsibilities. His task was not to create a salaried service, but to shape one which was already in existence into greater conformity with the Company's actual needs.

Cornwallis was also to wage war on unofficial perquisites and private profits. The most spectacular of these, the distribution of presents by Indian rulers, ceased by the 1770s, but there was still a luxuriant undergrowth of unacknowledged incomes, often involving extortion from Indians or defrauding of the Company, in every branch of the civil service.

In addition to their immense salaries or commissions on the revenue, Governors of Bengal enjoyed certain perquisites. Some were officially recognized: a small commission on issues by the

[1] I.O.R., B.P.C., 20 Jan. 1767, Range 1, vol. 41, f. 33.
[2] Verelst to Clive, 28 Sept. 1767, Ames MSS., I.O.L., Microfilm, reel 606; Marshall, 'Personal Fortune of Hastings', *Economic History Review*, 2nd ser., xvii. 292.
[3] Minute by Cornwallis, 1786, I.O.R., Home Miscellaneous, 79, pp. 417–22.
[4] This was said by John Stewart, I.O.R., B.P.C., 28 Nov. 1775, Range 2, vol. 12, f. 33.
[5] [G. Smith], 'Observations on the British possessions in India', P.R.O., 30/11/112, f. 140.

Calcutta mint, a commission on sales of imported coral, and a duty
on goods exported by the 'freight ships' from Calcutta.[1] The legal
status of the most valuable of the Governor's perquisites was, however, in doubt. This was the receipt of *nazrs* or *salaamis*, ceremonial
presents offered by Indian officials, revenue farmers, and *zamindars*. These payments had presumably been made to the Nawabs
of Bengal on occasions like the annual *punyah*, or letting of the
lands. The sums involved were very large. Clive declared the
receipt of two lakhs of rupees from *nazrs* during his second
Governorship.[2] Verelst kept £33,000 from his *nazrs*.[3] In the last
five years of his administration, the only period of which his
personal accounts survive, Hastings's *nazrs* amounted to about
£12,000,[4] although he was breaking the Regulating Act by accepting them.

Servants in the Revenue Department had very obvious opportunities for augmenting their salaries by perquisites. Before 1757
the Company's revenue resources had been limited to Calcutta.
Within ten years £58,000 had been added for the Twenty-four
Parganas, about £650,000 for Mir Kasim's cessions and about
£1,500,000 for the rest of Bengal and Bihar.[5] Considerable sums
over and above what the Company received certainly remained
each year with its European servants through whose hands the
collections passed.

The revenue system which the British inherited was an extremely complex one, varying greatly in different parts of Bengal
and Bihar. In essentials, revenue was paid, usually in cash, by
cultivators at certain times throughout the year to intermediaries,
who were responsible for handing on a proportion of it to the
Nawabs' government. Who these intermediaries were, how much
revenue they accounted for, and over what sort of area, were questions to which answers varied in different parts of the provinces.
At one end of the scale there had been a tendency in the late
seventeenth and early eighteenth century for enormous holdings
to be built up by which a single *zamindar* might be responsible for

---

[1] See above, p. 74.
[2] I.O.R., B.P.C., 20 Jan. 1767, Range 1, vol. 41, ff. 33–5.
[3] I.O.R., Home Miscellaneous, 824, p. 321; Verelst to Clive, 28 Sept. 1767,
Ames MSS., I.O.L. Microfilm, reel 606.
[4] Marshall, 'Personal fortune of Hastings', *Economic History Review*, 2nd
ser., xvii. 295.
[5] 4th Report, Secret Committee, 1773, *Reports*, iv. 98–100.

paying the revenue raised from thousands of square miles, inhabited by hundreds of thousands of people with a maze of under tenures. At the other extreme, some areas were subdivided into innumerable microscopic tenures in which a mass of small *zamindars* or *talukdars* rendered payments to government collectors. The biggest *zamindaris* of eighteenth-century Bengal were Rajshahi with some 13,000 square miles and Burdwan with 5,000; in the frontier districts of Midnapur and Chittagong there were thought to be 3,000 and 1,500 small *zamindars* respectively.[1] For certain districts at certain times the government appointed revenue contractors or farmers, who would replace the existing *zamindar* and bind themselves to raise a stipulated sum over a particular period of time.

The system was riddled with opportunities for personal gain, of which Europeans soon became aware. To become one of the revenue intermediaries responsible for a particular district could in certain circumstances be highly profitable. The level of profit depended on a capacity to collect rigorously from the cultivators or under tenure holders and to conceal the extent of actual collections from the government, so that a sizeable margin was left between what was collected and what was handed over. In the early years of the Company's rule Europeans were often tempted to undertake revenue farms. Mir Jafar's grant of the Twenty-four Parganas was openly farmed to groups of Europeans, a part, for instance, being let in 1762 to a syndicate which included Vansittart and Hastings.[2] The rates at which the lands had been let were later discovered to have been so low that Clive commented: 'If the gentlemen who formerly parcelled the pergunnahs amongst themselves did not acquire large advantages it is certain that the servants acting under them did.'[3] European farming spread to Burdwan, one of the districts ceded by Mir Kasim in 1760. The Rajas of Burdwan collected their revenue through a series of under farmers, among whom by 1762 were the famous firm of John Johnstone, William Hay and William Bolts, who were already

---

[1] N. K. Sinha, *Economic History of Bengal* (Calcutta, 1956–70), ii. 17.

[2] Committee of New Lands Proceedings, 13 Jan. 1762, I.O.R., Range 98, vol. 10. Three farms were held by Europeans at the first letting in 1759 (I.O.L., MS. Eur. G. 37, box 4).

[3] I.O.R., B.P.C., 20 Jan. 1767, Range 1, vol. 41, ff. 29–30; for further accounts of frauds in the 24 Parganas see ibid., 16 Feb., 29 Apr. 1767, Range 1, vol. 41, ff. 74–7, 154–7.

so deeply involved in Bengal's internal trade. Johnstone was in a particularly strong position to obtain lucrative farms for his associates since he had been appointed the Company's Resident at Burdwan and remained there for three years. In 1765 a subsequent Resident reported that the farms of the Johnstone firm had been relet to Indian contractors at 'a great advance', the implication clearly being that Johnstone had given the lands to himself and his friends at a rate that was much lower than the Company should have received. Johnstone denied that this was true.[1] Even if the Johnstone partnership had not defrauded the Company, which is not a very likely supposition, it was clearly most undesirable that the Company's servants should be in a position to strike bargains with themselves in contracting for the Company's revenue. Instructions were issued by the Directors in 1766 formally forbidding Company servants from being directly involved in farming revenue.[2]

In practice, however, European participation in revenue farms actually increased, especially after 1772, when the Company put much of Bengal under temporary farmers. But more circumspection was required than before. Farms in which Europeans were involved were generally held in the name of an Indian agent, usually that of the European's banian. The existence of clandestine European revenue farms was made public in 1775, when investigations were begun by the new Supreme Council. The Collector of Monghyr in Bihar admitted that he farmed part of the area under his jurisdiction through his banian;[3] the Collector of Sylhet did the same;[4] and a *pargana* in Burdwan was also farmed by a Company servant in the same way.[5] In some other cases where banians were found to be holding revenue farms it is, however, less easy to be sure that their masters were involved. The most notorious of these were the huge concerns, amounting to over Rs 500,000 of Cantu Babu, the banian of Warren Hastings, at that time Governor. There is no direct evidence that Hastings had any share in Cantu's farms, which, he alleged, were 'taken and

[1] I.O.R., Select Committee Proceedings, 14 Sept. 1765, Range A, vol. 6, pp. 584–5; I.O.R., B.P.C., 7 Oct. 1765, Range 1, vol. 38, ff. 383–5.
[2] Directors to Bengal, 17 May 1766, *Reports*, iv. 115–16.
[3] I.O.R., B.R.C., 11 June, 16 July 1776, Range 49, vols. 62, pp. 334–55; 63, pp. 51–4.
[4] Ibid., 15 Aug. 1775, Range 49, vol. 55, pp. 70–88.
[5] Ibid., 26 May 1775, Range 49, vol. 53, pp. 115–19.

held without my advice and almost all without my knowledge',[1] a conclusion confirmed by the thorough researches of Cantu's biographer. By 1772 Cantu, like other important banians, was certainly a man of great wealth and influence, perfectly capable of acting on his own initiative to further his own interests.

Revenue farming among the Company's servants in the Revenue Department may have been widespread at certain times; collecting more revenue than was actually accounted for to the Company was probably universal up to 1784 and beyond. It could take many forms from simple embezzlement of money before it reached the Company to the levying of extra cesses for the personal profit of the European collector or the extraction of presents from *zamindars*. Embezzlement on a large scale seems to have occurred during the Company's early revenue operations. Clive's investigations in his second administration led him to believe that over two lakhs of rupees had been collected from the Twenty-four Parganas but never accounted for to the Company,[2] and that two-and-a-half lakhs a year had been embezzled at Midnapur.[3] The possibility of placing extra cesses on the revenue for private gain arose from the Mughal system of calculating revenue on the basis of a fixed assessment to which additional cesses, called *abwabs*, were added. European revenue collectors, like their Mughal predecessors, were in the habit of adding *abwabs* which went into their own pockets. The most celebrated of all the cesses collected for private profit was one called 'mahtoot' (*mahtaut*), which attracted much publicity in Britain. It was a cess which had been levied throughout Bengal for the benefit of the Nawab and his revenue administrators. From 1765 at least until 1772 a considerable part of the 'mahtoot' was appropriated by the Company's Resident at the Nawab's court, who supervised the work of the Indian ministers there. About Rs 70,000 or Rs 80,000 was distributed to senior servants, the Resident also taking Rs 2,000 per month for his 'table' and a further Rs 2,000 a month as commission for providing the ceremonial dresses issued at the annual revenue settlement.[4] 'Durbar Crutch' was another name for a cess collected for private profit. It was rumoured that 'Durbar Crutch' was extracted from

[1] Ibid., 28 June 1775, Range 49, vol. 54, p. 896.
[2] Letter to F. Sykes, 23 Nov. 1765, N.L.W., Clive MSS., 223, p. 55.
[3] Bengal to Directors, 31 Jan. 1766, *Fort William–India House Corr.* iv. 384.
[4] 4th Report, Secret Committee, 1773, *Reports*, iv. 110–13, 216–40; Sykes to Hastings, 28 Jan. 1773, Add. MS. 29133, ff. 348–53.

many *zamindars* and revenue farmers in 1772 by Hastings and other Councillors who made the revenue settlements for that year.[1] 'Mahtoots' and 'Durbar Crutch' were also taken by local collectors from local revenue payers. A 'mahtoot' was said, for instance, to be in force at Rangpur in 1770.[2]

Offers of presents were probably the most obvious temptation faced by European revenue collectors. Many of their official acts were the occasion for *nazrs* or *salaamis*, ceremonial offerings individually of no great amount; but sizeable sums could be held out to them at certain times. Their decisions could enrich or impoverish *zamindars*, revenue farmers, or Indian officials serving under them, some of whom would certainly be willing to pay for what they might regard as the right decision. As an experienced revenue servant put it, 'The fluctuations of the revenue since the English . . . have opened the largest field for abuses . . . Annual settlements with zemindars, agreements with farmers upon long or short leases, beneficial farms, occasional abatements' could all be 'made subservient to private interests'.[3] Allegations of presents being taken from the payers of revenue are innumerable. Even before the Company acquired the *diwani* which gave it formal authority over most of Bengal, Clive believed that its servants were selling their protection to *zamindars*. He heard that William Billers, who committed suicide under investigation, extracted money from all 'the principal Jemidars' in Bihar.[4] George Gray, the Company's Resident at Malda, collected in 1764 what he called 'voluntary presents from zemindars and others whom by my situation I was enabled to assist or oblige'; many witnesses were, however, produced to show how payments had been enforced by violent extortion, involving torture.[5]

The history of the great *zamindari* of Burdwan provides a very well documented example of how occasions arose at regular intervals for presents to change hands during the first thirty years or so of British revenue administration in Bengal. The immediate reaction of Tilakchand, Raja of Burdwan, to becoming a tributary

[1] I.O.R., B.R.C., 5 May 1775, Range 49, vol. 52, p. 636.
[2] *Proceedings of Controlling Council*, xi. 205.
[3] C. W. B. Rouse, to Francis, 2 July 1776, I.O.L., MS. Eur. C. 7, pp. 459–60.
[4] Letter to F. Sykes, 25 July 1765, I.O.L., MS. Eur. G. 37, box 3.
[5] I.O.R., B.P.C., 30 Dec. 1765, 3 Mar. 1766, Range 1, vols. 38, ff. 566–91; 39, ff. 108–17. Clive to F. Sykes, 24 Nov., 21 Dec. 1765, N.L.W., Clive MSS., 223, pp. 53–4, 93.

of the Company in the place of the Nawab in 1760 was to bargain for the lowest possible assessment by offering presents to the Councillors who were going to make it with him.[1] When Residents were appointed to Burdwan on the Company's behalf, they too became the target for presents, offered to them by the Raja himself, the *zamindari* servants or the farmers of particular districts. During his years at Burdwan from 1762 to 1765 John Johnstone was alleged to have accepted many such offers,[2] including sums amounting to two lakhs of rupees from the Raja.[3] Fresh allegations were made about events which followed the death of Tilakchand in 1770. Large sums were said to have been paid out to confirm the succession of his infant son, Tejchand, and to enable one Brijar Kissor to win and retain the post of *diwan* of Burdwan and thus to control the management of the *zamindari*. John Graham, the Resident at Burdwan in 1770, was said to have taken over two lakhs, while two more were given to his successor Charles Stuart.[4] In 1775 Brijar Kissor was dismissed by the new members of the Supreme Council and replaced by the Raja's mother as the effective administrator of the *zamindari*, a service for which she was alleged to have paid over two lakhs to the new Councillors and their Indian allies.[5] Yet another change took place in 1780, when payments due from Burdwan to the Company fell into arrears and the Council decided to remove the Rani from the management and to replace her with a temporary administrator. The man chosen was Nobkissen, one of the richest members of the Indian community in Calcutta who had been closely associated with many Europeans over a long period. Nobkissen marked his appointment by making a loan to Warren Hastings of three lakhs of rupees, a sum which Hastings eventually kept as a present.[6]

The size of the Burdwan *zamindari* and of the potential profits to be made out of handling the revenue of a district which

[1] W. Sumner's evidence, 1st Report, Select Committee, 1772, *Reports*, iii. 163–4.
[2] See a series of letters from J. Ashburner to Verelst, 28 Oct. 1765 to 27 Jan. 1766, I.O.L., MS. Eur. G. 37, box 36, ff. 25–31.   [3] Account in ibid., box 10.
[4] I.O.R., B.R.C., 30 Dec. 1774, 6 Jan., 10 Mar., 31 Oct., 1775, Range 49, vols. 48, pp. 280–91; 50, pp. 1–30; 51, pp. 971–90; 56, pp. 521–612; West Bengal Archives, Miscellaneous Revenue Records, vol. 2, pp. 277–9.
[5] 'Memorandum of information given to Mr Hastings', Add. MS. 29198, f. 325.
[6] This episode is examined in my article 'Nobkissen versus Hastings', *Bulletin of the School of Oriental and African Studies*, xxvii (1964).

normally paid some forty lakhs of rupees a year (about £450,000) to the Company made its control a highly desirable object for which competitors were prepared to pay lavishly. Even if specific allegations about presents cannot usually be substantiated and many of them may well have been exaggerated or even fictitious, it is not difficult to see why Burdwan had the reputation of being a lucrative station for any Company servant concerned with its revenue. The stakes may have been higher in Burdwan than elsewhere, but a situation in which there were many rivals for the favours that it was in the power of the European revenue servants to bestow recurred in many other districts.

Every level of Bengal's revenue system before and after the British conquest seems to have depended on loans being available to enable the revenue payers to meet their commitments on time. Interest was charged on such loans at a very high rate, which made them an attractive if risky form of investment for Europeans. Loans by Englishmen to the Nawab himself never developed on a scale comparable to those at Madras, presumably because the Nawabs of Bengal controlled only limited resources after 1765. But much money was advanced to subordinate revenue payers, especially by Company servants in the Revenue Department who were in a position to protect their loans and to enforce payment of interest.

The practice of borrowing in advance of their receipts seems to have been universal among *zamindars*, their needs presumably providing much of the business of the bankers of pre-British Bengal. Shortly after Plassey, Englishmen began to explore the possibility of making such loans themselves. Luke Scrafton, Clive's first Resident at Mir Jafar's court, got back Rs 90,000 on Rs 50,000 which he had advanced to the *zamindar* of Rajshahi.[1] Clive disapproved of loans to *zamindars*. He forbade them[2] and ordered that interest on any loans made by Europeans should be limited to 12 per cent.[3] He was, however, prepared to allow exceptions for those whom he regarded as deserving (such as the captain of a country ship who had lost his money playing cards),[4] and his regulations seem generally to have been disregarded. Servants in the Revenue Department evidently regarded loans to *zamindars* as a

[1] Letter to Hastings, n.d., Add. MS. 29132, f. 63.
[2] Select Committee Proceedings, 25 Oct. 1765, *Reports*, iv. 115.
[3] Select Committee Proceedings, 31 Dec. 1766, ibid., iv. 115.
[4] Letter to F. Sykes, 9 Jan. 1766, N.L.W., Clive MSS. 224, p. 30.

customary perquisite. Two instances on which much information came to light were the loans of Captain David Mackenzie in Rangpur and a loan made to the dowager Rani of Burdwan. Captain Mackenzie, who was stationed at Rangpur with a detachment of sepoys, made loans to *zamindars* there in 1769 and 1770 at 60 per cent (5 per cent a month) rising to 168 per cent (14 per cent a month).[1] The dowager Rani, in whose name a portion of the Burdwan *zamindari* was managed, was charged 2 per cent a month, regarded as moderate interest on *zamindari* loans, on a sum of Rs 170,000 put up in 1773 by a syndicate of Europeans.[2]

Even higher rates could sometimes be obtained by those who had direct access to men at the bottom of the revenue hierarchy. In 1770 William Young, who was stationed in the Twenty-four Parganas, advanced money to certain *shikdars*, minor revenue collectors, who were to obtain paddy for him. He then discovered that the *shikdars* were using his money to make loans at 150 per cent to cultivators, who, he said, were 'glad to get money upon any terms' to pay their revenue before the next rice harvest. Young decided to take a share in these profitable transactions and demanded that the *shikdars* pay him 100 per cent. He lent money to them on other occasions at 90 and even at 180 per cent.[3]

Contemporaries believed that virtually every servant employed in the Revenue Department enjoyed unofficial profits of some kind or other. Even a very austere young man called Charles Boughton Rouse, who enlisted in Philip Francis's campaign of reform, admitted that he had 'gained private advantages which at the time I disapproved'.[4] The scale on which such private advantages were harvested was probably very large in the years immediately after Plassey, declining somewhat by the 1770s. There can be little doubt that very substantial deductions were made from the revenue of the Twenty-four Parganas, Burdwan, Chittagong, or Midnapur, when they were first acquired. For the first few years after the grant of the *diwani* of the rest of Bengal and Bihar, the only servants actively involved in the administration of the revenue

[1] *Proceedings of the Controlling Council*, vii. 17, 128; ix. 198, 208; x. 3, 23-4.

[2] I.O.R., B.R.C., 25 July, 27 Oct., 1 Dec. 1775, Range 49, vols. 54, pp. 1321-37; 56, pp. 324-448; 58, pp. 103-5; also a collection of papers on the loans in Bodleian, dep. b. 82.

[3] Calcutta High Court Records, Mayor's Court, *Young v. Gopaul Sircar and Beergoram Majunder.*

[4] Letter to Francis, 2 July 1776, I.O.L., MS. Eur. C. 7, p. 460.

of the new lands were a Resident at Murshidabad and a Super-
intendent for Bihar at Patna. Both posts were reputed to be
extremely valuable. Two of the greatest fortunes of this period
were made at Murshidabad and Patna by Francis Sykes and
Thomas Rumbold. In 1769 three lakhs of rupees in profits
'exclusive of all trade' were distributed among the servants at the
Murshidabad Residency.[1] From 1769 British revenue administrators began to be posted widely throughout Bengal and Bihar
as Supervisors, Collectors, or members of provincial Revenue
Councils. By 1773 Hastings believed that Collectorships had
become 'more lucrative than any posts in the service' and heard
that Collectors made at least a lakh a year on the side (part of which
was likely to have been gained by trading as well as from administering the revenue).[2] By the 1770s, however, it seems to have
been increasingly difficult to make very large gains from the
revenue. The resources of districts and *zamindaris* came to be
better known; obvious deficiencies drew comments and inquiries.
The possibility of being informed against by those from whom one
had taken money became a very real one, especially after the new
Councillors arrived in 1774 and began to collect information against
Hastings. But in some districts where supervision was less strict
expectations remained high. It was still being said in 1776 of
service in Bihar that 'every man that has any thing to do with the
revenue . . . has made a fortune'.[3] There was eager competition for
Collectorships there.[4] In Bengal itself expectations were generally
lower, but there were still some profitable districts. An attempt
was made in 1779 to buy out the Collector of Rangpur by an offer
of a lakh of rupees for vacating his collectorship.[5] Profiteering by
Collectors was still periodically exposed even during Cornwallis's
administration.[6]

The Company's Bengal trade had for generations been made to
yield private profits. In the Commercial Department, set up in 1774
under the new Board of Trade, such practices seem to have reached
new heights. The Court of Directors finally came to the conclusion

[1] This estimate is based on a statement in R. Goodlad to unknown, 26 Feb.
1771, Add. MS. 29132, f. 415.
[2] Letter to J. Dupré, 6 Jan. 1773, Add. MS. 29127, f. 62.
[3] D. Anderson to T. Graham, 30 Aug. 1776, Add. MS. 45439, f. 83.
[4] J. Scott to W. Hastings, 20 Oct. 1780, Add. MS. 29146, f. 171.
[5] R. Goodlad to G. Bogle, 24 Sept. 1779, Mitchell Library, Bogle MSS.
[6] A. Aspinall, *Cornwallis in Bengal* (Manchester, 1931), pp. 158-9.

that many of its commercial servants had joined in a systematic conspiracy to defraud the Company of some £200,000 by adding large perquisites for themselves to the price of the goods shipped from Bengal.[1] The allegations seem to have been substantially true. With their official emoluments kept to a very low level, and with poor prospects for success in the private trade to which they were still legally entitled, many of the commercial servants seem to have decided to take profits for themselves, either from the Company or from the Indians with whom they dealt, and thus to gain some sort of equivalent for what was being made in other branches of the service.

The methods by which private perquisites could be levied out of the Company's trade were well tried.[2] Commercial servants evidently continued to apply the Company's money entrusted to their care to their own purposes. In 1776 one of the assistants at Dacca revealed that over two lakhs, which should have been in the Dacca treasury, were missing. The Chief at Dacca, Nicholas Grueber, then volunteered the information that 'the deficiency will be found in the hands of my banyan'.[3] Grueber was able in time to refund what he had removed, but the Company lost the money taken by another servant at Dacca called David Killican. When Killican died insolvent in 1785, he was found to have appropriated very large sums, which should have been spent on the Dacca investment, to his own use.[4]

Commissions unofficially charged to the Company and 'dastur' levied from merchants or weavers seem to have been collected in some form or other at every commercial station. A documented instance is that of William Barton, who practised both fraud against the Company and extortion against the weavers. He added what he called 'aurung charges' for himself amounting to Rs 59,000 over three years to the cloth he supplied to the Company from Lakshmipur, and took Rs 48,000 in 'dastur' from the weavers. He is also alleged to have accepted a present of Rs 20,000 from one of his brokers as the price for not investigating complaints against him.[5]

---

[1] The figure of £200,000 is included in the Bill in *East India Company* v. *Aldersey et al.*, P.R.O., C 12/175/27.   [2] See above, pp. 160-2.
[3] West Bengal Archives, Board of Trade Proceedings, 24 Apr., 10, 21, 28 May, 8 Nov. 1776, vols. 7, pp. 114-18, 244, 328, 356-7; 9, p. 234.
[4] Calcutta Bar Library Club, Supreme Court Reports, xiv. 36-41.
[5] West Bengal Archives, Board of Trade Proceedings, 7 Aug., 14 Sept., 13 Oct. 1775, vols. 4, pp. 208-26, 445-59; 5, pp. 58-60.

When the misdemeanours of Grueber and Barton came to light in 1775 and 1776, the Board of Trade, who managed the Company's commerce, had, if perhaps reluctantly, to see that justice was done and the Company's interests protected. Within a few years, however, the Board of Trade was colluding with the servants at many commercial factories and residencies to defraud the Company. Warren Hastings was evidently aware of what was happening, warning one of the members of the Board of Trade that 'it is universally believed that every article of the investment is provided for the Company at 30 or 40 or even 50 per cent beyond its real cost',[1] but he chose to take no action. The frauds continued until information about them finally reached England. In 1786 the Court of Directors began a series of prosecutions against their commercial servants in the Supreme Court in Calcutta and in the Court of Chancery in London. Few convictions were obtained, but much was admitted, or at least not contested, and one of those against whom particularly serious charges had been brought chose to abscond.

It appears that the Board of Trade's members instituted a fund to supplement their salaries by deducting a certain part, usually 8 per cent, of the price paid to European contractors who provided the Company's silk and piecegoods. To ensure that the contractors did not suffer from the deductions, they were allowed generous prices for their goods as compensation. The real sufferer was of course the Company which had to pay the generous prices.[2] For some contracts specific bargains seem to have been made for overcharging which went far beyond an 8 per cent commission. Such collusion was particularly prevalent in the contracts for raw silk. Silk was sold at a certain price per 'seer' of some two pounds weight. Inquiries by the Company suggested that the average price of 'filature' silk (wound by European methods in the new silk works)[3] in the open market was at the most Rs 8. 12 annas per seer, while that for 'Bengal wound' silk was about Rs 7.[4] Yet Jacob

---

[1] Letter to S. Droz [June 1782], Add. MS. 29115, f. 110.

[2] Calcutta High Court Records, Supreme Court, Equity, *East India Company* v. *Barton, Blaquiere et al.*; *East India Company* v. *Aldersey et al.*, P.R.O., C 12/175/27. See also Aspinall, *Cornwallis in Bengal*, p. 33; H. Furber, *John Company at Work* (Cambridge, Mass., 1951), pp. 332–4.

[3] See above, p. 151.

[4] As well as statements in the Company's bills in the Supreme Court and in Chancery, see C. Stuart's calculations, West Bengal Archives, Board of Trade Proceedings, 18 July 1786, vol. 51, pp. 450–1.

Rider was allowed Rs 14 for filature silk and Rs 10 for Bengal wound;[1] for filature silk Thomas Henchman was paid Rs 13½ or Rs 12,[2] and James Keighley Rs 12. 6 annas.[3] The need for the contractors to invest in expensive new buildings and equipment was offered as a defence for the generous terms for filature silk, but much else was clearly allowed for in the price. Two of the contractors admitted that Rs 1½ per seer went as a perquisite into the pockets of the Board of Trade.[4] Collusive overcharging beyond a commission of 8 per cent, also occurred in the contracts for piece-goods. On contracts arranged in 1784 by William Barton, who had succeeded to the Presidency of the Board of Trade in spite of a record of proven dishonesty, 'the difference between the fair or real price and that charged' was said to be '35 or 40 per cent'.[5] Barton declined to stand trial on this and other charges and fled to Serampore, the Danish settlement.

Certain offices in the General Department also provided openings for large unofficial profits. Paymasterships in Bengal, as elsewhere, were recognized to be lucrative posts since they handled large sums of public money which could be turned to profitable private use. Contemporary opinion was inclined to accept this as a legitimate perquisite, so long as the paymaster could make repayment when he was required to do so. But with highly uncertain trading conditions existing in Bengal, paymasters were often caught with huge balances which they could not hope to pay off. In one dispatch in 1780 the Bengal Council had to record the death of two paymasters, owing six and four lakhs respectively, and the absconding of another against whom the Company had claims amounting to nine and a-half lakhs.[6] Storekeepers, commissaries, and other servants, who were responsible for building work or the supply of equipment or material had obvious temptations to overcharge or to deliver short quantities. 'Every man, now, who is permitted to make a bill, makes a fortune', Clive commented.[7] The worst abuses seem to have been committed in the great military

[1] Calcutta High Court Records, Supreme Court, Equity, *East India Company v. Barton and Bateman.*

[2] Ibid., *East India Company v. Barton and Henchman.*

[3] *East India Company v. Keighley,* P.R.O., C 12/977/29.

[4] Answers of T. Chapman and J. Worship in *East India Company v. Aldersey et al.,* ibid., C 12/175/27.

[5] Calcutta Bar Library Club, Supreme Court Reports, xxiv. 511.

[6] Bengal to Directors, 29 Nov. 1780, I.O.R., E/4/39, pp. 65–8.

[7] *Parliamentary History of England,* xvii. 361.

building programme, intended to make the Company secure in Bengal after Plassey. A huge new fort was built at Calcutta with three sets of barracks to lodge the army up-country. A disgraceful story of uncontrolled spending accompanied by pillaging of the Company soon came to light.[1] Very large sums were paid out for non-existent workmen said to be employed in the fort, and materials for it were overcharged by about 50 per cent. Public blame was put on Indian agents and on the Company's Engineer and a junior servant, both of whom absconded, but it was generally known that two councillors, William Mackett and Thomas Boddam, had connived in the frauds and taken a share in them.[2] The Company was swindled in all three barrack projects, but the frauds at Berhampur, near Murshidabad, were particularly gross, involving 'an amazing amount'.[3] The chief culprits there were the members of the Kasimbazar factory who carried out the work. They refused to produce their accounts, claiming that they had been destroyed, but one of them was shown to have overcharged for materials and to have received payment for timbers which he had never supplied.[4]

The alternative to having supplies or services provided by a salaried servant was to put them out to contract. The creation of contracts and agencies became increasingly frequent as the Company's needs grew. In theory, the Company was intended to benefit by inviting individuals to bid against one another to offer the cheapest terms; in practice, collusion frequently took place between those who submitted bids and the Company servants who made the award, so that extremely generous terms emerged. As was the case in Britain,[5] contracts were regarded as a form of patronage. Some of them were distributed to those whom the Governor wished to favour. In such cases terms were fixed which allowed the contractor to make a sizeable profit before sub-

[1] S. Wilks's narrative in 9th Report, Secret Committee, 1773, *Reports*, iv. 641–6, 653–61.

[2] The official version is in Bengal to Directors, 16 Jan. 1761, *Fort William–India House Corr.* iii. 296–7; for private accounts, see letters of T. Amphlett and H. Vansittart to Clive, 21 Dec. 1760, 19 Jan. 1761, I.O.L., MS. Eur. G. 37, boxes 28, 29.

[3] Verelst to R. Palk, 21 Sept. 1768, Ames MSS., I.O.L. Microfilm, reel 606.

[4] Calcutta High Court Records, Mayor's Court, *East India Company* v. *Williamson*.

[5] N. Baker, *Government and Contractors. The British Treasury and War Supplies 1775–83* (1971), p. 249.

contracting his concession to someone actually capable of executing it. The most valuable contract in Bengal was traditionally supposed to be the one by which the Company's army was supplied with bullocks. Allegations about inflated terms and fraudulent practices by the contractors were being made as early as 1760.[1] By the end of Hastings's administration the bullock contractor was thought to make a profit of some £17,000 a year.[2] The contract for supplying the Company with opium under its monopoly of 1773 was granted on terms so generous that the contractor could stipulate for £10,000 from a sub-contractor, who could himself stipulate for £17,000 from yet another sub-contractor, who was still able to make a handsome profit.[3] Other agencies and contracts during Hastings's administration, such as those for supplying elephants, boats, or medical stores, for shipping rice to Madras, for maintaining stores in Fort William, or manufacturing gun powder, also aroused suspicions of favouritism in the choice of contractor and liberality in fixing the terms.[4]

Any member of the Bengal establishment appointed outside the Company's provinces, to Oudh or to Banaras, counted himself exceptionally fortunate. Here perquisites and profits could be taken which the Company was powerless to prevent, while the Wazirs of Oudh or Rajas of Banaras found it very difficult to protect themselves against the depredations of well connected Englishmen. The Banaras and Lucknow Residencies were among the plums of the service and became the objects of intense lobbying in England as well as in India. A Resident was appointed to Banaras for the first time in 1764, immediately taking over the running of the mint for his own profit and obtaining revenue farms for his banian.[5] The Residency was re-established in 1775 and as British control over Banaras increased, so did the Resident's personal profits. In 1782 his private income was thought to be a lakh a year.[6] Part of this came from trading,[7] but the Resident was also involved in the collection of the revenue and able to extract large sums from those who paid it.[8]

---

[1] J. Carnac to Clive, 2 Nov. 1760, I.O.L., MS. Eur. G. 37, box 28; See also I.O.R., B.P.C., 31 May 1764, Range 1, vol. 37, f. 196.

[2] I.O.R., Home Miscellaneous, 362, p. 251; P. J. Marshall, *Impeachment of Hastings*, pp. 172–4. [3] Ibid., p. 169.

[4] Ibid., pp. 163–79; I.O.R., Home Miscellaneous, 347, pp. 192–5; 362, p. 251.

[5] W. Bolts, *Considerations on India Affairs* (1772–5), ii. 31–3.

[6] R. Johnson to Sir E. Impey, 4 Sept. 1782, Add. MS. 16263, f. 305.

[7] See above, p. 149.

[8] I.O.R., B.R.C., 13 July 1787, Range 51, vol. 8, pp. 1054–89.

Most Europeans went to Oudh as soldiers, but from 1773 there was a civilian Resident at Lucknow with a number of assistants, while favoured individuals were able to attach themselves to the Wazir's court and draw various allowances from him.[1] Valuable as Oudh was as a source of patronage for Hastings, he confessed himself 'distressed beyond measure' by what he heard of the behaviour of Englishmen at the Wazir's court. 'Lucknow was a sink of iniquity. It was the school of rapacity', he wrote. 'Beardless boys' were rejecting allowances of Rs 3,000 or Rs 5,000 a month as inadequate, and gambling away two lakhs of rupees at a sitting.[2] The Wazir's generosity was severely taxed. In addition to the very large official allowances which he was required to make to the Residents, they took a further Rs 12,000 a month as a personal allowance and Rs 25,000 a month for the expenses of the Residency. The Residents were also able to make large profits by manipulating the exchange on the money which they were required to remit from Lucknow to Calcutta.[3] The Wazir borrowed money from private Europeans, in some cases at 48 per cent (4 per cent a month).[4] By 1778 he had built up a debt to private English creditors of over twenty-six lakhs.[5]

By the standards of the nineteenth- or twentieth-century Indian Civil Service, the Bengal service in the eighteenth century with its almost universal resort to private perquisites stands totally condemned. By eighteenth-century standards there was much that was very seriously amiss in it; but there were also genuine differences between what was expected of a man in office in the eighteenth and in the nineteenth century. To judge men of Clive's or Hastings's era by the standards of 'the Guardians' would be unrealistic.

Eighteenth-century opinion had no doubts whatsoever about men who embezzled the Company's money, took payment for what they did not deliver, or rigged prices for their own advantage.

[1] See above, p. 188.

[2] *Warren Hastings' Letters to Sir John Macpherson*, ed. H. Dodwell (1927), p. 106.

[3] F. Russell's report on charges against J. Bristow, 28 Nov. 1785, I.O.R., Home Miscellaneous, 345, pp. 5–21; on the Residents' perquisites, see also E. Wheler to Hastings, 4 Sept. 1784, Add. MS. 29166, ff. 49–50, and J. Bristow to Chandler, 18 Aug. 1784, I.O.L., MS. Eur. F. 7, f. 219.

[4] N. Middleton to Hastings, 18 Nov. 1777, Add. MS. 29139, ff. 305–6.

[5] List dated 1 Nov. 1778, Add. MS. 29199, f. 242.

Had means of detection been surer and the obstacles to successful prosecutions less intractable, a considerable proportion of the Company's civil servants, for all their social pretensions, would have been convicted of fraud and peculation. But beyond a certain point neither the law nor convention offered clear guidance to men in office. In Britain, it has been said that 'the line between the officially recognized perquisites of office and the opportunities for financial profit presented by office was for much of the eighteenth century very indistinct and frequently crossed'.[1] In Bengal most civil servants until very late in the eighteenth century did not even acknowledge that they belonged to an administrative service. They regarded themselves as merchants, trading on their own and the Company's behalf. When they came to consider what was or was not permissible to a man who held office, uncertainties could arise for a number of reasons. The Company was often slow to decide whether a practice was acceptable. When it did decide, its decisions might conflict with long-established conventions within the service. For instance, even after the Company had declared all presents to be illegal, its servants continued to try to make a dictinction between honourable presents and dishonourable bribes. Where the Company's interests were not involved directly, most Europeans still thought that they should observe some standard of fairness and justice in their dealings with Indians. But, partly perhaps owing to the oblique way in which power came to the British in Bengal, any sense of responsibility for the welfare of the population as a whole was very slow to develop. Francis Sykes, for example, felt that no objections could be held against his profits as Resident at Murshidabad, since none of them would have accrued to the Company; 'it was this, whether it should go into a blackman's pocket or my own'.[2]

In a state of uncertainty different standards were put forward by different men. Some simply pointed to the risks which they ran. When accused by Clive in 1765 of taking presents from Najm-ud-daula and of other malpractices, George Gray replied that he had lived through the night of the Black Hole and had narrowly escaped from the clutches of Mir Kasim. 'The very idea of what

---

[1] N. Baker, 'Changing attitudes towards Government in Eighteenth-century Britain', *Statesmen, Scholars and Merchants*, ed. A. Whiteman, J. S. Bromley, P. Dickson (Oxford, 1973), p. 210.

[2] Letter to Hastings, 28 Jan. 1773, Add. MS. 29133, f. 349.

he has endured shocks his recollection and the precariousness of his situation and the vicissitudes to which he has been subjected have painted forth to him independence in too desirable colours to admit of his self denial', especially as no breach with what Gray called 'integrity' was involved.[1] That most resolute of fortune seekers, John Johnstone, thought it would 'have appeared absurd after so many years' services, after having risqued my life so often . . . had I refused this only honourable opportunity that is ever likely to offer of becoming independent, and to have trusted to the future kind offices of Lord Clive'.[2] Clive's own standard was certainly not a nineteenth-century one. For all the assured dogmatism of his judgements, his criteria are in fact rather elusive. What he discovered when he returned to India in 1765 made him weep for the 'lost fame of the British nation'.[3] Above all his strong sense of hierarchy and due subordination was outraged. He did not think that a man should necessarily be confined to his official emoluments, but what was permissible for someone who had served the Company with distinction for a long period of time was definitely not permissible for men who had yet to prove themselves. 'Fortunes should be acquired in the course of faithful and meritorious service' by those 'whose age or experience qualify them for high stations'; but those who showed 'a licentious and levelling spirit' should be put down with a firm hand.[4] He was in no doubt as to who was worthy and who was unworthy, but it is not always easy to share his sense of certainty, and he left himself very vulnerable to accusations of partiality. Not only was it permissible for he himself and for Carnac to receive presents after much active service, but it was also permissible for John Walsh on a flying visit to Bengal to take away over £50,000;[5] he drove men like John Johnstone out of Bengal, but he encouraged Sykes to seek some 'fair and honourable advantage to yourself' as Resident at Murshidabad,[6] an invitation which Sykes accepted in full measure. Whereas Clive was prepared to condone unofficial profits, if they were taken by the right man in the right circumstances, Hastings looked forward to a service in which perquisites were replaced by

---

[1] B.P.C., 17 June 1765, *Reports*, iii. 433.
[2] Ibid. iii. 435.
[3] Letter to Carnac, 6 May 1765, N.L.W., Clive MSS. 218, p. 10.
[4] I.O.R., B.P.C., 12 Feb. 1766, Range 1, vol. 38, ff. 53–4.
[5] See above, p. 165.
[6] Letter to Sykes, 7 July 1765, I.O.L., MS. Eur. G. 37, box 3.

official rewards.[1] Yet at the end of thirteen years of his government private gain was still rife throughout the service. Hastings was much happier to reward ability than to correct abuses. He lacked the ruthlessness of a reformer, a title which he specifically disclaimed.[2] As an old Bengal servant he felt a loyalty to the rest of the service. He prided himself on not having 'shewn myself an enemy to the Company's servants', even though 'my enemies charge the reverse to me as a crime'.[3]

Nevertheless, some signs of the official morality of the future can be found in the Hastings period. Hastings himself was well aware that new responsibilities required men with a new outlook:

. . . at this time, when the servants of the Company exercise the rights of sovereignty over a rich and extensive country, surely something more than a bare proficiency in writing and merchants accounts; a more liberal exercise of the understanding; a preparatory knowledge of the principles of government, and especially of our own constitution; some acquaintance with men and manners, are necessary to enable them to fill the parts of magistrates and legislators.[4]

His words were echoed by a young Scottish Writer who pointed out in 1770 that the Company's 'civil establishment in Bengal may rather be called an administration than a mercantile society', so that 'a classical education and . . . a talent for writing' were now more useful to a servant than skill in 'merchants accounts'.[5] By 1784 Hastings could pride himself on the number of men 'of cultivated talents, of capacity for business and liberal knowledge' that adorned the service,[6] although he would probably have had to concede that such men were only a small minority.

Hastings's great enemy Philip Francis was also an important influence on the future of the service. His intellectual sophistication and his withering contempt for much that he found in India, obviously made him a very attractive figure to serious-minded young men in Bengal. A number of those who had come under Francis's influence, such as John Shore, Charles Grant, and

---

[1] Letter to Cornwallis, Mar. 1786, P.R.O. 30/11/197, ff. 21–2.
[2] Marshall, *Impeachment of Hastings*, p. 185.
[3] Letter to S. Droz, [June 1782], Add. MS. 29115, ff. 110–11.
[4] *A Proposal for Establishing a Professorship of the Persian Language in the University of Oxford* (n.d. [1766–9?]), pp. 14–15.
[5] D. Anderson to W. Collow, 19 Nov. 1770, Add. MS. 45438, ff. 17–18.
[6] 'Letter to Nathaniel Smith', *British Discovery of Hinduism in the eighteenth century*, ed. P. J. Marshall (Cambridge, 1970), p. 189.

Charles Boughton Rouse, were later to have important roles in the government of British India. 'I should rejoice to prove myself deserving of your favourable opinion and to contribute so essentially to the happiness of the natives', Rouse told Francis.[1]

With the arrival of Francis and the new Councillors appointed in the Regulating Act of 1773 Bengal was briefly to experience something of the more critical approach to personal interest in government that was gaining ground in Britain. In 1786 Bengal was placed under a new Governor who was entirely committed to the new standards. Lord Cornwallis had already fought corruption and profiteering in the army supply system in America;[2] in Bengal he was determined to 'prohibit in every case what ever all perquisites or emoluments whether undefined or defined'.[3] He found most of the senior servants whom he inherited to be morally or intellectually disqualified from taking any useful part in the new administration, but a nucleus of servants existed, trained in the rival schools of Hastings and Francis, for whose talents and integrity he quickly acquired a high regard.[4]

The new Bengal army built up after Plassey was plentifully supplied with officers. There were about 500 of them in 1769 and and 1,069 by 1784. With Cadets being shipped out from home or appointed in India at a very rapid rate in the 1770s, the military service quickly became congested especially in its lower ranks.[5] Many 'supernumerary' officers, that is officers in excess of the established quota, were serving in the Bengal army by 1784, 140 of them with the artillery and the European infantry.[6] In a total officer strength of 1,069 there were no fewer than 790 subalterns.[7] With so many excess officers and so much competition, prospects for promotion were very bleak; some men were to have to serve for twenty years before they became Captains.[8]

The question of promotion was an extremely important one, because the rewards of junior officers in the Bengal army were

[1] Letter of 2 July 1776, I.O.L., MS. Eur. C. 7, p. 463.
[2] F. and M. Wickwire, *Cornwallis and the War of Independence* (1970), p. 76; R. A. Bowler, 'The influence of logistical problems on British operations in North America' (London Ph.D. thesis, 1971), pp. 255–6.
[3] *Cornwallis Corr.*, i. 541.   [4] Ibid., i. 318.   [5] See above, p. 17.
[6] I.O.R., Home Miscellaneous, 348, pp. 87 ff.
[7] Ibid., 361, p. 97.
[8] R. Callahan, *The East India Company and Army Reform 1783–98* (Cambridge, Mass., 1972), p. 23.

universally recognized as being very meagre. In 1767 Clive was told of 'scenes of poverty, misery and distress, particularly among the subalterns: some cannot appear abroad for want of clothes; others so shabbily, as to do little honor to a corps; many betake themselves to bed at meal times for want of victuals'.[1] The basic pay of a junior officer was Rs 4 a day for a Captain and Rs 2 for a Lieutenant. To this was added the much disputed allowance called 'batta'. Batta was originally paid to officers to help them meet the expenses of service in the field. It was assessed to different rates, but by the early 1760s all officers throughout the army were drawing what was called double batta, which meant that a Captain received three time his ordinary pay and a Lieutenant's pay was quadrupled. In 1766 Clive, acting on orders from the Directors, forced a reduction of batta. Double batta was now only to be paid to the troops in Oudh; troops in the field elsewhere would get single batta; troops in cantonment in Bihar half of that; and troops in cantonment in Bengal itself received no addition at all. The changes provoked what virtually amounted to a mutiny among the junior officers, who organized mass resignations, but were coerced by the use of sepoys. A supplementary 'gratuity' was, however, instituted later for the benefit of junior officers. Under the new scales a Captain's pay, gratuity, and batta varied, according to the station at which he was serving, from about £600 to about £250, while subalterns received between £350 and £150.[2] On such pay officers tried to maintain what they regarded as a decent style of life; even on campaigns Captains of the Bengal army felt that they could not be served by less than five servants or consume less than a bottle each of madeira and beer and half-a-bottle of arrack a day.[3]

Field officers were much better off; the Directors believed that they were 'on a more advantageous footing than any other military service in the world'.[4] With their pay, batta, and allowances, Colonels received about £3,500, Lieutenant-Colonels about

---

[1] Letter from J. Archdekin, 12 Sept. 1767, I.O.L., MS. Eur. G. 37, box 47, f. 89.

[2] 9th Report Secret Committee, 1773, *Reports*, iv. 519, 579–81; A. Broome, *A History of the Rise and Progress of the Bengal Army* (1850), pp. 550–9; H. Grace, *The Code of Military Standing Regulations of the Bengal Establishment* (Calcutta, 1791), i. 325–32; I.O.R., Home Miscellaneous, 362, p. 127.

[3] Broome, *Bengal Army*, pp. 552–3.

[4] Directors to Bengal, 20 Nov. 1767, *Reports*, iv. 583.

£1,500 and Majors about £1,000. In addition, field officers had
shares in the 2½ per cent commission on the *diwani* revenues
instituted in 1767.[1] The Commander-in-chief was awarded 7½
shares (which could mean £3,000 to £4,500 a year), Colonels
two-and-a-half shares (£1,000 to £1,500) and Majors a three-
quarter share (£300 to £400).[2] 'Off reckonings', profits from
clothing the troops, were divided into shares of Rs 1,500 for the
field officers.[3] Finally, there were the bazar duties levied on
markets to supply sepoys by their commanding officers. By 1766
it was being said that the collection of such duties was a traditional
'custom in the army'.[4] The officers' markets have left their names
in the many Colonelgunges and Majorgunges of Bengal and
Bihar. When the commanders of stations in Oudh were compensated for the loss of bazar duties by the Wazir, they received a lakh
of rupees a year.[5]

All officers could hope to add to their pay on occasions. Active
service raised hopes of great financial advantages. Indeed, the
degree of enthusiasm with which a European army in India fought,
and sometimes whether parts of it would fight at all, depended on
the prospect for rewards in prize money, from plunder from a
captured town, or from the munificence of an Indian ally. The great
windfalls were the donations of twenty-five lakhs made by Mir
Jafar after Plassey and after the defeat of Mir Kasim. But the
Wazir of Oudh also made a donation to the army which fought for
him against the Rohillas in 1774. Plunder was taken from Hugli
and Chandernagore on the Plassey campaign, and from the Raja of
Banaras's fortress of Bijaigarh, which yielded twenty-three lakhs
in 1781,[6] while Banaras itself paid a ransom in 1764. The value of
prizes could, however, be somewhat diminished by the complexity
of prize law which might involve many years of litigation, as was
the case with the Bijaigarh money. Whether the distribution took
place at once or was delayed, the senior officers took by far the
largest part. Since he was likely to have received personal presents
from Indian rulers as well, a single successful campaign could make

---

[1] See above, p. 185.
[2] See the division for 1767–70, 4th Report Secret Committee, 1773, *Reports*,
iv. 162–72; for that of 1784, see I.O.R., Home Miscellaneous, 348, p. 93.
[3] 9th Report Secret Committee, 1773, *Reports*, iv. 533; Grace, *Code*, i. 302–10.
[4] R. Barker to Clive, 3 Aug. 1766, N.L.W., Clive MSS. 54, p. 264.
[5] List of allowances from Wazir, I.O.R., L/PARL/1/20, no. 39.
[6] Marshall, *Impeachment of Hastings*, p. 106.

a commander's fortune for life. Of the twenty-five lakhs awarded for driving Mir Kasim out of Bengal, the army's commander, Major Thomas Adams, took three (as much as all the European privates and NCOs added together). What junior officers received was much less; a Captain got Rs 15,000 and a subaltern Rs 7,500, but it was still the equivalent of two or three years of normal pay.[1] A Captain's share in the Bijaigarh plunder of 1781 came to Rs 22,500.[2] As well as fighting formal campaigns, detachments of the army were also employed in a host of minor operations and skirmishes to enforce revenue collection within the Company's provinces. Army officers generally acted in support of the Company's civilian revenue collectors, but sometimes they even became collectors themselves. Such operations could be very profitable for the soldiers concerned. In Midnapur 'the officer who went to reduce the western jungles' was said to have 'settled a present for himself amounting to half as much again as the revenue which he settled for the Company'.[3] Captain Mackenzie, who commanded a force of sepoys on detachment with the Supervisor of Rangpur, lent money at between 5 and 14 per cent a month, collected extra cesses on the revenue for himself and speculated in rice.[4]

Oudh had the reputation of being by far the most profitable peacetime station for the army. By the 1770s two brigades of the Company's troops were serving there, drawing double batta, and the Wazir was being persuaded to take more and more English officers into his own army, allowing them handsome salaries and perquisites. Captain Mordaunt, the host at Zoffany's famous cock-fight, received an allowance of Rs 8,000 a month from the Wazir.[5] Most favoured of all were the military revenue collectors. The payments which the Wazir was required to make to the Company were secured by assignments on the revenue of particular districts. To ensure that the Company received its money promptly, Hastings persuaded the Wazir to allow British officers to take command of troops enforcing the revenue collections in these districts and even to become collectors themselves. The most notorious of these military revenue collectors was Colonel

---

[1] A copy of the agreement for the distribution, 22 Nov. 1763, is in I.O.R., Mayor's Court Records, Range 155, vol. 61.

[2] W. Palmer to D. Anderson, 15 Nov. 1781, Add. MS. 45427, f. 80.

[3] G. Vansittart to H. Vansittart, 26 Sept. 1767, Bodleian, dep. b. 100, p. 29.

[4] *Proceedings of the Controlling Council*, xi. 203–8.

[5] I.O.R., L/PARL/1/20, no. 39.

Alexander Hannay, who ran the district of Gorakhpur for a few years as his personal fief. The size of his fortune became a matter for amazed speculation both among Indians and Europeans.[1]

A committee of the Court of Directors complained in 1772 of the very large number of staff officers who were being appointed throughout the Bengal army and of the 'peculiar indulgences . . . at the expence of every other part of the service' which they appeared to enjoy.[2] A large part of these 'indulgences' seem to have arisen from the 'contingencies', expenses of offices charged to the Company. Hastings believed that 'contingent bills' were the most 'uncontroulable' source of the Company's expenditure.[3] In the year 1773–4 military contingencies came to eighteen lakhs of rupees.[4] Staff appointments also included commissaries, clothing agents, paymasters, and quartermasters, who could make the same kind of profits as their civilian counterparts from providing stores and other equipment or from handling money.

Army officers could also supplement their pay by activities which had no connection with their official duties. Engineer officers built up substantial practices as civilian architects. Men like Colonel Fortnom[5] or Captain Martin designed a large part of the expanding European quarter of Calcutta. But trade was by far the most common source of extra-curricular income. Some officers regarded trade as degrading and would take no part in it,[6] but there was a tradition of trading by the army before Plassey,[7] and it is likely that lack of opportunity and lack of capital were more important in restricting the number of officers involved in trade than serious doubts about its appropriateness for a military man. In Oudh, for instance, where there were relatively few other European traders to compete with them, army officers appear to have been very active. In 1772 Hastings called trade with Oudh 'a military

[1] Abu Talib, trans. W. Hoey, *The History of Asafu'd Daulah* (Allahabad, 1885), p. 57; the Wazir to Govind Ram, 13 Oct. 1779, *Calendar of Persian Correspondence* (Calcutta, 1919–49), v. 378–9. C. Alexander to D. Anderson, 12 Sept. 1782, Add. MS. 45424, f. 97.

[2] *Reports*, iv. 548, 596–7.

[3] 'Memoirs of State of India', *State Papers, Hastings*, ii. 24.

[4] I.O.R., Home Miscellaneous, 347, p. 131.

[5] He had 'been regularly bred an architect, surveyor and draughtsman' under an 'eminent builder' (Directors to Bengal, 9 Mar. 1763, *Fort William–India House Corr.* iii. 198).

[6] e.g. R. Smith to R. Orme, [Jan. 1767], I.O.L., Orme MSS., OV, 37, f. 25.

[7] I.O.R., B.P.C., 21 Jan. 1745, Range 1, vol. 17, ff. 466–7.

monopoly'.[1] One experienced Free Merchant believed that 'a soldier merchant' was 'the most powerful rival a man can have'.[2]

A man who reached the rank of Major in Bengal could expect with reasonable luck to make his fortune. He was likely to have the resources for trading, he could expect presents, he would get large shares in prizes, he would profit from off-reckonings and bazars, and in any case his normal pay was generous. Several senior officers became extremely rich: James Killpatrick, Thomas Adams, John Carnac, Eyre Coote, Richard Smith, Robert Barker, and Alexander Hannay are obvious examples.[3]

Very few men, however, became senior officers, and with the flooding of the service with Cadets in the 1770s, the prospect of ever becoming one grew more and more remote. An officer who was languishing for twenty years before he even became a Captain might sometimes be lucky: he might be posted to Oudh, take part in a campaign that paid well or get a lucrative staff appointment. But such chances only fell to a minority in a seriously over-crowded profession. For the majority the Company's commission at least gave them the status of a gentleman, but it gave them very little on which to try to maintain such a status. It is hardly surprising that the Company's junior officers should repeatedly have proved themselves to be an extremely refractory body in defending the few crumbs of advantage which the service offered them.

[1] *Memoirs of the Rt. Hon. Warren Hastings*, ed. G. R. Gleig (1841), i. 334.
[2] J. Fowke to Hastings, 6 Apr. 1772, Add. MS. 29133, f. 95.
[3] For further details, see below, pp. 239–40, 247.

IX

A Settling of Accounts

In 1780 the sponsor of an application for preferment in Bengal commented that his protégé was the 'next heir to a very handsome fortune' and thus 'perhaps the only person, who with his prospects, unaccompanyed by any follies or extravagances has ever gone to Asia for the laudable motives of seeing more of the world and turning what he is to see and be employed in to his advantage'.[1] This may perhaps do too much justice to the young man in question and too little to others. Nevertheless, few men went to Bengal who did not have some financial incentive to do so. A man who was able to live in Britain in what he thought a fitting style was most unlikely to uproot himself and go to India.

Service in India was commonly regarded as a sentence to exile in uncongenial surroundings with a very high risk of never returning home. Some enjoyed life in Bengal, usually because it enabled them to live with a panache and flamboyance which they could not have matched at home; a few were able to simulate some of the pleasures of English country life in rural Bengal. But the majority seem to have disliked Bengal: they disliked the climate, they disliked the sicknesses that recurred so frequently, they disliked 'the blacks', and the more sensitive disliked the forced extravagance of British society in Calcutta. To most eighteenth-century Englishmen and Scotsmen, with their very strong sense of belonging to a social group or a locality, exile, even to somewhere agreeable, was hard to endure. Happiness was to be found in living with one's family and one's 'friends'. But a man could not attain happiness unless he was self-supporting, 'A state of independency', as one Bengal servant put it, was 'the object of every liberal mind'.[2] If 'an independence' or 'a competence' could not be inherited or earned at home, some men were prepared to consider going overseas. For all its unpleasantness and risks, service in Bengal seemed

---

[1] J. Macpherson writing to Hastings of Archibald Seton on 12 May 1780, Add. MS. 29145, f. 91.

[2] L. Scrafton to Clive, 26 Jan. 1765, I.O.L., MS. Eur. G. 37, box 33, f. 83.

to offer the prospect of earning an independence with greater certainty and at greater speed than almost anywhere else. A boy who went to Bengal at sixteen or seventeen hoped to be home again before he was forty, 'free and independent like a gentleman' and able 'to enjoy myself, my family and friends in the manner I could wish'.[1] A Writer sailing to Calcutta in 1752 explained: 'I do expect it to be of fifteen or twenty years at least. In that time I may be made Governour. If not that, I may make a fortune which will make me live like a gentleman.'[2] Many put off their marriages until they returned.

For most who came back from Bengal living independently or like a gentleman meant living in the countryside, from the income of an estate or from the income of their Indian savings, either invested in government stock or lent out to other landowners on mortgage. Sons of merchants seem to have been as anxious to enjoy the charms of country life as sons of existing landowners and the sons of the clergy. Few appear to have regarded their fortunes as capital for further venturing in trade or manufacturing in Britain. Claud Alexander, the Company's Paymaster-General, who left Bengal in 1785, built a cotton mill and founded a new manufacturing town at Catrine in Ayshire;[3] but his letters home[4] show that his ambition too was to establish himself as a landowner. Clive's comment that 'it is absolutely impossible for gentlemen brought up in the luxury and indolence of Bengal to gain a subsistence in England'[5] was no doubt an unfair jibe, but it contained a grain of truth: after Indian service, most men hoped for ease and relaxation, not for a strenuous new career.

How much an individual felt that he needed for his independence varied with his temperament and his ambitions. An income appropriate to a gentleman in eighteenth-century Britain might be only a few hundred pounds or over £5,000, depending on what sort of gentleman one aspired to be.[6] Early in the eighteenth century John

---

[1] J. Grose to N. Grose, 23 Dec. 1770, I.O.L., MS. Eur. E. 284.

[2] S. Dalrymple to Sir H. Dalrymple, 1 Nov. 1752, S.R.O., Hamilton-Dalrymple MSS., bundle 56.

[3] J. Strawhorn, 'The background to Burns, II: industry and commerce in 18th-century Ayrshire', *Ayrshire Collections*, iv (1958), 187.

[4] In the possession of Boyd Alexander Esq.

[5] Clive to Directors, 1 Feb. 1766, *Fort William–India House Correspondence* (New Delhi, 1949–), iv. 393.

[6] G. E. Mingay, *English Landed Society in the eighteenth century* (1963), p. 10.

Scattergood was told that less than £20,000 would 'not do for a family'.[1] This was a sum at which moderate men still set their sights later in the century. Alexander Elliot, the son of an active Scottish politician, thought £20,000 'not enough to satisfy a man whose parts and ambition would make him wish to be perspicuous in the House of Commons, or whose vanity would lead him to a great show in houses, horses &c. &c', but 'certainly enough for a man who does not raise his future views so high'.[2] Another Scot, David Anderson, was aiming at a similar sum when he wrote of his hopes for 'a small estate in a pleasant part of Scotland and situated in a good neighbourhood with a house upon it fit for one who wishes to live like a gentleman of five or six hundred pound a year'.[3] At one point in his career Harry Verelst regarded £25,000 or £30,000 as 'sufficient to set down with myself and also to serve my friends'.[4] Some men appear to have settled down happily to the life of a small squire. Randolph Marriott, for instance, after thirteen years in India, married a young wife, spent £5,000 on a house with 135 acres in Yorkshire, and congratulated himself on having 'ground enough to employ me, and I hope sufficient for corn and hay for my horses, bread, bees and milk and butter for my family'.[5] But even in the early eighteenth century ambitions ran higher, and with purchasable estates becoming scarcer and land prices rising,[6] estimates of what was needed to make a man independent climbed upwards. In 1770 Lord Elibank warned his natural son William Young who was serving the Company in Bengal that '40,000 pound does not pass for a competency here'.[7] Less than a year later he was much more specific: 'Luxury has encreased to so uncommon a degree in England, that it is impossible to enjoy life without a very great fortune . . . to particulars, less than 100,000 pounds will not do here, without more philosophy than is to be

---

[1] J. Wendey to Scattergood, 23 Feb. 1716, I.O.R., Home Miscellaneous, 822, p. 26.

[2] Letter to his father, 7 Sept. 1772, National Library of Scotland, Minto MSS., M 14.

[3] Letter to his father, 11 Jan. 1778, Add. MS. 45438, f. 141.

[4] Letter to his sister, 27 Sept. 1762, Ames MSS., I.O.L. Microfilm, reel 606.

[5] Letter to Hastings, 10 Mar. 1770, Add. MS. 29132, f. 364.

[6] H. J. Habbakuk, 'The English land market in the eighteenth century', *Britain and the Netherlands*, ed. J. S. Bromley and E. H. Kossmann, i (1960), 155; T. S. Ashton, *Economic History of England: the eighteenth century* (1955), pp. 44–5.

[7] Letter of 17 Oct. 1770, S.R.O., GD 32/24/36.

hoped for in a merchant'.[1] Others thought that a gentleman could be happy on less. Clive hoped to see one of his friends return home with £40,000 or £50,000.[2] George Vansittart, the Governor's younger brother, put his own wants at £50,000 in 1774[3] and advised his nephew in 1786 to 'stay for 60,000'.[4]

There were, however, some individuals whose ambitions went far beyond an independence. Huge presents and great trading profits after Plassey offered at least the chance of a fortune comparable to those of the largest landowners at home or the most successful West Indian planters. With such a fortune a retired Bengal servant could buy a great mansion, a string of estates, and political influence in boroughs. He could hope to become one of the commanding figures in his county community and even to launch a bid for high office and titles in national politics. Clive set the pattern for such a career and thought that other men who had risen to the highest rank in the Company's service should also have grand ambitions. He urged Harry Verelst, whom he mistakenly believed to have £90,000 already in England with another £100,000 to come from Bengal, to spend £80,000 or £90,000 on an estate in Hertfordshire.[5] The assumption that a former Governor of Bengal should be one of the richest commoners in England was widely shared. Lord North thought that it would be not unreasonable for Warren Hastings to aim at a fortune of £200,000.[6]

Whether a man made a competence, however he chose to define it, or something more depended on many factors: good support at home from within the Court of Directors and in Bengal from a powerful patron, the luck to be in Bengal at a time when trading opportunities, either at sea or within the province, were buoyant, or when presents were being distributed lavishly and office could be turned to good account, skill and strong nerves in taking chances; but above all success depended on the simple fact of survival. The Company's civil servants are by far the easiest to account for, and the record of their life expectancy is a gloomy one. The over-all total is 645 civil appointments to Bengal, of whom

---

[1] Letter of 5 Apr. 1771, ibid., 32/24/38.
[2] Letter to his wife, 8 Sept. 1766, I.O.L., MS. Eur. G 37, box 3.
[3] Letter to R. Palk, 22 Mar. 1774, Bodleian, dep. b. 97, p. 32.
[4] Letter to H. Vansittart, jr., 30 Jan. 1786, ibid., dep. b. 103.
[5] Letter of 22 Dec. 1769, N.L.W., Clive MSS., 62, p. 18.
[6] L. S. Sutherland, *The East India Company in eighteenth-century politics* (Oxford, 1952), p. 298.

TABLE III

Civil servants appointed to Bengal		Died in India	Civil servants appointed to Bengal		Died in India
1707	5	5	1742	3	3
1708	—	—	1743	8	6
1709	18	8	1744	18	12
1710	12	9	1745	1	1
1711	11	7	1746	8	5
1712	6	5	1747	—	—
1713	—	—	1748	—	—
1714	3	2	1749	14	10
1715	4	3	1750	8	6
1716	5	3	1751	8	4
1717	10	6	1752	1	1
1718	10	6	1753	11	8
1719	—	—	1754	13	12
1720	—	—	1755	9	6
1721	3	3	1756	—	
1722	18	10	1757	9	7
1723	—	—	1758	15	8
1724	—	—	1759	18	12
1725	4	2	1760	13	6
1726	8	5	1761	5	3
1727	2	1	1762	10	6
1728	4	3	1763	28	16
1729	—	—	1764	13	3
1730	9	6	1765	26	17
1731	1	—	1766	30	20
1732	2	—	1767	15	9
1733	—	—	1768	4	3
1734	3	3	1769	34	13
1735	2	2	1770	46	20
1736	9	6	1771	19	13
1737	7	2	1772	31	12
1738	1	—	1773	41	16
1739	—	—	1774	6	2
1740	9	6	1775	11	4
1741	3	1			

Principal source: Bengal civil establishment lists in I.O.R. L/F/10/1–2.

368 or 57 per cent are definitely known to have died in India. The total of those who never returned may in fact be rather higher: some of the few individuals who cannot be accounted for probably died in Bengal and a number of those who remained in India after leaving the service for one reason or another probably never got home. Several who did return were so weakened by disease that they died shortly afterwards, while two or three were shipped home insane. Grisly as an average mortality of 57 per cent for the whole period 1707 to 1775 undoubtedly is, the averages per decade tell

an even more macabre story: 66 per cent of those who joined the civil service between 1707 and 1716 died in India; between 1717 and 1726 the rate was 60 per cent; it was 66 per cent between 1727 and 1736; 62 per cent from 1737 to 1746; and 74 per cent from 1747 to 1756. Thereafter the figures begin to improve: 59 per cent of those entering the civil service between 1757 and 1766 were to die in India, but only 44 per cent of those going out between 1767 and 1775. Before Plassey about two-thirds of all the Writers who competed so eagerly to go to Bengal could expect never to come back. It is only the large post-Plassey intake that brings the average down to 57 per cent. They were spared the warfare which cut deep swathes through the 1747–56 generation: forty-seven civil servants appear to have met violent deaths in the fighting in Calcutta in 1756, including the Black Hole, or in the war against Mir Kasim in 1763, when the staff of the Patna factory were wiped out. By the 1770s and 1780s the Calcutta community was said to be learning how to improve its diet and hygiene and to curb its 'irregularities'. It was becoming 'more rational, temperate and less subject to in-disposition'.[1]

If mortality among the civil servants, who lived in relatively salubrious conditions, was high for most of the eighteenth century, it must have been even higher for other Europeans. A return of casualties among the officers and Cadets of the Bengal army from 1770 to 1776 recorded six killed in action, nine drowned and 208 died of disease.[2] Thus over six years of peace, without a major campaign, about 6 per cent of the peacetime establishment of some 600 officers died each year. About 25 per cent of the European soldiers seem to have perished every year. To maintain the Company's European regiments at a constant number required annual renewal in the 1760s of at least one-quarter.[3]

Supposing that a man survived and that he had succeeded in amassing some kind of fortune by the means described in the earlier chapters of this book, he still had to clear one more hurdle before he could enjoy the delights of an independence at home. He had to get his money from India to England. The methods of 'remitting'

[1] *Memoirs of the Life and Correspondence of John, Lord Teignmouth*, ed. Lord Teignmouth (1843), i. 197.

[2] V. C. P. Hodson's transcripts of military records, National Army Museum, MSS. 6404/69/89.

[3] 9th Report, Secret Committee of the House of Commons, 1773, *Reports from Committees of the House of Commons* (1803–6), iv. 592, 636.

a fortune, the expression invariably used by contemporaries, merit close examination. Sums of money actually transferred to Europe were the true indication of a man's success. A lakh of rupees in the funds at home was worth any number of paper profits still to be realized in Bengal from banians, *gumashtas* or Europeans of doubtful credit.

For individuals the process of getting money back to England was greatly complicated by the existence of the East India Company's trading monopoly. Had this monopoly not existed, Englishmen in Bengal would have been able to remit their fortunes in much the same way as West India planters did: by investing their money in goods to be shipped on their own behalf or on that of British merchants for sale in London. Under the terms of the monopoly, however, with limited exceptions, British nationals were not permitted to ship their own goods from Asia to Britain. So, unless he was prepared to defy the law by trading with a British 'interloping' ship (of which there were very few in the eighteenth century), an individual in Bengal with a fortune to repatriate had two main alternatives. He could either place his money at the disposal of the Company itself, or he could make an arrangement with a foreigner, who was not of course bound by the terms of a British monopoly.

If he chose to deal with the East India Company, he might be able to take advantage of limited concessions for private trade on its own ships. In the seventeenth century, under a system called 'the old indulgence', returning servants were allowed to bring a stipulated quantity of goods back with them.[1] Special permission for individuals to ship goods in this way was still sometimes given in the eighteenth century,[2] but the practice seems to have died out. Others indulged were the captains, officers and part of the crew of the Company's European ships. A certain part of the cargo space on a return voyage was alloted to them as 'privilege' for their private goods. They could sometimes be persuaded to sell their privilege to men in India with goods to ship; by the late eighteenth century privileged cargo space was sold on a large scale and a considerable volume of goods were sent from Bengal to London in this way.[3]

[1] Directors to Fort St. George, 29 Nov. 1670, I.O.R., E/3/87, p. 394.
[2] Abs. Bengal to Directors, 29 Jan. 1726, I.O.R., E/4/2, p. 485.
[3] H. Furber, *John Company at Work* (Cambridge, Mass., 1951), pp. 281–2.

In addition to goods carried as privilege, the Company's ships also took precious stones from India to Britain on private account. This was an item in which the Company itself did not deal, but for a duty of 5 per cent (reduced by $2\frac{1}{2}$ per cent to encourage the trade) it would transport them on behalf of individuals. Pearls were sometimes shipped, but diamonds were overwhelmingly the most important of the precious stones exported by Europeans from India. In the first half of the eighteenth century the British acquired most of their diamonds in southern India, from the fabled mines of Golconda. Englishmen in Bengal who wished to make purchases had normally to act through an agent in Madras. Prices fluctuated and supplies were erratic, money often lying 'in the mines a considerable time'.[1] The chief factor affecting the sale of Golconda diamonds in Europe appears to have been the availability of Brazilian ones.[2] After Plassey, Bengal's need for diamonds outran Golconda's capacity to supply it. Clive, who had sent £30,000 out of his winnings in 1757 to be invested at Madras in diamonds,[3] found by 1765 that diamonds were 'not to be had; the sums of money sent out and private fortunes demand ten times the quantity'.[4]

By 1765, however, Europeans in Bengal were beginning to tap what they came to regard as their own supplies of diamonds. In the course of the campaign against Mir Kasim and his allies, the British established themselves at Banaras, the centre of the north Indian diamond trade and an outlet for the diamonds of Bundelkhand. William Bolts was apparently the first European to see the potentialities of Banaras as a source of diamonds,[5] but Clive quickly established an agent of his own there, a Free Merchant called John Chamier.[6] One of the Bundelkhand Rajas tried to open a direct trade with the British, allowing another agent of Clive's to visit his mines.[7] The Banaras trade was to produce a steady stream of stones for Clive, Verelst, Hastings, and a few other senior

[1] T. Pitt to Sir S. Evans, 5 Feb. 1706, Add. MS. 22849, f. 60; Pitt's correspondence in Add. MSS. 22848, 22849 and 22850 stresses the uncertainties and hazards of the south Indian diamond trade in the early eighteenth century.
[2] R. Adams to L. Barretto, 24 Jan. 1730, 22 Nov. 1731, I.O.R., Home Miscellaneous, 37, pp. 1, 116.
[3] G. Clive to Clive's trustees, 5 Jan. 1758, N.L.W., Clive MSS., 63, p. 17.
[4] Clive to J. Walsh, 7 Nov. 1765, I.O.L., MS. Eur. D. 546/5.
[5] W. Bolts, Considerations on India Affairs (1772–5), ii. 42.
[6] Clive to Chamier, 23 Aug. 1765, N.L.W., Clive MSS., 220, pp. 110–1.
[7] Clive to Walsh, 22 Mar. 1766, I.O.L., MS. Eur. D. 546/5, f. 136.

servants who kept control of it. The first Banaras diamonds sold well in Europe,[1] but after 1767 the inevitable fluctuations began. European demand was uncertain and Indian prices were often said to be too high. Nevertheless, there were still years in which diamonds from Banaras, for those who could get them, could prove a very advantageous way of sending money home. In a good year a rupee laid out in Banaras diamonds could realize 2s. 7d. or 2s. 8d. in London, whereas bills of exchange would give 2s. 3d. at the most.[2]

Either because only limited facilities were available or because (as in the case of diamonds) they were controlled by a very few, only a small proportion of the money available for remittance from Bengal found its way home through the Company's licensed trade. The Company did, however, offer a much more accessible channel for repatriating fortunes. That was by bill of exchange. The Court of Directors permitted the treasuries at its settlements to receive money from individuals in return for bills of exchange payable in London at various dates at rates fixed by the Company. From the Company's point of view such bills could be a useful means of raising ready money with which to finance its operations in India. From the individual's point of view bills on the Company offered complete security. The Directors could be relied on to honour bills drawn on them and, except at the very end of our period, to do so punctually. Before 1758 most bills seem to have been drawn payable within 61 or 91 days of being presented; after 1758 payment was normally made one year after sight, but by the early 1780s holders of the Company's bills were having to wait up to four years for payment. There were, however, some disadvantages in Company's bills. Publicity was one. It was impossible to keep sums remitted in this way a secret. Secondly, the quantity available did not always match the demand for them. The Company's willingness to grant bills depended on its assessment of its needs in India and of its capacity to discharge the bills in London when they were due. The Company could be put in a very embarrassing situation if bills from India were presented for larger amounts than

---

[1] e.g. J. Salvador to Clive, 19 May 1766, E. Crisp to Clive, 25 Sept. 1767, I.O.L., MS. Eur. G. 37, box 40, f. 102; box 47, f. 210.

[2] For examples of high returns for diamonds on Clive's shipments, see G. Clive to Clive, 11 Aug. 1767, I.O.L., MS. Eur. G. 37, box 46, f. 77; for similar returns on Hastings's shipments, see my 'The Personal Fortune of Warren Hastings', *Economic History Review*, 2nd ser., xvii (1964–5), 288.

it could meet out of its funds at home. From 1759 the Directors began to impose increasingly stringent quotas on the amounts that could be drawn on them in India; an upper limit of £300,000 was fixed by act of parliament in 1773 for all the British settlements.[1] Finally rates of exchange were fixed by the Company, which might or might not be advantageous for remitters. In determining rates the Directors had to consider a number of factors: how urgently they needed the money in India, whether individuals would offer it to foreigners or 'interlopers' if they were discouraged from lending it to the Company, as well as their professed desire to be generous to their servants and give them 'suitable encouragement';[2] on this principle Company servants were usually allowed a higher rate of exchange than that given to other Englishmen. Whatever considerations were being applied, the rate of exchange on Company bills fell throughout the eighteenth century, as Table IV shows.

TABLE IV

	Rate per current rupee for Company servants	Rate per current rupee for others
up to 1724	2s. 9d.	2s. 6d.
1724	2s. 6d.	2s. 4d.
1735	2s. 4d.	2s. 2d.
1738	2s. 3d.	2s. 1d.
1746	2s. 4d.	2s. 2d.
1750	2s. 3d.	2s. 1d.
1753	2s. 3d.	2s. 3d.
1760	2s. 3½d.	2s. 3½d.
1761	2s. 4d.	2s. 4d.
1766	2s. 3d.	2s. 1d.
1768	2s.	2s.
1769	2s. 2½d.	2s. 2½d.
1774	2s. 1d.	2s. 1d.

If a man with a fortune in Bengal could not get bills from the Company or if he did not find their terms to his liking, he could try to transfer his money to another British settlement in Asia and apply for bills there. Money was regularly sent to Madras or Bombay to await remittance and by the 1770s very large sums were being sent from Bengal to Canton. From 1769 the Company offered bills on London at generous rates of exchange for private money from India presented at its factory at Canton, where it was

[1] 13 Geo. III, c. 64, sec. 16.
[2] Directors to Bengal, 9 Nov. 1733, I.O.R., E/3/106, p. 59.

urgently needed to finance purchases of tea.[1] Over the next ten years, until war interrupted the trade, the Canton treasury received very large sums from Calcutta, carried there by 'country' ships bringing opium, cotton, and tin.[2] Company bills could also sometimes be obtained in small quantities for money presented at Benkulen in Sumatra, while for a few years in the 1770s enterprising Calcutta merchants arranged for private bills to be drawn on London in Egypt for money lent to them for voyages to Suez.[3]

One or two other channels for remitting through British hands existed. The survival of the Company's monopoly meant that relatively few men were prepared to offer bills on London for the use of money in India. Writers and others newly arrived in Bengal were sometimes an exception, able to draw on their connections in Britain to finance their first steps in India. The captains of the Company's ships were another. They were given permission to take up money for the running of their ships by offering 'certificates' on the security of the ship, which were repayable in London.[4] Captains' certificates were a highly regarded form of remittance, but the amounts involved were not very considerable. When the ships of the Royal Navy were stationed in the Indian Ocean their commanders were permitted to pay for stores and victualling by drawing bills on the Commissioners of the Navy in London.

If advantageous remittances could not be obtained through the East India Company or some other British source, it was usually possible to get money home through a foreign channel. The Portuguese, the Dutch and the French all maintained a trade with Bengal throughout the eighteenth century, while ships from Denmark, the Holy Roman Empire and Prussia also appeared in the Hugli. All the foreign companies at one time or another took money from British subjects in Bengal in return for bills drawn on their parent organizations in Europe. Links between individual Englishmen and the Danish, Prussian, and Imperial Ostend companies were indeed so close, both in Europe and in Bengal, that they can be regarded in some degree as organizations of British subjects who were able to evade the restrictions of the Company's monopoly by using a foreign flag.

[1] Directors to Bengal, 11 Nov. 1768, 30 June 1769, *Fort William–India House Corr.* v. 137, 219–20.
[2] See above, pp. 98–9.   [3] See above, p. 96.
[4] See an example of such a bond, on the *Boscawen* paying 6 per cent, in I.O.R., Mayor's Court Records, Range 155, vol. 60, p. 85.

A British subject who traded directly with a foreigner clearly broke the law. If he merely lent money to foreigners, he certainly disobeyed repeated instructions from the Court of Directors, who naturally disliked seeing the trade of their rivals financed by funds provided by men who lived in India under their protection or even in their service. But whether such loans were actually illegal was a hotly debated matter. The question was not finally resolved until an act of parliament in 1781 declared that this was so.[1]

In the first half of the eighteenth century there is little evidence that British subjects in Bengal felt obliged to resort to making large remittances through the foreign companies. Periodic Portuguese ships sailed from Bengal for Lisbon having taken British money repayable in Portugal.[2] From 1720 to 1730 the Imperial Ostend Company, with a number of English and Scots prominently involved, traded on a considerable scale in Bengal.[3] The Directors received information about money lent to the Ostend Company,[4] who paid 30 per cent on some of their bills.[5] Just before Plassey, bills for 'several thousand pounds' received from British subjects were said to have been sent home by the new Prussian Company.[6]

After Plassey the situation changed radically. The British community in Bengal now had very much more money to send home than the East India Company could accommodate, while the great increase in its territorial revenues meant that the Company had much less need to raise funds in Bengal on bills. The newly enriched inevitably turned to the foreigners. The Dutch were the first beneficiaries. Almost immediately after his first instalment of the post-Plassey presents had been paid to him, Clive handed over twelve lakhs of rupees to the Dutch factory in Bengal for bills which would yield £183,000 over three years. Three months later another three-and-a-half lakhs was sent directly to Batavia for bills worth £50,000.[7] Clive's example was followed by many others, the

---

[1] 21 Geo. III, c. 65, sec. 29.

[2] e.g. see accounts of a voyage that left in 1715 (I.O.R., Home Miscellaneous, 74, p. 473) and another in 1744 (copies of bonds and bills of exchange in I.O.R., Mayor's Court Records, Range 155, vol. 60, pp. 50–1).

[3] N. Laude, *La Compagnie d'Ostende et son activité coloniale au Bengal* (Brussels, 1944).

[4] Directors to Bengal, 16 Feb. 1722, I.O.R., E/3/101, p. 147.

[5] J. Fullerton to P. Woolaert, 5 Sept. 1734, I.O.L., MS. Eur. D. 602, f. 27.

[6] J. Payne to A. Mitchell, 4 Aug. 1757, I.O.R., D/106.

[7] Entries for 17 Aug., 7 Nov. 1757, Clive's Journal, 1756–8, N.L.W., Clive MSS., 350.

Dutch in Bengal receiving English money year after year until their factory was closed down by the outbreak of the Anglo-Dutch war in 1780. From 1764 the French company, trying to make good its losses in the Seven Years War, was also in the market for English money. The Swiss financier and future royal minister, Jacques Necker, was actively involved in schemes for raising loans in Bengal, mostly negotiated in London through the agents of men in India. Few Englishmen, including Clive who put £20,000 at the disposal of the French,[1] seem to have had inhibitions about lending money to a power which had threatened the very existence of the British in India. Necker was reputed to have raised twenty million francs from British sources.[2] The Company continued to borrow large sums until it was wound up in 1769. The French East India Company was succeeded by private French concerns who were permitted to send ships to Asia on their own account. Several of them offered terms for remittances to Europe in return for money advanced in Bengal. The War of the American Revolution cut off French trade and later the Dutch were involved in the war as well. But war enabled the Portuguese and above all the Danes, who remained neutral, to profit. In the last year of the war the Danes were able to borrow very extensively from the British community in Bengal and to take up much of the money that had previously gone to the Dutch or the French.

Thus there was no lack of opportunity for those who were prepared to commit their money to foreigners. But hard bargains were often driven by foreign companies, especially after 1757 when there was something of a seller's market for bills of exchange on Europe. In 1772, for instance, Dutch bills were thought to be 'too disadvantageous' to accept,[3] and in 1774 they were offering terms less favourable than those of the East India Company.[4] Englishmen also feared for the safety of money lent to some foreign concerns. The private French ventures after 1769 were to prove particularly vulnerable.

Transferring a fortune from Bengal to Britain was therefore a delicate operation. The availability of bills at the right time, rates

---

[1] R. Foley and Co. to G. Clive, 29 Sept. 1766, I.O.L., MS. Eur. G. 37, box 42, f. 97.

[2] H. Lüthy, 'Necker et la compagnie des Indes', *Annales: Economies, Sociétés, Civilisations*, xv (1960), 869.

[3] Clive to his attorneys, 20 Jan. 1772, N.L.W., Clive MSS., 61, p. 49.

[4] Sykes to Hastings, 13 Jan. 1774, Add. MS. 29134, f. 260.

of exchange and security had all to be calculated. Mistakes could make very serious inroads into a fortune. A prudent man tried to remit a considerable part of what he possessed to Britain well before he left Bengal, when he would take the bulk of the rest with him. But shortage of good bills when they were wanted might well mean that substantial sums would have to be left behind under the management of friends remaining in India. Such sums would of course earn interest at Indian rates, which is why some men left part of their fortune in Bengal as a matter of choice, but, as Clive put it, they were subject to the 'lukewarmness and the self-interestedness of those we depend upon for remittance'[1] and might never see their money again. No relationship was more corrosive of friendship than that of the returned Nabob, expecting instalments of his fortune by every ship, with his harassed former colleague who was trying to disentangle his affairs in Bengal.

If a man had succeeded in conveying the major part of his fortune to Britain without serious mishap, he would have overcome the last, but by no means the least exacting, of the obstacles which stood between him and his cherished independence. As previous chapters will have suggested, conditions for successful fortune-making were by no means uniformly good throughout the whole eighteenth century, and it was undoubtedly easier to complete the steeple chase and win a prize at certain times rather than at others. In the first half of the century the prosperity of Bengal's seaborne trade, on which the wellbeing of the British community largely depended, ebbed and flowed. After Plassey, profits on the seaborne trade were generally low for some years, but there was a great expansion of British participation in the internal trade of Bengal and huge sums were distributed in presents, compensation, and prize money by the Nawabs. In the 1770s there was a revival of trading by sea, but a decline in the profits which Europeans could draw from internal trade, as it came under closer regulation, and a drying up of presents. On the other hand, a considerable proportion of the Company's vast new resources of territorial revenue were now finding their way into private hands through the creation of new hierarchies of salaried offices and the levying of perquisites and unofficial profits of one sort or another. In times of opportunity, those who are able to survive and take their chances with dexterity can amass their fortunes and leave Bengal

[1] Letter to J. Call, 1 Mar. 1766, N.L.W., Clive MSS., 224, p. 67.

after some fifteen or twenty years' service; in times of stringency, men have to soldier on until the times changed or until death carried them off.

1707 to 1731

During the second and third decades of the eighteenth century the British-owned merchant fleet based on Calcutta grew very rapidly, its success on the routes to western India, the Persian Gulf and the Red Sea being reflected in the Company's receipts for consulage and tonnage duties.[1] The expansiveness of the period is also reflected in the will of a Company servant called Thomas Falconer, who left £6,000 to the East India Company, 'in consideration that in their service I got the fortune it has pleased God to bless me with', and £2,000 'to relieve such as are in real want and misery'.[2] Falconer left Bengal after seventeen years' service. The records of other Company servants suggest equally successful careers, one leaving in 1721 after eleven years' service,[3] two in 1722 after twenty-two and twenty-three years,[4] one in 1723 after only nine,[5] and two in 1724 after fifteen and fourteen years.[6] In 1730 there was another clutch of resignations: one man retired with twenty-one years in Bengal behind him,[7] while another left after nineteen years.[8] Also in 1730 the Directors dismissed Samuel Greenhill, who had been in the Bengal service for thirteen years, for dealing with the Ostend Company. In 1731 the Directors reacted to a serious deterioration in the cargoes received from Bengal by ordering a purge of the Bengal Council. John Deane, the Governor, and two other long serving Councillors[9] were ordered home, while another servant with nineteen years' service retired voluntarily.[10]

It seems reasonable to assume that all these men left Bengal in affluent circumstances, but specific information is available about some of them. One of those who left in 1722, Samuel Feake, bought an estate in Essex and later became Chairman of the Company. The assets of Edmund Crisp, who had left in 1724, were worth nearly £38,000 at his death.[11] Edward Stephenson

---

[1] See above, p. 55.   [2] Copy in I.O.R., D/99.
[3] Waterworth Collett.   [4] Samuel Feake and William Spencer.
[5] Gabriel Hanger, later an M.P. and 1st Baron Coleraine.
[6] Edmund Crisp and William Spinkes.   [7] Edward Stephenson.
[8] Edward Reynolds.   [9] John Lloyd and Charles Hampton.
[10] Philip Michell.   [11] Inventory in N.L.W., Clive MSS., 120.

followed his retirement in 1730 by buying the estate of Dawley from Lord Bolingbroke and eventually becoming the first Bengal Nabob to enter the House of Commons.[1] Greenhill's pursuit of a fortune was no doubt adversely affected by his dismissal, but he had still secured enough to enable him to purchase 'an estate of 5 or 600£ per annum' and to live 'a country life'.[2] Governor Deane was reputed to be very wealthy indeed. In 1726 he had asked for permission to send home goods on his own account,[3] and remitted £12,400 in Company bills in 1729–30.[4] He too was accused of trading extensively with the Ostend Company and with lending 'six lacks of rupees or £60,000' to the Dutch.[5] Sizeable fortunes were also made in the 1720s by some men who did not live to enjoy them. Governor Henry Frankland, who died in Bengal shortly after the Company had dismissed him in 1728, was said to have accumulated £90,000, although only £30,000 eventually reached his heirs in Britain.[6]

TABLE V

	£		£
1709–10	5,300	1720–1	2,143
1710–11	1,799	1721–2	11,204
1711–12	5,248	1722–3	36,578
1712–13	2,581	1723–4	12,868
1713–14	1,432	1724–5	13,852
1714–15	1,412	1725–6	18,798
1715–16	8,386	1726–7	18,098
1716–17	4,095	1727–8	29,827
1717–18	22,490	1728–9	86,756
1718–19	18,902	1729–30	71,038
1719–20	2,927	1730–1	68,026

Source: I.O.R., E/4/1–3.　　　　　　Total　£443,760

The increasing prosperity of the community as a whole is suggested by the bills of exchange drawn on the East India Company. Other forms of remittance cannot be calculated with any precision. A few thousand pounds from Bengal were probably

[1] R. Sedgwick ed., *The House of Commons 1715–54* (1970), ii. 445.
[2] R. Adams to J. Hinde, 2 Feb. 1734, I.O.R., Home Miscellaneous, 37, p. 223.
[3] Abs. Bengal to Directors, 19 Jan. 1726, I.O.R., E/4/2, p. 485.
[4] Mentioned in Bengal letters, I.O.R., E/4/3, pp. 78, 94, 197.
[5] L. Warnier to Directors, 26 Jan. 1733, I.O.R., Home Miscellaneous, 74, p. 518.
[6] J. Fullerton to W. Weston, 9 Feb. 1733, I.O.L., MS. Eur. D. 602, f. 9.

invested in some years in Golconda diamonds,[1] and it is likely that
the Ostend Company took considerable sums between 1720 and
1730, while the story of Governor Deane suggests at least one
large transaction through the Dutch.

1731 to 1756

In the twenty-five years from the early 1730s until the taking of
Calcutta in 1756 men continued to leave Bengal with large
fortunes and the remittances of the British community as a whole
were not markedly below the levels achieved in 1728. But there
is a more sombre side to the picture: successful fortunes were being
matched by bankruptcies. Calcutta's ships experienced several
poor trading seasons, while participation in internal trade or
profiteering in office had not yet developed to the point where they
could compensate for losses at sea.

Records of the careers of civil servants continue to suggest that
a number of men were able to leave Bengal at a time of their own
choosing, after a length of service and after having attained a rank
in the Company's service that imply that they were in affluent
circumstances. The notorious Hugh Barker, who fled from Bengal
on a French ship to avoid further investigation of his misdeeds,
seems to be the only candidate between 1731 and 1738. Barker
in fact died on the way home,[2] but he had already accumulated
enough to buy part of an estate in Buckinghamshire 'belonging formerly to Sir John Fortescue'.[3] In 1739, however, three
civil servants resigned after comparatively short spells of thirteen,
fourteen, and sixteen years respectively.[4] Another followed in
1741 with twenty-five years,[5] and two each in 1742[6] and 1743.[7]
A servant of twenty-seven years' standing was dismissed in 1745.[8]
Governor Thomas Braddyll retired in 1746 after thirty-one years
in Bengal. Another Governor, William Barwell, was dismissed in
1749 with another senior servant,[9] while two more servants

---

[1] Diamond imports from 1700 to 1732 into Britain are listed in Balkrishna,
Commercial Relations between England and India 1601–1757 (1924), p. 312.

[2] R. Adams to M. King, 14 Oct. 1737, I.O.R., Home Miscellaneous, 37,
p. 369.

[3] *Omichund v. Bate*, P.R.O., C 11/1055/16.

[4] Samuel Bennet, William Elliot, and John Hinde.   [5] Richard Eyre.

[6] Michael Cotesworth (31 years), William Price (16 years).

[7] Solomon Margas (25 years), Alexander Wedderburn (12 years).

[8] William Davis.   [9] William Kempe (19 years).

resigned in the same year.[1] A servant of thirteen years' standing came home in 1750;[2] one of fifteen years in 1751;[3] and one of twenty years was dismissed in 1752.[4] Like so many Governors, Adam Dawson, was dismissed on the orders of the Directors in 1753 and William Wogan, who had only been in Bengal for nine years but was reputed to be handsomely off came with him. From 1753 until Plassey no civil servant of any seniority left Bengal.

Additional evidence about the wealth of certain individuals is again available. When William Barwell died in 1769, his house and estate in Surrey were valued at £10,500 and he had £106,000 in Bank Stock and Annuities, South Sea Stock and East India Stock.[5] Thomas Braddyll bought a house and land in Essex for £19,500 and was reported to have died worth £70,000.[6] The Directors complained of 'Mr Wogan's raising such a fortune at Dacca as, it is reported he has brought home, although so young and low in the service', and believed that he had done it by supplying Dacca goods to the Dutch at a profit of 15 per cent.[7]

Before 1757, and after that date as well, Free Merchants were at a serious disadvantage by comparison with those in the Company's service. They were prevented from going outside Calcutta to obtain goods, were not usually given *dastaks* for goods they bought from Company servants or through Indian *gumashtas*, and were not allowed to take goods for freight on their ships until given permission by the senior Company servants. It is hardly surprising that any Free Merchant who could muster influence at home seems to have tried to use it to get into the service.[8] Nevertheless, some Free Merchants did prosper. In 1754 one John Brown was said to do 'more business in his accompting house' in a month than was transacted by the Company in a year.[9] The most widely respected Free Merchant of the pre-Plassey era seems to have been a Scot called David Rannie. Rannie was a shipowner

[1] Humphrey Bellamy, Richard Eyre, each with 19 years.
[2] Samuel Rooper.   [3] Edward Eyles.   [4] Wadham Brooke.
[5] Valuation in I.O.L., MS. Eur. D. 535, pt. i, ff. 22–3.
[6] *Gentleman's Magazine*, xvii (1747), 592; will in P.R.O., PROB/11/758, f. 301.
[7] Directors to Bengal, 31 Jan. 1755, *Fort William–India House Corr.* i. 85, 107.
[8] e.g. J. Fullerton to Dr. Littlejohn, 10 Dec. 1735, I.O.L., MS. Eur. D. 602, f. 39.
[9] S. Dalrymple to Sir H. Dalrymple, 6 Jan. 1754, S.R.O., Hamilton-Dalrymple MSS., bundle 56.

who often went to sea himself, as well as being a merchant capable
of organizing large purchases, as he showed in transactions with
the Prussian Company.[1]

The British community as a whole continued to make remittances through the East India Company's bills at approximately
the level of the late 1720s, until 1752, when a marked increase
began.

TABLE VI

£		£	
1731-2	87,497	1744-5	51,386
1732-3	83,843	1745-6	71,616
1733-4	97,375	1746-7	66,221
1734-5	54,558	1747-8	55,937
1735-6	33,761	1748-9	64,729
1736-7	47,831	1749-50	67,698
1737-8	51,708	1750-1	89,093
1738-9	43,675	1751-2	92,368
1739-40	73,819	1752-3	150,712
1740-1	27,865	1753-4	170,308
1741-2	44,898	1754-5	123,401
1742-3	61,388	1755-6	79,402
1743-4	49,753	Total	£1,840,842

Source: I.O.R., E/4/3-5; *Fort William–India House Corr.* i.

Diamond purchases at Madras should again presumably be
added to this total, and some allowance should be made for foreign
bills. There was little activity by the Ostend Company in Bengal
after 1730, but the Prussian Company was certainly taking money
for bills in the 1750s and the Portuguese and the Dutch were also
presumably giving bills.

In ugly contrast to the fortunes still being made, bankruptcies
were becoming increasingly common in Bengal in the 1730s and
1740s. Company servants were clearly stretching their credit to
the utmost, leaving themselves dangerously vulnerable to any
setback. In 1728 Governor Henry Frankland issued a warning
about the inability of some servants to pay their debts.[2] There were
rumours that the Bengal servants 'trade very high, especially the
Gov . . . r [Deane] and that they borough money of the black
merchants on the Company's creditt'.[3] One of the senior servants,

---

[1] Bolwerk and Nucella to Directors, 12 Nov. 1776, I.O.R., D/149; I.O.R.,
Mayor's Court Records, Range 155, vol. 70, p. 100.

[2] I.O.R., B.P.C., 8 July 1728, Range 1, vol. 6, f. 614.

[3] R. Adams to J. Jones, 24 Jan. 1730, I.O.R., Home Miscellaneous, 37, p. 5.

Richard Bourchier, was specifically warned that 'it is the opinion of your best friends that . . . you overtrade the marketts'.[1] Within a few years Bourchier and Mathew Wastell, another servant who had been in partnership with him, were declared insolvent. By that time Charles Bedford, whose affairs were entangled with those of the Company's Kasimbazar broker, 'Contoo',[2] was also a bankrupt as were two servants stationed at Dacca.[3] More disasters followed. Governor John Stackhouse was evidently in financial difficulties when the Company dismissed him from their service in 1739. He was reported to be 'above £40,000 in debt, poor man',[4] a charity not extended to him by one of his female creditors, who commented on the news of his death: 'there is a miserable wretch out of the world and happy had it been for me and for many others had he made his exit twenty years sooner.'[5] Samuel Fazakerly, 'whose effects will fall greatly short of discharging his debt' was allowed to return to Britain in 1739. In the same year another Councillor, George Mandeville, absconded to the French. Yet another Company servant was declared bankrupt in 1740,[6] and two more died insolvent in 1743.[7] When Humphreys Cole's mismanagement of the Company's factory at Patna was finally investigated,[8] he was found to be quite unable to meet the claims on him. John Smith died at Dacca in 1747 leaving debts of Rs 20,000.[9] A member of the Council, James Blachford, was reported in 1752 to be 'in very bad circumstances' and to be suffering from 'a distempered brain' for good measure.[10]

With so many failures it is hardly surprising that the British community in Bengal, and especially the Company servants, should have acquired a distinctly unsavoury reputation. One hostile observer in the 1730s thought that seven-eighths of them were 'deeply in debt' and doubted whether there were 'ten men amongst them who could safely be trusted with a loan of £500'.[11]

[1] Letter of R. Adams, 13 Feb. 1731, ibid., p. 69.
[2] See above, p. 161.
[3] John Cocke declared bankrupt in 1732 and Thomas Cooke in 1735.
[4] Cited in C. Gill, *Merchants and Mariners of the eighteenth century* (1961), p. 121.
[5] Mrs. Adams to H. Cole, 14 Dec. 1742, I.O.R., Home Miscellaneous, 37, P. 335.   [6] William Weston.
[7] Henry Rumbold and Sir Francis Russell.   [8] See above, p. 160.
[9] Bengal to Directors, 10 Jan. 1748, *Fort William–India House Corr.* i. 203.
[10] Bengal to Directors, 18 Sept. 1752, ibid. i. 610.
[11] Cited in Gill, *Merchants and Mariners*, p. 121.

Clive believed that the loss of Calcutta came as a blessing to its European inhabitants, who were on the point of 'an acknowledged universal bankruptcy'.[1] No doubt the Bengal servants did 'trade very high' and run great risks, as their critics alleged; no doubt too they were 'very extravagant and profane in their way of living'.[2] In the less certain times which set in from the 1730s several of them paid the penalty for their improvidence. But average annual remittances to Europe by bills on the East India Company alone of over £100,000 over the seven years before the capture of Calcutta hardly suggest a community on the point of collapse. Nor is this suggested by the growth of the settlement or by the value of the private European property taken by Siraj-ud-daula which was thought to have been worth some £450,000.[3]

1757 to 1769

Those who survived the capture of Calcutta or the subsequent exile to Fulta returned to a world which was shortly to be turned upside down by Plassey. Mir Jafar paid out some £1,750,000 in presents and compensation to Europeans and his successors were also to make liberal distributions over the next ten years.[4] Obstacles to full and effective British participation in the internal trade of Bengal with its high profit margins were soon broken down.[5] The Company began to receive large payments out of Bengal's revenues which could be tapped by individuals, either at source, if they were employed in the revenue service, or less directly by frauds and overcharging in projects such as the new Fort William.[6] The boom was to last for about twelve years after Plassey. But by 1770 or thereabouts declining profits in the inland trade, diminishing prospects for presents, and closer regulation of the perquisites of office by the Company were beginning to create new elements of uncertainty in the pursuit of a fortune.

For the Company's civil servants these twelve years were the only time during the eighteenth century when survival in Bengal virtually guaranteed that a man would return home with a fortune.

---

[1] Letter to H. Vansittart, 3 Feb. 1762, I.O.L., MS. Eur. G. 37, box 4.
[2] R. Adams to M. Wastell, 28 Oct. 1736, I.O.R., Home Miscellaneous, 37, p. 342.
[3] 50 lakhs were paid, but an addition of 20 per cent was apparently made to each claim (H. Vansittart, *A Letter to the Proprietors of East India Stock* (1767), p. 109).
[4] See chapter vii.   [5] See chapter v.   [6] See chapter viii.

Death and quickly won affluence produced a rapid turnover in the senior ranks of the service so that men with little more than ten years in Bengal found themselves on the Council and were able to contemplate retirement in another two or three years. Dismissal from the service had always been a hazard, especially for Governors of Bengal, and as the Directors became increasingly disenchanted with the way in which they were being served after Plassey, dismissals came thick and fast. Dismissal might disrupt carefully laid plans, but it does not seem to have inflicted serious hardship.

Mir Jafar's bounty enabled the Councillors who had both mismanaged relations with Siraj-ud-daula and failed to defend Calcutta to beat a hasty retreat. Presents had the great advantage over trading profits of being paid in specie which could be realized at once. In 1759 Governor Roger Drake and eight members of Council[1] took their winnings and departed. Most of them were presumably in comfortable circumstances, and one, William Watts, who had run very great risks and played a vital part in the Plassey revolution, was very well off indeed. When Watts died in 1764, he had two country properties in Berkshire, one of them bought for £40,000 from the Duke of Kingston, and a town house in Hanover Square.[2] His estate was rumoured to be worth £110,000.[3] Luke Scrafton was another to leave in 1759. He had been closely associated with Clive during the Plassey campaign, had served at Mir Jafar's court afterwards, and had clearly been well rewarded. Even though bills for £465,307 in all were drawn on London for the sailing season 1758–9, there was very much more money in Calcutta awaiting remittance than the Company could handle and much of it went to the foreigners.

Clive left Bengal in 1760. He took with him by far the greatest fortune ever made by an individual in India. In addition to the £230,000 in Dutch bills and the £30,000 in diamonds from Madras,[4] he sent off £41,000 in bills on the Company, £4,000 by

---

[1] William Watts, William Frankland, Matthew Collett, William Mackett, Richard Becher, Thomas Boddam, Charles Manningham, and John Cooke. Another Councillor, Edward Cruttenden, left in 1757 with a fortune of 'upwards of 50,000£ . . . the greatest part in money and Company's bonds' (letter to Clive, 16 Nov. 1757, N.L.W., Clive MSS., 805).

[2] P.R.O., PROB/11/903, f. 412.

[3] L. Scrafton to Clive, 14 Nov. 1764, I.O.L., MS. Eur. G. 37, box 32.

[4] See above, pp. 221, 225.

certificates on East India Company ships, £5,000 via Bombay and
£7,000 by a bill drawn on the Director Laurence Sulivan.[1] Before
he left he also secured what he hoped would be an annual income
of £27,000 from his *jagir*.[2] In his second period of service from
1765 to 1767, although Clive took no presents, did not trade, and
divided up 'all the advantages accruing to him as Governor . . .
amongst his dependants',[3] he was still able to remit home some
£165,000, including £54,133 by the Dutch company and £20,000
by the French.[4] Most of this consisted of accumulated arrears on
his *jagir* and what he called 'the conclusion of all my concerns in
India'.[5] On 31 July 1767, on reviewing his affairs after his arrival
in Britain, Clive calculated that his total 'stock' was now worth
£401,102.[6]

Clive was succeeded for a few months by Holwell, who acted as
Governor for part of 1760, until he was superseded by Vansittart.
Holwell was widely supposed to have put his five months as
Governor to very good account. According to one hostile witness
he had only been worth £20,000 when he took office, but left it
worth £96,000.[7]

By 1760 very large profits were being reaped from British
participation in Bengal's internal trade. In 1761 and 1762 members
of the Council were able to retire after only twelve and thirteen
years' service in Bengal.[8] Three more servants left in 1764, including William McGwire, who was already reported to have 'a pretty
fortune',[9] and Anselm Beaumont, who had been ruined in 1756 but
eight years later was able to make generous provision for his
friends and dependants.[10] Great fortunes had also been made by
those who were killed in the 1763 war. The inventory of William
Hay, partner of Johnstone and Bolts, abundantly confirms Clive's

[1] See Clive's Journal, N.L.W., Clive MSS., 350 and letters to his attorneys,
9 Nov., 25 Dec. 1757, ibid., 200, pp. 155–6, 169.
[2] See above, p. 165.
[3] H. Strachey to Morley, 15 Dec. 1766, I.O.L., MS. Eur. G. 37, box 43,
f. 225.
[4] List of remittances in ibid., box 79.
[5] Letter to attorneys, 27 Sept. 1765, ibid., box 4.
[6] 'Trial balance', ibid., box 82.
[7] J. Caillaud's defence of his conduct, I.O.L., Orme MSS., 'India', xii. 3253;
J. Carnac to Clive, 2 Nov. 1760, I.O.L., MS. Eur. F. 128, box 4/1.
[8] Samuel Weller and Culling Smith.
[9] H. Verelst to R. Becher, 9 Sept. 1761, Ames MSS., I.O.L., Microfilm,
reel 606.
[10] P.R.O., PROB/11/1016, ff. 43–5.

estimate that he had died 'in great circumstances'.[1] The inventory of William Ellis, Chief of the captured Patna factory, suggests that he died worth £100,000.[2] William Billers also seems to have been a rich man when he committed suicide at Patna in 1765.[3] Just how successful Vansittart had been is open to doubt. He had certainly aimed very high and traded on a huge scale.[4] He implied that he had achieved comparatively little,[5] but when he returned home in 1765 he was able to buy a valuable estate in Berkshire and to bring himself into parliament. He risked and lost large sums trying to create votes in an East India Company election in 1769.[6] Deciding that only another term in Bengal would give him the kind of fortune that he wanted, he was on his way back when the ship on which he was travelling was lost with all hands. His executors found that he possessed little in England, apart from the Berkshire estate and a house at Greenwich, but they still hoped to recover effects left at Madras (the scene of his early service) and in Bengal.[7]

No such uncertainties exist about John Johnstone. He had pursued a fortune with an enterprise and a ruthlessness which gave him one probably second only in size to Clive's. He is supposed to have been worth £300,000 when he returned to Scotland, where he bought three estates and built up a parliamentary interest.[8] Johnstone thought it prudent to leave Bengal during Clive's second administration. Six other senior servants agreed with him or were dismissed.[9] Although only two of this group had more than fifteen years' service, it would seem that they had already accumulated enough for a comfortable retirement. Only one of them was later to seek reinstatement and a return to Bengal.[10] Clive also persuaded William Sumner to resign the service.[11] Sumner was reported to have taken £90,000 home with him.[12]

---

[1] Clive to Walsh, 26 Sept. 1765, I.O.L., MS. Eur. G. 37, box 35, f. 167. For inventory, see I.O.R., Mayor's Court Records, Range 154, vols. 64, ff. 1–12; 66, pp. 147–52.

[2] Ibid., Range 154, vols. 64, ff. 20–1; 65, pp. 96–103, 106–9.

[3] Ibid., Range 154, vols. 65, pp. 192 ff.; 66, pp. 220, 224–9.

[4] See above, p. 115.

[5] *A Letter to the Proprietors of East India Stock*, p. 140.

[6] Sutherland, *East India Company*, p. 192.

[7] R. Palk to Hastings, 22 Mar. 1774, Add. MS. 29134, f. 335.

[8] C. L. Johnstone, *History of the Johnstones* (Edinburgh, [1909]), pp. 180–1.

[9] John Burdett, George Gray, Ralph Leycester, Randolph Marriott, Charles Playdell, and Ascanius Senior.   [10] Playdell.   [11] See above, p. 169.

[12] H. Verelst to R. Becher, 1 Oct. 1765, Ames MSS., I.O.L., Microfilm, reel 606.

Three more great fortunes were amassed before the end of the decade. These were made by Francis Sykes, Thomas Rumbold and James Alexander, who had all taken a rich harvest out of the early revenue administration, Sykes as Resident at Murshidabad, Rumbold at Patna, and Alexander at both. Both among his contemporaries in Bengal and among the public at home Sykes came to be regarded as one of the wealthiest men to come out of India. He settled at Basildon Park in Oxfordshire, becoming an M.P. and a baronet. In spite of a 'very sufficient and independent fortune' (as he called it), Rumbold was still 'ambitious of credit in life' and almost immediately sought a new career in India.[1] He eventually became Governor of Madras, and when he was able to add what he acquired there to his Bengal fortune, he was a very rich man indeed. In addition to his estate at Woodhall in Hertfordshire, his assets in cash, bonds, bills of exchange and outstanding debts amounted to £200,000.[2] Alexander, one of the relatively few Irishmen in the Bengal civil service, believed that he was worth about £150,000 when he left Bengal in 1772.[3] He acquired nearly 9,000 acres in Ulster, from which he hoped to derive an annual income of some £7,000,[4] and became the first Lord Caledon.

The great profits of the post-Plassey period went to the relatively senior civil servants. Due to the exceptionally rapid turnover of personnel in Bengal in this period, senior posts were often held by men still in their twenties. But Clive believed that fortunes were being made even more quickly. He complained of expectations that 'independency should fall to every man's lot, in a day, without the claim of service'.[5] There was an element of exaggeration in this. Inventories of deceased junior servants show that many of them were hopelessly in debt, mostly to their banians; but others had certainly been able to make a brisk start to the business of amassing a fortune. Two men, Henry Lushington[6] and John Wood,[7] who died after eight or seven years in Bengal, were both worth over four lakhs of rupees, or about £45,000. Alexander

[1] Letter to Clive, 23 Aug. 1770, I.O.L., MS. Eur. G. 37, box 60, f. 38.

[2] 'Inventory and account', 1 Apr. 1781, in the possession of Sir Anthony Rumbold.

[3] J. Alexander to W. Alexander, 20 Jan. 1772, Northern Ireland P.R.O., D/2432/1/7.

[4] Valuation of Caledon estate, June 1774, ibid., D/2433/32/2.

[5] I.O.R., B.P.C., 12 Feb. 1766, Range 1, vol. 39, f. 53.

[6] Inventory in I.O.R., Mayor's Court Records, Range 154, vol. 65, pp. 16 ff.

[7] Inventory, ibid., Range 154, vol. 68, pp. 71–87.

Campbell, who had come to Bengal from 'the lofty station of
a critical reviewer' in 1763, left it in 1767 with £30,000 and 'a
contented mind'.¹ Thomas Amphlett made £15,000 in little more
than two years before his death.²

During the twelve years or so after Plassey, the prospects for
civil servants who survived for any length of time were excellent.
No bankruptcies occurred comparable to those of previous
generations. But there were still pitfalls for the unwary. Warren
Hastings, for instance, traded very ambitiously during Vansittart's
Governorship, but resigned with him in 1764, leaving many of
his assets still to be realized. Sykes who tried to disentangle his
affairs for him reported that 'they turn out more to the credit of
his moderation than knowledge of the world. He is almost literally
worth nothing and must return to India or want bread.'³ Paul
Pearkes had received a Councillor's share of the Plassey spoils,
but when he died in 1760, with his 'affairs so scattered about' and
his accounts in confusion, little could be collected.⁴ The case of
Harry Verelst, Governor from 1767 to 1769, shows how conditions
were beginning to change for the worse towards the end of the
decade. Before he became Governor, Verelst had already sent
home some £47,000, but as the first Governor after Clive not
allowed to trade he anticipated that he would actually end his
administration poorer by £15,000 to £20,000, while deteriorating
trading conditions by 1769 made it very difficult for him to wind
up his old trading concerns.⁵ He appears to have ended his days
as a relatively modest country gentleman in Yorkshire.⁶

The twelve years after Plassey were also halcyon ones for army
officers. Promotion was rapid as the Company's army grew, while
prize money and presents were distributed lavishly after the
campaigns against Siraj-ud-daula and Mir Kasim. Major Killpatrick, who fought in all the actions of 1757 to die after Plassey,
left £60,000.⁷ Although Carnac was to suffer severe losses later,

¹ Verelst to Clive, 6 Jan. 1768, I.O.L., MS. Eur. G. 37, box 51, f. 35.
² Clive to T. Amphlett, 28 Sept. 1765, N.L.W., Clive MSS., 222, p. 57.
Inventory in I.O.R., Mayor's Court Records, Range 154, vol. 64, ff. 191–4.
³ Sykes to Clive, 28 Mar. 1768, I.O.L., MS. Eur. G. 37, box 52, ff. 108–9.
⁴ H. Verelst to his sister, 28 Feb. 1761 and to P. Bartley 7 Feb. 1763, Ames
MSS., I.O.L., Microfilm, reel 606.
⁵ Verelst to Clive, 24 Jan. 1767, 17 Feb. 1769, to T. Saunders, 20 Sept. 1768,
ibid.
⁶ Will in P.R.O., PROB/11/1139, f. 127.
⁷ Inventory, I.O.R., Mayor's Court Records, Range 154, vol. 61, pp. 96–7.

he was said to be worth £80,000 in 1765.[1] Thomas Adams, who
drove Mir Kasim out of Bengal, also left £60,000.[2] Eyre Coote had
two spells in Bengal between 1756 and 1762, which together with
his triumphs in the south enabled him to purchase large properties
in Ireland, an estate in Wiltshire, a country house in Hampshire,
and a London residence. Richard Smith had already made himself
independent and been able to invest £60,000 with the Nawab of
Arcot when he came to Bengal in 1764.[3] Six years later he left as
Commander-in-Chief with a fortune said to be of £200,000 to
£300,000.[4] Even enterprising surgeons could make quick fortunes.
William Semple, 'bred up a physician, was eminent in his way in
the West Indies but not liking his profession, he came to the
East to make his fortune which he has acquired in as short a space
of time as any body in this country ever did'; he apparently made
£30,000 by trade over three years.[5]

Opportunities for Free Merchants were more restricted in this
period than for those in the service of the Company. The seaborne
trade was generally depressed, and, although a share of the prosperity gained in the internal trade of Bengal certainly rubbed off on
them, Free Merchants were at a definite disadvantage in it. Lacking
political authority, they tended to act as the agents or managers
for the ventures of Company servants.[6] After 1764 efforts were
made to confine them once again to Calcutta. Acting as supercargoes on ships or contractors for services for the Company were
suggested as profitable lines for them.[7] Nevertheless, at least one
Free Merchant made a very large fortune. In 1765 Robert Gregory
returned to England, having, according to Clive, 'acquired a
fortune of £100,000 by trade only'.[8] Gregory had been a very
much respected figure in Calcutta, transacting a wide range of
business on land and sea. In Britain he became an active Director
of the Company, entered parliament and founded a notable
Anglo-Irish literary and political family. There is also evidence
of substantial if less spectacular prosperity in the inventories of

[1] Clive to his wife, 24 Aug. 1765, I.O.L., MS. Eur. G. 37, box 4
[2] Inventory, I.O.R., Mayor's Court Records, Range 154, vol. 63, f. 73.
[3] Letters to R. Orme, 7 Jan. 1767, [Jan. 1768], I.O.L., Orme MSS., OV, 37,
f. 12; 38, f. 35.
[4] R. Barwell to his father, 25 Dec. 1769, B.P.P., x (1915), 247.
[5] J. Grose to N. Grose, 15 Feb. 1769, 22 Dec. 1770, I.O.L., MS. Eur.
E. 284.   [6] Bolts, Considerations, i. 72–3.
[7] L. Scrafton to Clive, 9 Dec. 1765, I.O.L., MS. Eur. G. 37, box 37, ff. 30–1.
[8] Letter to his wife, 10 Feb. 1766, ibid., box 3.

other Free Merchants who died in the 1760s leaving estates worth some £20,000 or £30,000.[1]

In the years after Plassey lists of bills drawn from Bengal on the East India Company become increasingly inadequate as a means of measuring the volume of remittances home made by the British community. Far more money was accumulating than the Company were willing to accept. After several occasions on which bills from Bengal for large sums had arrived in London when the Company had difficulty in meeting them, quotas and restrictions were enforced. By 1768 these had reached the point where, with bills restricted to £70,000 and only offered at 2s. per rupee,[2] the Company's terms were seen 'in no other light than as a total prohibition'.[3] There were very few takers for bills until the rate was raised to 2s. 2½d. by orders of the following year.

TABLE VII

	£		£
1756–7	22,430	1763–4	168,846
1757–8	308,300	1764–5	248,072
1758–9	465,307	1765–6	95,825
1759–60	113,134	1766–7	156,414
1760–1	232,872	1767–8	145,011
1761–2	327,184	1768–9	47,051
1762–3	281,622	1769–70	54,880
		Total	£2,666,948

Source: *Fort William–India House Corr.* i, ii; *Reports*, iv. 60.

Shortage of bills on the Company created a scramble for other forms of remittance after Plassey. Clive was presumably not the only person in Bengal who tried to buy Golconda diamonds; by 1767 at least £100,000 was said to be waiting for unobtainable diamonds at Madras.[4] Bengal had by 1767 developed its own sources of diamonds, through Banaras.[5] Registers had to be kept of diamonds shipped from Calcutta; although these registers do not appear to have survived, totals for some years were copied

---

[1] e.g. Captain Alexander Scott, Peter Gallopine and Alexander Carvalho, I.O.R., Mayor's Court Records, Range 154, vols. 64, ff. 182–7; 66, pp. 121 ff., 283 ff.; 63, f. 30.

[2] Directors to Bengal, 16 Mar. 1768, *Fort William–India House Corr.* iv. 110–11.

[3] Clive to attorneys, 6 Feb, 1769, N.L.W., Clive MSS., 61, pp. T4–5.

[4] J. Call to Clive, 12 Mar. 1767, I.O.L., MS. Eur. G. 37, box 44.

[5] See above, p. 221.

into the dispatches home from Bengal. The over-all total of
Rs 658,055 (or about £70,000) over four years from 1765 to 1769
is not a large one,[1] and it is clear that the great majority of the
stones belonged to Clive or Verelst, whose agent John Chamier
must have kept a tight control over the European share of the
diamond market at Banaras.[2]

Bills on the foreign companies were a much more important
alternative to British bills than diamonds. Without searching
continental archives it is very difficult to offer more than guesses
at the sums involved. The Dutch had a reputation for driving hard
bargains, but their bills were regarded as punctual and secure.
They received £230,000 from Clive alone after Plassey and
another £54,000 from him in 1765,[3] while he negotiated for yet
another £60,000 in 1769.[4] After 1764 the French company began to
revive their trade in Bengal. By 1767 they were not only 'taking all
that is offered' at Chandernagore,[5] but their agents were approaching
men in Britain who still had money in Bengal or who could act for
others there, inviting them to draw bills on Bengal for which repayment would eventually be made in Europe.[6] John Johnstone was
believed to have brought home £70,000 left in India by this means.
It was thought that £1,200,000 in all was sent home by British
subjects through the Dutch and French companies between 1765
and December 1767.[7] 1768 was also a good year for the French.
One estimate of the value of the bills issued by Chandernagore in
1768 put them as high as thirty lakhs of rupees.[8] On the other
hand, the Dutch stopped taking bills on Europe by September
1768.[9] If the total of £1,200,000 for 1765–7 can be taken as well

[1] The annual totals (listed in *Fort William–India House Corr*. iv, v) were

1765/6	Rs 40,000	1767/8	Rs 306,890
1766/7	Rs 104,824	1768/9	Rs 206,341

[2] Chamier's purchases came to Rs 232,040 in 1767–8 and Rs 190,429 in
1768–9 (Verelst to Clive, 25 Mar. 1768, 10 Mar. 1769, I.O.L., MS. Eur. G. 37,
box 52, ff. 83–4; 56, f. 245).   [3] See above, pp. 235–6.

[4] Hope Bros. to G. Clive, 28 Feb. 1769, ibid., box 56, f. 219.

[5] C. Russell to Clive, 25 Sept. 1767, ibid., box 47, ff. 178–9.

[6] For an example of such a proposition, see J. D. Fatio to Clive 15 Aug. 1767,
ibid., box 46, f. 97.

[7] R. Barwell to his father, 9 Dec. 1767, *B.P.P*., x (1915), 16–17.

[8] J. Alexander to T. Saunders, 23 Nov. 1768, Northern Ireland P.R.O.,
D/2432/1/3.

[9] Verelst to Mrs. Beard, 25 Sept. 1768, Ames MSS., I.O.L., Microfilm,
reel 606.

informed, it is necessary to add substantial amounts to it for money lent to the Dutch between 1757 and 1765 and for sums taken by both in 1768 and 1769: a grand total of £2,000,000 for money remitted through the French and the Dutch by British subjects in Bengal between 1757 and 1770 may not be an unreasonable estimate.

1770 to 1784

In the early 1770s the period of easy fortune-making which had lasted since 1757 was being brought to an end by a number of unwelcome developments: Calcutta was affected by a sharp commercial depression in 1769; much of Bengal suffered severe famine in 1770; salt, and later opium, came under direct control by the Company; apart from a minor one in 1772, there were no further distributions of largesse by the Nawabs; the new Councillors arriving in 1774, after the passing of the Regulating Act, began to take what seemed to be an officious interest in perquisites and profiteering. Wealth could still be amassed: some individuals with conspicuous fortunes continued to leave Bengal in the 1770s or early 1780s, as did a very much larger number of men reputed to be able to live at home in reasonable comfort. But on the other hand, bankruptcies began again, and some began to face a prospect which was largely new to Bengal. As Europeans learnt to protect their health better and as official salaries improved in the Company's service, a number of men found that they could earn enough to support themselves respectably in India but not enough to give them any real chance of retiring in any sort of affluence to Britain. In the past it had been unusual for a man not either to have made his fortune or to be dead after twenty-five years at the most: several of those in the Company's service in the 1770s would still be in Bengal in the nineteenth century.

The financial prospects of a civil servant depended in the 1770s very much on the part of Bengal to which he happened to be posted. Calcutta had few attractions, except for those who had caught Hastings's eye and been given an office to which very high rates of commission had been attached.[1] Claud Alexander, the Paymaster General, was one of these. He made some £60,000 out of his office and the agency business which he ran with his younger

---

[1] See above, p. 183.

brother with which he bought the Ballochmyle estate in Ayrshire for £27,000 and later founded the Catrine cotton mills.[1] But most men in Calcutta felt that a fortune was likely to pass them by: living expenses were intolerably high, trading opportunities limited, and the chances of large perquisites, compared, for instance, with those in the Revenue Department, relatively restricted.

At the leading revenue and commercial stations things could be different, even in the 1780s. Dacca, Burdwan and above all Patna were thought to be lucrative postings. Senior civil servants could still get rich at Patna in a few years. George Vansittart, the younger brother of the former Governor, kept one of the most meticulous sets of personal accounts to have survived, calculating the size of his 'estate' on 30 April every year. In four years, mostly at Patna, he doubled his fortune, and was able to retire in 1776 with £100,000.[2] Ewan Law, who left Bihar in 1780, is said to have taken £150,000 with him.[3] William Young, who spent the later part of his career there, could congratulate himself by 1785 on having 'a quantum sufficient not only to live genteely but elegantly upon'.[4] The largest single fortune amassed in the 1770s was almost certainly that of Richard Barwell, rumoured probably with exaggeration to amount to £400,000.[5] A large part of Barwell's fortune was evidently acquired while he was Chief at Dacca and had opportunities to dip into the revenue and to farm the Company's salt.[6] The largest fortune made at Burdwan was probably that of John Graham, who appears to have had £70,000 awaiting remittance home when he was on the point of leaving India in 1774 with £25,000 already in Britain to be used in buying an estate in Scotland.[7] Outside Bengal itself, Oudh was an extremely lucrative station during the 1770s. The Residents and their assistants were all likely to do very well for themselves. Nathaniel Middleton, Resident at intervals between 1774 and 1782 was said to have

[1] See his correspondence with D. Anderson, Add. MS. 45424.
[2] Bodleian, dep. b. 98 and 99.
[3] W. Maxwell to D. Anderson, Dec. 1779, Add. MS. 45427, ff. 74–5.
[4] Young to Murray, 10 Sept. 1785, S.R.O., GD 32/24/54.
[5] J. Woodman to Hastings, 16 Aug. 1780, Add. MS. 29145, ff. 383–4. Indications of the size of his fortune in his correspondence are substantial if less spectacular: he had £67,581 in Britain in 1774; added another £32,400 in 1776, £40,000 in 1779 and £40,000 was sent after him when he left India in 1780 (*B.P.P.*, xii (1916), 76; xiii (1916), 298; xviii (1919), 23, 45).
[6] See above, p. 143.
[7] R. Mayne to J. Graham, 11 Jan. 1775, S.R.O., GD 29/2122/4.

amassed 'the largest private fortune on this side Sir Thomas Rumbold's'.[1]

Under the old dispensation, any man who had held the office of Governor of Bengal for thirteen years should have made a fortune beyond even the dreams of Clive's avarice. Under the new dispensation a man of common prudence who had enjoyed the Governor General's salary of over £25,000 should have been extremely wealthy. Warren Hastings could in fact command a fortune of £75,000 when he finally resigned from his office in 1785, a sum roughly comparable to those made by men of moderate seniority who had served half as long as he had done.[2] A fortune of this size after so many years with such plentiful opportunities seems to confirm the reputation which Hastings enjoyed among his contemporaries for moderation in financial matters. The truth is, however, more complex. In the first four years of his administration, 1772 to 1775, he clearly made the best of the perquisites available to him as Governor, remitting £122,000 (a sum which exceeds all his official emoluments by £25,000). After 1775 he received little beyond his official salary, on which huge as it was he was incapable of living; the only significant private addition to his fortune came from keeping three lakhs of rupees from Nobkissen offered to him in 1780 as a loan.[3] In the last ten years of his administration Hastings was able to send home another £96,000, so that his remittances amounted to £218,000 in all. Had he been able to keep the major part of this intact until he returned home, he would have been a very rich man. But unfortunately for him, he allowed enormous inroads to be made into it for generous gifts and loans to his friends and relatives, and for political expenses to defend him in office. By 1785 only £75,000 was left. The story of Hastings's fortune is one of mismanagement and lack of realism rather than of abstinence and renunciation.

With a much larger intake into the civil service and more men surviving their early years in India, the number of servants retiring in the 1770s or early 1780s after careers which suggest that they were comfortably off, if not notoriously so, increased. About fifty

---

[1] J. Macpherson to L. Sulivan, 16 July 1782, Macpherson MSS. in possession of Sir Cyril Philips.

[2] See my 'Personal Fortune of Warren Hastings', *Economic History Review*, 2nd ser., xvii. 284–300, on which this paragraph is based.

[3] See above, p. 195.

civil servants can be identified who at first sight appear likely to have fallen into this category.

By the 1780s, however, there were a number of men of considerable standing in the civil service who had no prospect of going home with any kind of fortune. In 1785 out of 260 civil servants no less than 150 were Junior or Senior Merchants, that is men with at least eight years' service who had been the Writers allowed to go to Bengal in such numbers in the late 1760s and early 1770s. At the best of times the Bengal establishment did not 'afford employment and proper situations to so great a number',[1] but by 1785 a major retrenchment had been launched against the proliferation of offices and the inflation of emoluments of Hastings's administration. As some compensation, a system of pensions was introduced for those deprived of office. A Senior Merchant could either remain in Bengal on £1,400 a year or go back to Britain for three years on half that; a Junior Merchant had the option of £960 in Bengal or £480 in Britain.[2] Thirty-five applications for pensions were received during the first year.[3] The Directors, however, insisted that a 'subsistence' of £400 and £300 was adequate for the two grades.[4] Thus those who were not well placed in the service and who in the more rigorous climate of the Cornwallis era stood little chance of winning a well paid office, such as a Collectorship, had a number of unpalatable choices before them: they could cling on to a minor office in Bengal (if they were fortunate enough to have one), live on a pension in India or admit defeat and come home to a very limited 'subsistence'. Many chose to come home, but others soldiered on in Bengal. In 1805 there were still twenty-one civil servants in the *Bengal Calendar* who had been appointed before 1775. They included men like Jacob Rider, who had come to Bengal for the first time in 1763, Edward Fenwick, who arrived a year later and had held no office since 1788, although he was paid a special allowance to compensate for his 'extreme poverty' and 'mental derangement', or the redoubtable William Brooke, a Writer of 1769 who was to die in the Company's service in Bengal in 1833.

The problems of an overcrowded service and lack of promotion

[1] Bengal to Directors, 25 Oct. 1785, *Fort William–India House Corr.* ix. 591.
[2] National Archives of India, Secret Department of Inspection, Letters Issued, i, pp. 35–6.
[3] Ibid. i, p. 159.
[4] Directors to Bengal, 21 Sept. 1785, *Fort William–India House Corr.* ix. 268.

were even more acute for the army officers than they were for the civil servants. Men could remain as subalterns for up to twenty years on pay which was much lower than the basic salaries of the civil service.[1] War against the Marathas in 1778 and the dispatch of Bengal contingents to fight against the French or Mysore in southern India after 1780 must have brought some relief, but peace had returned by 1783. Large military fortunes seem to have been few and far between. Sir Robert Barker retired as Commader-in-Chief in affluent circumstances in 1772; Captain Charles Marsac made enough in Oudh to buy Cavendish Park in Oxfordshire,[2] and Colonel Hannay[3] and a number of others also did well there; William Popham commanded at the storming of both Gwalior and Bijaigarh and was duly rewarded in prize money; but it would be hard to think of many others.

Bankruptcies, which had laid low so many in the 1730s and 1740s, began to recur. In the 1770s men who traded ambitiously in uncertain conditions could burn their fingers badly. The list of notable bankrupts included both civil servants, for whom many branches of trade were still legal, and Free Merchants. Samuel Middleton was a Company servant whose chequered career eventually brought him the office of Resident at the court of the Nawab of Bengal. In the past the Residency would of itself have been the guarantee of a fortune, but Middleton also traded on a huge scale by land and sea. When he died in 1775 he left over Rs 1,500,00 in debts. His banian acting as his executor was eventually able to discharge about half of them, leaving some £85,000 unsettled.[4] The Free Merchant James Lister, who died in 1773, appears to have conducted operations on a scale approaching Middleton's. On his death his executors were able to collect more than seven lakhs of rupees and to pay off those to whom he owed money on bond. Other sums due to the estate from trading ventures at sea and within Bengal, put at eight lakhs more, proved very difficult to realize, and Lister's so-called 'book' creditors, which included General Carnac who had entrusted four lakhs to him, suffered severely.[5] Joseph Price, probably the largest Bengal

---

[1] See above, p. 208.
[2] J. M. Holzman, *The Nabobs in England* (New York, 1926), p. 153.
[3] See above, p. 212.
[4] See above, p. 43.
[5] Inventory in I.O.R., Mayor's Court Records, Range 155, vols. 2, pp. 7–22; 3, pp. 10–19, 21–4; Sykes to Hastings, 20 Dec. 1774, Add. MS. 29135, f. 394.

shipowner of his time, ended his life a bankrupt.[1] In 1775 five Company servants and Free Merchants joined together in an ambitious undertaking which they called the Bengal Commercial Society. The Society sent a number of ships to the Red Sea, playing a prominent part in opening the trade to Suez, and developed sugar plantations near Calcutta; but within two or three years it had broken up leaving its members with considerable losses.[2] Another group of Company servants who tried to grow sugar cane and operate a distillery also failed disastrously.[3] David Killican, a very enterprising Calcutta merchant, died insolvent in 1785, involving many others in his failure.[4]

The frequency with which trading ventures ended in loss moved Francis to write in 1782: 'Exclusive of public employments or contracts with the India Company, there is no fair occupation for the industry of Europeans in Bengal. Every enterprise they engage in, whether of foreign commerce or internal improvement, leads them into distress if it does no[t] end in their ruin.'[5] This was unduly pessimistic. It was certainly true that the older ways of winning a trading fortune were becoming less attractive. Voyages to the western Indian Ocean no longer paid well, while profit levels in the internal trade had fallen and many of its most tempting items, such as salt, betel nut, or opium, were either prohibited to Europeans or had become Company monopolies. On the other hand, trade to the east, to Canton, Manila, Malaya, and Indonesia began to grow before the American War and was to develop very rapidly thereafter, while European silk works, indigo and sugar factories were increasing in number.

The initiative in opening up new avenues for trade was for the most part taken by the Free Merchants, some of whom were being enriched by them. In the past they had suffered much discrimination from the Company's servants on matters like the right to have *dastaks* or to live outside Calcutta. In the early 1770s the prospects for a Free Merchant to earn even 'a competence' were said to be

---

[1] J. Woodman to Hastings, 16 June 1777, Add. MS. 29227, f. 566.

[2] This episode is examined in greater detail in my 'The Bengal Commercial Society', *Bulletin of the Institute of Historical Research*, xlii (1969).

[3] Ibid., p. 185.

[4] Evidence in 'the goods of David Killican', Calcutta Bar Library Club, Supreme Court Reports, xiv. 36–50.

[5] *Original Minutes of the Governor and Council at Fort William* (1782), pp. ii–iii.

worse than ever,[1] but as the lure of increased official emoluments combined with prohibitions drove more and more of the Company's servants out of trade, the Free Merchants were to come into their own. John Prinsep, whose varied enterprises were described in a previous chapter,[2] eventually left Bengal with a fortune of £40,000.[3] John Fergusson was even more successful. In 1785 he was described as 'the only merchant in Calcutta (for few if any of the Company's servants merit the appelation)', a man 'of great integrity and unblemished reputation, generous and humane'. He retired with 'an easy fortune honestly acquired' in 1789.[4]

In spite of restrictions imposed by the Company and after 1773 by act of parliament, a large volume of remittances from Bengal to London was maintained from 1770 to 1784 by bills on the East India Company. To raise supplies in Bengal to support a war being fought by the Madras Presidency, bills on London for very large sums were drawn in 1770–1. Bengal itself was involved in a series of wars after 1778 and the Governor and Council were obliged to borrow ever larger sums from the European community. Ingenious schemes were devised to attract money, such as a 'remittance loan' launched in 1781, whereby one-fifth of the principal was to be repaid in London every year,[5] or the 'investment loans' of Rs 10,000,000 raised in 1782 and 1783, which were to be used to buy the cargoes for London and to be repaid out of the produce of the sales.[6] But as the flow of bills to London from Bengal became ever larger, it was obvious that the Company was in no position to pay then off for several years. By 1784 fears about the Directors' intentions towards those who held bills drawn on them reached the point where men would 'trust Dutch, Dane, and Devil first'.[7]

From 1769 the East India Company was doing its utmost to attract money from its Indian settlements to Canton, where it could be used to buy tea, by offering bills from Canton on London

---

[1] D. Anderson to his father, 28 Dec. 1770, Add. MS. 45438, f. 24; also J. Archdekin to Clive, 5 Mar. 1771, I.O.L., MS. Eur. G. 37, box 61.

[2] See above, pp. 152, 154–5.

[3] 'Three Generations in India', I.O.L., MS. Eur. C. 97, p. 19.

[4] G. Smith to H. Dundas, 7 Dec. 1785, 30 Nov. 1789, I.O.R., Home Miscellaneous, 434, pp. 227, 318–19.

[5] Bengal to Directors, 29 Nov. 1780, 30 Apr. 1781, I.O.R., E/4/39, pp. 60, 308.

[6] Bengal to Directors, 15 July 1782, 16 Apr., 23 Oct. 1783, *Fort William–India House Corr.* ix. 315, 401, 418–20.   [7] Furber, *John Company*, p. 227.

at favourable rates of exchange. This policy was highly successful: Canton was able to draw bills for just over £3,000,000 between 1769 and 1783.[1] The Company's records do not make it clear how the money should be divided between the Bengal, Madras and

TABLE VIII[2]
Company bills 1771–84

£		£	
1770/1	1,086,255	1777/8	244,356
1771/2	47,220	1778/9	108,584
1772/3	212,697	1779/80	234,604
1773/4	41,075	1780/1	122,823
1774/5	215,045	1781/2	302,474
1775/6	201,679	1782/3	1,419,969
1776/7	212,926	1783/4	979,768
		Total	£5,429,475

Source: I.O.R., L/AG/18/2/1, p. 15.

Bombay communities. Only one-third of the 'country' ships calling at Canton were owned at Calcutta,[3] but it seems reasonable to suggest that about half of the money offered for bills, or about £1,500,000, came from Englishmen in Bengal; there is evidence that large sums were remitted from Calcutta to Madras to catch ships going to Canton.[4]

The tight control over the supply of Banaras diamonds which Clive and Verelst had exerted before 1770 through their agent John Chamier seems to have been relaxed somewhat in subsequent years. A number of European diamond merchants competed against one another.[5] But the supply of diamonds was still limited and still only available to a few senior civil servants and army officers.

[1] The annual totals were

£		£	
1769/70	41,743	1777/8	240,915
1770/1	85,522	1778/9	219,100
1771/2	135,857	1779/80	541,435
1772/3	227,999	1780/1	476,090
1773/4	50,374	1781/2	369,139
1774/5	17,894	1782/3	239,662
1775/6	131,226		
1776/7	230,943	Total	£3,007,899

Source: *Reports*, iv. 68; viii. 370–1; E. H. Pritchard, *The Crucial Years of Anglo-Chinese Relations 1750–1800* (Washington, 1936), p. 400.

[2] The totals include 'certificates' drawn by captains of Company ships (see above, p. 224).   [3] See above, p. 99.

[4] e.g. R. Barwell to M. Barwell, 20 Mar. 1779, *B.P.P.*, xviii (1919), 23.

[5] J. Fowke to Hastings, 9 Mar. 1772, Add. MS. 29133, f. 64.

Warren Hastings invested heavily in diamonds, which eventually produced some £70,000 for him in Britain.[1] George Vansittart shipped diamonds worth £15,000.[2] John Graham and another Scottish servant, James Lawrell, also obtained them, as did Sir Robert Barker. After 1776 the return on Indian diamonds sold in Europe was very low and few appear to have been exported until 1782, when there was a revival of interest.[3] It seems unlikely that the total value of all the diamonds shipped from Bengal to Britain between 1770 and 1785 amounted to more than £200,000.

Until the outbreak of war in 1778 and 1780 respectively British subjects could still send large sums home through French concerns or through the Dutch East India Company. A list of bills of exchange granted to British subjects by the Dutch in Bengal between 1773 and 1785 amounts to £775,000.[4] Allowing for the years 1770 to 1773, remittances by the Dutch company may perhaps have been worth £1,000,000 in all. French remittances after 1770 are much more difficult to estimate. The company stopped trading after 1769, but private French concerns in fact sent a larger number of ships to Asia than the company had been able to do in its last years. A number of very complicated schemes were devised to enable such concerns to finance their Bengal voyages from British sources. British banks in London, who could offer money on behalf of clients in Calcutta, or Englishmen in Bengal, who helped to arrange loans for the French, played an important part in these schemes.

At the centre of many of them was Jean-Baptiste Chevalier, formerly employed by British private traders on the Assam border,[5] but now chief of the French factory at Chandernagore. In 1773 Chevalier and Jean Law, Governor of Pondicherry, supplied the French government with a huge consignment of Bengal saltpetre, sent to Mauritius in three British country ships, in which the ambitious Calcutta merchant Killican had a quarter share worth six lakhs of rupees.[6] In 1775 Chevalier was responsible for

---

[1] 'My 'Personal fortune of Hastings', *Ec. Hist. Rev.*, 2nd ser. xvii. 287–8.
[2] Bodleian, dep. b. 99, pp. 179–80.
[3] *Ec. Hist. Rev.*, 2nd ser. xvii. 289; Furber, *John Company*, p. 230.
[4] Ibid., p. 79.
[5] See above, p. 122.
[6] See the 'case' drawn up for Killican in S.R.O., GD 29/1868; also Killican to G. Graham, 14 Sept. 1777, GD 29/2061/11.

providing the cargo for three French ships coming to Bengal: the *Boine*, the *Duc d'Aiguillon*, and the *Duc de la Vrillière*. He evidently borrowed extensively from British subjects. The London bankers Mayne and Needham arranged for bills worth £234,000 to be secured on the *Duc d'Aiguillon* and the *Duc de la Vrillière*, and the firm had £175,000 due to be paid to them after the sale of the *Boine*'s cargo. In the same year Mayne and Needham received payment for bills worth £204,000 from what was presumably yet another French Bengal ship.[1] As an additional inducement for Englishmen in Bengal to commit their money to him, Chevalier appears to have entered into a partnership with Samuel Middleton and a surgeon called James Ellis. Bills for large amounts were issued by this Anglo-French consortium, whose credit was badly shaken by Middleton's death and insolvency.[2] A purely British concern, called Campbell and Anderson, also offered bills, also of doubtful security, on French ships.[3] At the London end Mayne and Needham clearly had a large business in making arrangements for British money to be available for French ships in Bengal, but French concerns, such as Louis Tissier, who acted for Admyrauld & Son of La Rochelle, the promoters of two ships for India in 1774,[4] or Bourdieu and Chollet of Paris and London,[5] were also active.

The outbreak of war between Britain and France in 1778 rudely interrupted this brief flowering of French private trade. Chandernagore was captured and Chevalier was sent home a prisoner of war with many claims on him still unsettled, even though his creditors together with those of Law had been paid 3,000,000 *livres*.[6] Chevalier's British creditors continued to pursue him and were finally offered the principal of what they were owed, interest being cancelled.[7]

It is hard to estimate how much British money eventually came

---

[1] R. Mayne to J., G., and T. Graham, 5, 10 Jan. 1775, to J. Graham, 11 Jan. 1775, S.R.O., GD 29/2122/2–4, and copy of a bill, S.R.O., GD 29/2122/9a; H. Lüthy, *La Banque Protestante en France* (Paris, 1961), ii. 452–3.

[2] R. Barwell to R. Leycester, 20 Sept. 1776, *B.P.P.*, xv (1917), 120.

[3] G. Vansittart to R. Palk, 4 Mar. 1774, Bodleian, dep. b. 94, p. 66.

[4] Proposal by them, Add. MS. 29227, f. 167; R. Mayne to J. Graham, 3 Feb. 1775, S.R.O., GD 29/2122/5.

[5] R. Barwell to A. Beaumont, 26 Feb. 1773, I.O.L., MS. Eur. D. 535, pt. ii, f. 134.

[6] Lüthy, *La Banque Protestante*, ii. 455.

[7] D. Killican to G. Graham, 10 Oct. 1780, S.R.O., GD 29/2061/18.

home from Bengal between 1770 and 1778 as a result of private French ventures. In 1776 no less than fifteen French ships were reported in the Hugli and it was thought that they had given bills worth £10,000 in all.[1] But as the sums handled by Mayne and Needham show, a single rich ship could carry home a comparable sum on its own. In addition to ships actually calling at Bengal, the British at Calcutta also helped to finance French ships sailing from Pondicherry or going to Mauritius, as in the case of Law's and Chevalier's saltpetre deal. In all £1,000,000 might be an approximate total for all remittances.

Danish trade with India has been the subject of an admirable study, which makes it possible to estimate the value of British remittances with much greater certainty.[2] Before the 1770s Danish contacts with Bengal have been called 'irregular and insignificant', but they flourished during the American War as the trade of Britain's enemies was closed down and those seeking foreign bills were forced to turn to the Portuguese or the Danes. British remittances not only financed the trade of the Royal Danish Asiatic Company, but they were also used by an increasing number of private Danish ships, which were permitted to go to Asia under licence of the Danish crown after 1772. Between 1772 and 1778 five ships belonging to the Danish Company touched at its settlement at Serampore in Bengal, but, with the exception of one of the ships, only a small part of their cargo originated in Bengal and bills issued at Serampore amounted to less than £50,000 (although some British money from Bengal went to the more important Danish settlement at Tranquebar on the Coromandel Coast). From 1778 to 1783 four more Danish Company ships came to Serampore together with no less than thirteen private ships from Denmark. Two more private ships were fitted out in India. In all Dr. Feldbaek calculates that nearly Rs 10,000,000, or about £1,000,000 was sent home by British subjects on Danish ships during the years of war from 1778 to 1783. Assuming that three-quarters of this money was subscribed in Bengal and one-quarter in Madras for Tranquebar, Bengal's Danish remittances would have been worth about £750,000.[3]

---

[1] [J. Price], *Five Letters of a A Free Merchant in Bengal to Warren Hastings* (1783), p. 65.

[2] O. Feldbaek, *Indian Trade under the Danish Flag 1772–1808* (Copenhagen, 1969).   [3] Feldbaek, *Danish Trade*, pp. 13–74 and appendices.

'An independence' was the goal which those embarking on an Indian career hoped to achieve. It was an elastic term which meant different things to different people: the most ambitious aspired to a great manor house dominating the locality around it; others hoped for the conventional delights of rural simplicity with a few acres; private soldiers would perhaps be content with enough to open a public house. However they might choose to define it, few men attained their independence from Bengal. The most obvious reason was that relatively few who went there ever came back. Even the civil servants, who led the most sheltered lives, and whose chances of survival seem to have been the highest, were cut down for most of the eighteenth century at a rate comparable to that of subalterns on the Western Front in the First World War or the crews of British bombers in the Second. In the worst decade, 1747 to 1756, 74 per cent of the civil servants posted to Bengal were to die there.

Of those who did return, some still found that an independence had eluded them, because they had either mismanaged their affairs, or been unlucky in Bengal, or because they had been forced by ill-health or by dismissal, to which the Directors of the Company frequently resorted, to leave India at an unfavourable moment. The civil servants had by far the best opportunities for enriching themselves, but of the 178 civil servants who appear to have returned to Britain before 1785 the circumstances of at least forty-nine seem to be dubious. To attempt to divide careers into successful and unsuccessful ones is, of course, a highly arbitrary procedure, especially as the evidence in most cases is very scanty; but the forty-nine are men whose reasons for leaving Bengal, or whose length of service there, do not suggest that they had been able to improve their fortunes to any considerable extent. A number of wealthy army officers returned home, especially in the twelve years or so after Plassey, but they were only a very small fraction of the total corps of officers. Free Merchants had suffered serious discrimination from the Company's servants until the 1770s. As a result, the rich merchant living in retirement in Britain on a fortune amassed in India is much more a figure of the nineteenth century than of the eighteenth, with a very few exceptions, such as Gregory or Fergusson. Only a trickle of its former private soldiers was repatriated by the Company, and it would seem doubtful if they had been able to save more than a few pounds.

Calculations based on a section of the aristocracy suggest that mortality among the adult males of the British upper classes was falling markedly during the eighteenth century. Of the group of peers studied, 44·7 per cent died between fifteen and fifty (roughly the age of service in India) from 1680 to 1779; before the 1770s 60 per cent or 70 per cent of the civil service would die in Bengal between the age of seventeen and forty. A man aged twenty in the sample who stayed in Britain could expect another forty years of life;[1] a young man who went to Bengal could expect to die there. Had accurate knowledge of the prospects for survival and the prospects for a fortune been widely disseminated, fewer men who had any alternative open to them in Britain would perhaps have decided to go to Bengal. Fortunately for the East India Company, however, there were always enough conspicuous fortunes made to tempt the hopeful.

Money often outlived the men who made it. The estimates so far given in this chapter for remittances from Bengal show that the sums involved were considerable, even if a large proportion was only to be enjoyed by widows, fatherless children or other heirs. An over-all estimate for the total amount of money sent to Britain on behalf of individuals might be of the following order:

	£
Bills on the East India Company	10,381,025
Company bills via Canton after 1769	1,500,000
Bills via the French and the Dutch after 1757	4,000,000
Bills on the Danes after 1778	750,000
Diamonds after 1765 from Banaras	275,000
	£16,906,025

Additions should be made to this figure for foreign bills before 1757, private British bills, 'certificates' on Company ships before 1770, diamonds via Madras, Company bills from British settlements other than Bengal or Canton, licensed and 'privileged' trade on Company ships, Portuguese trade, and other sources. These items probably contributed at least another £1,000,000, making a very tentative total of £18,000,000.

It seems probable that some £3,000,000 was sent home before

---

[1] T. H. Hollingsworth, 'A Demographic Study of British Ducal families', *Population in History*, ed. D. V. Glass and D. E. C. Eversley (1965), pp. 361–3.

1757 and about £15,000,000 over the twenty-seven years between 1757 and 1784. An average of rather more than £500,000 a year received by individuals from Bengal is certainly an impressive sum. The obviously comparable form of income is that drawn from the West Indies by absentee planters and others living in Britain who had claims on property in the islands. An estimate for the sums going to 'annuitants and proprietors non-resident' from Jamaica in 1773 was only £200,000.[1] But £500,000 a year from Bengal needs to be seen in relation to the national income of Britain as a whole, which for 1770 has been put at £140,000,000.[2]

A detailed study of the uses to which Bengal fortunes were put once they had arrived in Britain is outside the scope of this book. It seems generally to be accepted by economic historians that relatively abundant resources of capital existed in eighteenth-century Britain and that an over-all increase in capital accumulation was not a major factor in the development of industry late in the century. What was needed was the diversion of comparatively small sums into manufacturing or communications. There is little to suggest that money made in Bengal was directly used in these ways, except by isolated individuals like Claud Alexander.[3] The prestige of the Company's service, even in the early eighteenth century, and the ability of the civil servants to control most of the roads to wealth, ensured that fortunes were generally made by men whose families were already of some social standing and valued land as the supremely desirable possession. Money acquired in India was used to buy more land, to build on it or to lend to the government in return for an income with which to support life in the country.

[1] R. B. Sheridan, 'The wealth of Jamaica', *Economic History Review*, 2nd ser., xviii (1965), 304-5.
[2] F. Crouzet, 'Editor's Introduction', *Capital Formation in the Industrial Revolution* (1972), p. 24.
[3] See above, p. 215.

Conclusion

From the point of view of the men whose doings have been described in this book, the last chapter with its attempt to summarize their experiences in terms of lives lost and money sent home would perhaps be an appropriate point at which to end. But the efforts of several hundred Englishmen in eighteenth-century Bengal to win fortunes for themselves had consequences that went far beyond their individual successes or failures. Their trading became an important part of the pattern of British trade as a whole, not only in Bengal, but also in other parts of Asia, while their ambitions intruded at many points in the launching of a British territorial empire. Finally, not only was the future of the British in Asia shaped by the private pursuit of gain, but the future of Bengal was also at stake.

By the end of the period with which this book has been concerned British commercial operations in Asia were taking a form that has been aptly described as 'a working association between a monopoly corporation and various forms of free enterprise'.[1] Within another thirty years those spheres previously reserved for the monopoly corporation—the East India Company—were to be successfully invaded and after 1833 the Company was to cease to exist as a trading body, finally ceding victory to 'free enterprise'.

The vigour of British private economic activity in the late eighteenth and early nineteenth centuries can be traced, via the developments described in this book, back to the later seventeenth century and the Company's decisions to tolerate participation in the 'country' trade by its servants and by Free Merchants. At intervals during the eighteenth century, conflict was to break out between particular interests and those of the Company, but in general the two worked together without excessive friction, as separate public and private spheres evolved. Private traders were encouraged to extend their inter-Asian seaborne trade further and further, partly along Bengal's traditional shipping routes to the western Indian Ocean and partly along routes of their own. The

[1] V. T. Harlow, *The Founding of the Second British Empire 1763–93* (1952–64), ii. 488.

rise of trade between Calcutta and Canton in the 1770s is perhaps the most obvious example of mutual interdependence: had the Company not been willing to grant bills on London from Canton, the shipowners would not have been able to finance their voyages; but had the shipowners not been willing to venture on this route, the Company would have been deprived of a most valuable source of funds with which to buy tea. Even before Plassey, private traders had begun to explore the possibilities of Bengal's internal trade. Plassey gave them opportunities to build up a major stake in it. After some twelve years of virtually unrestricted private participation, the Company intervened to draw up a new demarcation between public and private. The Company placed saltpetre, salt, and opium under its own control, but this still left room for a large private European sector in commodities like raw silk, sugar, and indigo, to which others like jute and tea were to be added in the nineteenth century.

By 1784 some of the institutions of the nineteenth century were already coming into existence. Some part of the wealth which British subjects were able to accumulate from office-holding and from trade remained in Bengal to be managed by increasingly elaborate private companies and banks, and to be invested in ships and plantations. The victory of free trade in the nineteenth century would hardly have been possible without the successes of private trade in the eighteenth century.

The fact that British political supremacy in Bengal was both preceded and accompanied by a striking growth in British private activities within the province obviously invites speculation about possible connections between the two. Such connections are not at first sight difficult to suggest. Enormous advantages came to private individuals from the political revolution in Bengal and, as they became aware of the potentialities, the temptation for senior civil and military servants to fish for presents, prize money, and enhanced trading privileges by dabbling in politics must have been a very strong one. It is also not difficult to see how increased trade by individual Englishmen could by itself provoke the conflicts with successive Nawabs out of which the revolution in Bengal was to develop. A larger volume of private trade meant that more goods were claiming exemption from the Nawab's customs, that more of his wealthy subjects were being attracted to Calcutta, where they virtually passed out of his jurisdiction, and that intrusion by Europeans into government monopolies and 'farmed' trades became increasingly likely.

Detailed examination of the events between 1756 and 1765, which led to political domination of Bengal by the British, confirms that private interests and ambitions did indeed have a role in them of some importance. The avalanche was set in motion by Siraj-ud-daula's attack on Calcutta in 1756. In part, no doubt, this was the irresponsible act of an inexperienced ruler; in part too it was the consequence of an unusual degree of incompetence by the Calcutta Council. But it can also be seen as the final culmination of tensions between the British and the Nawabs which had a long history. Private traders must bear a considerable share in the responsibility for this state of tension. Their salt trading had led to confrontations in 1727 and 1741, and their willingness to extend the protection of the *dastak* at a price to more and more Indian merchants had been the subject of frequent expostulations and was to be brought up again by Siraj-ud-daula when he launched his attack. But if the private traders had certainly given the Nawab strong grounds for wishing to see the influence of Calcutta curbed, there is no evidence to warrant the conclusion that they were uppermost in his mind when he moved against the settlement. Many of his grievances appear to have been directed against the Company itself. Nor does it seem possible to establish that private British interests were in a particularly expansionist or aggressive phase in the 1750s which might have led to new provocations being offered to the Nawabs.

The disaster which the British community had in some degree brought upon itself in 1756 was turned to triumph by Plassey with its deluge of presents and restitution, followed by the opening of the internal trade of Bengal to European participation on a huge scale. But although it is easy to see what private ambitions had to gain from the Plassey revolution, it is by no means easy to prove that they were able to bring it about. The role of Clive was crucial; whatever other men might want, the army was under his control. He showed himself perfectly capable of resisting private pressures for renewing the war on the Nawab, until he was convinced that a revolution was both feasible and in the Company's interests. He was well aware that huge private benefits would accrue from his great stroke, but they appear always to have been a subsidiary object for him.[1]

[1] See above, pp. 166–7.

The Bengal Nawabs were very seriously weakened by the consequences of Plassey, but their final emasculation required two
further crises: the deposing of Mir Jafar in 1760 and the defeat of
Mir Kasim in 1763. The hand of private interest can be detected
in both. If the suspicions against Holwell were well founded, even
less restraint was placed on self-interest in the negotiations with
Mir Kasim before his accession than had been the case with Mir
Jafar in 1757.[1] In the events that led to war with Mir Kasim in
1763 the role of private traders was very prominent. The Nawab
evidently felt himself to be threatened by the British in many
ways, and it is certainly likely that conflict would have broken
out on some other issue. Nevertheless, the immediate cause of the
failure of all attempts to achieve a stable relationship between the
Nawab and the Company was the intransigence of the private
traders.[2]

But if the machinations of private interest appear at many points
between 1756 and 1765, events were being shaped by other factors
as well. The Nawabs were being subjected to pressures from the
Company even more powerful than those which individuals were
able to exert. The Company was insisting on greater trading
privileges for itself, on its right to eliminate the French by force,
to interfere in the Nawab's choice of ministers, and to receive ever
larger subsidies for its troops, which ultimately required the outright cession of territory to maintain them. Secondly, assuming
that private interests wanted political change for their own purposes, there was still a gap between what they wanted and what
they could achieve. Change required military force on the British
side, which was not available in decisive strength in Bengal until
the arrival of Clive's expedition from Madras at the end of 1756.
Even then, as Clive was to show, the army was not always the
pliant instrument of interested parties. Finally, to portray Nawabs
like Siraj-ud-daula and Mir Kasim as no more than the victims of
British provocation is to suggest that events were much more
predictable from the British point of view than was in fact the
case. Individual Englishmen in pursuit of their own gain certainly
contributed an important element to the instability in which
Mughal rule over Bengal collapsed; but their activities are not a
complete explanation of this instability nor can they be seen as the
conscious architects of the new British order which replaced it.

[1] See above, p. 170.   [2] See above, p. 124.

Histories of European expansion overseas often devote much space to what is usually termed the European 'impact' on indigenous societies. For much of the eighteenth century it would be more appropriate to discuss the impact of Bengal on the British. Bengal was not a *tabula rasa* for British enterprise to exploit in whatever way seemed most advantageous to it. For most of the century British ships sailed along routes established by Asian shipowners, carrying among their cargo to Bengal's traditional outlets a high proportion of freight entrusted to them by Asian merchants. British participation in Bengal's internal trade at first involved no major changes either in the pattern of distribution or in the commodities handled. The highest profits were usually made when the British were able to take over a system of control and regulation devised by the Nawabs or their officials and to operate it on their own behalf. Political power was at first made to yield profits either by the time-honoured practice of extracting presents, or by milking the revenue system in ways pioneered by Mughal *amils* and *faujdars*. Innovation in the form of trade to new ports, the development of new commodities or the improvement of existing ones, or the creation of new hierarchies of salaried offices came late and uncertainly. Yet if the British up to 1784 were to a large extent being shaped by what they found in Bengal, they were presumably not without some capacity to shape it in return.

Any attempt to assess the consequences for Bengal of the activities described in this book has to contend with serious deficiencies of knowledge. Relatively little is known about many aspects of Bengal's social and economic history, especially for the period before the British conquest. There is an almost total lack of reliable data about population, output, or the volume of trade. There is, however, no shortage of comment by contemporary Englishmen on what they thought was happening in Bengal. Much of this is starkly pessimistic. To those in Britain, like Edmund Burke, who studied such statements, it seemed that Bengal was being 'ravaged' and was undergoing an 'annual plunder'.[1] Many historians have agreed with him. In a recent distinguished introduction to modern Indian history 'private financial greed' and 'public policy' are said to have brought about 'the ruin

[1] These phrases occur in the 9th Report, Select Committee, 1783, *Reports from Committees of the House of Commons* (1803–6), vi.

of Bengal'.[1] This book certainly does not provide grounds for any extensive revision of such assessments. By far the most important side of the British presence in eighteenth-century Bengal, 'public policy', lies completely outside its terms of reference. If Bengal was to be significantly changed by the British, such changes were likely to be brought about by the East India Company, through the level at which it set its revenue demand, its choice of the men through whom the revenue was to pass, its working of the customs system, or the way in which it obtained its investment. The consequences of 'private greed' are likely to have been more restricted. Modern scholarship has, however, tended to endorse two of the main accusations made by contemporaries like Burke. The repatriation of private fortunes to Britain has been seen as a major element in what is termed the 'drain of wealth' from Bengal, while private British trade has been portrayed as having been conducted in a way that was highly damaging to Indian merchants in particular and to the population of Bengal in general.[2] Material in this book prompts some tentative reconsideration of both points.

Various attempts have been made to define and to quantify the 'drain of wealth', since the concept was first formulated by Harry Verelst, Philip Francis, and Burke.[3] Its main elements are normally said to have been in the Company's exports to Britain, inasmuch as they were paid for by a surplus of territorial revenue and not out of imports, the Company's remittances from Bengal to the other Indian presidencies and to China, and the repatriation of fortunes by individual Englishmen. Whether all or part of the £500,000 a year received in Britain from Bengal on private account between 1757 and 1784 is regarded as having been 'drained' depends on the definition of 'drain'. Only a minute part of the private remittances produced a physical transfer of specie out of Bengal, and only a relatively small part directly involved the shipment of goods. The great bulk of remittances were made by bill of exchange

---

[1] P. Spear, *India: a Modern History*, 2nd edn. (Ann Arbor, 1972), p. 197.

[2] There is much material offered to substantiate both charges in N. K. Sinha, *Economic History of Bengal* (Calcutta, 1956–70), i; there is a cogent summary in T. Raychaudhuri, 'Writings on Modern Economic History', *Contributions to Indian Economic History*, i (1960), 123–5.

[3] See discussions in H. Furber, *John Company at Work* (Cambridge, Mass., 1951), pp. 305–12; C. J. Hamilton, *The Trade Relations between England and India 1660–1896* (Calcutta, 1919), pp. 135–48; K. N. Chaudhuri, 'India's International economy in the nineteenth century: an historical survey', *Modern Asian Studies*, ii (1968), 31–50.

for money advanced in Bengal to the British East India Company or to foreign companies, who used it to defray the costs of their Bengal establishments and to purchase cargoes for export. Thus the transfer of fortunes to Britain certainly contributed indirectly to Bengal's surplus of exports over imports, and by some definitions to the 'drain'. It may also have contributed indirectly to the shortage of specie, about which there were so many complaints in Bengal from the late 1760s, in that the British and foreign companies would presumably have been obliged to import more silver with which to pay for their exports if private British money had not been available in Bengal for bills.

On the other hand, the effects of private remittances may not have been uniformly malign. Had British fortunes not been available to finance it, the total of Bengal's foreign trade and therefore of the demand for certain commodities would probably have been lower. If they had not been certain that they could raise money by bill of exchange, the promoters of a number of European ships, especially perhaps those of the Danes and the private French concerns, presumably would not have come to Bengal at all. It can also be argued that what Bengal lost in imports was matched by invisible imports of the services of Europeans. The value of some of these had become apparent by 1784, as the Company's army proved itself capable of defending Bengal against incursions from the Marathas or any other invader. Others were perhaps to produce administrative or economic improvement in the future. But what Bengal gained in the short run from the services of most British subjects who went there before 1784 is not very obvious.

By most definitions part of the annual remittances of £500,000 cannot be included in any 'drain', since it was spent on military and civil expenses in Bengal. To prove convincingly that the 'loss' of the rest without apparent equivalent seriously damaged the economy of Bengal, more needs to be known of the province's total income. The tribute paid in the early eighteenth century to the Mughal emperors raises very similar problems. In amount, at one crore of rupees, it was nearly double the volume of private remittances and the mechanism for transferring it was also largely by bill of exchange, but it too was said to produce acute shortages of specie.[1]

[1] Sinha, *Economic History*, i. 151, 232–3; J. Steuart, *The Principle of Money applied to the Present State of the Coin of Bengal* (1772), p. 63.

Attempts to substantiate allegations that private trade drove Indian merchants out of business and impoverished the artisans and cultivators who worked for the British are equally hampered by ignorance of basic facts about Bengal's economy. The scale of British activity certainly grew throughout the eighteenth century, but it is very hard to estimate what proportion of Bengal's trade or manufacturing was under their control at any particular time. Nor is it at all clear whether increasing British involvement led to an over-all increase in the output of certain commodities and in the volume of trade, or whether they merely took a larger share of more or less static quantities.

Asian merchants first felt the effects of private British enterprise in Bengal's seaborne trade, as a considerable part of it began to travel on British-owned ships. Some Asian shipowners based on Bengal in the early eighteenth century were probably put out of business, although a number of Indian and Armenian ships used Calcutta as their home port and Indian businessmen often took up shares in European ships.[1] If there was for a time a net decline in the number of Asian ships operating from Bengal, this does not mean that opportunities for Bengal merchants to trade overseas declined. The reverse seems to be true. The British Calcutta fleet provided Asian merchants with a large volume of cargo space. It is likely that through the persistence of British shipowners and the relatively privileged position which they enjoyed in the ports of the western Indian Ocean, Bengal's exports to Surat, Persia, and the Red Sea remained at a higher level for rather longer than would have been the case had they depended solely on Asian ships. It is also hard to see how the great increase in the export of opium and piecegoods to Indonesia, Malaya, and China in the 1770s could have been achieved by Asian ships alone.

Within Bengal itself certain trades passed more or less completely under European control (although this did not of course eliminate Indian participation in many profitable forms), Indian merchants faced greatly increased European competition in others, while in a final category there was no significant European involvement. Salt and opium from about 1760 are the most obvious examples of the first type. Certain regional trades, such as Sylhet's

---

[1] Gokul Ghosal and Madan Dutt owned a third of the ship *Rumbold* on a voyage to China in 1769 (Calcutta High Court Records, Supreme Court, Equity, *Rumbold and Wilkins* v. *Joynarain Gosaul and Muddun Dutt*).

chunam or betel nut grown in eastern Bengal, seem also to have been European monopolies for a time. Purchases of silk and piece-goods by the East India Company and by private Europeans grew throughout the eighteenth century. Asian merchants who dealt in Bengal textiles presumably found smaller quantities available for them and fewer weavers or silk winders who could accept their orders. The problems of the Asian merchants were particularly acute in the late 1760s as the Company began to plough its *diwani* revenues into much larger investments. In 1767 the trade of 'Armenian and Mogul merchants' was said to be 'much impeded to their great loss and detriment',[1] while the Gujarat silk merchants were believed to be having difficulty in obtaining supplies.[2] By the 1770s, once the effects of the great famine had begun to wear off, the situation seems to have eased, presumably because of some increase in production. Exports of silk by Asian merchants revived somewhat in 1776 and 1777,[3] and it was estimated that the East India Company and the British private traders were only taking about half the annual output of cotton cloth at Dacca in 1776.[4] The huge trade in food grains was the largest area left virtually untouched by Europeans, as were other bulk trades, such as those in raw cotton (except for imports by sea from western India) or the coarser piecegoods worn by the mass of the population.

Any assumption that the whole of Bengal's internal trade passed into British hands is patently untenable. The British did, however, succeed in entrenching themselves in certain trades where they hoped for high profits. After 1757 direct competition within such trades between an Indian merchant and the East India Company or a British private trader was not likely to be advantageous for the Indian merchant. The British had too many weapons, such as their *dastak* or the political control which they could exercise over the producers. But if overt competition was hardly practical, collaboration could be highly profitable.

Collaboration could take many forms. Some Indian merchants appear to have done no more than pay a commission to a European for the use of his name and his *dastak* privileges, while carrying on their own trade much as before. Others might enter into a

---

[1] I.O.R., B.P.C., 5 Oct. 1767, Range 1, vol. 41, f. 409.
[2] Verelst to Clive, 5 Feb. 1768, I.O.L., MS. Eur. G. 37, box 51, f. 158.
[3] K. M. Mohsin, *A Bengal District in Transition: Murshidabad 1765–93* (Dacca, 1973), pp. 33–5. [4] See above, p. 150.

formal partnership with a European or become his banian. As has previously been suggested,[1] service as a banian did not necessarily imply any significant loss of independence by those who served. The banian might appear on the surface to be merely the manager of his master's trade, but it was likely that in reality he had provided most of the capital and was taking the decisions about how it should be used. The role of *gumashta* was a more obviously servile one, but there were no doubt still opportunities for a *gumashta* to trade on his own behalf as well as on his master's. For those who did not wish to be actively involved in trade, collaboration with Europeans could take the form of loans to individuals or to the newer corporate enterprises. There were at least eight Hindu names among the founding members of an Insurance Society set up in 1780.[2]

The rewards of collaboration could be high. *Gumashtas* were often said to extract profits from their masters' dealings that went well beyond the commission or wages allowed them. In joint trading ventures a banian's terms varied from receiving a commission on business which he transacted for his master to paying his master a commission on his own profits. But the greatest fortunes seem to have been made by those who were banians to the first European office-holders and accompanied their masters to their new postings, managing their households, organizing their trade, and taking a proportion of their presents, deductions from the revenue or whatever other perquisites might be going. Investors in European enterprises received interest rising to 12 per cent with higher rates for loans on respondentia to finance shipping ventures.[3]

Collaboration could be highly profitable, but many Indian merchants even after Plassey had no need to collaborate. A large part of Bengal's trade was unaffected by British competition, and even when they were actively involved (unless they were prepared to entrust goods to *gumashtas* for long periods), British traders usually acted merely as wholesalers, disposing of commodities in bulk, which then passed to consumers through a chain of Indian merchants. Many of these merchants were responsible for large transactions. In the salt trade, for instance, a group of substantial Indian dealers grew up to handle sales by private Europeans or by

[1] See above, p. 45.
[2] Calcutta High Court Records, Supreme Court, Equity, *Blume* v. *Blythe et al.*
[3] See above, p. 71.

the Company after 1772. One such concern purchased over
100,000 maunds (over 3,000 tons) from the Society of Trade in
1766.[1] By 1773 a single Indian merchant, Gokul Ghosal, the former
banian of Harry Verelst, was due to receive nearly 350,000 maunds
of salt from the Company.[2]

That many Indians were greatly enriched by the British conquest of Bengal is undeniable. Most of the families who were to
dominate the rich social and intellectual life of mid-nineteenth-
century Calcutta trace their origins to the later eighteenth century.
But if finding the winners presents no problems, it is more difficult
to identify the casualties. It is often suggested that the late
eighteenth century was a period of very rapid social mobility in
Bengal, as established merchants were driven to the wall by
British competition and 'new men' rose through service as banians
or *gumashtas*. Contemporary British comment certainly gives that
impression. It was habitual for the British to heap abuse and contempt on the men from whose skills they derived so large a part
of their fortunes. Banians were repeatedly denounced as men of
base origins who made their fortunes by cheating their masters.
Widely accepted as the stereotype of the banian as a penniless
adventurer has become, it is not altogether a convincing one. What
Europeans needed from their banians were the resources of capital
and the commercial skill of an experienced merchant. There is
some evidence in individual cases to suggest that this is what a
number of banians in fact were. The willingness of members of
the Sett and the Basak cotton-merchant families to enter European
service in the mid-eighteenth century drew comment.[3] The famous
Cantu Babu, banian to both Warren Hastings and Francis Sykes,
had been a successful silk merchant at Kasimbazar.[4] Nor are
assumptions about a holocaust of merchants particularly convincing either. Such assumptions would seem both to overestimate
the extent of British commercial participation in the eighteenth
century and to underestimate the merchants' powers of adaptation,
which must have been well developed under the Nawabs. In short,
it would seem that there was a considerable degree of continuity

[1] Select Committee Proceedings, 15 Aug. 1766, *Reports*, iii. 522–3.
[2] I.O.R., B.R.C., 30 July 1773, Range 49, vol. 40, pp. 2715–17.
[3] See above, p. 45.
[4] I owe this information to the kindness of Cantu's descendant, Maharajkumar S. C. Nandy of Cossimbazar.

between the independent merchants of the early eighteenth century and the collaborators of a later period.

Nevertheless, it would be pointless to deny that some casualties occurred. The dexterity of a small group of Muslim and Armenian merchants in navigating through the perilous seas of the Nawabs' courts had been rewarded by valuable farms and monopolies. Such grants stood directly in the way of ambitious British traders, who particularly relished the prospect of dispossessing the Armenians, whose share of Mir Kasim's favours seemed to make them dangerous rivals.[1] The future held little for such men. It was also widely believed that many Indian bankers or 'shroffs' were suffering from the rise of the British.[2] But it is likely that any decline in Indian banking was at the most a selective one. The businesses which languished were presumably those that depended most on the older administrative and commercial centres, such as Murshidabad. The bankers to the Nawabs, the Jagat Seths, were certainly very hard hit by the transfer of the revenue headquarters to Calcutta. Elsewhere Indian banking seems to have flourished on increased European business, especially in Banaras and Calcutta. In the absence of an effective European banking system, 'native money monopolists' in Calcutta as late as 1786 were said to be able to dictate terms to the whole British community by combining to force up the discount rate on the certificates with which, due to the shortage of specie, salaries were being paid by the Company.[3]

For the mass of the population of Bengal the change from Mughal to British rule was likely to have made itself felt through changes in the demand for revenue, discussion of which lies outside the scope of this book, except in as far as it was enhanced by the personal rapacity of European revenue administrators. But the activities of the British traders could have had an effect on those sections of the population who worked in certain industries or who cultivated certain crops. Europeans also dealt extensively in some

[1] G. Gray to Carnac, 3 Nov. 1761, I.O.L., MS. Eur. F. 128, box 3/8; H. Vansittart to Hastings, 2 May 1762, Add. MS. 29132, ff. 172–3.

[2] e.g. H. Verelst's minute, I.O.R., Select Committee Proceedings, 11 Aug. 1769, Range A, vol. 9, p. 428; W. Harwood's evidence, 9th Report, Select Committee, 1783, *Reports*, vi. 267; A. Majed Khan, *The Transition in Bengal 1756–1775* (Cambridge, 1969), pp. 175–7.

[3] National Archives of India, Proceedings of Secret Department of Inspection, 14 Mar. 1786.

items of common consumption, salt being the most important. It is usually assumed that the effect of European trading on the people of Bengal was to create poverty by holding down the rewards of the producers while forcing up prices to consumers. On the surface another, less pessimistic, interpretation is at least possible. Increased demand for certain commodities might have enabled producers to obtain higher prices and might have created more productive employment by encouraging more men to become artisans or to grow more profitable crops.

Although there appears to be no firm evidence, it would seem likely that more men were induced to take up weaving or silk winding or to grow mulberries or poppies in certain areas in response to increased British demand. In other respects, however, it is difficult to take an optimistic view of the effects of early British enterprise. The price of commodities in which the Europeans dealt certainly rose, but the indications are that little of this reached the producer. The rewards of the *mulangis* in the salt pans around Calcutta remained stationary during the 1760s.[1] Dacca weavers were thought to be receiving less in the 1770s than in the 1740s and 1750s.[2] Before Plassey, cultivators of poppies in Bihar for the manufacture of opium were said to get at least Rs 2 per seer for them. In 1785 a European, who claimed to have made a close investigation of prices paid in various parts of Bihar, came to the conclusion that 'the general medium' was now Rs 1. 9 annas.[3]

The ability of Europeans to hold down prices suggests that producers had few opportunities for effective bargaining with them. Many cultivators and artisans were bound to the service of the Company or of private traders by arrears accumulated in previous years. The prices at which they worked appear to have been based on a customary rate with allowances for changes in the cost of raw materials or food. Under such a system of control the standard of living of the producers is not likely to have risen. Whether it fell presumably depends on whether the British were simply employing well-established methods of coercion used by other merchants in the past or whether the cultivators and artisans had enjoyed real freedom to extract the highest prices from a reasonably open

---

[1] See above, p. 157. [2] Sinha, *Economic History*, i. 167–8.
[3] Cf. G. Sanyal, 'Ramchand Pandit's Report on opium cultivation in 18th-century Bihar', *B.P.P.*, lxxxvii (1968), 182–3, and I.O.R., B.R.C., 19 Aug. 1785, Range 50, vol. 59, p. 360.

market before Plassey. Studies of the textile industry suggest that weavers at least were not under the effective control of merchants in the seventeenth century and for much of the eighteenth in Bengal.[1] Increased trading by government officials and the grant of privileges to favoured individuals in the last years of the Nawabs may have brought more restrictions, but it still seems likely that the kind of control which the East India Company thought it necessary to apply and which private Europeans tried to imitate was more rigorous than anything which had existed before. Increased British trade thus probably offered increased employment but on terms which left little scope for bargaining for improved living standards.

Consumers of salt throughout Bengal had to pay more for it as a result of the intervention of British traders. So did the consumers of betel nut. It would, however, be more difficult to prove that the price of other necessities had been directly affected.

It must again be stressed that this discussion has not tried to offer a reconsideration of the over-all effects on Bengal of the beginning of British dominance. It has been concerned with what can reasonably be deduced about the consequences of private activities. Here the balance of probabilities seems rather less dramatic than is often assumed. When Englishmen sent their fortunes home, they certainly contributed to Bengal's surplus of exports over imports. But in the present state of knowledge it is not self evident that this contribution was on a scale to inflict major damage on the province. British enterprise in Bengal during the eighteenth century depended to a very large degree on Indian co-operation in providing commercial skill and finance. British fortunes were therefore matched by Indian ones, as the opulence of part of the Indian community in Calcutta clearly showed. Indeed, it seems likely that opportunities for secure and systematic accumulation of wealth were greater under the British than they had been under the Nawabs. Some of those who prospered were no doubt men who had been enriched by sudden windfalls, but most of them were likely to have been men of substance already or to have come from substantial families, who had done well out of trade or administration in the relatively open society of

[1] K. N. Chaudhuri, 'The structure of the Indian textile industry in the seventeenth and eighteenth centuries', *Indian Economic and Social History Review*, xi (1974), 147–60.

Mughal Bengal. A real degree of hardship was inflicted on the mass of the population by the rise in salt prices. In other respects, however, the consequences of private British enterprise are likely to have been less decisive. An increased demand may have been created for labour, but under the conditions which Europeans were generally able to enforce, those who worked for them evidently could not effectively exploit this demand to improve their living standards.

Such conclusions are not only prosaic and unexciting by comparison with stories of pillage and destruction, but they are also tentative and may well be displaced by new research on the history of Bengal. But a verdict of change within fairly narrow margins still seems the most probable one. Eighteenth-century Bengal was not like sixteenth-century Mexico, a society totally isolated from contact with Europe and likely to be devastated by alien diseases and transformed by European mining and farming. It had a complex and resilient economy which had handled a large volume of overseas trade for centuries. British merchants, especially when they were armed with political power, could win handsome profits for themselves, but it is hard to see how they could have laid Bengal waste in the space of a few decades.

There is, on the other hand, little evidence to suggest that European enterprise had as yet set in motion any significant process of economic development. Some marginally improved technology had been applied to ship construction and navigation and to the processing of silk, indigo, and sugar. The new agency houses, banks and insurance businesses were presumably organized more efficiently than their Asian counterparts. But in an economy where labour was cheap, abundant and highly skilled in its hereditary occupations, while interest rates on capital were very high, there was very little incentive to introduce expensive new technology.

By 1784 it was still too early to predict whether European enterprise would galvanize the economy of Bengal into taking new courses, would stultify its development, or would remain an isolated enclave in a stagnant agrarian society.

Main Manuscript Sources Consulted

India Office Records

Correspondence Reports and Memoranda: series D.

Despatches to and from Asia: series E/3 and E/4.

Factory Records, Calcutta: series G/7.

China and Japan: series G/12.

Egypt and Red Sea: series G/17.

Persian Gulf: series G/29.

Sumatra: series G/35.

Surat: series G/36.

Home Miscellaneous series.

Writers Petitions: series J/1.

Bengal Civil Establishment lists: series L/F/10.

Bonds and Covenants: series O.

Additional Factory Records, China: series R.

Bengal Secret Consultations and Select Committee Proceedings: Range A.

Bengal Public Consultations: Range 1 and 2.

Bengal Revenue Consultations: Range 49 and 50.

Miscellaneous Revenue Records (Customs and Committee of New Lands): Range 98.

Bengal Mayor's Court and Supreme Court Records: Range 154 and 155.

India Office Library

Richard Barwell letter books: MS. Eur. D. 535.

Letters of Robert Clive to John Walsh: MS. Eur. D. 546/5.

John Fullerton letter books: MS. Eur. D. 602.

Papers of John Grose: MS. Eur. E. 284.

Papers of John Carnac: MS. Eur. F. 128.

Papers of Robert Clive: MS. Eur. G. 37.

Letters of Philip Francis: MS. Eur. C. 7, F. 5, F. 7, G. 4.

Collection made by Robert Orme: Orme MSS. OV, and 'India'.

Harry Verelst letter books (originals in the Ames Library of South Asia): microfilm, reel 606.

John Fullerton papers: microfilm, reel 674.

British Museum

Evidence to House of Commons, 1767: Add. MS. 18469.

Letters of Thomas Pitt: Add. MSS. 22848–50.

Papers of Warren Hastings: Add. MSS. 28973–29236.
Letters of David Anderson: Add. MSS. 45417–40.

Public Record Office
Chancery proceedings: C/11, C/12.
Wills: PROB/11.

National Army Museum
Transcripts made by V. C. P. Hodson: MSS. 6404/69.

National Library of Wales
Papers of Robert Clive: Clive MSS.

Scottish Record Office
Papers of John, George and Thomas Graham: GD/29.
Letters of William Young: GD/32/24.
Letters of Stair Dalrymple: Hamilton-Dalrymple MSS.

Northern Ireland Public Record Office
James Alexander letter books: D/2432/1.
Letters to Robert Cowan: D/564/B1/5E.

Bodleian Library, Oxford.
Papers of George Vansittart: dep. b. 66–109.

Mitchell Library, Glasgow
Letters of George Bogle: Bogle MSS.

National Archives of India, New Delhi.
Secret and Separate Proceedings.
Proceedings of the Secret Department of Inspection.

West Bengal Archives, Calcutta.
Board of Trade Proceedings.
Committee of Grain Proceedings.

Calcutta High Court
Records of the Mayor's Court.
Records of the Supreme Court, Plea side.
Records of the Supreme Court, Equity.

Calcutta Bar Library Club
Supreme Court Judges' MS. notes: Supreme Court Reports.

Algemeen Rijksarchief, The Hague.
Shipping lists in Koloniaal Archief series.

Unpublished Theses

S. AKHTAR, 'Zamindars in Bengal 1707–72' (London, Ph.D., 1972).

G. BHADRA, 'Some Socio-economic aspects of the town of Murshidabad 1756–93' (J. Nehru University, M.Phil., 1971–2).

R. A. BOWLER, 'The influence of logistical problems on British operations in North America 1775–82' (London, Ph.D., 1971).

S. CHAUDHURI, 'Trade and commercial organisation in Bengal . . . 1650–1720' (London, Ph.D., 1969).

W. E. CHEONG, 'Some aspects of British trade and finance in Canton' (London, Ph.D., 1962).

R. W. FERRIER, 'British–Persian relations in the seventeenth century' (Cambridge, Ph.D., 1970).

K. P. MISHRA, 'The administration and economy of the Banaras region 1738–95' (London, Ph.D., 1971).

R. RAY, 'Agrarian change in Bengal 1750–1850' (Cambridge, Ph.D., 1973).

Index